graphic designer's
print
+color
HANDBOOK

ROCKPORT

graphic designer's
print+color
HANDBOOK

GLOUCESTER MASSACHUSETTS

ROCKPORT PUBLISHERS

CONSTANCE SIDLES . RICK SUTHERLAND . BARB KARG

First published in the United States of America by Rockport Publishers, a member of Quayside Publishing Group
33 Commercial Street
Gloucester, Massachusetts 01930-5089
Telephone: (978) 282-9590
Fax: (978) 283-2742
www.rockpub.com

Library of Congress Cataloging-in-Publication Data

Sidles, Constance J., [date]
    Graphic designer's print and color handbook / Constance Sidles, Rick Sutherland, Barb Karg.
        p.   cm.
    ISBN 1-59253-191-1 (pbk.)
    1. Color printing. 2. Digital printing. 3. Color computer graphics. 4. Image processing—Digital techniques. 5. Color in design. 6. Graphic design (Typography) I.
Sutherland, Rick. II. Karg, Barbara. III. Title.
Z258.S57 2005
686.2'3042—dc22   2005008435
                                                                    CIP

ISBN 1-59253-191-1   3371 +311 5/06

10 9 8 7 6 5 4 3 2 1

Cover Design: Peter King & Co.
Design: Peter King & Co.
Layout and Production: Joan Lockhart
Technical Illustrations: Brian King

Printed in China

Grateful acknowledgment is given to Barb Karg and Rick Sutherland for their work from *Graphic Designer's Color Handbook* on pages 8–77, 164–285, and 306–321; and to Constance Sidles for her work from *Graphic Designer's Prepress Handbook* on pages 78–163, 286–305, and 322–429.

CONTENTS

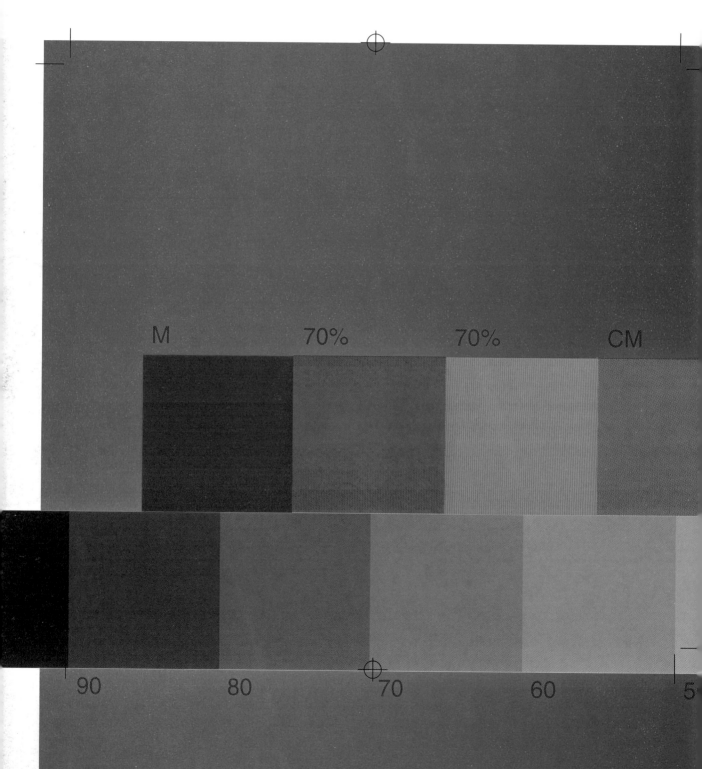

M   70%   70%   CM

90   80   70   60   5

INTRODUCTION

Graphic design and communications media have been for centuries a far more intrinsic influence on the evolution of our society than we ever imagined.

Johannes Gutenberg's creation of movable type in the fifteenth century made information and knowledge accessible to the masses, but his is an oversimplification of a revolutionary process that profoundly appealed to human responses and visual interests. While Gutenberg's invention created a means for mass-producing the printed word, it also created an enduring medium for producing emotionally evocative and effective color design, as evidenced by the brilliant illustrations of Gutenberg's early Bibles still in existence.

We are blessed with an amazing visual sensibility that serves not simply as a biological necessity for survival but also as a means of highlighting, analyzing, and appreciating the modern world. It is this very sensibility that the graphic designer speaks to by creating imagery that appeals to our colorful and inquisitive nature. Without the influence of graphic designers, the aesthetic and intellectual growth of society would be clouded by shades of gray.

The accessibility of computers, graphics programs, and the Internet is creating a combination of challenges and opportunities for graphic designers. Increased accessibility has diluted some elements of the design market, and many people with a modicum of talent and experience have invested thousands of dollars on computers and programs, and proclaimed themselves "graphic designers." Our opinion of this concept is the same as we would imagine Gutenberg's reaction might have been upon finding that his Bibles were being industriously illustrated by a stablehand who had recently purchased a cheap box of paints and a stick of charcoal. This is a technological trend that will not go away, but it does offer the opportunity to distance yourself from the pack. Excellent design and execution of color and type has been done, and will always be done, by those who understand and take full advantage of the remarkable processes available today.

The purpose of this book is to offer meaningful insights into the world of color graphic and print reproduction in real-world settings. Our goal is to provide practical, hardworking information that will serve you professionally by helping you better serve your clientele.

1

THE PRINCIPLES OF COLOR

UNDERSTANDING COLOR IS THE KEY TO SUCCESSFUL GRAPHIC DESIGN, whether it's in or out of the digital world. Color is empowering, but it's also unpredictable because it's subject to so many variables from print to print, monitor to monitor, press to press, and domestic to international locales. Designers must learn how to balance the variables, mixing and matching colors so that a project is eye-catching and satisfying to a client.

All successful graphic designers become students of color. Every color has unique properties and problems. The trick is learning how to mix and match.

Color Theory:
WHAT DO YOU SEE?

AT A MONDAY MORNING MEETING, the production manager of a design agency holds up a picture containing a red square. Seated around the table are ten graphic designers. He asks the designers to write down the square's color, then reads each answer aloud: "Cherry, burgundy, Bombay, pimento, burnt orange, magenta, tomato, mauve, rose, and Pantone 186."

People agree on color as often as they agree on whose grandmother makes the best chocolate chip cookies. The above scenario is a typical color conundrum, whether between designer and client, sales rep and prepress operator, or broker and printer. Color brings life to the world around us, but it is subjective, and if there is one guiding rule, it's that one person's crimson is another's cranberry.

When you think of color, what first comes to mind? Your favorite color? The color of your car or your dog? Maybe it's the color of the jacket you're wearing.

The principles and theories regarding color are well researched, in fields as diverse as art, sales, and psychology. Colors can be loud, calm, fresh, neutral, dark, rich, stimulating, or mysterious. They can be vibrant or muted, warm or cool, and they are used in every imaginable combination. This diversity is particularly evident in the art world, where personal and professional opinions about color are rampant.

From ancient times to the modern age, color has played an important role in the visual arts. When gazing on the art and architecture of past civilizations, you can't help but become entranced by the lush, verdant colors artisans used to solidify their place in history. Artists from Egypt, Greece, Rome, and China created colorful images that remain beautiful and expressive thousands of years later. The true brilliance of their creations is that they understood how color works on the mind and in the environment. They learned how to combine colors, and how to apply them in abundance or in more subtle ways.

Color means different things to different people around the world. In some societies, colors are dictated by tradition and customs, such as wearing a white or red wedding dress. Certain colors are considered sacred, while others are forbidden. Everyone has a theory about color—its uses and abuses. Ultimately, how you think about color is personal. You will increase your value as a graphic designer by honing the color theories and instincts that you develop. Learn from past and present masters by studying their successes and failures, and in time, you'll become your own best color critic.

Artists and artisans understood the effectiveness of melding colors to create conceptual designs long before the advent of modern color theories and technical explanations of light waves and color spectrums.

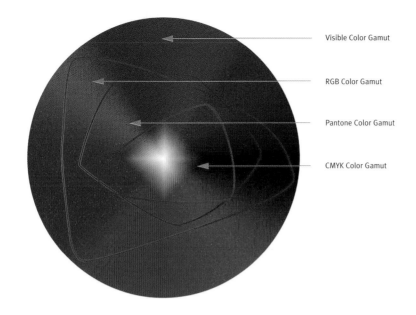

Visible Color Gamut

RGB Color Gamut

Pantone Color Gamut

CMYK Color Gamut

The color gamut of computer monitors is a fraction of the color range that the human eye can perceive. The color gamut for CMYK printing is even less, with a range of about four thousand colors, compared with the nearly ten million we can see in nature.

Running the Gamut

COLOR GAMUT IS A TERM that describes the range of colors that can be produced by any given process or device, such as computer monitors or proofing systems. The dynamic range of human vision is about ten million colors, far greater than any known printing process can reproduce. This number is elastic and depends on the visual acuity of the individual. Interestingly enough, visual color deficiency—or color blindness—is far more prevalent among men, with 7 percent of the male population having some element of the condition. About 0.4 of 1 percent of women are similarly affected. This can be useful to bear in mind when you're reviewing proofs in a group or asking a press operator to make minor color adjustments on press.

Inabilities for some people to recognize minor changes in reds, blues, and yellows are not uncommon, and subtle color alterations in any or all of these colors that may be very apparent to one person, may appear to be unchanged to another. Having your color vision tested can be interesting and enlightening. The Internet contains a number of sites that offer simplified color testing programs. In depth color vision tests are also available from opticians.

Understanding that these often minute variations in individual color acuity are a fact of life can help relieve the sometimes frustrating process of trying to convince a client or press operator that the variations you see really exist, even if they don't see it exactly the same way you do.

Visual Adaptation

Our sense of sight is incredibly adaptive and works in conjunction with our brains to provide us with rational visual information. The adaptation illustration shown here is one example of how our vision helps us to keep our world in perspective.

This chromatic adaptation illustration demonstrates the fluidity of human vision and our eyes' ability to compensate for our environment. The left half of the fruit image appears too yellow, while the right half is too blue.

Now, stare at the black dot in the center of the yellow/blue adapting patches for thirty seconds without wavering. Then look at the black spot in the center of the fruit image. You'll notice that the two halves nearly match.

When you play with color, you walk a fine line between method and madness. So how do you know which colors are best? This plate shows how colors can work well together. The cool blues and blacks complement the warm oranges and reds. Yellow ties it all together.

Colors can be ritualistic, spiritual, and superstitious, but, above all, colors trigger emotion. The soft hues and surrealistic color transitions in this photograph have a calming, dreamlike effect.

Choosing and Using Color

WHETHER YOU'RE NEW to the design field or an experienced professional, color can be a tough customer. On any color job, you must strike a balance among a wide range of variables, such as hue, density, and saturation. How you choose and use color has much to do with instinct and experimentation.

Playing with color is much like choosing sides in *Star Wars*. When you're one with the Force, everything looks bright and hopeful, but when you dip into the dark side, it all becomes murky and chaotic. To become a successful color connoisseur, you need to understand the psychology and evolution of color. Practice combining colors; learn about hue, saturation, and density; and above all, fine-tune your color instincts.

Color Psychology

WHAT MAKES PEOPLE CHOOSE the colors that surround them? Is it a random choice, a conscious choice, or a subconscious choice? Perhaps, it's a combination of all three. We choose colors for many reasons, but most commonly because they are pleasing to the eye, they blend well with our surroundings, and even because they bring out the color of our eyes. But again, it's all about perception. Just because we like a certain color, doesn't mean anyone else will. Beauty, in this case, is definitely in the eye of the beholder

Color Perception

THE PERCEPTION OF COLOR is further complicated by the fact that colors mean different things to different people around the world. Colors are often associated with a variety of events or occurrences, including rites of passage, Mother Nature, loyalty, illness, spiritual enlightenment, and superstition. In Western culture, for example, white symbolizes cleanliness, virtue, and chastity, whereas in China, white is associated with mourning and grief.

Some colors, such as black, have negative connotations that are hard to dispel: "The dark side," "blacklisted," "the Black Plague," "black magic." Conversely, green evokes positive notions such as energy, life, growth, and money. "The grass is always greener..." is a state of mind often associated with green.

The psychology of color is subject to extreme differences of opinion. To prove this, ask several of your colleagues to write down objects or phrases associated with a certain color. When you read the answers, an interesting dynamic will emerge. For example, list everything you associate with red, and you'll run the gamut from roses, to stop signs, blood to tomatoes, red alerts and "seeing red." It's a color that suggests heat, love, passion, and danger. In symbolic terms, red is a warm color that in many cultures symbolizes strength and power. Whether consciously or not, individuals have innate and specific reactions to color.

Red is a highly visible color that traditionally symbolizes strength, passion, and power. With its thousands of shades and hues, red is also a color that people seldom agree on. The differences in tone can be subtle or dramatic, as these three images illustrate.

Large percentages of the four process colors can lead to dramatic, highly saturated images. In this image, 80 to 90 percent magenta is mixed with the same amount of yellow to create a deep, vibrant red.

The meaning and symbolism of colors vary by culture, but the following values often associated with specific colors:

RED:
passion, strength, power, danger

YELLOW:
playfulness, wisdom, optimism, jealousy

ORANGE:
creativity, warmth, adventurousness

GREEN:
healing, life, prosperity, regeneration, nurturing

BLUE:
loyalty, integrity, rejuvenation, trustworthiness, sadness

PURPLE:
royalty, mysticism, imagination

BROWN:
earth, nature, stability, balance

WHITE:
chastity, purity, virtue

BLACK:
mystery, death, rebirth, determination

In psychological terms, the values associated with certain colors can have a huge impact on the look and feel of a project. Some colors can project beauty, such as the reds, yellows, oranges, and browns of autumn. The deep hues of purple and blue can project richness, royalty, and elegance.

The meaning and use of colors will have a guaranteed impact on your projects—one way or another. Working with color will turn you into an amateur color psychologist, and the more experience and insight you glean out of a client's reactions, the better prepared you'll be for the next color challenge.

Some ancient societies believed in the healing capacity of color; while red was thought to stimulate energy, blue helped to cure colds and reduce bouts of hay fever. Even though this concept is regarded with a certain amount of skepticism in modern society, premature babies with jaundice are often treated and cured by exposure to blue light, which can trigger positive metabolic reactions.

One interesting attempt at using color to influence behavior is the bubble gum pink color sometimes used in jail and prison holding cells. The color seems to quell violent behavior, although studies have indicated that the effect is relatively short term.

An infinite number of intangible color associations will trigger a variety of responses in individuals. Traumatic events associated with a particular color can permanently affect an individual's reaction to that color. A sense of well being is often experienced by people who subconciously associate related colors, much the same way that the smell of baking cookies is reminiscent of soothing childhood memories.

When it comes to color, digital technology has opened a Pandora's box. Not long ago, designers manipulated color images without a color monitor. This frog, with its many percentages of greens, would have been nearly impossible to color correct on a grayscale display.

Color Evolution

BACK IN THE STONE AGE of graphic design and production, before computer systems became commonplace, color artwork went to press in numerous ways. Colors were specified on tissue overlays, cut out of rubyliths, or even drawn in colored pencil accompanied by pages of scribbled directions.

From the time the job left your hands, until the first proofs arrived from the printer, you held your breath. Often, yellow became butterscotch, your reds turned to pink, and that lush fern green transmuted into something commonly associated with nausea.

These days, you still hold your breath when delivering a job to the printer, and you still lose sleep wondering if the pale coral band bleeding off the top of each page should have been red. However, the processes you use to create, select, and display your colors from prepress to finished product have changed dramatically.

Designers now learning the trade have benefited from growing up with sophisticated hardware and software. However, if you've been around long enough to remember rubyliths, you probably found the digital color transition frustrating and time consuming, as all of the tried-and-true color palettes you developed over the years now required different percentages and specifications. Matters weren't helped by the primitive state of early desktop hardware. Because color monitors were small and expensive, many pioneering designers got by with monochrome displays, specifying color percentages on screens that could show only shades of gray. The trick was to create a digital file containing swatches with known color percentages, and then have it printed in color. You could then use the printed colors as visual references.

Anything related to color takes practice. Even Michelangelo had plenty of screw-ups on the Sistine Chapel before pronouncing it a masterpiece. Draw from your background, create samples, and build new color bases. You already know that greatness is the result of experimentation.

While color has evolved on many different levels, one factor remains constant. Color is an expensive commodity, and when used improperly, it is costly to repair. As you'll see in following chapters, you can employ many solutions to ensure proper color selection and display. But you need to understand how color works, both mentally and digitally. Rubyliths and tissue overlays served us well, but they pale in comparison to a whiz-bang color palette, a Pantone deck, and a 21-inch color monitor.

Understanding color balance will help you avoid making bad color choices. The right side of the ferns may look reasonable on the screen, but in reality, half of the yellow was eliminated due to some heavy-handed color manipulation.

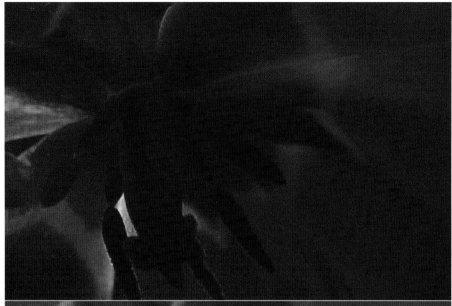

Mastering color takes time and practice, but the best designers learn to experiment with different levels of CMYK to create new combinations and appearances. Sometimes, the most striking images are created by accident. Side-by-side comparisons of the flower and entryway show how different an image can become when all of the yellow is removed.

Color Confidence

THE BEST DESIGNERS exude a well-developed confidence when it comes to color. They've studied how colors work on the page and in digital form. They've learned to mix their own colors and create color palettes. Most importantly, they've learned about the printing process. It cannot be overstated: A designer who wants to be successful with color must learn how the printing process works.

Many designers don't have a clue about what happens to their project once it arrives in the printer's hands. All they know is that the FedEx driver collects the package and delivers it to printing land, where Merlin magically colors and prints everything to perfection. It's a sad and fatal tale. Don't hesitate to ask questions of your printing representatives. You will gain valuable insight into the process, along with immeasurable confidence when communicating with clients.

Chapter 7 examines this process in-depth. Learning the mechanics of color is important, but it is equally important to learn how printers will handle your project. Color experience is a valuable commodity among everyone in design, print, and Web production. If you don't have the confidence to produce color, other designers will, and as a result, their clients and printers will be more confident in the final product.

Find Out What the Client *Really* Wants

THERE IS NOTHING MORE EDUCA-TIONAL—or amusing—than watching the color dance between client and designer as they discuss a job. It's a tense and uncomfortable time for both parties, as neither can agree on a hue, shade, tint, or density.

Every designer on the planet has endured the following situation. After weeks of preliminary meetings, the designer presents several logos to the client, who chooses the one they like. However, they request that the letters be royal blue. The next week, the designer gleefully presents the new logo, but the client winces in horror: "I said 'royal blue' for the lettering. That's not royal blue." The designer takes a long look at the lettering and determines that it's definitely a deep royal blue.

Sheepishly, the designer retrieves a color swatch book and points out the royal blue. The client skims through the book, selects a sky blue, plunks it down in front of the designer, and adamantly states, "*That* is royal blue."

The best advice any graphic designer can heed is to find out exactly what your client wants. In addition to calming your color fears, it will save time and production costs, while demonstrating your professionalism.

As a rule, always have color samples, swatches, or a Pantone deck on hand to present to your client. Ascertain what kind of look they're striving to achieve. If it's an advertisement in a retirement magazine, garish colors are most likely inappropriate. For an annual report, they may want to use corporate colors. The best approach is to listen and give them space and time to select the colors they're looking for. If they ask for recommendations, give them several choices. If a client changes their mind faster than their socks, run a color proof page with a variety of colors and let them choose the one they like. It's important to remember that battling with your client by voicing radical color opinions, or by being stubborn about their color choices, will most likely cost you an account.

Successful color work requires careful communication between designer and client or employer. Miscommunication can burn budgets and scar reputations. Before beginning any color project, be certain that everyone is envisioning the same color. You can do this using a Pantone book, CMYK color swatches, or other color references.

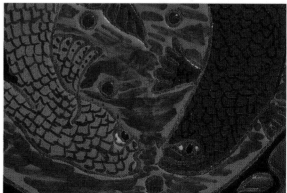

The Effects of
Ambient Lighting

LIGHTING HAS A SIGNIFICANT effect on the way you and your clients see color. Many designers create a work environment that provides a great deal of natural light, which can be ideal for accurately creating, choosing, and viewing colors. Clients and readers often don't have the luxury or need to work in natural light, and much printed material is viewed under the harsh fluorescent lighting common to modern offices.

Fluorescent lighting is generally colder and bluer than natural light, and thus tends to emphasize cool colors and subdue warm ones. Incandescent lighting tends to be more yellow and, thus, enhances warmer colors. Natural light, which is replicated in viewing booths and on pressroom viewing tables, is primarily neutral and creates minimal color cast. A pale yellow image that matches a color swatch under controlled lighting can virtually disappear under fluorescent lights, an effect known as *metamerism*.

Ambient lighting can have a significant impact on how your color images appear. Reflective images, such as this example, appear to have different colors under various lighting conditions.

These images illustrate the effect of metamerism.

The four red squares are all the same color, but when seen under incandescent light and natural light, the differences are unmistakable.

Metamerism

METAMERISM, as noted previously, occurs when objects match under certain lighting conditions but don't match under others. Proofs and press sheets produced with different pigments, dyes, and substrates can appear to be good matches in controlled natural light, but will be dissimilar under fluorescent or incandescent lighting. When proofing and press checking critical color matches, it's best to view the materials under different light sources. Stepping back a few feet from a viewing booth—and into the fluorescent lighting of most pressrooms—can provide a good representation of how a press sheet will appear in the office.

In this example, the identical blue square is shown under different lighting conditions. The square on the left is shown under incandescent, the middle square under fluorescent light, and the one on the right under natural light.

It's never too soon for a designer to discuss these issues with a client so that they have a reasonable understanding of the many ways that light sources visually affect color images. Sharing this knowledge will go a long way in assuring your clients that you have their best interests in mind and that voodoo doesn't play a part in the process. This is also a fact of life that good print reps and press operators should be intimately familiar with.

Using Common Sense

GRAPHIC DESIGNERS, like most creative folks, can be an assertive bunch, and everyone has an opinion. Some go down in flames as a result of stubborn pride. But the most successful designers can attribute their success to being open minded, learning from their mistakes, and using common sense.

Working with color is a privilege, not a curse. If you approach it with that attitude, you've won half the battle. While color can definitely push the limits of your patience, nothing is more gratifying than feasting your eyes on a colorful job well done.

When you're sitting down to a new color project, the first and most important task is analyzing the job. Objectivity and common sense will help set the tone. If you want to create a powerful impact, you can use a bright color scheme, as shown in the vegetable tray. The stylized pear image shows a more subtle use of color.

Defining Which Colors to Use

Whether you're a beginner or an advanced designer, it's crucial to keep each job in perspective, being mindful of your clients' wishes, budgets, and deadlines. Before diving into any color project, analyze the project on a practical level. Remove yourself from the glitz and glamour of the final product and use common sense as your base. Remember what your client asked for, and then ask yourself the following questions:

1. Who is the audience for this project?

2. What tone does the client want to project?

3. What colors are appropriate for the feel of the project?

4. What is the budget for this project?

5. Is it four color, two color, or is there a fifth color?

6. Does this project require a traditional or modern presence?

7. Is this a selling piece or an informational piece?

8. Will this project require staying power or is it a quick-turn piece?

9. Has the client chosen colors from a sample book?

10. Is this client open to suggestions?

11. Is there money for spot varnish or special paper that will improve color quality?

12. Under what lighting conditions will the final piece be viewed?

Asking these questions is a great way to understand what your client is trying to achieve. Working with color can be fatal to a designer/client relationship if it's not handled with care. This means setting aside preconceived notions and using a commonsense approach.

Warm versus Cool Colors

COLORS ARE PERCEIVED on a cerebral and physical level in many ways and through literally thousands of shades. In the design world, colors are typically divided into groups of warm, cool, and neutral colors. Warm colors are considered to be reds, yellows, and oranges. Cool colors include greens, blues, and purples, while neutrals run the gamut from browns to grays to black. Depending on whom you talk to or what you read, white is considered a neutral color, cool color, or noncolor.

Developing a trained eye will help you better understand warm versus cool colors. It's as easy as driving down the road, noticing the color of each house, and proclaiming it warm, cool, or neutral. The groupings listed above are a general rule. The waters get muddy when you begin mixing percentages to create new colors. At that point, a cool color can quickly become a warm one.

For example, 100 percent magenta is an extremely cool color. Adding percentages of yellow to magenta has a warming effect. Increasing the yellow to 100 percent, and decreasing the magenta by fixed percentages will result in a continuing change in warmth, until you reach the relative coldness of 100 percent yellow.

The primary process colors—cyan, magenta, and yellow—are inherently cool. Adding percentages of one color to the other has an overall warming effect. Adding percentages of yellow to magenta is a perfect example of this phenomenon.

Learning the subtle differences between warm and cool colors will enhance your ability to combine and contrast elements, while also creating a solid color palette. The overall effect of the chrysanthemum image is cool, with bright magenta highlights and mid-tones. The close-up photo illustrates contrast between the warm reds of the flower petals and the cool yellows of the pollen within.

Color Combinations

If you're stumped when combining color, take inspiration from the world around you. Sometimes, the least likely colors work in harmony. When you find combinations that work well together, add them to your repertoire.

IF YOU COULD BE ANY COLOR of the rainbow, what color would you be? Cool ice blue? Elegant royal purple? Flashy metallic gold? It may be a silly question, but it's worth asking as it gives insight into the type of colors you feel comfortable with and that work well together.

Even color aficionados differ on which colors are warm or cool or which combinations work best together. Colors can work in harmony, or they can clash. Your choices depend on the look you're striving for and the aura you're hoping to project.

Beyond the warm and cool designations, colors are typically lumped into categories such as natural, rich, muted, and calm. Natural colors are a perfect definition for the term "subjective." What you might consider natural, the next person will deem unnatural. Natural colors are often associated with the great outdoors: green grass, blue sky, brown tree trunks, or orange leaves. These are terrific no-nonsense colors that appeal to most individuals and are a safe bet for designs.

This photograph presents an interesting combination of warm browns and cool greens and reds. The contrast helps to enhance the poignant impact of the image. (Photo courtesy of Audrey Baker.)

Color is Mother Nature's gift to designers, and as luck would have it, glorious greens, blues, oranges, and browns are soothing to even the most discerning eye. In the first set of images, you can see the range of warm color combinations. The second set illustrates the cool combinations found in a single green leaf.

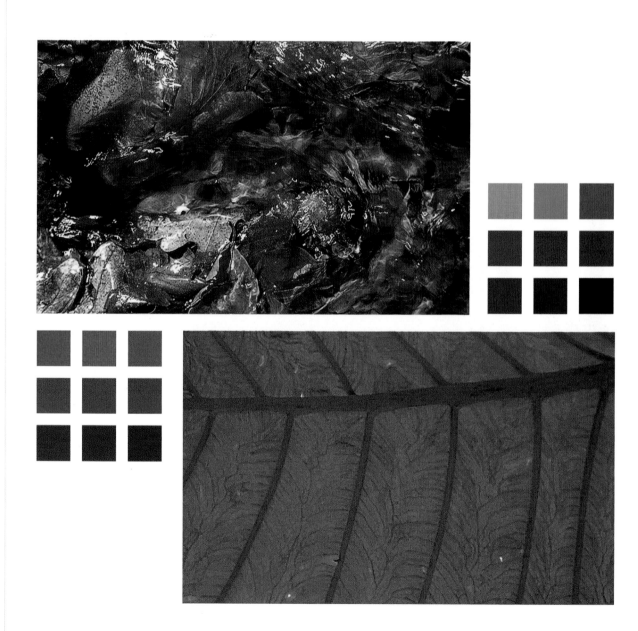

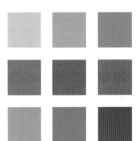

Rich shades of purple, blue, red, green, or burgundy are comforting but can quickly overwhelm the eye. Take care to use them with purpose and within the context of your message. Both sets of images convey a range of rich color combinations in different hues and saturations.

Rich Colors

REDS, PURPLES, ROYAL BLUES, FOREST GREENS, AND BURGUNDIES with deep tones are examples of rich colors. Various percentages of black dictate how dense these colors can be, and how well they will print. The historical colors of royalty, these tones convey depth and weight. They work well in contrast and in combination with highlight color, but you should be careful not to overuse them. A page enveloped in rich color can quickly overwhelm a design. This can reduce the information you are trying to convey, and make the finished piece feel excessively dramatic and overdesigned.

Small percentages of color can make a big difference to the outcome of your project. Relatively minor fluctuations in color density, whether in solid color blocks or a smattering of stones, can make a big difference. These colored blocks illustrate only a 3 percent fluctuation in percentages of cyan, yellow, and magenta. How many variations of gray do you see in the stones?

Muted Colors

MANY DESIGNERS HAVE TROUBLE working with what they consider to be calm or muted colors. Here, instinct and judgment must dictate your color selections, and playing the color percentages comes to the forefront. Percentages of base colors can vary greatly, as neutrals colors are most prone to shifting on press.

If you have a job that requires loads of muted color, your best insurance is to run a test proof with your printer. Set up a page containing different color blocks with different percentages, and it will make your job infinitely easier.

Muted colors can combine to present an effective image and feel. A simple wall can contain dozens of subtle shades from pale yellow to rusty orange to dark brown.

Colors That Make a Statement

CLOSE YOUR EYES and think about what you've seen in the last twenty-four hours. What sticks out in your mind and why? Is it the green pasture you strolled through, the swirling beige coffee you drank this morning, or those blue guys on a television commercial? No matter what you saw or where you saw it, certain colors made an impact. Color has a way of seeping into your brain and staying there, whether it's a Caribbean sunset or a burnt roast.

What makes something memorable? Words, expressions, and color. Just ask anyone in advertising. The same rules apply to design, whether it's in print or on the Web. Depending on your medium and project, the use of bold colors, patterns, and letters can have enormous impact and longevity.

Creations with bold color and unique imagery often become embedded in our memories. Playing with strong colors is fun, but it's easy to cross the line into garish.

The Yellow Factor

FOR SOME BIZARRE REASON, people are mad for the color yellow. While yellow as a stand-alone color may be too perky for some designers, it is very practical for most media and a crucial element to mixing colors. Designers find that yellow causes much trouble both in proof and final product. It is a key component in many color mixes and it's a tough mix to get right. Whenever you're designing a color job, keep a printed sample of yellow color blocks handy. It's a great reference and reminder of what could happen if yellow is misused.

These blocks give a range of yellow percentages from 20 to 100 in increments of 10 percent. The second set of blocks shows the same increments of yellow with 20 percent cyan added to each.

Opposites Attract
(I.E., THE GREEN/RED FACTOR)

MANY DESIGNERS will argue that colors must be complementary in order to be pleasing to the eye. However, the radical design faction will argue to the death, that contrasting colors are the only way to use color. In this instance, both parties are correct—but it depends solely on the type of project you are working on.

Colors at the opposite end of the spectrum, like red and green, have caused arguments for years. Some people see spots, while others see Christmas. Obviously, colors that are closer together on the color wheel work well together. Colors at opposing ends of the wheel can also work well together if used in the proper context.

Contrasting colors is tricky business, and the more you use them in a single project, the more garish they become. However, when used for a specific purpose, the resulting piece can be wildly successful.

Contrasting colors make a strong statement and can work well together in the proper context. The red/green combination is a common occurrence in nature, but a little goes a long way. The goal is to highlight, not nauseate.

On a traditional color wheel, complementary colors are diametrically opposed. In this case, the combinations are red/green, violet/yellow, and blue/orange.

SUMMARY

BUILDING THE FOUNDATIONS of a solid clientele depends on your knowledge and understanding of color and color combinations. Discovering and sharing the concepts, impact, and possibilities of color can be one of the most rewarding elements of graphic design. As a design professional, it's important to explore the variety of available resources from which you can expand your color repertoire. Graphics handbooks are invaluable tools for ideas, along with books on interior and exterior design, architecture, and landscape design. The natural world can also provide endless inspiration. Visiting wild animal parks and botanical gardens, or even local attractions, with a designer's eye for color can lead you in effective, unusual, and exciting directions.

2

COLOR CORRECTION, MANIPULATION, AND PROOFING SYSTEMS

YOUR SCREEN IS FILLED WITH COLOR. The images are glorious, perfectly adjusted, and ready for mass consumption. But are they really? Are those "perfect" photographs the real thing, or simply a trick of the eye? You didn't bother running proofs of any of them, why would you if the images appeared to be perfect? If you're a rookie designer, you wouldn't, and that could be a costly mistake. What you see is not what you get, and if you didn't take the time to create and test your color percentages, and didn't run a sample proof, you're in for a very unpleasant surprise.

Color imagery and proofing are kindred spirits. They rely and thrive on one another, and any designer worth their Sharpie pays heed to this all-important relationship. Knowing how to manipulate color is vitally important, and proofing those manipulations is also crucial. If you learn one thing as a designer, it's that color is a fantasy world, and the only way to bring it to reality is to back up your actions with hard evidence.

Many designers create their own color palettes, such as the one shown here. All three rows begin with 100 percent yellow, adding 10 percent increments of another process color until both are at 100 percent. The top row is yellow mixed with magenta, the middle row is yellow mixed with cyan, and the bottom row is yellow mixed with black.

Creating a Trusted Color Palette

DESIGNERS LOVE EXPERIMENTING with color because it offers freedom, movement, and creativity. However, those enticements often come at a high price. Before attempting any color-manipulation or color-correction process, it's important to develop a palette of tried-and-tested colors that you feel comfortable with and you know will print superbly.

Learning the nuts and bolts of color means learning how to mix and match colors using percentages. In most graphics software, you can easily create such a palette, saving it for use on future design jobs or tailoring it to specific projects. It's a good idea—and well worth the effort—to experiment with mixed percentages of the four process colors, for example taking 100 percent magenta and adding increments of 10

percent yellow, until you reach red. Then do the same thing with 10 percent increments of cyan and black. This will provide a solid base for any palette, especially as you add new mixes with each new project. Duplicating these mixtures on a single page, and having the printer run a proof, will give you a fabulous archive of color swatches that you can refer to at any time.

You can also add variations of colors you've already created to the palette. For example, if you have a particular shade of teal, you can create a list of percentages for that color beginning at 100 percent and moving down to 10 percent. As you will quickly find out, the combinations are endless.

Experimenting with percentages always yields new and exciting combinations. Any premixed color is also fair game for your palette. These rows are examples of already mixed shades reduced in 5 percent increments. The top row starting color is a mix of 72 percent cyan and 38 percent yellow. The middle row starts at 43 percent cyan and 76 percent magenta. The bottom row starts at 56 percent magenta and 87 percent yellow.

This forest pond, with its varying shades of garish yellow and blurry pastel pinks, screams overexposure. Working with the brightness and contrast will help, but in the long run, these images require lots of tinkering with hue, saturation, and density settings.

Color Correction and Manipulation

MANIPULATING AND CORRECTING COLOR IMAGES is like dancing with the devil—you never know when you'll get burned. As with all color work, the key to avoiding problems is to manipulate color percentages, learn the color-editing functions of your graphics program, and run a proof with your printer. Images can suffer from any number of color maladies, including oversaturation, over- and underexposure, extreme shadows and highlights, subtle color variations, and in many cases, poor original art.

This image is a perfect example of oversaturation. The murky magenta and blue tones overwhelm the image, making it blurry and hard to adjust. Adding to the difficulty are the subtle highlights, deep shadows, and the blown-out yellows in the sun.

Saturation

HEAVILY SATURATED IMAGES ARE TRICKY to manipulate. What appears to be a slight adjustment on screen can result in huge differences in the printed product. You can try experimenting with these images, but your best insurance is to create a ganged sample page and have your printer run a test file. Make notes of the modifications performed on each image and then compare them to the proof. Only then can you continue adjusting images with reasonable certainty.

Remember that oversaturated images in the design stage will probably become even more saturated on press due to dot gain. Once on press, the only cure for oversaturated images is to reduce the amount of ink applied to the paper, which can have a negative effect on all of the other elements of your design.

Everyone loves silhouettes, but they're a nightmare for designers. If you're lucky, manipulating brightness and contrast can do the trick, but most of the time you'll need to heavily manipulate hue and saturation, taking care to prevent the image from becoming murky and plugging up on press.

Images with heavy shadows
are equally tough to manipulate, as this poorly constructed
image shows. Working with
shadows takes a lot of practice, as it is very easy to over-
work the shadowy areas and
have them posterize on press.

Subtle color variation is the
ultimate trickster when color
manipulation is required. The
complex browns and yellows in
this image make it extremely
difficult to shift certain portions without shifting others.
As a rule, you should avoid
making radical corrections
and try to retouch only the
glaring problems.

Poor original art is a common
complaint among designers.
This blurry image has bad
exposure, saturation, dust and
scratches, and a moving target.
If you are compelled to fix
such an image, take solace
in knowing that it can't look
much worse.

This image, heavily saturated with blue and black, is a perfect example of how difficult manipulations can be. The original version (top left) is murky and needs adjustment. However, the progression of accompanying images from top to bottom shows what happens as you lift cyan in 10 percent increments.

The magenta in this image is oversaturated to such an extent that it glows. At first glance, it's too garish, but reducing the saturated magenta by even 10 percent can turn this image around. The trick is making sure that the background blues don't turn purple.

This original image (above), though captivating, suffers from a massive dose of yellow. Manipulating the yellow is complicated because the entire image is affected. This is the type of image you want to proof, no matter the cost, because even the slightest color adjustment will be dramatic. The image at left has 30 percent of the saturated yellow removed.

Highly overexposed images, such as this beach shot, require careful adjustments. You can modify brightness and contrast only after increasing the midtones, in this case, by approximately 20 percent. The before and after images are quite startling.

Over- and Underexposure

AT FIRST GLANCE, MOST OF THESE images appear unusable, but with the surge in photo-manipulation technology, many can be salvaged. In some cases, you'll get lucky, and a simple brightness or contrast adjustment will do the trick. Or you can use the more-sophisticated Levels or Curves functions in Adobe Photoshop to independently modify highlights, shadows, and midtones. However, with many images, you'll have to execute multiple manipulations with all four process colors to achieve the desired effect.

Underexposed images are common and can be easy to adjust. This image, taken on a cloudy day, is remedied by manipulating the brightness, contrast, and sharpness of the image. Notice how the colors leap from the page.

Extreme Shadows and Highlights

THIS IS WHERE COLOR RETOUCHING gets interesting and frustrating. Images that contain extreme shadows or highlights are problematic, even under the best circumstances. The unfortunate byproduct of dealing with these images is that no two are alike. Shadows are often in danger of becoming posterized, and highlights can become bright white splotches on the image. Practice makes perfect when it comes to retouching these images, and the more you manipulate, the better you'll get at adjusting them for optimal reproduction.

Food photography suffers from highlight anxiety on a daily basis. Reflections from a camera flash wreak havoc on just about any surface. These peppers were retouched by adjusting the brightness to reduce the white glare and contrast to even the color saturation.

When adjusting for shadows, you need to be careful that you're not distorting the entire image. With a photo as dense and shadowy as this, you have to work slowly to adjust the midtones and brightness in small increments.

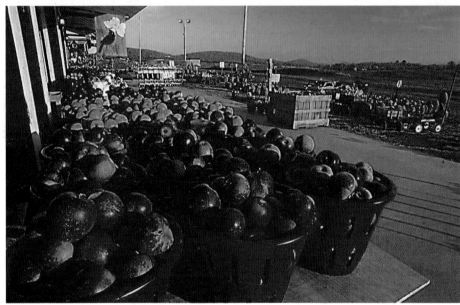

Shadows on faces are common, and fixing them is not always easy. In an image like this, compromise is the better part of valor. The original is muddy and saturated. You can bring out the warrior's beautiful expression by using Adobe Photoshop to modify brightness and midtones, but doing so while maintaining the richness of the blue sky can be tricky.

Some images that contain extreme shadow and highlights cannot be manipulated effectively. In this case, the image is still effective without any adjustment.

As you can see in these four comparison photos, a minute adjustment of 5 to 15 percent less magenta can make a significant difference. The first image is the original; the three that follow have respectively had 5, 10, and 15 percent magenta removed.

Subtle Color Variation

OVERADJUSTING IMAGES that contain similar tones and shades can be devastating, because ink densities on the press have a significant effect, and subtle variations that are possible on the computer may not fall within the press's CMYK gamut. Use care when retouching any images with subtle color variation.

No matter what images you're color correcting and manipulating, it's important to send a sample to your printer for proofing. In addition to offering relief from color uncertainty, it will help secure your professionalism in the design field. What follows are the different types of proofs available to you and your client.

Reproduction of skin tones can be controversial and subjective. As illustrated in this series of model photos, skin tones that could be construed as too pink or too yellow if photographed separately prove to be accurate representations of natural color variations when shown together.

Images of food are among
the most demanding projects
for designers. The key to success is excellent photography
that conveys palatability,
freshness, and festivity.
These are examples of good
photographs that need
little overall retouching
or manipulation.

Running proofs early and often is the key to any successful color project. You should always check questionable images; even one that looks reasonably good on screen can have disastrous results on press. This before-and-after representation of an image is a perfect example of why designers should make the proofing process part of their regular routine.

Types of Proofs

Types of Proofs

- DESIGN LAYOUT PROOFS
- SCREEN-BUILD PROOFS
- PAGE PROOFS
- GANG PROOFS
- IMPOSITION PROOFS
- CONTRACT PROOFS

PROOFING ON ANY PRINTING PROJECT CAN NEVER BEGIN TOO SOON. "Proof early and proof often" is sound advice and pays dividends in successful press runs. Proofing follows a pattern of succession and can be broken into the following categories:

Design Layout Proofs

THE FIRST PROOFS GENERATED IN PRINT projects are those produced during the conceptual and design stages. It's common here to perform preliminary scanning of critical images for color correction and manipulation. These images are generally sent to color prepress houses or the printer, and serve a dual purpose: They can be grouped on single sheets as printed proofs, and they can be adjusted electronically. Designers who use established color-management systems often bypass hard proofs at this stage, and work directly with electronic scans.

Basic design proofs are generally produced on monochrome laser printers and low-end color printers, with place-holders designated as *position only* (POs) or *for position only* (FPOs), for the high-resolution scans to follow. This stage is rarely used for final color approval.

Screen-Build Proofs

IF YOU PLAN TO USE A CMYK PROCESS to replicate Pantone spot colors, you may be in for an unpleasant surprise. Many Pantone colors can't be accurately translated into four-color process because the gamut of CMYK isn't large enough to replicate the spot-color pigments. For jobs with high expectations, it's worth the expense to send your printer a file with small blocks of screen-built colors for proofing. If the results don't meet your expectations, you'll have time to make adjustments in the early stages of the project before going to the expense of final contract proofs and last-minute changes.

You should also consider the eventual impact of making final color adjustments on press. Adjusting four-color images on press will also affect screen-built spot colors. For example, if the press operator adds more magenta to an image, any colors built with magenta will also show a color shift. If accurate Pantone matching is essential, consider adding it as a fifth spot color.

Screen-build proofs can be a simple series of blocks proofed on a single sheet. This provides a valuable visual reference and allows you to make minor percentage adjustments before committing the project to the final contract proofing stage.

Four-color images and screen-built color blocks can be ganged together on a preliminary color proof before committing the project to the final proofing stage, where changes and corrections can be costly.

Gang Proofs

SIMILAR TO SCREEN-BUILD PROOFS in intent, gang proofs are scanned and scaled photos of four-color images grouped onto a single sheet for color proofing. For images that may require color retouching and manipulation, this is a cost-effective approach to achieving the final proofing results you're seeking, without the expense of reproofing an entire job with scattered four-color photos. This can also be done in concert with screen-built blocks, and can put you on the right track with screen percentages and color images at the same time.

For jobs with multiple Pantone color-matching criteria, another option is to print the job using the patented six-color process described later in this chapter. This increases the color gamut on press tremendously and provides far more accuracy for screen-build matches.

Ganging images on a preliminary high-resolution proof can save time and money on corrections at the final proofing stage. Scanned and scaled images can be electronically placed in random order to best fit the most economical proof size and then reviewed for color.

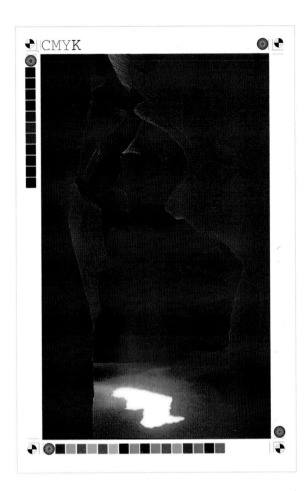
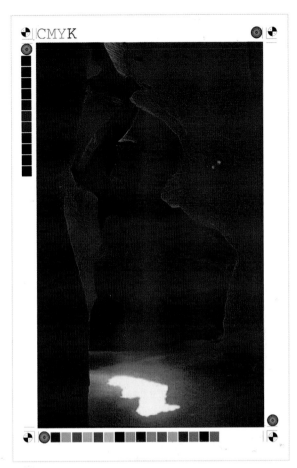

Proofing Systems

MODERN PREPRESS PROOFING systems are an integral part of the evolution of prepress technology. Major manufacturers such as Kodak, Agfa, Fuji, Hewlett-Packard, and Creo are part of the pack, and the range of proofing technologies can be overwhelming. High-resolution proofing is generally quite accurate, and most printers and prepress houses maintain consistent quality standards. All proofing systems are subject to a wide range of variables, and no single proofing system is inherently superior in all respects. Two separate printing houses—using identical proofing systems to produce final proofs of identical electronic files—can produce output that displays significant differences in color and fidelity. These variations are caused by differences in hardware settings, exposures, chemical maintenance, machine maintenance, and handling.

These proofs are examples of the same file processed and proofed by two different printers using the same proofing system. Most printers adjust their proofing system to closely match the capabilities of the printing presses they use.

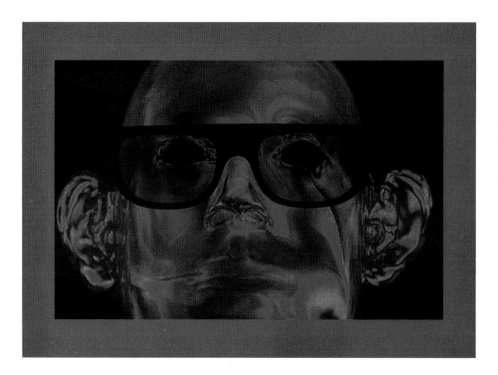

Many proofing systems reproduce Pantone colors as CMYK builds, even if the spot colors are to be printed separately on press. To ensure that the printer is aware of this, you should clearly mark your additional color locations on the proof.

Proofing Purposes and Expectations

Proofs to Your Printer

Remember that if you are unable to run separated proofs from your files, your printer probably won't be able to run separated files either. Supplying separated lasers is critical to ensuring good communication and avoiding costly errors when the job is in the printer's hands. Many printers won't even accept a job if separated lasers aren't included in your submission package. Those that do will often send you a change order for additional costs if they encounter problems.

BEFORE ANY RESPONSIBLE PRINTER puts a job on press, they will expect the client to sign-off on a proof. The purpose of a proof is to represent what will be printed on press, within the predictable limitations of the proofing system. It's important to establish these limitations with your printer as early as possible—preferably before sending the job out (see Chapter 7 for more information on working with your printer). Printers use a variety of systems that can produce proofs with color gamut and brightness that be either less or more than what's possible on press.

Proofing Spot Color

ONE IMPORTANT ELEMENT WITH many proofing systems—and virtually all digital proofing systems—is that spot colors printed separately from the process colors will be proofed either as composite CMYK or as a separate proofing pigment. This may not precisely represent the specific spot color you've chosen. The Chromalin proofing system allows the proofer to mix specific pigments that will match formulated colors with good accuracy, but this can be pricey because it adds considerably to the time and effort required to precisely match pigments. For critical color matching and client approval, the cost can be justified. The key to saving money and time is to clearly identify your color breaks and, if possible, mark them on the proofs you receive so that all parties will be aware of each spot color's placement. To ensure that there are no surprises on press, you need to communicate your specifications and run your own separated laser proofs.

Separated Proofs

Along with electronic files, you should supply your printer with separated laser proofs. This ensures that the printer is aware of each color to be printed, and shows that your separations were accurate before they left your possession. Shown here is a four-color job with a fifth color in addition to the black, cyan, magenta, and yellow.

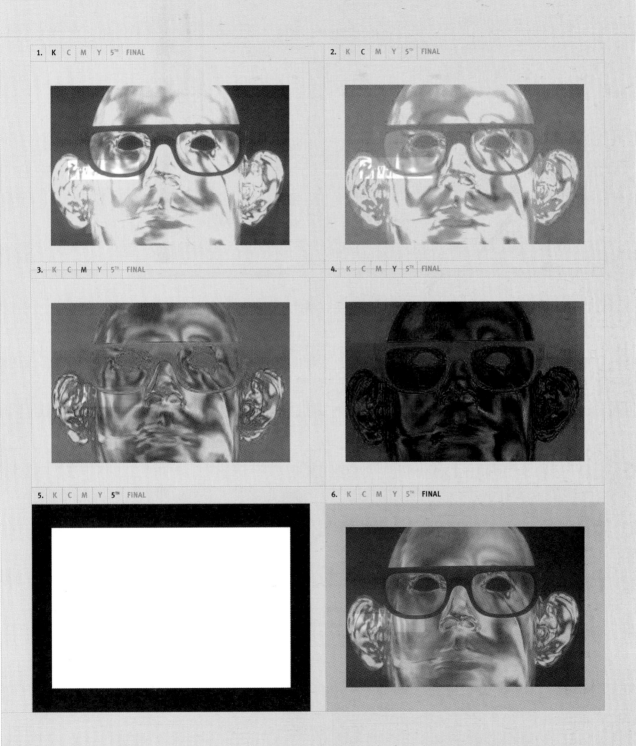

1. K C M Y 5ᵀᴴ FINAL

2. K C M Y 5ᵀᴴ FINAL

3. K C M Y 5ᵀᴴ FINAL

4. K C M Y 5ᵀᴴ FINAL

5. K C M Y 5ᵀᴴ FINAL

6. K C M Y 5ᵀᴴ **FINAL**

Reviewing Proofs

REVIEWING PROOFS IS EASILY ONE OF THE MOST CRITICAL STAGES for ensuring a high-quality final color product. Once you've signed off on a proof, your printer has every right to assume that the job is okay to print, and the last thing you want to say during a press check is, "Oops, I missed that on the proof." This is particularly dangerous when your client has enough confidence in you to okay the proof without their involvement, as is often the case with reruns that involve only minor changes. Missing the most mundane color alterations, such as a changed date in the small print, can turn an expensive project into an even more-expensive disaster. While printers occasionally complain about clients who are "red pencil happy," they are not responsible for client errors that don't get caught.

Light booths with color-corrected light sources (5,000 degrees Kelvin) present the most accurate and repeatable conditions for reviewing color proofs. This is true in your review of color proofs and at the time your job goes to press. (Courtesy Heidelberg USA, Inc.)

Lighting and Proofing

PROPER LIGHTING CONDITIONS are important for proofing and reviewing critical color matches. Viewing booths with 5,000 degree Kelvin corrected lightbulbs are an industry standard, and provide lighting that has the least effect on color appearance. Proofs viewed under fluorescent or incandescent lighting will reflect the cooler colors of fluorescence, or the warmer colors of incandescence.

Lighting and the Pressroom

ANOTHER ELEMENT TO BEAR in mind when analyzing color under various lighting conditions is that most pressroom viewing tables are also fitted with color-corrected, 5,000-degree Kelvin lights. The color you see when reviewing proofs under controlled lighting conditions will be the same color you see when your job is on press.

In this example, the original photograph (top) and the proof viewed under fluorescent lighting (bottom) show significant color variation. The differences are due to the ambient light in combination with variations in the dyes and substrates used to make the prints.

Metameric Influence on Proofing

COMPARING COLOR PROOFS TO PHOTO-GRAPHIC PRINTS under uncorrected lighting conditions can show the effects of metamerism. If ambient light alters the color you are viewing, other variables can exacerbate the differences. Dyes used in different proofing systems are not identical, nor are the proofing substrates. Dyes and finishes on photographs also vary depending on the manufacturer. A proof and an original photograph can appear to be closely matched under corrected lighting, while quite dissimilar under other artificial lighting. By the same token, it's possible for a proof and photograph to display a good color match under fluorescent light and display a significant color shift under corrected lighting. Viewing color proofs under corrected lighting is the only accurate and repeatable method of assessing them.

The same images seen in the color-corrected light of a viewing booth show the proof to be an accurate representation of the photograph. The light source minimizes color influence, providing the most accurate and repeatable environment for good color analysis.

Fishermen claim that Mother Nature owns the land, but their mistress is the sea. That is, perhaps, never more evident than on the Oregon Coast, a glorious stretch of land carved by everchanging time and tide.

On sunny days, its craggy outcrops and sandy shores are kissed by succulent waves. When consumed by fog, the land is reminiscent of coastal Maine, the vague sillouettes of boats fading into the mist like ghostly pirate vessels hunting the high seas.

The quaint coastal villages of the Oregon coast are born of the sea and the local color, both of which are in abundance. The everpresent crash of waves against is in sharp contrast to the sounds of technology so evident in big cities. In towns ranging from Coos Bay to Astoria, the folks one meets are neither opportunists or escapists. They are coastal and they spawn from all walks of life, joining together to celebrate their love for the ocean and all that it represents.

Fisherman spin their yarns faster than a Sunday coffee klatch. Some fish for profit, some for sport, but all will tell that their love for the sea is rooted in respect for the everchanging watery landscape and all that it provides.

Page proofs show content and elements from the designer with position-only placeholders for the four-color process images to be added during the prepress stage. Always make the FPO notation big and easy to identify, so you avoid the risk of printing the low-resolution file.

Page Proofs

PAGE PROOFS ARE FULLY COMPOSED proofs of each page, with all design elements in place. Four-color images can be shown as position-only placeholders in a single color to signify that the final images will be placed at the prepress stage. Page proofs are commonly shown to the client in single pages or as *reader spreads*, which indicate the page sequence of the final job.

Imposition Proofs

YOUR PRINTER CREATES IMPOSITION PROOFS from processed files. These show all of the images and elements as they will appear on the press sheet, and are often folded, collated, stitched, and trimmed to final size to represent the finished product. Imposition proofs show position, content, and color breaks.

Bluelines

Bluelines are used as imposition proofs and are often employed as final proofs for simple one- and two-color jobs. As the name implies, these proofs are manufactured with a blue toner that becomes progressively darker with increased exposure to intense light in a vacuum frame. They are exposed using the same film that will be used for producing the press plates. Color breaks can be shown effectively by reducing exposure times, which results in a lighter shade of blue. One caveat here is that the lighter shades of blue representing a lighter color in a two-color job will often look similar to screens printed in the darker color. If these bluelines will be used as final proofs before a press run, it's always a good idea to clearly mark the color breaks. Blueline proofs will also discolor rapidly when exposed to direct sunlight, so care should be taken when transporting them.

Digital Imposition Proofs

Digital imposition proofs are usually made in conjunction with direct-to-press systems and have come a long way in fidelity and color. While still far from being final-proof quality, these imposition proofs offer a four-color continuous-tone representation of the elements that will be imaged onto plates. These proofs are imaged on both sides directly from the prepress system and will accurately portray color breaks.

Bluelines can be exposed incrementally to show color breaks, but they should be clearly marked to avoid confusion. Some printers will mark up color breaks on bluelines before showing them to you. Others will not take responsibility for this step. When they don't, it's up to you.

Fishermen claim that Mother Nature owns the land, but their mistress is the sea. That is, perhaps, never more evident than on the Oregon Coast, a glorious stretch of land carved by everchanging time and tide.

On sunny days, its craggy outcrops and sandy shores are kissed by succulent waves. When consumed by fog, the land is reminiscent of coastal Maine, the vague sillouettes of boats fading into the mist like ghostly pirate vessels hunting the high seas.

The quaint coastal villages of the Oregon coast are born of the sea and the local color, both of which are in abundance. The everpresent crash of waves against is in sharp contrast to the sounds of technology so evident in big cities. In towns ranging from Coos Bay to Astoria, the folks one meets are neither opportunists or escapists. They are coastal and they spawn from all walks of life, joining together to celebrate their love for the ocean and all that it represents.

Fisherman spin their yarns faster than a Sunday coffee klatch. Some fish for profit, some for sport, but all will tell that their love for the sea is rooted in respect for the everchanging watery landscape and all that it provides.

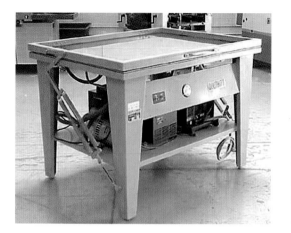

Analog proofs are created using film and proofing material in a vacuum exposure frame similar to this one. These proofs are still common and many believe they offer the most accurate color representation. However, accurate digital proofing systems are quickly becoming more prevalent.

Contract Proofs

AS THE TERM IMPLIES, signing off on a *contract proof* is the indication of an agreement between the client and the printer that the proof will represent the result of the project on press—within the predictable limitations of the proofing system. Contract proofing systems fall into two categories: Analog and digital.

Analog Proofing

ANALOG PROOFS are still common, although they are fading in importance as fully digitized systems become more accessible. This proofing system requires the use of film in a vacuum frame for exposure, one color at a time. These proofs represent the same halftone dot structures that will be produced on the plates. Analog proofing systems have long been considered to be the most accurate of all proofing systems—a notion that is coming under fire as digital proofing becomes more sophisticated.

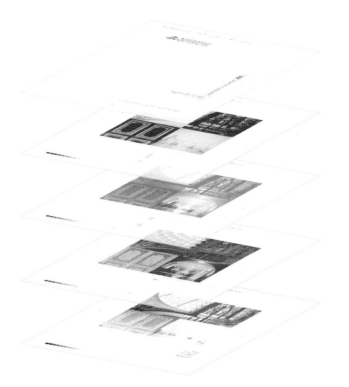

Film Overlay Proofs

Film overlay proofs, often referred to by the 3M trademarked name *Color Key*, have been with us for decades and produce proofs in loose layers that require wet chemical processing. These were part of the analog proofing system before the term was even coined. Film overlay proofs are exposed in a vacuum frame with a single pigmented color representing each of the process colors, then chemically developed, assembled, and taped to a substrate in the manufacturer's predetermined sequence.

With each of the process color pigments fused to an acetate base and the acetates loosely overlayed, a certain amount of air is trapped between each layer. The combination gives the final proof a hazy, grayish cast. This layering and air trapping also allows light to bounce within the layers, creating a *softer* looking dot that is most noticeable in highlights.

Film overlay proofs are the least expensive of the analog proofing systems. A benefit to the system is that additional colors can be added to represent specially formulated ink mixes. While these don't accurately depict each color, the layers can be lifted to ensure accurate color breaks. Many printers still use film overlay proofs, which will probably hold a share of the analog-proofing marketplace for years to come.

Film overlay proofs are loose layers of analog proofing material assembled in predetermined sequences and usually attached on one edge to the substrate. This image shows the progression of black, magenta, cyan, and yellow, and the final results.

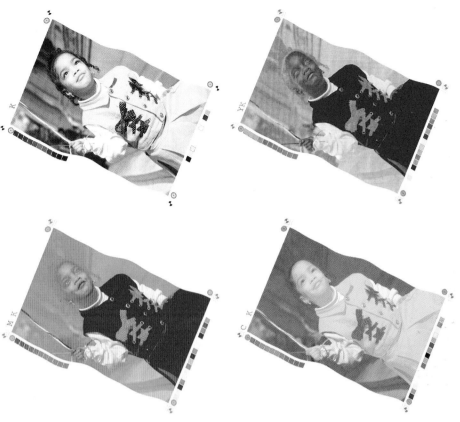

Occasionally, film overlay proofs are assembled out of sequence, resulting in a slight shift in the final color. Most printers strive to maintain proper sequence, but this is not an uncommon mistake. As you can see, the same image with colors out of sequence shows a significant difference in the final proof.

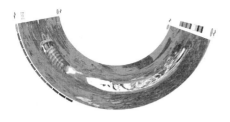 

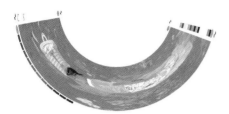 

Laminate proofs should be clean, with registration targets and color bars in place. These images show the manufacturer's recommended sequence of yellow, magenta, cyan, and black.

Laminated Proofs

Laminated proofs, which have largely displaced film overlay proofs, were first developed with wet chemical processors, but are now produced with a dry proofing process that does not require use of chemicals or processors. This proofing system is still assembled one color at a time on a single substrate or carrier. Some of these proofing systems allow for a sheet of the actual job stock to be used as the proofing surface. The layers of wet chemical and dry proofing systems are laminated to the substrate in specific sequences (yellow, magenta, cyan, and black). These sequences are determined by the manufacturer, and strict adherence is required to ensure proper color. Occasionally, proofs are accidentally assembled out of sequence, which may result in mild to radical shifts in color.

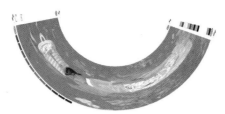

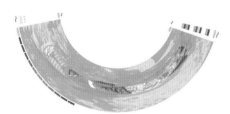

Laminate proofs are sometimes inadvertently assembled out of sequence. This can result in a noticeable color shift that will adversely affect the balance of color. This is difficult to detect because the proofing layers are laminated tightly together, but the overlapping color bars will likely show their own slight color shift.

Common Denominators of Analog Proofs

All of these systems depend on accurate film assembly and the careful attention of the proofing operator. For years, the people who exposed and processed proofs also burned and developed the plates for the press. Minor slips in these processes, either on the part of the *stripper* who assembles the film layers, or the proofer who assembles the proofs, can result in images out of register on the proof. One common problem with the analog system is damage to the emulsion side of a color. This is often seen in the form of white specks, or holes that appear in that color after the proof is assembled. The emulsion side of any proofing material is highly sensitive, and susceptible to scratches during the assembly process.

Proofs can occasionally slip in the vacuum exposure frame, causing slight but noticeable registration problems. These problems are usually caught and corrected before presentation to the client, but the occasional out-of-register proof can still slip through. If images look out of register, check the targets, and always ask for a revised proof. In this image, you can clearly see that the cyan is out of register.

Areas of pigmented proofing material can flake off during processing, resulting in pinholes and gaps in the final proof. In this example, the magenta pigment was damaged, which can be difficult to detect on the proof before assembly. While this may not represent flaws in the film or affect final printing, these mistakes should be corrected and a new proof, as illustrated on the right, should be supplied.

The *emulsion* side of proofs that carries the process color pigment is quite sensitive, and is sometimes scratched during processing and handling. In this example, the cyan proofing material was accidentally scratched on the left side with a rough fingernail. Remaking the proof, as illustrated in the third image, is the best way to ensure that there are no problems with the film.

In some cases, proofing artifacts result not from the proofing material itself but from scratches on the film that generates the proofs. This is usually noticeable because the scratches allow light to pass through the film and are thus exposed on the proofing medium. In this example, the film used for the cyan plate has been damaged. The only recourse is to reproduce the cyan film and remake the proof.

A common problem with analog proofing systems is contamination by minute dust particles trapped between the film layer and the proof surface. These particles interfere with the contact of film and proof, creating a ring-shaped distortion in dot size and dot pattern. Called *halation*, this usually occurs only in the particular color being exposed, and can be difficult to interpret. Fortunately, the solution is usually simple and experienced prepress professionals will eliminate the problem by examining the film and wiping it clean of debris.

Digital Proofing

COMPUTERIZED DIRECT-TO-PLATE technology is coming on strong. Just as computer-to-film systems eliminated the need for the much slower flatbed cameras of years past, direct-to-plate systems have eliminated the need for film. One factor hindering the acceptance of direct-to-plate has been the lack of adequate proofing systems. Plates are processed for printing only one color each. This means the hardware and software for plate production is designed to handle the digital information and accuracy of a single color. The production of four-color digital proofs presents essentially four times the technical difficulty. Although the pigments and substrates of digital proofing systems are not identical to ink pigments and paper substrates, recent technological advances have resulted in digital proofs that can be matched with remarkable accuracy.

Foreign particles trapped between layers of analog proofs when exposed in a vacuum frame can cause halation, shown by a small ring of distorted dot patterns in the final proof. These are sometimes overlooked at the proofing stage and are one reason why you should inspect proofs carefully.

Earlier digital proofing systems produced representations of the final output, which allowed content proofing, but didn't present a truly accurate medium for color. Current digital systems for contract proofs produce *dot-for-dot* proofs that—like analog proofing systems—provide an accurate representation of the data that will be imaged to the plates. These images are typical examples of what you can expect from modern digital proofing and direct-to-plate printing.

Proofing Systems and Press Operations— Running the Gamut

ANALOG PROOFING SYSTEMS can produce a gamut of approximately six thousand colors, about half again the gamut achievable in offset printing. The simplest explanation for this is that analog proofing systems are manufactured with dyes bonded to plastic surfaces that produce a brighter, purer reflection of CMYK than do printing inks and the substrates that they are applied to. Modern digital proofing systems offer a color gamut of about four thousand—very close to that of high-quality four-color offset printing.

SUMMARY

THERE ARE A NUMBER OF PROOFING systems used in color reproduction that provide dependable representations of color design. Developing a trusted color palette that can be proofed and reproduced with predictable results will increase your faith in color choices. Familiarizing yourself with the proofing systems that are used for your color design work, and sharing that knowedge and experience is invaluable for establishing confidence and building long-term relationships with your clientele.

3

COLOR IMAGES

If you've ever found yourself toiling in front of a monitor trying to get the last little screen pixel of a photo to look perfect, you know that scanning and software systems today are powerful enough to do almost anything with color. But that power comes with a price—usually hours of seat time that can swallow whole production schedules in a single gulp.

In the days before desktop publishing, pointillist painter Georges Seurat used to paint like that, dot by dot. It took him years to get anything out the door. Neighbors used to hear his wife yell at him, "Georges, are you done yet?"

"Non."

"But Georges..."

"Tais toi (shut up)!" And quiet would descend. But it wouldn't be a happy quiet.

You too can achieve the lasting effects of the master painter, but only if you live in a time capsule. Otherwise, you should make every effort to avoid the need to turn bad art into good. In other words, you should select great originals in the first place.

How can you tell when you've got good originals? The best color originals are the ones that control three factors: composition, sharpness, and color.

(FACING PAGE)
This photo has all three of the necessary factors for good reproduction: The composition is appropriate for a photo that has no type on it; the focus is good, so details are sharp; and the colors look saturated because there is a full range of tone from highlight through midtones to deep shadow.

(FAR LEFT)
Notice how good the lighting is on this photo. It brings out perfectly the intricacies of the carving. You can see the details because of the play of light and shadow that highlights the carving. If the lighting were more direct or the photo not in pin-sharp focus, the details would fade into the background.

(LEFT)
Many outdoor photographers prefer to shoot on cloudy days because they don't have to worry about introducing too much contrast from bright sun and dark shadow. Photos shot in this kind of light can be a little tricky to reproduce, however, because they do lack contrast, so they can come out looking flat. Avoid this by making sure that the photo you select does have a bright highlight somewhere in it, and a dark shadow. Can you find the highlight and shadow in this picture?

Composition

When you evaluate the composition of a photo, don't look just at the artistic merit of the piece. Ask yourself how you plan to use it, and then make sure your photo has the necessary elements to succeed technically. Here are some considerations:

DIRECTION

Is your photo facing the right way? Directional considerations can have great meaning to a designer. Should a model face into the gutter or out? Should the weight of the composition be on the left or right? Luckily, software programs make it quite easy to flop photos. But, if you'll pardon the pun, this capability is a two-edged sword. With it you can create monumental goofs, which once happened to a textbook publisher.

(ABOVE)

At first glance, the photo above looks eminently floppable. Nobody is famous, the building is almost completely symmetrical, and hieroglyphs can be read from left to right or right to left. Why not flop? The reason is that this building is the Temple of Hatshepsut, and this view shows the place where terrorists slaughtered a group of tourists some years ago. While the building is not as famous as the White House, it's well enough known worldwide to merit a ban against flopping.

BEFORE YOU FLOP ANY COMPOSITIONS, THINK VERY CAREFULLY ABOUT WHETHER ANYONE WILL NOTICE.

- CHECK ESPECIALLY FOR PRINTED TEXT IN THE PICTURE.

- BE CAREFUL WITH FOREIGN SCRIPTS THAT MAY LOOK DECORATIVE BUT REALLY DO SAY SOMETHING.

- LOOK FOR SUBJECTS THAT HAVE AN INHERENT DIRECTION. *Americans place their right hands, not their left, over their hearts when saying the pledge of allegiance, for example. The British drive on the left side of the road, etc.*

- AVOID FLOPPING ANYONE OR ANYTHING FAMOUS THAT HAS RIGHT- OR LEFT-HANDEDNESS.

The publisher was making a presentation to a school board some years ago, during a competitive bid for a new history book. He was bragging about how the authors had gone to great lengths to use original sources, even in the illustrations. As an example, he opened his book to a section on ancient Egypt and showed the board how the designer had used a real illustration from a papyrus in the British Museum. Unfortunately, the hapless publisher failed to realize that one of the board members was a former Egyptologist. She pointed out that the illustration had been flopped.

The publisher's response was that so few people would notice the flop that it wouldn't matter. Even more unfortunately for the publisher, however, another board member was an African-American who had been fighting for equality all his life. When he heard that an African picture had been flopped and that "it didn't matter," he went ballistic. End of sale.

(ABOVE LEFT)
Famous people—even when they're statues—have left- or right-handedness. Michelangelo's David holds his right hand down, not his left.

(RIGHT)
Pictographic languages such as Japanese may look just as beautiful to our Western eyes whether they're flopped or not. But don't forget that the pictographs can be read by millions of people, so do not flop them.

There certainly seems to be no earthly reason to hang onto all the driveway pixels in the foreground here. Take a look at how much the composition is improved when you crop out all that superfluous data. But before you throw those pixels into the trash, ask yourself what you would do if a cat food company decided they wanted a photo that had plenty of halftone space on the bottom in which to put an advertising slogan? Save the full frame somewhere because you never know.

CROPPING

Almost always, after you have scanned an original into your computer, you will want to crop it. This is definitely something you should do early in your design, because cropping reduces the number of pixels your computer has to manipulate. In other words, a cropped picture uses up less disk space. Not only does this free up disk space for more designs, it also lets your software programs run more smoothly and faster.

When you do crop, however, be careful what you throw away. Rather than trash your original scan, save the cropped version under a different name. You're still getting rid of pixels, but if you change your mind and decide to reinstate the cropped-out portions of your art, you can. If you trash the pixels permanently, you're doomed to use the cropped version forever.

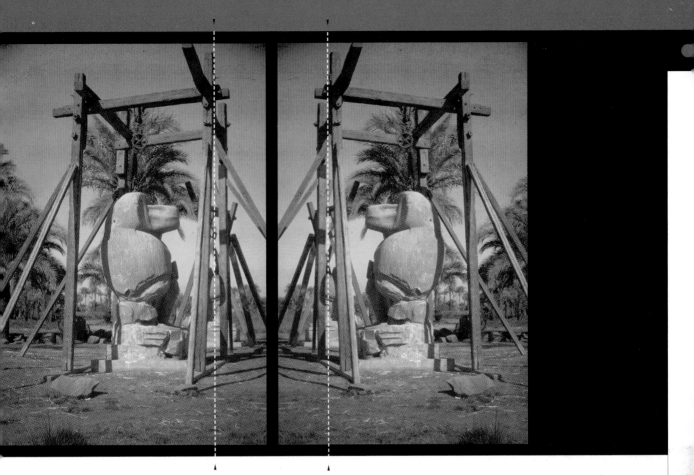

MOVING

If you do need to crop your original, rotate it, or manipulate it in some other way, do so using the original scan. Then save the changes as a new version with a new name and import the finished version into any layout you design. Don't import the original scan itself, which may have many more pixels in its bitmap than you actually use.

The computer doesn't really care what you do with the pixels, but it must still make decisions about each pixel that it has in a file. Even if the computer's decision is, "Don't use it," the computer still has to think about it. This takes time and memory, which can be particularly aggravating if you're transmitting your designs or if you're RIPing them on a high-resolution imagesetter.

(ABOVE)

This photo needed to be straightened (i.e., rotated) and flopped. After performing these operations in an image-manipulation program such as Photoshop, you should save a separate, new version before importing it into your layout program. By saving a new set of pixels, you keep the RIPing computer from wasting time rotating and flopping the pixels when it's trying to output a final, high-resolution design.

Type on Art

Overprinting or reversing out type in the digital world is as easy as importing graphics, keystroking your type, adding a few layers, and poof! You've got art. More than that, you've got design. Through the wonders of powerful software programs, you can make type and graphics magically appear on your computer screen, move them around, show color—all at the mere touch of a few fingers. Who needs to worry about photo composition when you can control all the elements in your design at will?

The problem is, computers seem incredibly smart but they're actually really dumb. They just do what they're told. So if you tell a computer to put red type over a dark-blue portion of a photo, it will do so. What does it care if the design makes your readers' eyes bounce around worse than a Volkswagen on a washboard road?

But if you care about your readers, you must pay attention to how your type is arranged on your art. Here are a few things to watch out for:

TYPE ON A PATTERNED BACKGROUND

Whether you overprint black type on a colored background or reverse it out, choose an area of color in your photo-composition that is flat and smooth, not patterned.

Studies have shown that we read text not as individual letters, but as blocks of shapes, usually two to five words at a time. If the pattern of the background interferes with the patterns made by the type—the ascenders, descenders, round shapes, angles, etc.—we are forced to look at each letter individually. This not only slows down our reading speed, but it tires out the eyes. Readers get discouraged by this and may give up on reading your message at all. If the background pattern and type actually blend with each other, readers may not be able to distinguish the shape of the letters at all. This is especially true if your type is smaller than 12-point, or if it is a font designed with fine serifs.

If you must use a photo with a strong pattern, you can improve readability by enlarging your type and using a sans serif font with thick strokes. If it is still problematic, you can knock out a box from the background photo and float your type within the box.

Another way still is to screen back the photo itself; so all the colors are much paler than in the original. You can do this by choosing a portion of the photo to screen back (in effect, creating a pale box for the type), or you can screen back the entire photo. If you use this technique, screen back the photo so that the deepest shadow has a total density of 30 percent. This may cause the lightest portions of the photo to disappear altogether, a sign that perhaps you should choose a different photo.

When you're printing black type over a black-and-white illustration, make sure there is enough contrast between the type and the art. There should be at least a 70 percent difference in tones. Here solid black type is generally readable over grays that range from 0 to 50 percent density.

But if you tried to screen back the type to print 40 percent black, you would have a problem.

OVERPRINTING TYPE ON A FLAT BACKGROUND

Even if you are careful about choosing a flat area of color to overprint type, you may still overprint something that is unreadable. You've got to consider the density of the type versus the density of the background.

Choose a place in the photo where the colors are pale enough so that readers can see the black type clearly. If the color of the background and the color of the type are the same, black type over a black-and-white illustration for example, then follow this rule of thumb: Allow at least a 70 percent difference between the density of type and the density of the background. So if you're overprinting solid black type (100 percent black), then you should not let the background get any darker than 30 percent gray.

If you're overprinting black type on a colored background, the total density of CMK (cyan, magenta, and black) should not exceed 90 percent in any combination, as long as the percentage of black stays below 30 percent. So you can safely overprint black type on a background with densities of, say, 40 percent cyan, 20 percent magenta, 30 percent black. Or you could use 60 percent cyan, 20 percent magenta and 10 percent black.

Notice that yellow has not been mentioned. That's because our eyes do not perceive yellow density very well. So generally you can use any additional percentage of yellow without affecting the readability of overprinted black type.

REVERSED-OUT TYPE

If you plan to reverse out type from a photo background and print the type in white, the background should have a total density of at least 40 percent. Without this, there won't be enough contrast between the white of your type and the white of the underlying paper. Choose an area of your photo that has enough pixels in it to provide the contrast you need.

(ABOVE LEFT)

The total density of CMYK in the water is 95 percent. Black type overprinted here is not easy to read.

(ABOVE CENTER)

Here the total density of CMYK across the butterfly ranges from 105 percent in the highlight, to 126 percent in the midtones, to 168 percent in the shadow. Black type is legible here because the density of black ink in the butterfly is less than 30 percent.

(ABOVE RIGHT)

The total density in the sky is 39 percent, making it difficult to read reversed-out type. By contrast, the total density in the water is 144 percent.

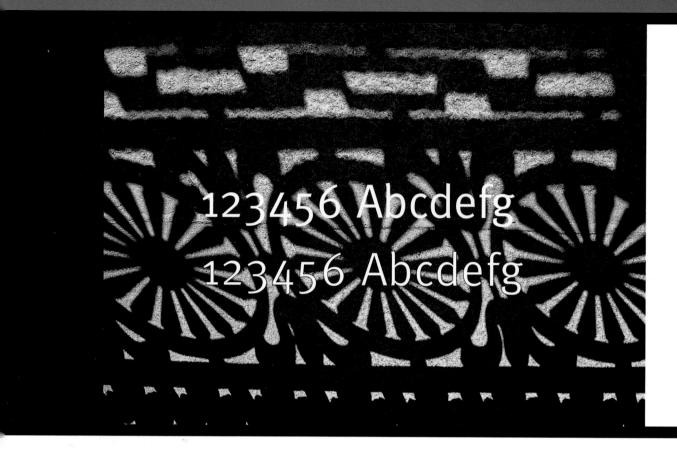

123456 Abcdefg

123456 Abcdefg

123456 Abcdefg

(ABOVE)

Outlining the type helps hold letter shapes whether the type is placed in a dark or a light part of the photo.

(FACING PAGE, TOP LEFT)

The colors in the sky here are very dense (215 percent of CMYK) as is the color of the type (200 percent CMYK). In addition, blue and red are on opposite sides of the color wheel. Look at the halo effect in the negative, or blank areas around each letter. Then take two aspirin and call me in the morning.

If you want to reverse type out of a photo that has lighter and darker areas in it, consider outlining the type with a hairline of black. The hairline will hold the shape of each letter in the lightest parts of the photo and won't interfere with the appearance of the reverse in the darker portions of the photo.

OVERPRINTING COLORED TYPE

Be careful about the colors you choose when you print colored type on a color photo or illustration. Some color combinations cause the eye to "bounce" from color to color because the negative space around each letterform is filled in by the background color. This creates a halo effect around each letter. The effect is worse if the colors you choose for the type are similar in density to the colors you have in the background, and those colors appear on opposite sides of the color wheel. Rich red letters on a dark blue sky are very difficult to read, for example.

If you try to output this kind of combination on a computer monitor (for instance, if you are translating a print campaign into a Web campaign), you will create a page that is almost impossible to read. That's because a computer monitor actually emits light, intensifying the halo effect. It's like shooting laser beams straight into your eyeballs. Powerful, yes, but also painful.

Sharpness

Unless you have a particular reason to use a soft-focus or out-of-focus picture, you should choose originals that have the sharpest details you can find, because the printing process degrades details. You lose information during every step of production, beginning with photo development and running all the way through scanning and final output. To ensure the sharpest detail, check out these considerations:

SIZE

The sharpness of a printed piece is affected by the size of the original. In simple terms, big printing requires big originals, if you want to hold detail.

So be careful when you decide that you don't need to use a full-frame original but want to blow up a portion of it to an enormous size.

Think of it this way: When a photo is digitized, a scanner chops it up into a given set of numbers. These numbers are called pixels. Once a photo has been scanned and turned into a set of numbers, the amount of numbers in the scan cannot be increased in any satisfactory way. But you can always throw away some numbers! For example, if you don't like the left-hand portion of a photo, you can throw out those pixels and never deal with them again. But you can't add them back in if you change your mind. Once pixels are gone, they're gone for good.

(TOP RIGHT AND CENTER)

This 35mm transparency looks fine when enlarged by 300 percent. But look at the graininess when we try to blow it up too big.

(BOTTOM)

Resampling up is a mathematical process that your computer can use to create new pixels. This is done most often when a photo has been scanned at a low resolution, losing detail. A designer may wish to increase detail by telling the computer to add pixels. The computer does this by interpolating the new pixels from the data in adjacent pixels. This, however, cannot add detail if the detail is not already there. For example, all the upsampling in the world won't restore the writing on the spools on the left side of this photo.

*The amount of detail your computer can pro-
duce is related to the number of pixels it starts
out with. Like butter on a knife, the computer
spreads its pixels over any size area you
desire. But also like butter, if you don't start
with a goodly number of pixels, you won't give
your readers much for their eyes to feast on. A
really good photo, shot with larger-format film,
should show little or no grain when enlarged.*

*This black-and-white photo was originally
scanned from an 8-by-10-inch (20-by-25-
centimeter) print. The scanning resolution
was set at 300 dots per inch to keep the file
size manageable. When the image size was
reduced to 3 inches wide, the resolution
became 700 pixels per inch. At this resolution,
can you see any grain?*

It is true that some software programs
allow you to "resample up," meaning
more pixels can be added to the file.
But are these pixels good pixels? The
computer resamples up by averaging
adjoining numbers. In other words, it
guesses how the new pixels should
look from the data it already has, but
it can't add anything really new.

The nature of pixels dictate why it's
important not to enlarge your final
output too much. Pixels living on your
computer disk don't have any fixed
size, they are just numbers. When you
tell the computer to output its pixels
onto a substrate—let's say a sheet of
paper on a digital press—the computer needs to know how far you want it
to spread its pixels. It could cram all
the pixels into a quarter-page photo in
a book, or it could spread them out
over a large poster on the side of a

bus. However much the computer
spreads its pixels, the amount of
pixels it has to work with does
not change.

It's kind of like spreading a pat of
butter on bread. You can spread that
butter on a cracker and get full, dense
coverage. Maybe you have even more
butter than you need and should have
started with half a pat (i.e., you
should throw some pixels away). You
can also spread the same pat of butter on a foot-long baguette and hardly
be able to see any butter on the
bread. Maybe you should have started
with more butter.

The best way to increase the number
of pixels a computer has at its dis-
posal is by scanning at an appropri-
ately high resolution so you have
plenty of pixels (but not so many that
you can't run your software programs

(LEFT)

To check for sharpness, look at fine detail in areas such as curved or straight lines, hair, eyes, grass, or leaves. Do these areas look sharp or fuzzy?

(BELOW)

If you must use a fuzzy, out-of-focus photo such as this one, try sharpening it in Adobe Photoshop. Sharpening works best when the details that are out of focus exhibit broad differences in color. Look at how much better the photo on the right appears after sharpening.

efficiently; see Chapter 5). This will create the maximum number of pixels available in your scanning device.

But if you start with a scan of a small picture, say a 35mm transparency, even if you scan at a high resolution, the scanner is marching across only 35 millimeters of information. Adding more pixel-capacity is not going to add details that aren't in the film already. Enlarging a 35mm original too much causes the final output to look grainy or out of focus.

On the other hand, if you start with an 8-by-10-inch (20-by-25-centimeter) transparency, the scanner can still chop up the photo into the same small bits of numbers that it used for the 35mm original. It just has more data to work with because the area it scans is bigger. In effect, there's more butter on the knife.

In a practical sense, if you enlarge an original transparency by more than 1,000 percent, you will start to see graininess and loss of detail.

Similarly, if your original is a piece of reflective art (as opposed to transparent art), you also need to pay attention to the size of the original. However, if you're using a photographic print, it is not an original. A photographic original is the negative from which the print was made. In most cases, the print has already been enlarged. But enlarging a photo does not add more

information to it, it just makes the picture bigger. So be careful when you select a photograph to reproduce. Check out the grain on the print itself. If you see any, it might be better to get a smaller print with less grain, if possible.

Scan the print at full size and at the highest resolution that is practical. This will give you the greatest number of pixels with the least amount of grain.

(BELOW)

Using unsharp masking can improve the sharpness of a photo that shows clear lines between one tone and another. However, you can go too far using sharpening tools. Stop short of creating black lines around your subjects.

FOCUS

To check whether a picture is in focus, always use an eight-power or greater loupe or a magnifying lens. Don't rely on putting a transparency into a viewing screen of one sort or another—such systems merely take you farther away from the original.

Looking through a loupe, check areas in the photo that have fine lines or edges. Can you see everything clearly? If the main subject in the picture is a person or an animal, most photographers choose to focus their cameras on the subject's eyes, so look there too. Can you see pin-sharp detail?

If your photo is slightly out of focus and appears a bit fuzzy, you can use editing software to fix it without too much trouble. The tools that do this fall into two broad categories: One set of algorithms looks at adjacent pixels of different colors and increases the differences between them. This is called sharpening. The other kind of tool looks for edges within a picture—continuous lines of pixels of one color. Then it increases the contrast between those pixels and the ones on either side of the edge. This kind of sharpening is called "Unsharp Masking."

(BELOW)

Not even sharpening can make an out-of-focus photo look completely sharp.

(RIGHT)

Even when a photo is in focus, sometimes it's hard for the reader to see it very well if the colors and patterns of the main subject blend in with the background. Sharpening can help set the main subject apart from the background.

Unsharp masking can really help a fuzzy photo that has edges in it, because the program adjusts only those pixels, leaving the pixels in more graduated tones alone. So you get an increase in the effect of lines without increasing the linear look overall. You can also control the amount of contrast and the number of pixels that exist between edges before the program kicks in and does anything about it.

Using unsharp masking can produce dramatic results, but you can definitely go overboard. Too much unsharp masking makes a picture look like someone drew cartoon lines around the subjects. When such pictures are printed on a digital press, the effect can look like a poor trapping job, with colors overlapping each other to form dark boundary lines.

You should realize, too, that tricks such as sharpening or unsharp masking cannot really substitute for lack of detail in the focus. Once again, the computer can work only on the pixels that it has in its file. If details aren't in the original, you can't tell the computer to make them up.

Sometimes a photo is in perfect focus but you still can't distinguish the subject very well. This happens when the colors and shapes of a subject blend in with surrounding background. Think of an owl in a tree or a white rabbit in the snow. You can create more separation between subject and background by using unsharp masking to draw lines between the two. The lines should provide enough definition so that you can see the subject as a separate object, but not enough so that you begin to see the lines as lines.

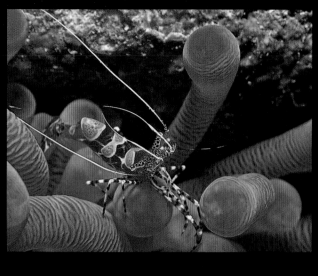

DEPTH OF FIELD

Depth of field is the apparent amount of distance from the foreground through the background within which a picture stays in focus. Depending on the film speed and exposure used to take the original photo, you can have a lot of depth of field or practically none.

Ideally, what you should look for is perfect focus in some part of the picture and out-of-focus in other parts. It is this contrast between detail and fuzziness that helps the human brain interpret the visual data our eyes see as three-dimensional. Remember, all printing is a two-dimensional trick to simulate the real world of three dimensions. So whatever mimics real life adds to the verisimilitude of print.

Try this experiment. Stare at an object about 2 feet away from you. While you focus on that object, try to look at the background behind it without taking your eyes off the object. Can you see how out of focus the objects in the background appear? Now, without moving your head, focus your eyes on the background. Can you see how the object in the foreground becomes fuzzy?

That is the effect you're trying to re-create in two-dimensional print.

Bear in mind, however, that a printed piece is viewed by readers who have never seen the original. All the readers have to look at is the printed matter that lies before them. So as you design your two-dimensional piece, try to back off from the original a bit and look at your design as though you were a reader seeing it for the first time. If there is too much foreground or background that is out of focus, the sheer color of those areas is enough to distract the reader from the main subject.

On the other hand, if nothing is out of focus, the scene looks unreal. So tied are we to this method of interpreting visual stimulus that if you composite two photos together without blurring one somewhat, people will be able to guess every time that you have composited an artificial piece.

(ABOVE LEFT)

The pale yellow highlight in the background adds nothing to our depth perception here. Crop out as much as possible, or color it to match the rest of the background.

(ABOVE RIGHT)

Notice how the out-of-focus background serves to draw our attention to the seeds in the center of the picture. This is how we would see them in nature, and that is why this picture looks so real.

(ABOVE)

The screen-like appearance of the subject's jacket can cause a moiré pattern when scanned as a conventional halftone. If you use a stochastic screen to scan this picture, the moiré pattern won't appear. Stochastic screens are made of tiny, randomly occurring spots that have no pattern, so they cannot conflict with any patterns that may appear in the original photo.

SCREEN LIMITATIONS

Sometimes everything about a photo is perfect but the finished piece prints with an unintended event. Maybe the smoothly curved tones you saw in the original came out as bands when the job printed. Or perhaps a closely patterned jacket on a model came out with additional patterns that weren't in the original.

These kinds of problems are the result of using a grid-type screen to create printable dots from the original. The pattern of the screen (which produces dots arranged on a grid) creates a pattern that the eye can sometimes see. So smooth tones, especially in curved metallic subjects, or finely patterned textiles are reproduced with extra screen patterns.

If this creates a problem for your design, try using a stochastic screening mode instead. (see Chapter 5) Stochastic screening uses tiny spots of ink or toner arranged in a randomized array. Since the spots are very tiny, the breakup of tones into bands is reduced. And since the spots are randomly placed on the paper, there is no screen pattern to conflict with the subject's pattern. However, not every output device supports stochastic screening, so check with your printer ahead of time.

(BELOW)

Sometime you might need to reproduce a previously printed image that has been screened as a halftone. If you apply your own halftone screen to print it again (left), the new screen angles will conflict with the old screen angles. You will get a moiré. Try using a stochastic screen (right) instead. Stochastic screens have no pattern, so they cannot conflict with halftone screen grids.

Graphic Designer's Print and Color Handbook

Color

Color is the most important factor for good reproduction, even if the color is only gray. That's because all of the detail in print, all of the shadows, and all the highlights are expressed by pure color. Golf clubs glint in the sun because the metal heads look grayish but the reflections are white. A model touting plastic surgery looks old and wrinkled because the creases in her face are expressed as darker and lighter areas of skin tone colors. To make sure your color is giving you every last ounce of punch, check out these points:

EXPOSURE

Sometimes detail is obscured in the original because the photo is too dark (underexposed) or too light (overexposed). Photo-editing software is great for bringing out shadow detail in underexposed photos and for bringing out highlight detail in overexposed photos. By working on the brightness and contrast of a photo, you can make details appear that you never thought were there. You can lighten dark areas and darken light areas. But you cannot create new details that aren't already in the original.

If you must use an overexposed or underexposed photo, look at it under strong light on a light table. If you can see any detail in the shadow or highlight, the photo can probably be salvaged. Whether it's worth saving is another issue.

(BELOW)

When you check a photo for range of tone, look for detail in the shadows, in the highlights, and for plenty of midtones in between.

(FACING PAGE TOP LEFT)

Not every photo has to show detail throughout its range of tones. Here the dense shadows of the kelp in the foreground draw the eye into the mysterious depths of the sea. The effect would be spoiled if we could see every detail of the shadows.

I learned this the hard way when I worked on a coffee-table book about seabirds of the northern Pacific. Many of the birds in the book were rarely seen by anyone, let alone by a professional photographer with the right equipment under the right lighting conditions. In fact, several of the photos were one-of-a-kind pictures of birds never before published. These rare photos had been taken by scientists who belonged to the point-and-click school of outdoor photography. Many of the transparencies consisted of overexposed frames showing black X's with feet hanging down. One memorable underexposure pictured a black blob in a brown hole. The only way you could even tell it was something

living was that it had a small glint in a dimly perceptible eye. Everything else was just solid black.

When I saw the transparencies, I nearly had palpitations. "We need better photographs," I gasped when I could get a breath.

"There are none," said the art director. "Not a single one in the entire world. These are the best and only ones in existence."

Well, we worked with them. Whatever detail was in them, we brought out. They still looked like black X's and blobs when we printed them, but we had no choice. In this case, a bad picture was better than no picture.

RANGE OF TONE

The best photos have a full range of tones from darkest shadow to lightest highlight, with plenty of midtones in-between.

To check for range of tone, take a look at the photo first in the deep shadow areas. Ideally, there should be some detail visible in the shadows, although sometimes you may want the very deepest shadows to be completely black. This is a judgment call and depends on the kind of effect you are trying to create.

After you check the deep shadows, look at the highlights. Bright high-lights should appear white enough and yet still have a little color in them to give them some shape. Sometimes you'll see very small, round highlights that are totally white. These are called specular highlights and are caused when smooth surfaces reflect white light directly back to the camera. You should generally set your scanner to blow out all pixels in these highlights, leaving the space completely blank. If you set your scanner to read some pixels in specular highlights, your resulting range of tones will be so spread out that no press will be able to print all the changes in tone from bright to dark.

(ABOVE)

The small, completely white highlights on this statue (above center) are called specular high-lights. They reflect light directly back to the camera and print with no halftone dots at all. They can add a sense of reality to a photo. See how three-dimensional this statue looks com-pared to the statue on the right, which has no highlights at all. The statue without highlights looks flat and dull.

(ABOVE LEFT)

This is a histogram of the photo on page 100. Notice that it shows pixels on both extremes of shadow and highlight, but the majority of pixels fall in the midrange.

(ABOVE RIGHT)

This is a histogram of the photo on page 101. It lacks pixels in the deep shadows and bright highlights. All its pixels are in the midrange, creating a photo that will print looking flat.

HISTOGRAMS

If you want to check on a picture's range of tone exactly, you can ask your computer to display a histogram. Histograms are diagrams that show the mathematical distribution of pixels from dark to light in a given color channel. A well-balanced histogram should show some pixels at the extreme ends of darkest and lightest, but the majority of pixels should show up in the middle. A photo that has a poor tonal range lacks pixels on the outside extremes of a histogram.

Some photos have too big a range of tone. The darks are really dark, the highlights really light. There are plenty of midtones, but the photo gives the feeling of being stretched out over too big a spectrum. This kind of photo is too contrasty. A histogram of a contrasty photo shows how stretched out it really is. Photographic film has a bigger range of tone than printing ink or toner. In effect, ink or toner can reproduce the equivalent of only four f-stops of a camera. If a photo has a bigger range than four f-stops, you will not be able to reproduce it well; the photo simply has more tones than the press.

Changing a picture's range of tones is easy, up to a point. A picture that is heavy on the midtones but lacks deep shadows and bright highlights can be

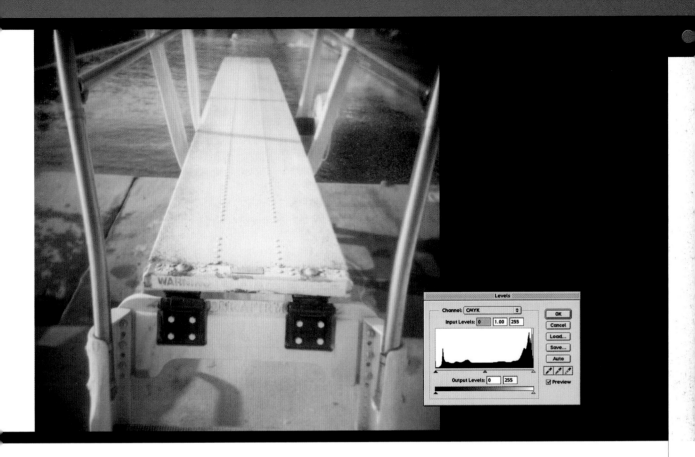

changed by first identifying the deepest shadow and brightest highlights that are on the film, and then making them deeper in the one case, whiter in the other. The computer will then spread out the available pixels that express all the tones, in effect stretching them over a wider spectrum. For photos with minor problems, this actually works, in the sense that a photo looks better afterward. But for photos with too little range in tone, stretching out the pixels can make the picture look odd and artificial. My advice is, try it but save a copy of the original. You may need it.

Compressing a picture's range of tones is also easy. In fact, most photos should be compressed to some extent, just to compensate for the press's inability to reproduce as many tones as film can. With a really contrasty photo, however, compressing the tones will cause more detail to be lost in the shadows and the highlights. You're left with the choice of living with the lack of detail, or finding a different photo.

(ABOVE)

Some photos have too much range of tone. The deep shadows are so dark you can't see any detail. However, the brightest highlights show no detail, either; yet there are plenty of midtones. Such photos have too much contrast and may be tricky to reproduce. If you do use a contrasty photo, make sure you have a good design reason for your choice. Here the strong lines and saturated colors create a compelling image, even if the range of tones is too great.

(ABOVE)

Photos taken in early morning light or late afternoon can show a yellow color cast. One way to check for this is to look at colors that should be neutral gray, pure white, or neutral beige. In this photo, all three of these neutral colors have shifted to yellow.

(RIGHT)

When using contrasty photos, be prepared to spend time altering shadows and highlights. It's usually best in these cases to ignore the deepest shadows and brightest highlights and work instead on the midtones. In this photo, the model's face can and should be lightened, but everything else should probably be left alone.

COLOR CAST

Photos should have no overall color cast. You can check this by eye. Simply gaze at the original without magnifying it in any way. Can you see a color shift overall?

Sometimes a photo can show a color shift because, when the photo was shot, the ambient light itself was skewed. Photos taken in the late afternoon or early morning, for example, look too yellow or too red. Photos taken under indoor incandescent light show a similar shift to yellow and red. Photos taken under indoor fluorescent light show too much green.

Sometimes a photo's color shift is due to the way the film is made. Film manufacturers know that any given film emulsion cannot capture the full spectrum of visible light, so they make a choice about the colors that a given film ideally will portray. This can result in an overall color shift in a photo when colors are present that are outside the film's ability to "see." Most common is a color shift to the cold side of the spectrum—a photo looks greenish or bluish.

Film emulsions are somewhat limited in their ability to "see" certain portions of the visible spectrum. This can result in an overall color cast, in this case, too much blue.

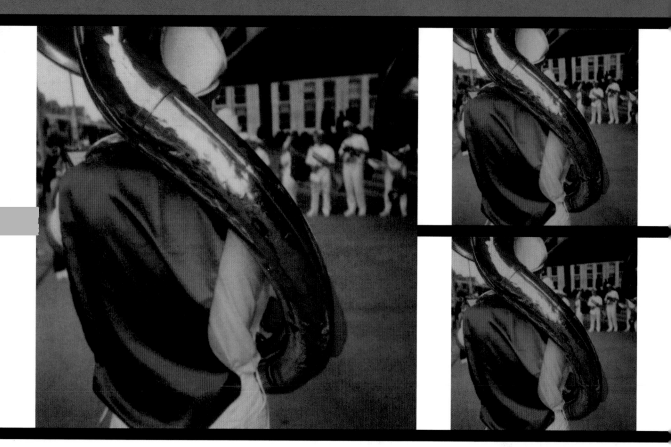

The original photo (above left) has an overall blue cast. When this problem is addressed, a new problem is created: The other colors look wrong. You can spend a lot of time correcting a photo like this, as you try to compensate for a cascade of problems. Ask yourself if the photo is worth it.

You can easily alter a picture's color cast by telling the computer to look for similarly colored pixels in the midtones, shadows, or highlights. By fiddling around with these controls and checking the results on your monitor, you can create a color balance that is more pleasing. Bear in mind that the computer will change all areas that have these color tones, unless you laboriously construct layers and masks that de-select areas that you don't want to alter. That, of course, will start you down a slippery slope where making one change cascades into the necessity of making another. You can spend a long time sliding down this slope, if you're not careful.

My grandmother had a saying for situations like this: "If you see a spot on the wall, don't wash it off. Hang a picture over it. If you wash one spot, the rest of the wall will look horrible, and you'll end up washing all the walls of your house, and your ceilings too."

WRONG HUE

Sometimes a photo looks okay overall, but you wish you could tweak one color a little more. You can, either by selecting a small area and working on it in a separate layer, or by selecting one hue and changing that everywhere it occurs in the photo.

When you do this, be aware that fixing a color may mean adding more intensity to it, or reducing the intensity of the other colors. Let's say, for example, that you think a photo has too much cyan in it. The problem actually may be that it doesn't have enough yellow. Try changing both colors one at a time and see which result you like better.

It is a real art to determine exactly which adjustment will help a photo the most. Mastering this art is also enormous fun. So watch the clock.

(BELOW)

The grays in this photo are not neutral (top). Here's what happens when you take out blue (middle). Here's what happens when you add more yellow (bottom).

PASTELS

You wouldn't think that true pastels would be difficult to achieve in digital printing, but they are. On the one hand, digitally created dots are much tinier than offset printed dots, so your control of very pale colors is greater. However, digitally applied dots have a hard edge that keeps them from blending seamlessly. This is not banding, where bands of color show up in steps. The hard-dot effect is more subtle, but it is real.

In offset printing, when ink is applied to paper, it sinks into the substrate to some degree. As it soaks in, little threads of ink spread out into the paper fibers, making the dot grow in size. This dot gain has the bad effect of altering the color balance of the design, so printers go to great lengths to control it. But dot gain has a good benefit too, softening the edges of the halftone dots and making the colors blend together into more of a continuous tone effect. This can be especially helpful when you're trying to print soft colors like pastels.

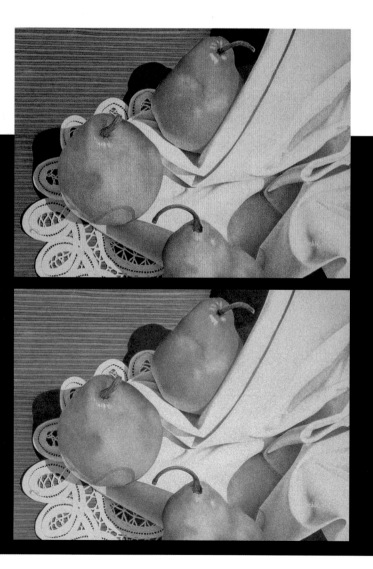

(LEFT)

Subtle pastels can be very hard to reproduce with conventional halftone screens because the digital process makes hard-edged dots that are not softened on a printing press. Stochastic screening can help by giving the computer more dots to work with. You still have hard-edged dots, but at least the stochastic screen can show more subtle variations in tone.

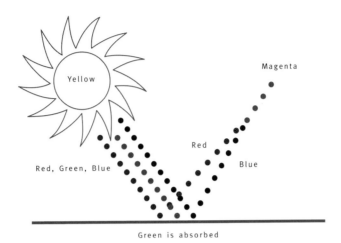

Yellow

Magenta

Red

Red, Green, Blue

Blue

Green is absorbed

Toner or waxy dyes, on the other hand, do not sink into the paper. So the dots retain their hard edges. With these forms of digital output, you don't have to contend with excessive color balance changes due to dot gain, which is good. But you also lose the softening effect of feathery dot edges.

The best way to get around this problem is to go to stochastic screening. The randomized array of dots that defines a stochastic screen mimics a softened dot because stochastic dots are much, much smaller than traditional halftone dots, and there is no discernible pattern in the colors created.

FLUORESCENTS AND OTHER BRIGHT COLORS

The gamut of colors available to printers is much less than the gamut of colors available to computer monitors. Ink and toner chemists say that this is mostly due to the fact that all printed colors in all printing processes are subtractive. What does that mean?

White light is made up of three primary colors: red, green, and blue. When white light hits ink, the pigment in the ink absorbs—or subtracts— some wavelengths of light and reflects back the wavelengths that are left. The color we see thus contains less intensity than the original beam of white light and expresses a more restricted part of the visible spectrum.

(ABOVE)

White light contains the three primary colors: red, green, and blue. When white light strikes this magenta ink film, the ink subtracts a third of the spectrum (in this case, green). The light reflected back is red and blue, which we perceive as magenta.

Most printing inks and toners are designed to subtract one-third of the spectrum of visible light. Cyan ink or toner, for example, subtracts red light and reflects green and blue light—and it appears turquoise (or cyan) to us. Magenta ink or toner subtracts green; yellow ink or toner subtracts blue.

Theoretically, if inks and toners were perfect, each of the three process colors would subtract a full third of the visible-light spectrum. In the real world, however, even the best inks and toners are imperfect and let some improper wavelengths of light "leak" back. So colors are not pure; they are contaminated by other parts of the spectrum.

What all this means is that inks and toners simply cannot duplicate all the colors of nature. Really bright greens, oranges, and purples are not in their gamut. Neither are highly saturated reds. As for bright colors that don't appear in nature—such as fluorescent yellow, pink, or turquoise—forget about it.

There is no perfect way to get around this problem, whether you're printing on digital output devices or conventional presses. Printers try, though, using various tricks. Some add a custom-colored ink to the traditional CMYK (cyan, magenta, yellow, black) inks. By chemically mixing a new color, you can achieve a wider range of hues. Some printers make extra passes through the output device, adding more ink density by just adding more ink. This can be effective for spot colors and solids especially. But printers can never entirely overcome the inherent limitations of the physical process of printing inks or toners onto paper.

(BOTH PAGES)

Ordinary process inks and toners can reproduce only a limited gamut of colors. One way to brighten up your colors is to add custom inks and toners. On these pages, we used CMYK inks to reproduce one version of the art (images on left). Then we replaced process magenta and process yellow with fluorescent substitutes (images on right). Look at the difference in vibrancy.

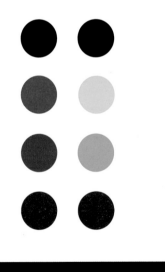

REFLECTIVE ART

If your original is a piece of reflective art, rather than a transparency, you might have a little extra challenge in reproducing the colors. That's because scanners "see" the artificial colors of paints, crayons, etc. as natural and try to digitize them accordingly. If the art is made from colors that do not occur in nature (such as fluorescent paints, for example), the scanner will do its best to interpret the colors; results may be mixed.

One way to improve color fidelity is to shoot a digitized version of the art using a high-end digital camera. This may give better results than shooting a color transparency of the art, simply because the digitizing process is closer to the original with a digital camera. The translation of color from one medium to another happens only once here.

When you digitize reflective art, you may notice that certain physical elements of the original may become distorted. Lumpy paint may cast unwanted shadows, for example. Or textured paper might appear as mottling that confuses the reader. Conversely, smooth-but-glossy paper might cast reflections back at the scanner's eye, introducing meaningless highlights. It's best to anticipate these problems and ask your artist, if possible, to use a smooth, matte surface for the original substrate. If that is not an option, then you should expect to spend some seat time making adjustments after the image is scanned.

Sometimes when you shoot reflective art or fabric, you get unexpected colors from the camera. This happens because the camera lens can sometimes "see" paints or dyes differently than the human eye does. This problem is called metamerism. It's a pesky problem because you never know when you're going to get it, and you can correct it only in prepress. Allow for some extra time. However, before you get started on your career to color-edit the *Mona Lisa*, you have to decide how important an exact color match really is. If the art is being reproduced in a catalog, for example, exact color matches may be crucial.

(LEFT)

When an illustration is drawn on textured paper and the art is scanned, the paper can contribute unwanted effects that you may need to correct by hand.

If the art is being used to illustrate a magazine article, perhaps it doesn't have to be as exact as you might like. After all, readers won't see the vibrant original art; they'll see only a reproduction.

This issue came up at trade magazine where the art director did not communicate her final design vision to her production manager. She just handed over a painting the size of a playing card. It was a piece showing the White Rabbit, done in beautiful oil pastels. "I want this scanned," she said.

Ordinarily the production manager scanned small pieces of art on her flatbed scanner. But usually these pieces were snapshot photos of organization members at trade shows, dressed in funny hats. This was clearly Art with a capital "a". So the production manager went to great expense to get the digital version exactly right, sending the painting to a service bureau for drum-scanning. When the scan came back, the colors were off. Everything looked dull and dirty. So the production manager sent the proof back for retouching. Two scans later, she was finally satisfied and showed the contract proof to the art director.

"Oh good," said the art director, "I've been needing that to drop into our April calendar. I picked it up at a garage sale and thought it would look really cute. I didn't really care how the colors came out, but hey, these colors are fantastic."

Just one more rabbit hole for the production manager to go down, right along with the budget.

(ABOVE)

Sometimes artist's paints or fabric dyes absorb light in unexpected ways, such as reflecting back to the camera lens a different color than our human eye sees. This phenomenon is called metamerism. Greens, for some reason, are often at fault. The only solution is to correct the colors by hand. On the left is the original scan of a Chinese embroidered picture; on the right is the color-corrected version.

COLOR MANAGEMENT

The staff of a newly launched adventure travel magazine—of which I was part—gathered around the designer's table as she opened the package of proofs from the color separator. We were eager to see the photos for a story about apes in the wild that the publisher's wife had written. Several of the photos had been taken by the publisher himself.

We all stared as the proofs were unveiled. One picture in particular drew our attention, a close-up of a gorilla squatting in a nest of green leaves. The gorilla was scowling horribly. "Aren't gorillas supposed to look warm?" asked the designer. "This one looks like his space heater just blew out, and he is not a happy camper."

We had to agree. The leaves of the nest were all very bluish. So were the plant stems. Even the gorilla's fur had a blue cast to it. If this had been live film, the poor creature would have been shivering. The two vervet monkeys on the next proof appeared even colder—the baby monkey huddled in his mother's lap actually had blue fingers.

The group turned to me. I was the production manager. I was responsible for color quality. "I'll call the separator right away," I said. "He won't get away with this!"

The color separator was surprised that we weren't happy with the color. "The photos were all perfectly exposed, no special problems. They should have been fine."

"Well, when we looked at the originals on our light table, they all looked much warmer than the proofs do now," I replied.

There was a long pause. "Your light table? You mean the kind with an ordinary light bulb behind a panel of translucent plastic? Didn't you use a viewing booth?"

"What's a viewing booth?" I asked.

"I'll be right over," said the separator. When he arrived, he set up a little color-corrected projector and put our slides into it, one by one. In every case, the colors looked much bluer than I had remembered.

"That's your problem," he said. "Your light bulb is not color-corrected, so the color of the light has shifted. It makes all your slides look warmer than they really are."

What I came to think of as the "Bad Monkey Incident" took place more than twenty years ago. It taught me a valuable lesson—if you want to get good color, you have to pay attention to good color management. In the modern digital world, color management consists of two main ideas: color calibration and proofing.

Color calibration is crucial when you must reproduce a picture with the challenges presented by this one. The original photo was illuminated both with ambient light from outdoors (filtered through the door curtain) and incandescent light bulbs inside the house. Reflections from the doorway, wallpaper, and woodwork add to the mix of light sources. The net effect is to skew otherwise neutral colors to the red, yellow, and blue sides of the spectrum—simultaneously. Add in the need to reproduce good skin tones and wood tones, and you've got a potential mess. If your monitor isn't calibrated with your supplier's monitor, you could easily get totally different hues when this picture is reproduced.

Color Calibration

In simplest terms, color calibration means making sure that you see color in the same way that everyone else in the production cycle does, including your service bureau, color separator, and printer. In a way, this sounds simple. After all, color is nothing more than wavelengths of light exciting the optic nerve, which transmits the stimulus to the brain, where it is interpreted. But because we see color as both an outside stimulus and an inside interpretation, color perception really is a mysterious process.

For one thing, consider why we humans can even see color at all. Many other mammals cannot. Scientists speculate that we evolved the ability to perceive color as a way to find food. If you can see that a banana is green, you don't waste time climbing up to pick it. Instead you go for the yellow one with just a hint a brown spots sprinkled across the skin.

However, in the real world, if we were to perceive all colors in the true wavelengths that reach our eyes, we'd never pick any bananas at all. That's because a ripe banana in bright sun has a different hue than a ripe banana in shade.

A banana growing on a tree in Guatemala is a different color than that same banana sitting on a produce table in your supermarket. Yet we perceive that all the ripe bananas in all the different lighting conditions are yellow. Somehow our brains adjust the real wavelengths we see into categories of color that we recognize.

While this system may be great for finding food, it's not particularly accurate for matching color on press. You can see this for yourself by trying a little experiment. Take a square of khaki-colored cloth and view it under a 60-watt incandescent bulb. Match the color to a swatch from a Pantone® color swatch book. Then take the cloth outside in bright sun and match it again to a new color swatch. Do this again under fluorescent light. Now bring together the three color swatches and see if they are exactly the same. When I do this, I find that khaki looks more like brown in sunlight and more like green in artificial light.

(ABOVE)

When we look at objects in the real world, we don't really see the colors that are present. Rather, our brains automatically interpret the actual wavelengths of light that strike our eyes. In the real world, these bananas would all look yellow to us. But notice how many different colors are really present in this bunch. The lesson here is that we can't depend on our eyes to see color images accurately, unless we view the images under the proper lighting conditions.

A good way to check if your desktop system is accurately calibrated is to look at a scan that should have neutral colors. Gray is a good neutral to check, because it readily shows when the color balance is off. Is either half of this photo truly neutral?

A good viewing booth system consists of a light table with a color-corrected bulb, a neutral-gray surround, and overhead lighting with 5,000 K bulbs, all located in a room with no windows. If possible, you should dim all other lights and wear neutral clothing yourself.

COLOR-CORRECTED ENVIRONMENTS

Because our brains interpret colors so expansively, you should always view color in a color-corrected environment when trying to match originals to proofs. The best environment is a viewing booth with a neutral-gray surround under 5,000-degree K lighting.

Viewing booths designed specifically for the graphics industry control color quality, light intensity, evenness of illumination, and surrounding conditions. They allow us to see neutral gray as truly neutral. By using neutral gray as a set point, we see all the other colors in their truest hue.

Never, ever hold a transparency up to the light bulb in your office and make color decisions about it. Whether the bulb is incandescent or fluorescent, it skews the colors of everything you're viewing. Incandescent bulbs skew the colors toward yellow. Fluorescent bulbs can skew colors toward green or even pink if the bulbs are old.

Some people have daylight-corrected bulbs in their office and think that those show colors "truly." They don't. Although many such bulbs are advertised as achieving as much as "91 percent natural daylight," you have to ask yourself, what kind of daylight?

The color balance of a given photo is affected by many factors, including the ambient light present at the time the photo was shot. Take a look at the statue on the left: Each shot was taken under different lighting conditions (sunny day, cloudy day, nighttime). Notice how different the hues look in the stonework and even in the background vegetation.

Daylight in the morning and evenings is skewed heavily toward red and yellow. Daylight on rainy days can be bluish. In smoggy cities, daylight is orange. At high latitudes in the fall or spring, daylight is yellowish.

In addition to viewing color in the proper surroundings, you should also get your eyes tested as you get older. People's color vision changes over time, and you should be aware of how yours is affected.

Now that I've hit that magic age of seventeen (at least in tortoise years), I find that my color vision perceives more yellow than it used to. For me, global warming has a special meaning—the whole world is getting much more warmly colored.

MONITOR CALIBRATION

Controlling the way you view color is only the first step in running a good color-management system. The next thing you need to control is your desktop monitor. You need to make sure that your vendors' monitors show color the same way that yours does. Each of you needs to adjust, or calibrate, your monitor to the same standard.

Here, too, it's important that you view color in a consistently neutral environment. Don't put your monitor in a room painted with Federal Blue walls and expect to see very warm colors accurately on your monitor. The ambient light bouncing around off the walls is bouncing off the monitor too, affecting the colors you see. For the same reason, you should keep your monitor in a room with no sunlight. Sounds grim, but the color of sunlight changes with every passing cloud. If your room is filled with sunlight, then the colors you see are also changing rapidly throughout the day. Overhead illumination can also affect colors. If at all possible, you should consider replacing the overhead light bulbs in your office with 5,000-degree K, color-corrected bulbs.

Once you have adjusted your environment, it's time to adjust your monitor. The first thing to do is to remove any colorful wallpaper from the background of your monitor. Boring gray is what you want, all the better to see the colors of your designs accurately.

After your monitor has had a chance to warm up, you should adjust the brightness level. This is what controls the level of black that your monitor can show. Put up a solid black onto your screen and play with the brightness knob until you see a true black, but not one that is so dark that it is surrounded by a halo of gray. Now you need to calibrate the color gamut of your monitor so it meets industry standards. Monitors are surprisingly variable in the colors they can display. Different manufacturers produce monitors that might emphasize colors more to the blue or to the yellow side of the spectrum. Even individual monitors made by the same company can vary. Monitors can also change over time. You need to make sure that all the monitors throughout your production process are displaying the same colors in the same way. Theoretically if everyone in the production cycle does this, then everyone should see the same colors. This ability of digitized color to be always and ever the same is one of its most powerful appeals. Think of it: A world where, once you calibrate your monitor and set your colors, they will always look that way, whether you gaze upon them today or a year from today, whether you look at them in Peoria or your printer views them in Prague.

This almost never happens in the real world. For some reason, people seem strangely reluctant to take the time to calibrate their monitors together. Or if they do, they don't do so regularly, despite the fact that phosphors in color monitors can deteriorate over time.

Failing to match the color of all the monitors in the production process is like failing to synchronize watches before beginning a crucial mission. Even the federal government knows that everyone has to be in the same time frame: At the Social Security Administration's vast complex that constitutes the head offices in Baltimore, a security guard presses a special button once a day. All the hands of all the clocks in the building start whirling around madly. Then they all stop at the same time. "That's so nobody can claim that they were late coming to meetings because their clock was slow," explains the guard. Hard as it may be to believe, we could learn something from the government's commitment to consistency. Not only does the SSA calibrate their clocks, they do so to one standard.

Software programs exist that can calibrate monitors to a standard. But to what standard? Remember that the goal of calibration is to print a final design that expresses the colors you expect. Therefore, when you calibrate your monitor, you should always do so based on the system that your outputting service or device uses. Don't make them adjust their system to your monitor. Instead, you adjust your monitor to them.

The reason is that if you calibrate your monitor to the output device's calibration, then what you see on your monitor is pretty much what you'll get in print. Which is the point.

(FAR LEFT)

When viewing images on a monitor, set the background as neutral gray, not psychedelic rainbow. Take a close look at the image of the horse on these two monitors: The horse with the bright surround looks darker but really isn't.

(ABOVE)

Make sure the brightness level of your monitor is set correctly. You should be able to see a solid black square as neutral black (monitor on left) but not so dark that you begin to see a halo around the square (monitor on right).

(LEFT)

Different monitors display colors differently, even when set on the default calibration. Make sure your monitor has been calibrated properly, and that it matches the monitors of all your vendors.

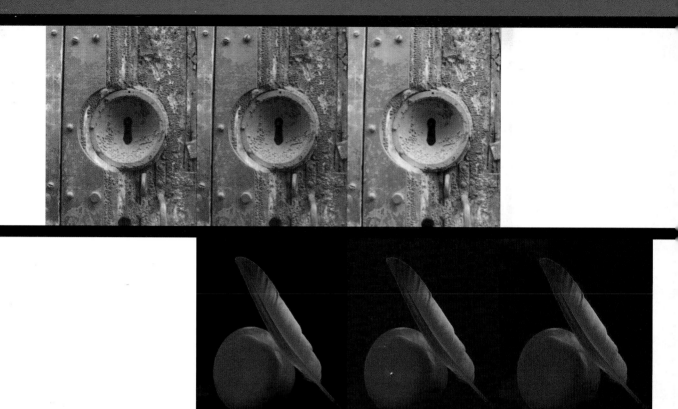

Properly calibrated color systems make neutral colors look truly neutral. Wood should look in balance, not skewed to yellow, pink or blue, as here. Blacks should also look neutral, but if a calibration system is skewed to red or green, even dense blacks will take on the same color cast.

NEUTRALS

The quality of your overall color management system is revealed when printing neutral hues: grays, whites, blacks, and beiges. A system skewed even slightly toward cyan, magenta, or yellow will give these neutral hues a noticeable color cast.

This becomes an important quality issue when you print certain subjects. Skin tones, sand, gray pavement, stone, and cloudy sky are especially sensitive to color shifts away from purely neutral, as is any image with white. Images with deep shadows containing a lot of black are also surprisingly sensitive to color shifts.

The reason these neutral colors are so easily skewed is that they are created by an even balance of C, M, Y, and K dots. If one of these colors is too heavy or too light, the entire hue of the subject shifts.

So when you color-calibrate your system, don't go by just the numbers of your calibration program. Take a look at the neutral hues in your designs and make sure they are truly neutral.

(RIGHT)

Look what you can do when your color calibration is perfect. This anemone is a quiet riot of blues, pinks, yellows, and grays, and yet, because every color is perfectly balanced, we see it all as white. This is how white really looks in nature, which is why this photo looks so spectacular in print.

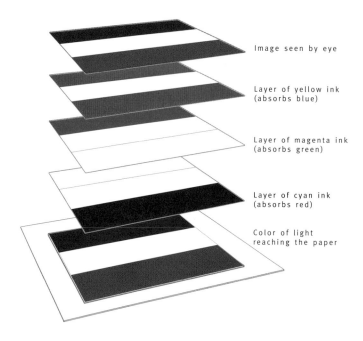

Image seen by eye

Layer of yellow ink
(absorbs blue)

Layer of magenta ink
(absorbs green)

Layer of cyan ink
(absorbs red)

Color of light
reaching the paper

(ABOVE)

We see all printing via reflected light. How does this work? Take a look at the red stripe in this Hungarian flag. White light (consisting of red, green, and blue wavelengths) first passes through a film of yellow ink (laid down on the paper). The yellow ink absorbs blue light, subtracting blue from the white light. Next the white light passes through a film of magenta ink, which absorbs green light. When the remaining light strikes the white paper under the ink, it is reflected back through the magenta and yellow ink films. The only color left of the original white light is red. So we see the top stripe as red. Similarly, on the bottom stripe, the yellow ink film subtracts blue light, and the cyan ink film subtracts red light. All that is left for the white paper to reflect is green light, so we see the bottom stripe as green.

Proofing

Unfortunately, even with all your monitors calibrated, it still may be difficult to print your designs so that they match exactly what you see on your desktop. It's a matter of physics: You can see many more colors on your computer monitor than you can print, and the colors are brighter. That's because your monitor does not show you color in the same way that paper does. We see ink on paper because the inks absorb light from a beam of white light that is shined upon it. When the inks reflect back the light to our eyes, they subtract (i.e., absorb) certain wavelengths. We see only the colors that are reflected; the other wavelengths of the color spectrum are lost in the ink.

In contrast, a computer monitor emits light through red, green, and blue phosphors, so its color spectrum is limited only by the temperature or energy of its power source. We can't see the entire spectrum of light, as we could from a brighter, stronger power source. But we can see many more colors than we can from a reflective system like ink on paper.

Thus, what you see on your monitor is not what you get on press. Your monitor shows you emitted light. The press shows you reflected light. Your monitor makes colors by adding three primary colors together. The press makes colors by subtracting three colors and by doing so imperfectly. Your monitor uses red, green, and blue. Your press uses cyan, magenta, and yellow.

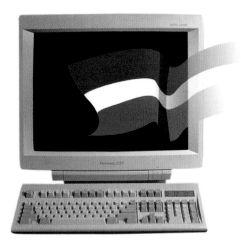

When you think about all these differences, it's really a wonder that printed pieces resemble desktop designs at all. Well, okay, on some jobs they don't. But that's often because the designer didn't take the time or trouble to make an accurate proof. Making a color proof can help stabilize color communication between you and the printer because a proof communicates color in the same way that your final output does: on paper. It is the second essential tool you need to output good color.

In the analog world, color proofs have always been the standard that printers use to match color on press. Color proofs are more than just a guide. They are legally binding. Once a client approves a proof, called a contract proof, the printer is obligated to match it to the degree he promised

when the client and he agreed to do business. Some printers agree to match the proof exactly; others agree just to come close; still others, the ones we call the down-and-dirty bunch, agree to produce color that only "pleasingly" resembles the proof. Because so much depends on the accuracy of the color proof, many high-end color separators maintain a proofing press on their premises. They use this press to print a couple of copies of proofs plated from the same film that the regular printer is going to use. So if the proof is okay, everybody in the production loop knows that the film is okay, and thus the plates are good and the job will match on press.

(ABOVE)

We see all color on a computer monitor as emitted light beamed directly to our eyes. How does this work? The phosphors in the monitor screen are energized with electricity and emit that energy as light. We see the red stripe of the Hungarian flag because in that section of the computer monitor, the red phosphors have been excited and emit their energy as red light. We see the green stripe because in that section of the monitor, the green phosphors have been excited. The white stripe appears as white because the red, green, and blue phosphors of the screen have all been excited. When they all emit light, the colors combine to form white.

Notice that the physics for seeing color on a monitor is completely different from the physics for seeing color on the printed page. That's why it is absolutely critical that you okay all final color by using printed color proofs.

Of course this process is extremely expensive. So years ago people looked for a cheaper way to proof color off-press. DuPont's Cromalin® proofs were one way. Separators would composite all the original negatives of a job into printing signatures, and then they would make four new negatives from the composites: one negative each for cyan, magenta, yellow, and black. Using those negatives (the same ones that would later be used to make the printing plates), they would expose a sticky, light-sensitive paper using each negative in turn. As each color was exposed, the separator would sprinkle C, M, Y, or K powdered toner onto the sticky surface and rub it on.

When these off-press proofing systems came on the market, printers didn't like them at first. They complained that the toner colors looked different from printing ink. But over time, they got used to seeing the differences, and both printers and designers were able to adjust their eyes so they could make a good comparison between the proof and the press.

Then the digital revolution hit. All of a sudden, you can send digitized files all over the world and not have to use film at all. Instead of negatives, we have numbers. The numbers are used to output the printing plates.

Since it seems ridiculous to use an analog proofing system in an otherwise all-digital printing world, designers began to push to use digital proofs. Various proofing systems came onto the market to address this need. In essence, the digital proofing systems employ the same technology as digital printers (see Chapter 9). That's because they *are* digital printers. So you can proof with ink-jet, laser, thermal-dye, and dye-sublimation systems. They all produce different quality proofs and they all do it by assembling little tiny color specks into simulated halftone dots. Printers were very uncomfortable with this idea at first. They hated the fact that a digital proof does not show the physical dots on a plate. Instead, the proof portrays abstract numbers stored in the computer and output especially for the proof. The problem is, if a page looks bad on press, the printer can't haul out his loupe and check to see if the right halftone dots are present in the proof or not. There might be dots there, all right, but the dots are generated separately by an entirely different machine: the digital platemaker. So the dots in the proof aren't the same dots as the ones on the plates.

Although conventional printers still struggle with this issue today, digital printers do not. Because digital printing is designed to generate one copy at a time, each and every time it prints, a digital press can make a proof as easily and cheaply as a real copy. In fact, you might say that a proof *is* the real copy, as long as it's made on the same paper as the final job.

Paper proofs are still important in the digital printing world because you need to verify how your design is going to look when the inks or toners are applied to paper, as compared to how the design looks on your computer monitor. But it's so easy to generate a single copy from your disk, the whole concept of proofing is different. You don't have to worry about paying for makeready on a proofing press. You don't have to try to match colors from one kind of off-press proofing technology to colors created by another kind of on-press printing technology. If you need to change your layout, you simply change your pixels and generate a new printout. You can even ask the printer to do the output on the exact paper you'll be using.

One printer who specializes in making extremely large, one-of-a-kind posters on a digital press does away with the concept of proofing altogether. Instead he insists that his clients come down to the plant and use his computers. He says he just finds it simpler to sit beside the client and make color corrections with his equipment on the spot. If a customer is fussy about a particular color, he can output it right then and there and change the color immediately by typing a new command into the computer. In the most literal sense, proofing and printing are the same thing.

Digitally printed, large-format signage like this can be proofed on the same equipment and with the same paper as the finished job. Proofing such a large piece with conventional equipment would be prohibitively expensive, but in the digital world, the final proof can be no more and no less than the final output.

5

RESOLUTION

When the ancient Egyptians invented hieroglyphics five thousand years ago, they never caught on to the concept of vowels. They wrote only consonants. For example, their word for "answer" was spelled "w-sh-b." But "w-sh-b" was also how scribes spelled the word "bull."

The Egyptians could appreciate that it might be a problem if you wrote home to your farm supervisor demanding an answer and he sent you bull instead. So to clarify their meaning, scribes drew a little picture at the end of a word, in this case, either a man holding his hand to his mouth or a bull walking along.

We professionals in the graphics business might do well to copy the Egyptians' practice when it comes to communicating about resolution. That's because the technology (and the jargon) for printing has overlapped that of computers. As a result, we have allowed ourselves to become very sloppy when it comes to our vocabulary.

Screen resolution, for example, can mean the amount of detail on your computer monitor. But it can also mean the number of lines per inch that your printing press is laying down on paper, or the number of dots your laser printer can squeeze into an inch.

(RIGHT)

Screen resolution can mean several things: the number of squares of red, green, or blue that your computer monitor—or screen—can display (measured as screen dots per inch); the number of screened halftone dots that a press can print (measured in lines per inch); or the number of screened ink spots a laser printer can apply (measured in dots per inch).

Understanding Terminology

Pixels sometimes refer to the squares of color on your monitor, or sometimes to the amount of data needed to print a graphic element. Dots can be halftone spots of ink on paper, or arrays of toner dots on paper.

Usually these quirks of expression are merely annoying—until your client asks you why your designs aren't coming out the way you said they would, and you realize that you, your printer, or some faceless black hole in cyberspace has messed up your resolution and your quality. It's at times like these that you might find yourself wishing you could hand out answers instead of dishing out the bull.

(BELOW)

Pixels sometimes refer to squares of red, green, and blue on your computer monitor. But technically, pixels are nothing more than a grid of zeroes and ones. The zeroes and ones tell the computer to turn off or on each pixel in its memory. That is how the computer stores information of all kinds, including images. When the computer outputs its zeroes and ones, it can do so in many formats: on paper, plastic, metal, monitor screen, audio, etc.

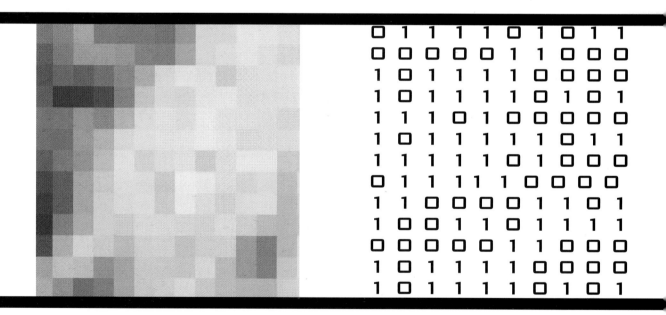

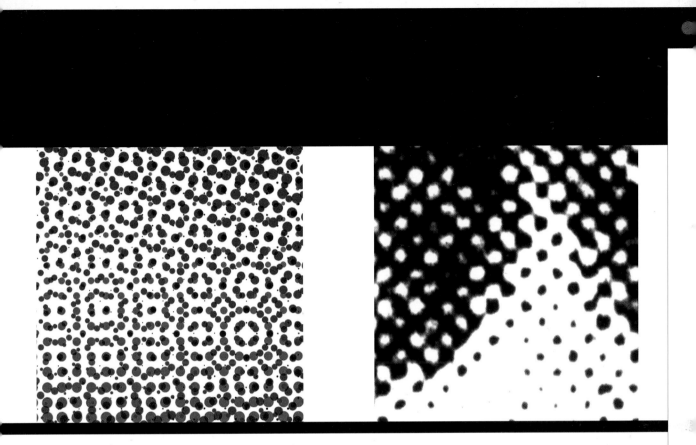

In the old days of printing, before the desktop revolution, sloppiness of jargon did not spoil the resolution of your finished piece. That's because the vendors determined how much resolution you needed. So you, as the customer, could throw around terms without knowing their exact meaning, leaving it to the vendors to figure it all out for you.

In an all-digital world, however, you are responsible for creating your own prepress materials. Ignorance about prepress terminology and concepts can be catastrophic.

To make your prepress art come out the way you expect, it is essential to understand the meaning of resolution. Only then can you determine exactly how much data you need to define the optimum amount of detail for a particular layout. In other words, you must answer the question: How much resolution is best?

(ABOVE)

Dots can be printed as halftone dots that are output by a printing press (above left), or as toner dots output by a laser printer (above right).

How much resolution is best?
The answer mainly depends on the resolution
of your output device.

How Much Resolution Is Best?

In digital prepress, there is no one right answer. Rather, the answer mainly depends on what resolution your output device is capable of. You can find out this information by checking with your printer, or—if your final output is an in-house device—by checking with the manufacturer.

Let's say, for example, that your digital design is going to be output on a conventional offset press. What is the maximum resolution the press can achieve? Depending on the quality of the paper, the resolution might be anywhere from 85 lines per inch to 300 lines per inch.

If you're outputting your prepress on a computer monitor, for a Web page for example, you are limited by the resolution that most monitors are capable of. You are also limited by the amount of time it takes to transmit the data to other computers. Nobody likes to hang around for too long while a computer image downloads. By trial and error, Web page designers have settled on 72 dots per inch as an industry standard because it's the default resolution of a Macintosh monitor (the default resolution for a PC monitor is usually 96 dots per inch). That means that the resolution of your scan of the original art should also be no more than 72 dots per inch.

Notice that offset presses and computer monitors describe resolution using different units of measure. Presses measure resolution as lpi, monitors as dpi. In fact, print production professionals have three main ways of discussing resolution: lines per inch (lpi), dots per inch (dpi), and numbers of pixels.

LPI

Lines per inch is a term that originally referred to the amount of resolution used when screening a continuous-tone original into a halftone print.

A continuous-tone original is a photo or an illustration, made with dyes or paints that create the image by using a continuous gradient of tones from dark to light. For example, if you load a paintbrush with watercolor paint and paint a swash of color across a paper, you'll see a continuous gradient of color gradually going from dark to light tones. A paintbrush can paint continuous tones, but a printing press cannot print them.

Printing presses can lay down ink only in very small areas at a time. If a press attempts to lay down a large amount of ink at once, it plops down on the paper in a shapeless glob.

Early in the history of printing, print-ers realized that to print large areas of ink—in other words, pictures—they would need to break up continuous tones into small pieces they could control on press. At first, printers used hatch marks of lines to create the illusion of tones. Lots of hatch marks together looked solid from a distance; fewer hatch marks looked pale. To etch the hatch marks, however, took a long time and had to be done by hand.

(ABOVE, LEFT)
A paintbrush can paint a continuous range of tones from dark to light. A printing press cannot.

(ABOVE, CENTER)
Engravers broke up continuous tones into hatched lines that presses could print.

(ABOVE, RIGHT)
A halftone screen really was a screen of inter-secting lines, through which a camera lens converted a continuous-tone original into a series of halftone dots.

Screened halftones are created with different-size dots, all spaced evenly apart. Large dots create the illusion of dense color; small dots create the illusion of pale color. When the dots touch each other on all sides, the color prints solid.

DPI

Eventually printers began to use screens or grids placed over a camera lens to break up the continuous tones of art. When the camera lens looked at a continuous-tone picture such as a photo or painting, the grid of the screen broke up the tones of the picture into dots. The dots were all evenly spaced, but their size was determined by the density of tone. Dense tones had big dots; light tones had small dots. The dots didn't look evenly spaced because they were all different sizes. But they really were evenly spaced, as measured from the center of one dot to the center of another.

This process of creating tones using dots from a screen was called halftone screening. The results were much more satisfactory than hatching. For one thing, the process readily lent itself to mass production—all you had to do was fit the appropriate screen over a camera lens and shoot your original art through the screen.

Printers also discovered that they could create the illusion of continuous tones better if they used finer screens to produce more dots. They measured the fineness of the screens by counting the number of lines per inch across one direction of the screen. Over time, printers came to standardize the fineness of the halftone screens they used, measured in lines per inch or lpi. The screens that were most commonly used were 85 lpi (called an 85-line screen), 100 lpi, 120 lpi, 133 lpi, 150 lpi, and 300 lpi.

85 lpi

120 lpi

150 lpi

What determined the fineness of screen was a paper's ability to hold a printed dot on the surface, without the ink soaking into the paper and spreading out. A screen with 85 lines per inch was good for printing dots on newsprint. It produced some detail, but more important, it allowed enough room for each dot to expand as it soaked into the porous newsprint paper. Finer screens—up to 300 lines per inch—could be used on paper with better ink holdout.

Designers began to forget exactly what these screen measurements represented. Instead, they developed a seat-of-the-pants way to specify the fineness of resolution they wanted. It was based on their experience with different printers and different grades of paper. As a rule of thumb, designers knew that an 85-line screen was okay for newspapers but much too coarse for magazines.

Designers settled on 133-line screens as reasonable quality for magazines because they knew that most grades of coated papers could hold dots that fine. Really fine printing with 150-line screens produced extremely high-quality detail and color and required higher-grade papers; 300-line screens pushed the limits of offset printing to the maximum.

Speaking loosely, people often substituted "dots per inch" for "lines per inch". Remember, the screens used to make halftones were grids of crossing lines. Wherever the horizontal lines crossed the vertical lines, the screen would break up a continuous halftone into dots. It was convenient to refer to screen resolution as dots per inch because when the job was printed on an offset press, the ink that was printed came out in dots.

(ABOVE)

Finer resolutions produce finer details, but only up to a point. If your printer is capable of printing only 120 lpi, finer-screened halftones will only plug up the press.

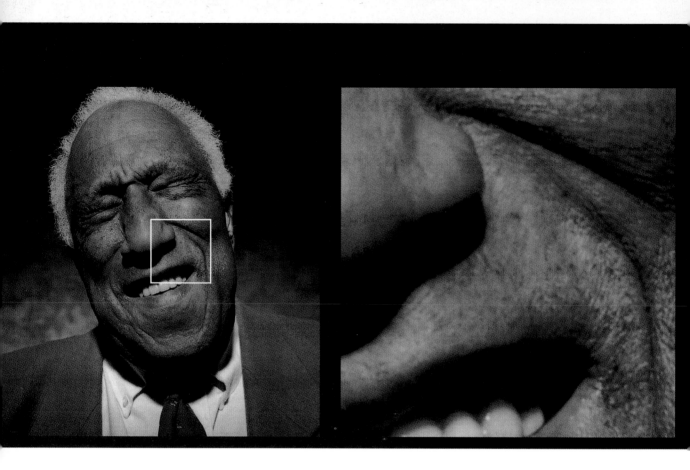

BITMAP IMAGES

When our industry began to create halftones using imagesetters and desktop systems to process art digitally, we continued to use the same terminology as before. Halftones are still "screened," even though no physical screen exists anymore. Computers instead use mathematical algorithms to break up the continuous tones into halftones. Fineness of screens is still measured as lines per inch or dots per inch. But the lines and dots from an imagesetter are completely different from physical screens.

When a computerized scanner makes a digitized halftone, it has to figure out how to turn continuous tones into dots. It does this by scanning the original art and creating cells made up of very tiny spots, with the color of each cell stored in a file on the computer. As the scanner's "eye" scans across the original picture, the computer converts each square of tones it sees into numbers. The numbers describe the color of each square. The resulting array of colored cells is called a bitmap image.

Why does the scanner need to divide the original continuous-tone picture into cells or squares? Think of it this way: A bitmap image is rather like a paint-by-number kit.

Remember those? When you bought a paint-by-number kit, you'd get a white canvas with areas outlined. (The areas could be any shape, though, not just squares.) Each area had a number printed in it corresponding to a little can of paint. You'd load up your paintbrush with the proper color and fill in the numbered area. When you were done, you'd have a picture. Usually the "resolution" of the picture was pretty coarse and would have a lot better "resolution" if it had divided the paint-by-number areas into tinier bits of color. But who would have had the patience to fill in millions of squares?

In today's world, the computer has that amount of patience. As it scans your original art, it can create thousands or millions of squares of colors.

Before the computer can do this, however, you must tell it how many little squares you want it to use (resolution). The answer is measured in dots per inch. You determine this when you set the scanner modes. For example, if you select 600 dots per inch, then the scanner divides the original into 600 little squares per inch as it moves across the original.

(ABOVE)

Scanners break up the tones of a continuous-tone original for the same reason that paint-by-number crafters paint small areas of color: You've got to apply the color using some scheme of painting small amounts that, from a distance, create the illusion of continuous tones.

LASER PRINTER

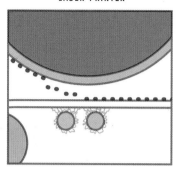

INK-JET PRINTER

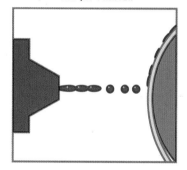

COMPUTER MONITOR

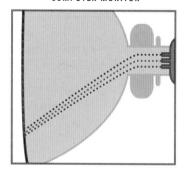

(LEFT)

A computer doesn't care how it displays the pixels stored in its memory. It's happy to output pixels by interfacing with the software in a laser printer, which converts pixels to toner dots. Or the computer can interface with an ink-jet printer, which converts pixels to sprayed-out droplets of ink. Or the computer can direct its own monitor to display the pixels by lighting up squares or phosphors on the monitor screen.

The "dots" are not really printing dots. They are a spreadsheet of numbers arrayed in a grid or cell. Each number in the grid tells an output device either to color in a tiny portion of the grid, or to leave it blank. These tiny portions are the dots in "dpi."

These dots can be depicted or applied by various output devices. Laser printers, for example, apply little blobs of toner in a grid. Ink-jet printers spray little droplets of ink. A computer monitor turns on little phosphors that emit red, green, or blue light. All these applications are measured as dpi and all come from the same source: pixels.

8.5"

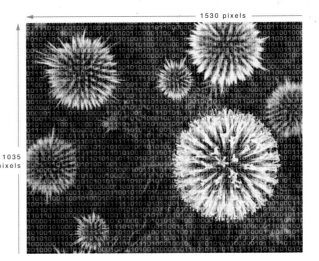

1530 pixels

1035 pixels

PIXELS

In a nondigital world, a picture has a fixed size. You can measure it with a ruler, so many inches long, so many inches wide. You can cut it up into pieces (cropping it). But the images that appear in the picture don't change their size.

To a computer, picture size is different. A computer doesn't care very much about the length and width of a picture. A computer does care about how many numbers it has in its files. It is these numbers which enable it to output a picture to some device, whether it's a laser printer, a piece of film, a Web page, or something else.

These numbers are called pixels. They consist of collections of bits, or zeroes and ones. When grouped together into an image, pixels form a bitmap image. In this form, they fill a file on a computer drive. Thus, they have no physical width or length. In fact, they have no physical existence at all.

Unfortunately, when computer people were naming their inventions, they loved the word pixel so much that they also used it to identify the little boxes of red, green, and blue (RGB) that appear on your computer monitor. If you take a loupe and look at your monitor, you will see rows of red, green, and blue, separated by lines to form squares. Each of these squares is called a pixel. But it is not a true pixel. A true pixel is a set of numbers.

(ABOVE LEFT)
Original art has a fixed, measurable size. Digital art does not.

(ABOVE RIGHT)
Digital art is measured in terms of numbers of pixels stored in computer memory. The pixels can be output at any linear size you want.

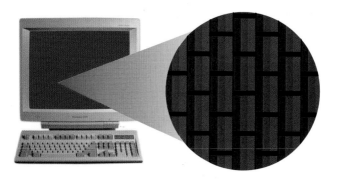

If you look at your monitor through a loupe, you will see thousands of little squares of red, green, and blue phosphors separated by black lines. These phosphors are screen pixels that the computer tells to light up. Each square can be lit to a certain intensity as well, creating millions of colors.

To distinguish a numerical pixel from a square that represents it on your monitor, we should probably invent a new word for the screen version. Not pixel. Maybe spixel (for screen pixel), or squarxel (for square pixel). Unhappily, the time is long past when we can invent a new word for something in such common use. We're probably stuck with pixel. But at least we should call the pixels we see on our monitors "screen pixels." It's an important distinction because it has to do with image size.

Image Size

No one ever looks at real (i.e., numerical) pixels in their true form. If you did, all you'd see are strings of zeroes and ones.

When you want to see a bitmap of pixels on your computer monitor, the computer asks itself where you would like to see the bitmap, and how big a picture it should show you. You can tell the computer to show you the bitmap image on your computer monitor, or on some other output device, such as your laser printer.

Using the control bar, you can tell your computer monitor to output (or display) its pixels at different screen resolutions. The higher resolutions can display more colors and more detail. But the number of pixels displayed is the same, because pixels are pure numbers, not squares on a screen.

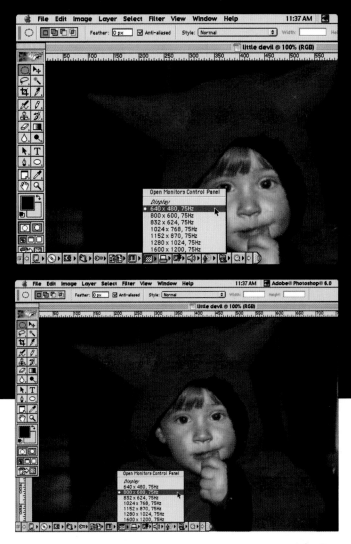

When you tell your computer to show you a bitmap image on your monitor, usually the computer depicts one numerical pixel by using one screen pixel. You can alter this on your monitor by clicking on the control bar and opening up the window for screen resolution (the icon looks like a little checkerboard). On my iMac, I can choose to view my monitor screen with 640x480 pixels, 800x600 pixels, or 1,024x768.

Altering my screen resolution does not affect the real pixels at all. They're still living, inviolate, in the computer's database.

What limits the computer's ability to show resolution on any output device is the number of total pixels that were input into its file for any given image. The input can be from a scanner, a Photo CD, an E-mail image, etc. This data is expressed by the number of pixels along the height of the image and the number of pixels along the width. An image measuring 640 x 480 pixels has 640 pixels along the height and 480 pixels along the width, for a total of 307,200 pixels. All the information about the picture—the colors, the detail—is contained by these 307,200 pixels.

If you decide that you'd rather change the number of pixels in an image, you can throw data away and reduce the number of pixels you have. This may be a good idea because manipulating large numbers of pixels takes a lot of memory from the computer. Let's say you have scanned in a color picture, but you really only need black-and-white. You can throw away all the data used to create the colors, thereby shrinking the database considerably.

Unfortunately, you cannot go the other way very effectively. You cannot increase the number of pixels stored in your computer for any given image.

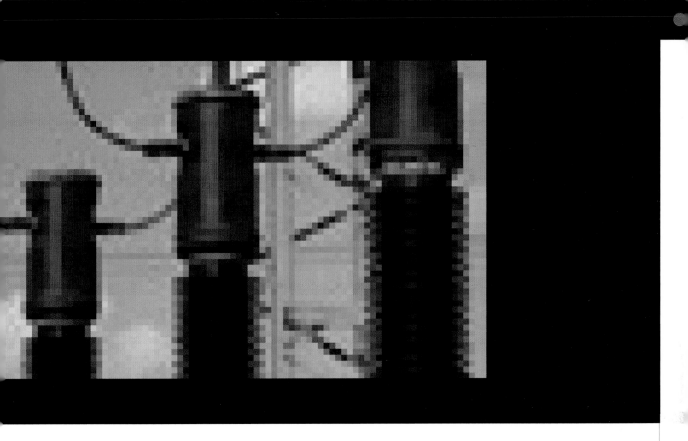

(However, note the discussion about resampling in Chapter 4.) If you tried to tell your computer to add pixels, it wouldn't know what to do. Put a zero here, a one there? How many zeroes? In what order? Your poor computer has no way of answering these questions. On *Star Trek*, when the crew did this to the computerized android, Commander Data, his eyes would start to flit back and forth in a Nixonian manner, and then sometimes he would topple over.

The best way to increase the number of pixels your computer has to work with is to give it more pixels in the first place when you scan the image. How many pixels should you give it?

(ABOVE AND FACING PAGE)
If you want to reduce the resolution of an image, you can always throw away pixels from a stored image, but it's difficult to add new pixels to increase resolution effectively. The computer must guess how to add the new pixels, but it can't know for sure. Sometimes you can improve an image slightly, but if you try to add too many pixels, the results look horrible. That's why it's best to scan your originals at the highest resolution you think you will need.

In the picture above, the resolution is too coarse. When the computer is told to add more pixels, it tries its best, but the image (facing page) just doesn't look right.

100%

50%

(RIGHT)

To determine the best resolution for your images, you first need to calculate the linear reduction (or enlargement) of the original. You do this by measuring one side of the original and calculating the percentage that side changes as you reduce or enlarge your scan. It doesn't matter which side of the original you choose to measure; just be sure you use only one side. Here, the original measures 3.25 inches (82 cm) wide and must be reduced to a measure of 1,625 inches (41 cm) wide, or a reduction of 50 percent.

Choosing the Right PPI

The first thing you might try is to scan at the highest possible resolution available. But you find that this leads to enormous files. For example, an 8-by-10-inch (20-by-25-centimeter) picture, scanned at 1,200 pixels per inch (ppi) contains (8 x 1200) x (10 x 1200) = 115,200,000 pixels. How big is the resulting file? If you have a 32-bit system, that's four bytes per pixel. So the raw image would be 4 x 115,200,000, or 460 MB. Such enormous images will burn up your disk space quickly and slow the output considerably. If the output is an imagesetter used to produce final film, you can spend a lot of money on this big of a file—service bureaus with expensive imagesetters often charge by the minute.

You might think that the expense is just a cost of doing business. But, in fact, a file with resolution this fine is a waste of money because most output devices can't use this much data. In effect, they throw large portions of it away.

Rather than waste money producing resolution that nobody can print, it's far better to calculate how many pixels per inch you really need for your images in the real world. There are only three numbers we need to calculate, and two of them are very easy.

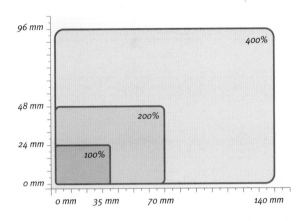

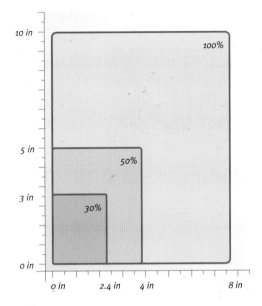

ENLARGEMENT RATIO: 35mm NEGATIVE

REDUCTION RATIO: 8 x 10 INCH PHOTO

LINEAR ENLARGEMENT RATIO

The first (easy) number we need to know is the linear enlargement ratio. This is defined as the linear size of the final outputted artwork divided by the linear size of the original artwork. So if we are going to print our original 8-by-10-inch (20-by-25-centimeter) picture at a final output size of, say 4 by 5 inches (10 by 13 centimeters), the linear enlargement ratio would be: 4 inches final width divided by 8 inches original width equals one-half (0.5).

Note that we are choosing the linear measurement of the original, not the area. Note, too, that we chose to use the width measurement. We could also have chosen the length; it makes no difference.

SAMPLING RATIO

The second (easy) number we need to know is a sampling ratio. This is a "fudge factor" used to ensure that each output halftone dot is backed up by more than one bitmap pixel. Just set the sampling ratio to a value between one (for smallest feasible files at slightly lower resolution) and two (for bigger files at higher resolution). For output to a conventional offset press, use one and a half. It works. For output to a computer monitor for a Web page, use the number one. If you're in doubt, use two for the sampling ratio—you can always reduce the size later in Photoshop, or just accept a little bit of extra, wasted disk space and RIPing time.

8 x 10 ORIGINAL

Printer Resolution

The final (not so easy) number we need to know is the printed resolution. This requires some expert knowledge of the particular printing process you are using:

1. If you are using a conventional offset press, the printed resolution is determined by the press's and paper's ability to hold ink on the surface of the paper. The resolution can range from 85 to 300 lines per inch. Ask your printer what number is best, based on the equipment and paper to be used to produce your work.

2. If you are using a toner-based system, such as a laser printer, the laser printer has to draw each individual halftone dot as a bundle of many laser-printed dots. There are

quite a few ways to do this, and some experimentation may be necessary for you to determine the effective resolution of your output device.

As a rule of thumb, the effective halftone resolution of a laser printer is not much better than one-quarter of the manufacturer's quoted dots-per-inch resolution. Thus, a 600 dpi laser printer will achieve a halftone resolution roughly equivalent to a 150 lines-per-inch screen (600 divided by four equals 150).

3. If you are outputting your design to a computer monitor, the lines-per-inch resolution is the same as the manufacturer's stated pixels-per-inch resolution. In most cases this number is seventy-two or ninety-six.

linear reduction ratio		sampling number		resolution of output device		scanning resolution
0.5	**X**	**1.5**	**X**	**150 lpi**	**=**	**112.5 ppi**

Scanning Resolution

Once you have determined the three numbers you need, here is the magic formula to calculate how many pixels per inch you need to scan your images:

Scanner pixels per inch equals linear enlargement ratio times sampling number, times the effective resolution of the output device.

So if you're wondering how many pixels to scan that 8-by-10-inch (20-by-25-centimeter) image we first talked about, here is what you do:

1. Decide how big the final outputted image is going to be. In this case, we said 4 by 5 inches (10 by 13 centimeters). This gives a linear reduction ratio of one-half (0.5).

2. Decide on the sampling number. We're going to be outputting on a laser printer, which doesn't have very good printing quality, so a sampling number of one and a half should be more than adequate.

3. Decide the effective resolution of the output device. Our laser printer is a low-end model capable of 600 dots per inch. The effective resolution of this printer, we have learned through experimentation, is 150 lines per inch.

Therefore we need to scan our 8-by-10-inch (20-by-25-centimeter) image at a resolution of 112.5 pixels per inch (0.5 times 1.5 times 150). If we're unhappy with the detail on the resulting image, we might try raising the sampling number to two. Then we would scan at 150 pixels per inch. Anything more than that is a waste of disk space.

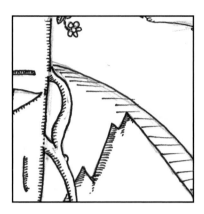

File Compression

Images, especially color images, are big data hogs. Not only do they require a lot of memory to store, they require quite a bit of memory just to look at them, and even more memory to manipulate them. The problem is exacerbated any time you want to send an image anywhere, whether it's over the Internet or to your ink-jet printer.

To deal with this problem, software programmers came up with the idea of compressing data. Think of it this way: Let's say you have scanned a line drawing into your computer. Wherever the image is black, the computer bits are on; wherever the image is white, the computer bits are off. Vast areas of the bitmap are nothing more than long strings of zeroes that show all the white space.

Rather than make the computer store each zero separately, why not write a little program that tells the computer, "Hey, right now you're going to show 1,082 zeroes in a row (where there is a lot of white space). Then you'll show eighteen ones (where there is a little black). Then another 582 zeroes." You can see how much shorter such a command would be than making the computer actually store 1,082 zeroes followed by eighteen ones, and another 582 zeroes.

Many programmers saw the advantage of compressing data, but they all did it in a different way. The result is that there are many compression programs on the market today. Some of the most common are TIFF (Tagged-Image File Format), BMP (used for Windows), GIF (CompuServe's Graphics Interchange Format, used mainly for pages of hypertext markup language, or

HTML), JPEG (Joint Photographic Experts Group, also used commonly on HTML pages), and PICT.

Some of these programs are lossless, meaning that when they compress the data, they don't throw any of it away. When you reopen the file and uncompress it, it reverts to the same bitmap it had originally. Some compression programs, notably JPEG, are lossy. That means they throw data away when they compress it. When you uncompress a JPEG file, the software recreates the data in a set way. But it doesn't duplicate the original data exactly. So JPEG images look a little different from the original.

You can save your bitmap data in many different formats. Be aware, however, that some service bureaus and printers may have trouble with certain formats. This is especially true if they are still using older imagesetters. So always, always check ahead before you compress anything. You don't want to find out that your format causes the imagesetter to crash on the day that you have to get your job printed, bound, and out the door before the last mail pickup at 3 p.m.

That would cause heads to roll just as surely today as screw-ups did in Pharoanic times three thousand years ago. Some things never change.

(TOP) PRE-COMPRESSED

(BOTTOM) POST-COMPRESSED

Lossy compression programs, such as JPEG, throw away some of the pixels and then restore them later when the image is decompressed. The restored pixels aren't always the same as the original ones thrown away so details in restored JPEGs can look slightly different from the original.

A BIT OF COLOR

Each screen pixel on your monitor is either on (one) or off (zero). So each pixel can show two levels of meaning. But you can't express any shades of color or intensity at that level. So computer engineers grouped pixels into collections of eight bits, or two permutations of eight zeroes and ones strung together. An eight-bit system can create 256 levels of color (two to the eighth power, or two times two times two times two times two times two times two times two). Why did engineers stop at eight bits? Because the human eye can see only about 256 levels of gray.

Now, if you make each pixel capable of showing three colors (red, green, or blue), then you increase an eight-bit system to twenty-four bits. This yields 16,777,216 colors. Bird eyes might be able to resolve more shades than that, but our eyes can't.

(RIGHT)

Sometimes vignettes that are supposed to fade gradually from dark to light do so in steps that you can actually see. This is called banding.

(BELOW)

The human eye can see approximately 256 shades of gray, ranging from solid black to white. The eye can perceive as many shades in each of the primary colors too, meaning that we can see as many as 16,777,216 colors.

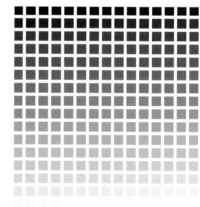

Banding

When you create a design where color is supposed to gently fade off into nothingness, like General Douglas MacArthur saying goodbye to Congress, sometimes bad things happen. The general doesn't go gradually. In print, this is called banding. Instead of a smooth, continuous-looking fade, banding creates a kind of stepping-stone look in a vignette or in a design where one color blends into another.

There are four reasons why you can get banding in digital printing:

1. **Not enough bits in each pixel.** The first rule of no-band printing is: Do your initial scans with a bit depth of at least eight bits. Here's why:

In programs such as Photoshop that deal with raster images, each pixel carries several channels of information. The number of channels determines the kind of image you have. A grayscale image has only one channel (the gray level). An RGB image carries three channels (red, green, and blue). A CMYK image carries four channels (cyan, magenta, yellow, and black).

Each channel has a "bit depth," which determines the number of shades resolved in that channel. For most halftone images, a bit depth of eight is plenty. This yields 256 shades of gray (two to the eighth power), which is about as many as the human eye can see.

You are almost certain to run into banding problems if you are given files with a bit depth of less than eight pixels.

In such cases, banding is almost inevitable. Therefore, such files are not suitable for high-quality images. If you receive such a file, you can increase its bit depth in Photoshop and then use smoothing filters. But the results are unlikely to be top quality.

2. **Too much file compression.** The second rule of no-band printing is: Be careful about using lossy compression schemes. Here's why:

Lossy compression programs, such as JPEG, throw away some information to make the file size smaller. To do that, the program looks at pixels and in effect says, "Here's a tone, here's the same tone. Let's compress the data. Okay, here's another tone and another and another that we can compress in the same way. Oops, here comes a tone that's too different. Let's make a new compression tone." At that point, you might get a band not present in the original, uncompressed image.

Alternative file formats, such as GIF and TIFF, compress tones without throwing away data. The resulting files are bigger than JPEG files, but they preserve every pixel that was in the original.

TIFF: 3.6MB

(LEFT)

Sometimes lossy compression programs can cause banding when images are decompressed (left). The solution is to use a lossless compression program (right).

(RIGHT)

The reason that designers use lossy compression programs, even though they can cause banding problems and changes in detail, is that lossless compression programs don't compress as many pixels. So the files are much bigger.

GIF: 964K

JPEG: 132K

VIGNETTE TOO LONG = BANDING

3. **Gradients spread across too great a length.** The third rule of no-band printing is: Use short blends and vignettes. Here's why:

Digital imagesetting devices create ink halftone dots by building them up out of smaller digital dots. They do this by creating a grid and placing various amounts of digital dots onto the grid to synthesize different-size halftone dots. Depending on its size, each halftone dot can be created by one digital dot on the grid (resulting in a very, very small halftone dot), two digital dots, three, all the way up to the largest number of digital dots that the imagesetter is capable of outputting (resulting in an array of halftone dots so big and so densely spaced that the ink color is solid).

When these synthesized dots are asked to produce a continuous gradient of tones, they do not arrange themselves randomly.

All the 50 percent dots clump together in the middle of the blend, all the 40 percent dots clump next to that, all the 100 percent dots clump together on the solid end, etc. As the dots go from percentage to percentage, they do so in steps.

SHORTER VIGNETTE = LESS BANDING

ENLARGED DETAIL OF A BANDING STEP

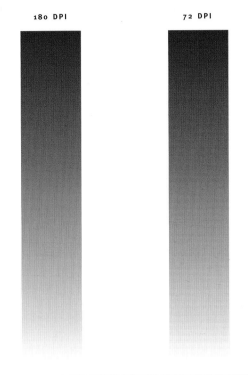

180 DPI   72 DPI

If the steps are spaced far apart because the vignette or blend is stretched across a great width, we can see the steps as bands. If the steps are packed closely together across a short distance, we can't see them.

4. **Not enough resolution.** The fourth rule of no-band printing is: Use an imagesetter and a line screen with plenty of resolution. The more dpi and lpi you have to work with, the smoother your blends and vignettes will look, simply because the steps between shades will be more finely drawn and harder to see.

(ABOVE)

Banding can be minimized if the resolution you choose is high. That's because higher resolutions use more pixels, so the steps between bands of tones are smaller and less visible.

(FACING PAGE, LEFT)

Vignettes made of halftone dots can show banding as the grayscale steps from one tone to the next. This is especially true if the vignette is stretched across a long distance. If the vignette is shorter, the banding becomes less noticeable.

1.

calculate number of shades available

$$dpi^2 \div lpi^2 = \underline{A}$$

dpi of monitor or output device

lpi of printing device

HOW CAN YOU TELL IF YOU'RE LIKELY TO GET BANDING?

Basically it boils down to whether you've got too few dots or too big a blend. You can calculate this for yourself.

1. Figure out the number of shades available in your blend, by acquiring two numbers: the dpi of your digital outputting device (an imagesetter, a computer monitor screen, etc.); and the lpi of your final printing device (an offset press, a laser printer, etc.). Remember that the lpi of a digital printing device is not the same as its dpi. The lpi of a digital printing device is really the effective halftone screen frequency (measured as lpi) that its digitally synthesizing toner or ink-jet heads can create. To get the effective lpi of your printing device, consult the manufacturer. Most desktop laser printers, for example, have an effective lpi of 150.

2.

measure length of vignette in points

#inches x 72pts = _B_ pts

3.

divide length of vignette
by # of shades available

B ÷ A = _C_   **if _C_ > 1 banding
may
result**

Once you have found out these two numbers, plug them into this formula:

(dpi squared) divided by (lpi squared) equals total shades available.

This formula applies to a vignette that goes all the way from 0 percent black (i.e., white) to 100 percent black (i.e., solid). If your vignette is going to shade from, say 30 percent to 70 percent black, you've got to multiply the total shades above by 40 percent (because that's all the tones you'll be using).

2. Measure the length of your vignette, in points (72 points equals an inch).

3. Divide the length of your vignette by the total shades available.

If the number you get is greater than one, you will probably see banding. Let's consider an example.

Suppose your imagesetter is capable of 1,200 dpi, and you ask it to produce a halftone vignette 5 inches (13 centimeters) long, going from solid black to white, screened at 100 lines per inch.

First, you need to figure out how many tones are available by squaring the dots per inch and dividing it by lines-per-inch squared: dpi squared is 1,200 times 1,200, or 1,440,000. Lpi squared is 100 times 100, or 10,000. 1,440,000 divided by 10,000 equals 144. You have 144 tones available.

Next, measure the length of the vignette in points: 5 inches times 72 points equals 360.

Next, divide the points (360) by the number of tones available (144), and you get 2.5. The number is greater than 1, so you will get banding.

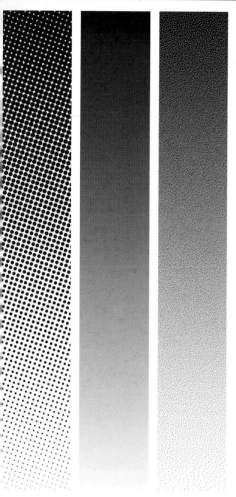

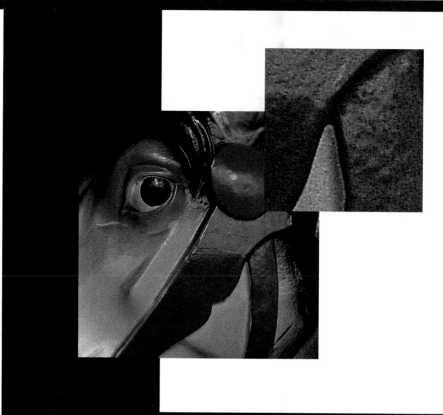

(ABOVE LEFT)

Conventional halftone screens (left) often show banding (center), while stochastic screens (right) don't. That's because halftone screens are arranged in a grid pattern, but stochastic dots are random.

(ABOVE LEFT CENTER)

Conventional halftone screens use a grid of evenly spaced dots. The dots are large in dense areas of color, and small in pale areas of color.

TO AVOID BANDING, YOU CAN DO ONE OF SEVERAL THINGS:

1. Stretch your vignette over a smaller distance. If you make the sample vignette above 2 inches instead of 5 and work the formula, you will get a final ratio of 1 instead of 2.5. So you won't see banding.

2. Use more dpi. If you use an image-setter with a resolution of 2,400 dpi, you will have 576 tones available: (2,400 times 2,400) divided by (100 times 100). When you divide the length of the vignette in points (360) by 576, you get 0.625, a number less than 1. So no banding.

3. Reduce your lpi. If you printed your halftone at a very coarse 60 lpi, you would have 400 tones available: (1,200 times 1,200) divided by (sixty times sixty). When you divide 360 points by 400 tones, you get 0.9. So no banding.

4. You can also try two general tricks: You can add noise to disguise the banding, or you can make the contrast of the blends bigger (although in our example, going from 1 to 100 percent is as big as you can make it).

5. You can use stochastic screening instead of conventional halftone screening. Stochastic screens employ randomized dots, so no banding pattern ever appears.

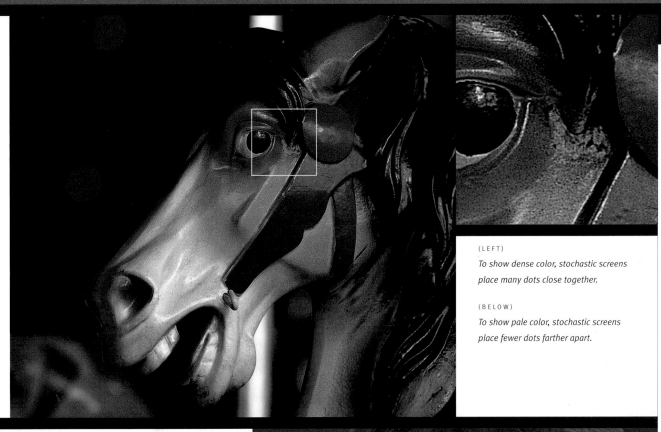

(LEFT)
To show dense color, stochastic screens place many dots close together.

(BELOW)
To show pale color, stochastic screens place fewer dots farther apart.

Stochastic Screening

Like halftone screening, stochastic screening is a method of converting continuous-tone images into dots that can be printed on a press.

The difference is that instead of chopping up an image by using a grid, stochastic imaging chops up the image by converting it into millions of really tiny dots. The dots are all the same size (unlike halftone dots, which are different sizes). But they are arranged in a randomized way so that we can see no pattern. Stochastic dots may be close to each other or farther away (unlike halftone dots, which are evenly spaced).

When many stochastic dots clump together, the color is very intense. When few stochastic dots clump together, the color is pale.

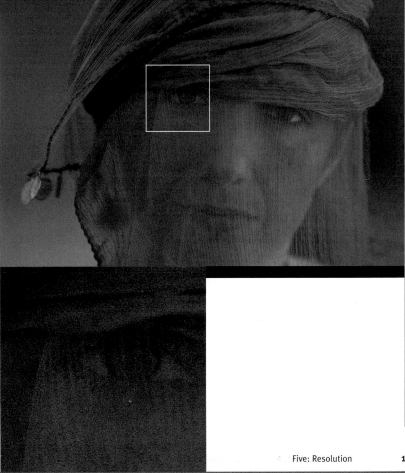

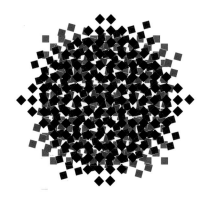

(ABOVE)

When angled halftone screens are used to reproduce a small geometric pattern, the angles of the screens can conflict with the angles of the pattern and can cause a moiré. Stochastic screens have no pattern and produce no moirés.

(ABOVE RIGHT)

Halftone screens are angled to prevent one ink printing directly on top of another.

(RIGHT)

Stochastic screens (right) can show more detail than conventional halftone screens (left).

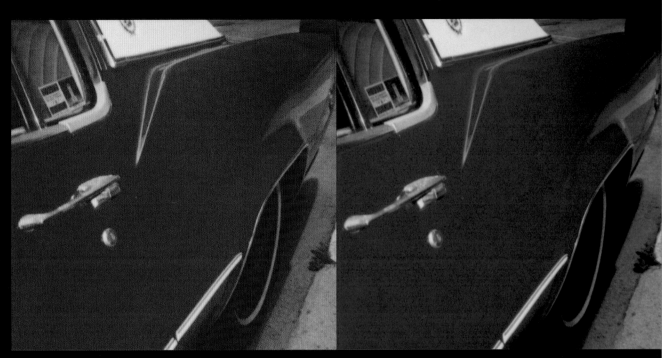

(ABOVE)

Because conventional halftone screens are made up of dots on a grid, they butt against each other in square patterns. When you try to reproduce subjects that have a lot of smooth, curvy shapes, such as metal cars, a square grid may not create the subtle modeling effects that you need. This may be especially noticeable in digital printing, because the halftone dots do not sink into the paper, as they would on a conventional press. The grid pattern is thus not soft-ened by dot gain. Stochastic screening might be a better choice.

(ABOVE AND LEFT)

Because stochastic screens use very tiny dots, they can print delicate shades of color with finesse (above). Halftone screens use larger printing dots that do not provide as many tonal gradations (left).

Stochastic screens are more forgiving about registration. An image that prints noticeably out of register with halftone screens (left) is not noticeably affected with stochastic screens (right).

THE ADVANTAGES OF STOCHASTIC SCREENING:

1. **More detail.** Stochastic dots are tinier than the dots used to make halftone dots, so stochastic screens can show greater detail.

2. **No screen angle conflicts.** Because stochastic screens have no grid pattern, they have no angles. Without angles, stochastic screens never show moirés.

3. **Less banding.** With smaller, randomized dots, stochastic screens do not show banding when one tone blends into another. This trait can be especially helpful when showing curved, shiny surfaces, such as those on cars, or when showing delicate midtone blends, such as skin tones.

These colors look smoother and more continuous than images separated with halftone screens.

4. **More control.** Because stochastic dots are so tiny, you can control certain colors better, especially those on the pale end of the scale, such as pastels.

5. **Easier registration.** Stochastic screens are far more forgiving on press than halftone screens, when it comes to registration.

THE CHALLENGES WITH STOCHASTIC SCREENING:

1. **Harder to print.** Not every printer or output device can print stochastic screens. You need output devices that can produce the incredibly tiny dots. This is especially true for digital devices. So check ahead with your printer to make sure your job can print.

2. **Different software algorithms.** To make stochastic dots random takes powerful software. It is not a simple thing to make random dots look really random—our eyes keep insisting on finding patterns or shapes. Just go outside and look at the stars some night: The stars are distributed randomly in our sky, yet we see constellations such as the Big Dipper, Pegasus, Cassiopeia.

Since programmers knew that you wouldn't want a spoon, a horse, or a W appearing in your image, they devised software that would compensate for our desire to see patterns. Different software publishers came up with different programs. Make sure that everyone in your production flow can support your screening software.

3. **Proofing.** Even if your printer can output stochastic screens, you may not be able to proof your designs on your office laser or ink-jet printer, if the resolution they offer is too large to print stochastic dots. Ask your printer for some help with proofing.

4. **Dot gain.** If you're printing with inks, as opposed to toners, you may have to contend with excessive dot gain. That's because stochastic dots are so small that any dot gain at all is usually a significant proportion of the total size of the dot. This is an especially big problem on a conventional offset press, a small problem on a waterless press, and no problem at all with toner technology. Ask your printer how you should compensate for dot gain, if necessary.

(RIGHT)

To be random is not the same as to look random. The stars in the sky are scattered randomly, but our eyes try to see a pattern, such as the Orion constellation here. To look random, stochastic screens employ highly sophisticated mathematical programs that randomize dots in such a way that our eyes see no pattern whatsoever.

6

COLOR IN PRINT: GETTING THE RESULTS YOU WANT

The three primary process printing colors are cyan, magenta, and yellow. A separate black plate produces a truer black than the relatively muddy combination of CMY and allows for reproduction of detail that the combined colors cannot match. (From left to right: 100C, 100M, 100Y, 100CMY, and 100K.)

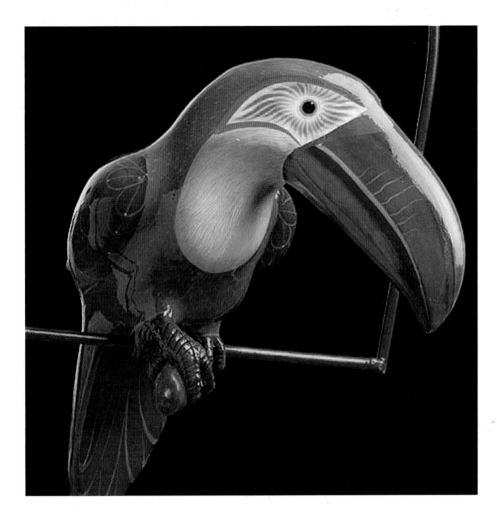

This toucan may look brilliant on your monitor, but how will it look in press proofs, when printed, or when displayed on the Web? What you see in RGB is not representative of the final CMYK result.

But That's Not the Way It Looks on My Monitor

ACCURATE COLOR REPRODUCTION IS one of the primary goals of printing technology. It can achieve this goal, in part, because the human eye is relatively easy to fool with the right props. Think of really good color printing as one of the most exhaustive and expensive illusions ever created. For all of their flair and dizzying props, Siegfried and Roy can't hold a penlight to the printing industry's achievement in convincing us that the colors we see on the printed page are as real as those created in the natural world.

The color you see on your monitor or television is inherently different from color reproduced in print. Your color monitor emits light by firing electron guns at phosphors embedded in the screen in the primary colors of red, green, and blue (RGB). At full intensity, these three colors combine to produce white. The absence of RGB produces what appears to be black. With myriad variations of RGB, we can produce the array of colors available on today's color monitors.

In the natural world, the primary colors of red, green, and blue (RGB) interact with one another in unlimited combinations. This simplified illustration represents the effect of the primary colors at maximum intensity. All three colors combine at full strength to produce white.

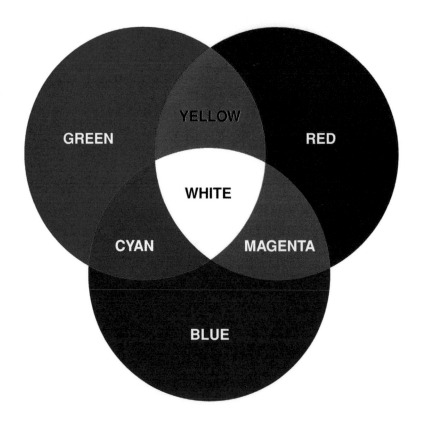

Although this photo is reproduced in CMYK, the images on the monitor will always be RGB. RGB is known as additive color; CMY is referred to as subtractive color, and represents the secondary colors of RGB. CMY combines to produce black, but most printing processes add a black (K) plate for better-quality reproduction.

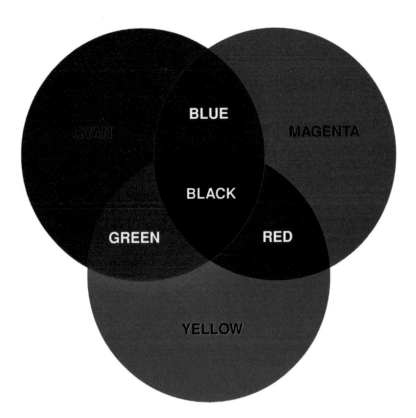

Secondary RGB Colors—
OUR BELOVED CMY(K)

Additive Color

THE RGB PRIMARY COLORS produced by monitors are commonly known as *additive colors*. The *secondary colors* of RGB—produced by mixing any two primary colors and excluding the third—are cyan, magenta, and yellow. For example, green and blue produce cyan, red and blue result in magenta, and green and red produce yellow. By varying the intensity of RGB, we can run through the gamut of colors available—within the constraints of the monitor—until the eventual result is the strongest color possible: white.

The beauty of RGB is that it closely relates to how we perceive color in the natural world. However, while it is the basis for media that project color, such as your computer monitor and television set, it is useless in print reproduction, which employs CMYK *subtractive* colors. Conversely, no matter how often you convert a design on your computer system to CMYK, it will always be RGB on your screen.

Secondary Colors Turn
the Tables in Print

IN PRINTING REPRODUCTION, the secondary RGB colors—CMY—take the lead, reducing RGB to simple reds, greens, and blues. In print, the combination of magenta and yellow produce red; yellow and cyan result in green; and cyan and magenta combine to give us blue. While the three primary printing colors produce black, this combination alone lacks the snap and detail of a separately applied black ink. Because of this, the print industry has added black (K) to the primary subtractive color lineup. Think of it as the Special Forces member of the CMYK printing process, with several obvious missions and a surprising number of covert talents.

Black ink for commercial printing is manufactured in a variety of pigmented compositions. Process black, which is used in four-color process printing, is a relatively neutral color and is pigmented so that it doesn't shift the hues of the other three primary colors. Most ink manufacturers also produce intense blacks for black-and-white printing. These generally contain blue toners that help produce a colder, stronger black.

Most of the detail in this image is carried by the black printing unit as illustrated in the black-only image. Process black is neutrally pigmented so as not to alter the subtle color variations created by the three primary printing colors of cyan, magenta, and yellow.

Process black is relatively neutral. Black inks designed for black-and-white printing often contain blue toners that add intensity and "pop," as illustrated by the box on the right.

Subtractive Color

SUBTRACTIVE COLOR REFERS TO COLOR in most of our natural world, and in print production. Whereas RGB colors are projected directly from the monitor, CMYK pigments in printing ink absorb ambient light, reflecting the results back to your eyes. The reflection's accuracy depends on the light sources in the immediate environment. Understanding these light sources is key to understanding good color reproduction and, most importantly, to making good color decisions. We will discuss the full effect of light in greater detail in Chapter 8.

The modern multicolor printing press is a combination of mechanical units designed to print process colors in rapid succession. The four towers of this sheetfed press contain the inking system, plates, and cylinders for each printing unit. (Courtesy Heidelberg USA, Inc.)

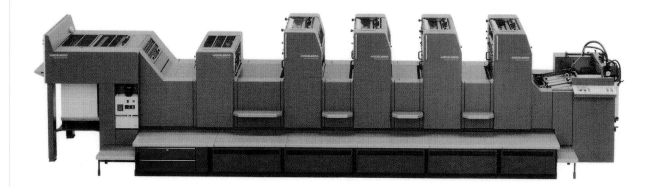

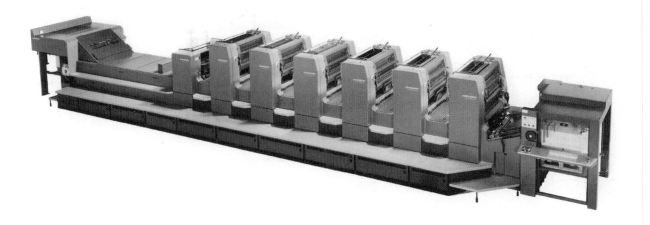

The Color Printing Process One Step at a Time

Today's four-color printing process requires consistent color sequences. This printing press is running with black ink in the first printing unit, cyan in the second, magenta in the third, and yellow in the fourth. The fifth and sixth units can be used for printing spot varnishes or specially mixed additional colors. (Courtesy Heidelberg USA, Inc.).

AS A GRAPHIC DESIGNER, it pays for you to have a basic understanding of how color is printed. With this knowledge, you'll be able to better mix and match colors, make repairs, and avoid potential disasters. A little press knowledge goes a long way toward putting you ahead of the competition.

In four-color print production, cyan, magenta, yellow, and black inks are applied to the paper in microscopically thin layers. With modern multicolor printing presses, these applications of ink occur in rapid succession. Printers establish and maintain strict sequences for printing each of the colors. The color sequence is important for several practical and economic reasons. Modern printing presses can operate at incredible speeds, requiring many related systems to function nearly perfectly in the blink of an eye. Many printers use a standardized printing sequence of black ink in the first printing unit, cyan ink in the second, magenta in the third, and yellow in the fourth. When producing projects with a great deal of black ink coverage, the black ink will often be moved from the first printing unit (*first down black*) to the fourth printing unit (*fourth down black*). We're not talking about football strategies, but the decisions can be equally important to producing the desired results.

Whether sheetfed or web, the offset press is the standard for high-quality and economical four-color printing. Understanding the process in a real-world setting is a key to achieving your desired results. For the following example, we'll focus on commercial sheetfed multicolor offset presses.

The moment the operator pushes the Feed Paper and Print buttons, a sheet of paper begins a swift and complicated journey. When entering the first printing unit, the sheet is pulled between two rotating cylinders. On the surface of one cylinder is a rubberized blanket covered with a thin coat of ink representing a reversed duplicate of the image on the printing plate. This image is delicately pressed onto the paper's surface as it passes through the cylinders under highly calculated and consistent pressures.

In this standard printing sequence, black is the first color printed and has the highest tack, or stickiness, of the four process colors, allowing the subsequent inks to stick to it with optimum dot fidelity.

The second color in sequence is cyan, with a slightly lower tack, printing over the black.

The third color is magenta, with less tack than cyan, printing over both black and cyan.

Yellow has the lowest tack, and is printed over the black, cyan, and magenta. Lower tack allows the ink to print smoothly over the three previous colors. It also causes more dot gain, which is largely unnoticed. The four process colors are now combined, one after the other, in the blink of an eye, to create the final process-color image.

Properties of Printing Ink for the Technically Disinterested

JUST LIKE THE PAINT you use on your bathroom walls, ink combines a pigment with a base *vehicle* that allows the press operator to move the pigment from the ink can to the press ink fountain, inking rollers, plate, rubber blanket, and finally to paper. Once on the paper, the vehicle's job is done and it's time to get rid of it. Ink contains additives that enhance elimination of the vehicle through evaporation and absorption into the paper, along with additives that harden and dry the pigments as they rest on the paper's surface.

Beyond the pigment color, several other differences distinguish the four process-color inks. The first ink to be printed is the stickiest. This stickiness is referred to as *tack* and plays a significant role in the successful, reasonably accurate application of the subsequent colors. It's much like a peanut butter and jelly sandwich. You probably apply the peanut butter first, then the jelly. Peanut butter sticks to the bread, and the jelly sticks to the peanut butter. Try it the other way around, and you wind up with jelly on the bread, and peanut butter all over the place.

We're as consistent with our sandwich assemblies as printers are with their ink sequences. Each ink applied to the paper is successively less sticky. Almost universally, yellow has the lowest tack, and is the last primary color to be printed. Understanding the reason for this also helps explain some of the inherent difficulties of in-line multicolor printing.

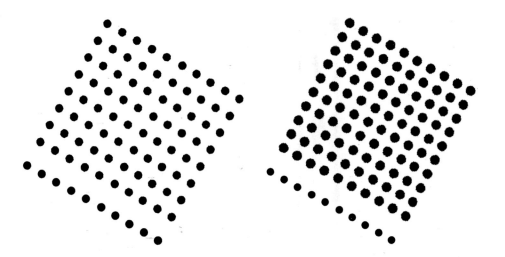

The fibers in uncoated paper absorb and spread ink pigments. On the lower left is an enlargement of hypothetically perfect 20 percent dots. On the right, the same dots are printed on uncoated paper with a significant increase in dot gain.

A Dot's Gain Is Our Loss

SUCCESSIVELY LOWER TACKS IN PRINTING INKS cause successively greater problems in printing dots with optimal detail. The stickier the ink, the better its ability to maintain the dimensions of dots on the printing plates. Lower ink tack increases dot size, as the less-sticky edges of the dots tend to flow outward. This phenomenon is commonly referred to as *dot gain*.

Dot gain is a fact of life for printers, and controlling it is a key challenge. Sophisticated printers even consider it in their proofing processes, building dot gain into their proofs. They manage dot gain by applying industry standards and thoroughly testing their own systems.

Uncoated paper causes much more dot gain than coated paper. This is because its spongy surface fibers absorb ink outward from the dot's edges to a greater degree. You should avoid screen frequencies greater than 133 lines per inch on uncoated papers because the dots tend to run together. In this case, a high screen value doesn't necessarily result in greater detail. On uncoated papers, you can significantly increase detail simply by decreasing screen values, such as from 175 lines per inch to 133 lines per inch.

A composite proof, as shown here, can match what was expected when the job went to press.

Excessive dot gain, as illustrated here, can cause a muddy, oversaturated effect. Too much ink and/or improperly adjusted printing pressures can increase dot gain to an unacceptable level.

Optical Dot Gain

DOT GAIN ALSO HAS AN ILLUSORY aspect, called *optical dot gain*, which causes us to see faint shadow images. This results, in part, from minute shadows being cast onto the surface of the paper from printed dots. Another factor is light passing through the paper's surface and reflecting back from minute amounts of ink that have soaked into the sheet. The eye perceives this as an overall increase in density on the printed sheet.

The Challenge of Yellow

BECAUSE YELLOW IS SUCH A LIGHT color, its effect on color images is based more on saturation and density than on carrying fine detail. Even with a printer's loupe, it's difficult to see a ten percent yellow dot, even though the same dot sizes can be quite visible in any of the other process colors. As a result, the yellow printing unit is the least affected by the dot gain caused by low tack. One challenge in keeping the yellow unit printing reasonably well isn't so much in maintaining detail as it is in keeping the yellow dots from completely filling in. A dot gain of as much as 50 percent is not uncommon with low-tack yellow ink in the fourth printing unit.

Dot gain is a fluctuating phenomenon that varies from
press to press and color to
color. Because yellow is normally printed at the end of the
color sequence, the gain in dot
size is greater than it is with
the other process colors. It's
also the least harmed by
significant dot gain. The
yellow in these images convey
color and saturation without
the necessity of carrying
fine detail.

Ink Density

ANOTHER POWERFUL INFLUENCE on dot gain is the amount of ink applied to each sheet of paper, a factor known as *ink density*. Fortunately, this is a measurable quantity, and it is generally kept within predetermined optimal ranges. We can make most of our fine-tuning color adjustments within this range, and achieve wide variations in the final color. Ink manufacturers mix as much pigment as is reasonably possible into all of their colors and try to formulate strong colored inks without compromising the handling characteristics that are necessary to get the ink onto the paper in the first place.

Pushing the upper limits of ink density can produce brighter, more vibrant color. Increased color density also tends to produce a warmer overall color effect. However, it also increases dot gain and can result in oversaturation and loss of detail. With the right printing project, some images can benefit from increased brightness and warmth and won't being excessively harmed by loss of detail. In this case, little damage is done by pushing the limits. We often encourage clients and press operators to crank it up. This usually sends the latter into a cold sweat, but with proper attention and care, it can produce spectacular results.

The drawbacks of pushing ink density include increased drying time—the bane of print estimators and pressroom managers—and the potential transfer or *setting off* of ink onto the backside of overlying sheets in the delivery pile. Again, with attention to detail, these risks are often well worth the extra effort.

The other end of the density range is running the ink *spare*. This can be practical in projects that have been poorly scanned, or those that require a high level of detail. Lighter ink density tends to make the ink stickier on the printing plates and blankets, enabling greater dot fidelity. Lower ink densities also create cooler color schemes.

The downside is that increased stickiness tends to tear coatings and fibers from the paper's surface. This can cause a speckled look, while contaminating the press's inking system with paper particles that often come back to haunt us in the form of *hickeys*. A hickey is an inked image of a particle surrounded by a white halo. The halo appears because the particle blocks ink transfer to the blanket.

Ink densities of many images
can be pushed to the limits
to brighten or enhance color
when fine detail is not an
issue. The illustration of the
soccer player can be printed
beautifully at levels that
will plug the detail of photographs, as seen in this
image of a skier.

Lowering ink density can reduce dot gain and increase detail. This can be a quick fix to the expensive alternative of pulling the job for color correction. A better approach is to anticipate dot gain on dense images and make corrections at the proofing stage.

Additives on Press

THE PRESS OPERATOR CAN ADDRESS some of these drawbacks by adding a softening agent to the ink fountains, which reduces the tack to more acceptable levels. Another approach is to add some neutral ink base to the ink fountains, which lightens the color while allowing the press operator to run sufficient ink densities to prevent tearing the paper coating. Running ink too lightly almost invariably results in a washed-out appearance. It's generally unwise to run ink too lightly on any printing job, but the practice has a place in the highly subjective color process.

A primary reason for maintaining the same printing sequence is consistency and predictable results. While process printing inks are generally thought to be transparent, the sequence of printing each layer of ink has a noticeable affect on the final appearance of the printed sheet. Printing in a consistent sequence of black, cyan, magenta, and yellow will produce similar results, time after time. If we were to switch the sequence to black, then magenta, cyan, and yellow, the finished result would be visually different, even with identical ink densities. One reason is that our ink tacks are formulated for a consistent sequence. By switching ink sequence, we've also switched our ink tack requirements, and we're back to spreading peanut butter onto jelly.

Subtle changes in ink
densities of cyan, yellow,
and magenta can be made
on press to achieve pleasing
color balances. However,
press operators and pressroom managers will happily
explain the ramifications of
pushing the limits too far.
Here, the printer added yellow to the first image and
magenta to the second. The
third image is printed with
standard overall ink density.
The correct color is subjective.

Color Balance

MANAGING COLOR BALANCES—while remaining within reasonable ink density ranges—is much like driving on a freeway. You can drift a bit to the left or a bit to the right with relative impunity, but start crossing the lines and you can get into trouble. Trust your printer on the locations of the lines. They've probably encountered every problem imaginable by crossing them too far, and a good printer won't let you do it.

The reality of color printing is that successive ink applications on in-line multi-color presses reduce print quality and fidelity. The challenge for today's printer is to keep the losses in dot accuracy to a minimum and experienced printers do a remarkably good job of it.

Paper:
THE MEDIUM AND
THE PRICE YOU PAY

Sheetfed presses are designed to print *cut sheets*—paper manufactured in rolls and then trimmed on guillotine cutting machines to specific parent sizes.

PAPER IS THE BASIC MEDIUM FOR COMMERCIAL PRINTING applications and the variety of stock available is staggering. Paper can be the most expensive element of printing projects. Prepress costs on most projects are generally stable and consistent from job to job, but the length of the press run and choice of paper have the most influence on production costs. Successful printers work hard to establish ongoing relationships with paper vendors, and these relationships can translate into significant savings for the print buyer. All other elements being equal, the printer who can negotiate the best paper prices will also give you the best prices. Because paper is an outsource purchase for the printer, you will always be paying for a markup. This can range from 10 to 30 percent, and is usually a moving target. Most of the time, printers who know they are competing for a particular project will revisit the markup on the paper as a first step in lowering prices. When the very best quality is desired and the customer's budget is not limited, premium-quality paper is always the best choice. For situations where the budget is more sensitive, considering a comparable stock in a lower grade may be the best option. Print reps can be very helpful in offering suggestions, and good printers can work wonders with less expensive papers.

Web paper rolls can be huge, standing 3 to 5 feet high and weighing thousands of pounds. Fork trucks with pole attachments maneuver rolls into position for feeding through the presses.

Paper Availability: The "Here Today, Gone Tomorrow" Trap

PAPER LINES COME AND GO AS QUICKLY as automobile styles, and the paper swatches you got from your vendor a year ago may be unavailable today. Paper manufacturers often unleash a wave of hip new paper finishes and colors, only to have them fall flat in the marketplace. It's common to see graphic designers who have created an entire image package based on a new hypothetical paper line like "Extravaganza Marquis" in the "Bubblewrap" finish and "Twinkletoes" shade. A few phone calls later, and guess what?

It's available, but not in that shade; the stock is available in cut sheets, but no one has envelopes; or the entire line has been discontinued.

Paper manufacturing is a competitive industry, driven by the basic laws of supply and demand. A hot new paper that is well received by the design community can generate tremendous revenue for the manufacturer. New offerings are produced in limited supply on a regular basis, and many new paper lines don't trigger much positive response. Without demand, there's no point in producing a supply that will sit on the warehouse floor.

Web presses feed paper through the press from a continuous roll of stock. Paper is trimmed and folded to size after it is printed.

Taking Stock

If your budget is tight, consider lowering your choice of stock grades before dropping design elements. Beautiful printing is done every day on number two and number three grade stocks. A good design produced by a good printer will look terrific, and few will be the wiser. One of the most memorable images ever printed, an Afghan girl in *National Geographic*, was printed on a number three grade coated sheet.

You should always double check with your print rep before committing to any paper with a special finish, color, or an obscure source. You'll save much time, grief, and last-minute scrambling for substitutions by verifying that the paper you have in mind is sitting on a vendor's shelf—preferably with your name on it.

Another consideration is the longevity of a paper line. Even though a paper line may be available right now, it may not be around at all in six months. This can present a problem if you're working on a project that may take several months to get to press. For projects that are unlikely of a concern. On the other hand, if your client anticipates regular reprints that will require matching stock, your safest bet is to stick with the tried-and-true stocks, of which there are myriad excellent choices from a wide variety of excellent sources.

Standard printing paper weights and finishes can appear to be confusing to the uninitiated, but they can also be simplified into a few categories. These papers are the real workhorses of the printing industry, as they are readily available and generally perform with consistent results.

The Machiavellian Paper Weight Principle

LET'S GET THE BASICS OUT OF THE WAY. Paper is categorized by *basis weight*, a term that takes on relatively bizarre characteristics in application. Basis weight is the weight of five hundred sheets of a given grade of paper, in that particular grade of paper's standard parent size, which varies from grade to grade. There are explanations galore for this system, most of which only serve to justify its existence while avoiding common sense. The best explanation is that it's a tradition. In a fast-paced world where technology becomes obsolete within a few months and information is flooding us from all directions, it can be amusing to ponder that an 8 ½ x 11- inch sheet of 50-pound offset paper feels just like a sheet of 20-pound bond. What follows are the reasons these issues may be important to you.

Bond

BOND PAPER IS RELATIVELY INEX-PENSIVE and is generally used in cut 8 ½ x 11-inch sizes for letters, copying, and business forms. It sees enormous use in the business environment, and is often used for quick printing and simple letterheads. The parent size sheet of bond paper is 17 x 22 inches. Five hundred sheets of 11 x 17-inch 20-pound bond paper weighs 20 pounds. This paper comes in a reasonably smooth finish and a variety of often-garish colors. It is perfectly adequate for the purposes it's designed to fulfill.

Writing Paper

WRITING PAPER IS A HIGH-GRADE BOND PAPER, often made with a percentage of cotton and used for stationery packages designed to convey a luxurious image. It comes in a variety of finishes and colors. Finishes can be smooth, laid, eggshell, or linen. The colors generally range from bright white to a variety of neutral hues. This is the paper for classy image packages, and is generally available with matching envelopes and cover weights for business cards. The parent size of writing paper is the same as bond; 17 x 22 inches. Five hundred sheets of 24-pound writing paper this size 24 pounds. Writing papers are often watermarked, which can be an important element in conveying an upper-crust image. Maintaining the correct orientation of the watermark on finished letterheads is always a major concern for printers.

The spongy surfaces of uncoated textured paper tend to increase dot gain and line size. Whether laid, linen, or felt finished, they require increased printing pressure to impress the ink image into the *valleys* of the finish, which ultimately adds to the gain. Fine line screens with sharp detail are better reproduced on smooth coated stock.

The Parent Size Conundrum

A SIGNIFICANT AND OFTEN DETRIMENTAL ELEMENT of writing papers is the combination of *parent* size and watermark. Although the basic parent size is 11 x 17 inches, these papers are also available in larger sheet sizes, 22 1/2 x 34 inches and sometimes up to 23 x 35 inches. These sizes often create limitations in the image area that can be printed, particularly if the paper is watermarked and the design calls for bleeds. All sheetfed printing presses require a *gripper* allowance for mechanical pincers to hold the sheets. The gripper is generally 3/8 inch and represents a "no print" zone on the leading edge of each sheet. Images that bleed also generally require an oversized press sheet to allow for trimming.

Printers will try to squeeze as much image area as possible onto any given press sheet, but the end result is sometimes a slightly undertrimmed letterhead. The answer is to print letterheads that have bleed designs on a larger parent size, which results in a good deal of wasted paper and higher costs for long runs. When writing papers are available in 23 x 35-inch parent sheets, the sheet can be cut into thirds for the press, and the letterheads can be printed *two-up* on the press sheets. This solution offers tremendous savings in paper costs, and usually maintains the watermark in a *right-reading* orientation.

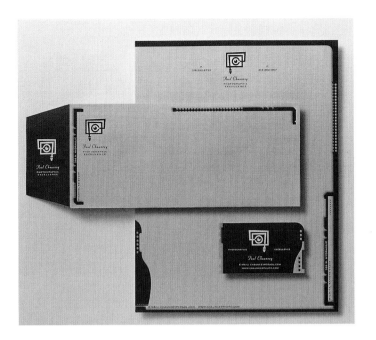

For the best results in envelope printing, print on flat sheets and then have the sheets converted into finished envelopes. This will ensure consistency across the print run.

Many image packages (envelopes, letterhead, and business cards) are designed so that the envelopes print in four colors or with bleeds. This can present one of a printer's most interesting challenges. Depending on the nature of the bleed, many printers can get away with printing premanufactured envelopes on small presses. Envelopes present an inherently unstable printing surface because of the uneven multiple layers and slight variations in their manufacture. This can create a difficult proposition for the press operator, and the results are sometimes less than desirable.

For critical jobs with bleeds, and for virtually all four-color jobs with high expectations, the practical approach is to have your print rep quote the job to print on flat sheets and then have the sheets converted into finished envelopes. Printers experienced with this process will probably include prediecutting the printed sheets on a letterpress before sending them to the envelope converter. This helps ensure accuracy and first-class results. Without the diecutting, most converters will not guarantee a conversion accuracy of less than ⅛ inch. This can be a tricky area for graphic designers striving to quote accurately for clients, and often leads to discord that can travel from the client to the designer, to the printer, to the envelope converter, and then right back up the ladder. It's always best to know your printer's capabilities and to ask for samples and assurances.

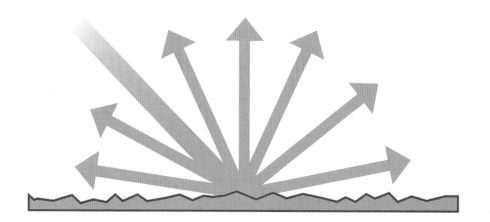

The surface of uncoated papers, as seen in this exploded side view of a single sheet, is rough and uneven. Ambient light in the viewing environment is absorbed and reflected from these surfaces and scattered in many directions, resulting in the dull appearance of ink on these types of paper.

Printing on Writing Paper Surfaces

WRITING PAPER IS GENERALLY VERY WELL MADE under strict quality controls and provides a stable printing surface. For four-color designs, or designs that have a great deal of definition, it's best to choose smooth surfaces. One drawback is that the increased printing pressure required for these papers can cause slight distortions as the press sheets travel through successive printing units. This can lead to misregistration, and the printed images can shift from sheet to sheet as the job is being printed. Linen finishes tend to offer a less spongy surface than laid finishes because the process that produces the cross-hatched linen look also produces a smoother surface.

Laid

Linen

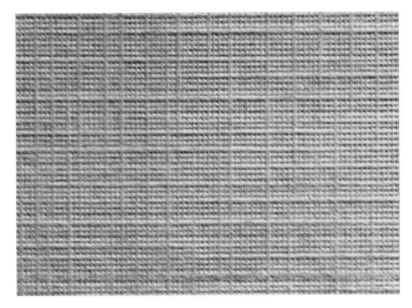

Laid finishes, as illustrated on the top, tend to be spongy, and excaserbate dot gain. The linen finish on the bottom has a pattern that is reminiscent of a weaved linen cloth material. The application of this finish is stamped by hard rollers during the paper making process and produces a hard uncoated printing surface, which will print finer detail in comparison with the laid finish.

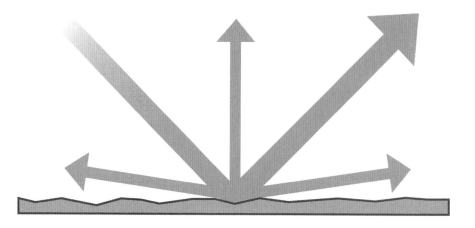

The surfaces of highly calendared uncoated, matte, and dull-coated papers are much smoother than standard uncoated paper and diffuse light in a less exaggerated fashion. The result is more vibrancy in printed images.

Color and Appearance on Writing Paper

WHEN CHOOSING SPECIALLY MIXED colors for writing papers, bear in mind that these papers are uncoated, so you should choose colors using the uncoated pages in the color guidebook. Writing papers are usually available in a variety of relatively neutral colors. The choice of color stock will also affect the ink colors you choose. For critical color matching, it's always a good idea to ask your printer for an ink *drawdown* on a sheet of the job stock. Many ink companies will do this as a service for the printing companies they work with. Some printing companies have the personnel and equipment to provide the service for you directly, though there may be nominal fees for these samples. If you have an established relationship with a printer, you can often receive this service at no charge, particularly if the printer knows that they will be producing the job for you. You'd be surprised at the little extras your print reps will try to provide for you, assuming you offer some reasonable incentive.

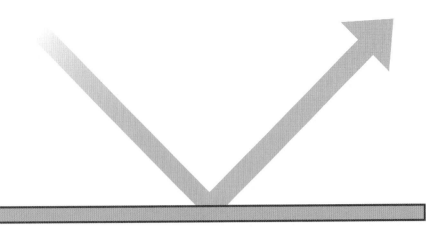

Quality coated papers present a smooth surface with great reflective qualities. The combination of clay coatings that hold ink pigments on the surface, and more direct reflection of the viewing light, results in images that shine.

Text Papers

TEXT PAPERS ARE AVAILABLE in an array of textures and colors. Some are manufactured in finishes and colors identical to those in writing paper lines, and are excellent choices as companion brochures for stationery image packages. The basic parent size of text paper is 25 x 38 inches. Text paper is available in 60, 70, and 80 pound weights, and in cover weights of 65, 80, and 110 pounds. All are appropriate for booklet covers and business cards.

Offset and Book Papers

THESE PAPERS ARE SIMILAR IN APPEARANCE and print characteristics. The basic parent size of book paper is 25 x 38 inches, which is ideal for book production because it provides ample image and trimming area. Surfaces range from vellum to smooth finishes.

These papers are uncoated and subject to dot gain, which makes ultra high-resolution images difficult to reproduce. The maximum line screen effectively used on these uncoated papers is 150, with 133 generally being the most acceptable choice.

The quality and price of offset and book papers covers a tremendous range. The lower end of the spectrum will provide adequate results for spot-color and black-and-white projects. Solids and screens tend to have a mottled appearance, halftones are subject to plugging, and *show through* is common. Papers at the high end of the scale are very opaque with good ink holdout. These are often highly *calendared*, a process through which the paper is passed through a series of calendaring, or polishing, rollers in the finishing stages.

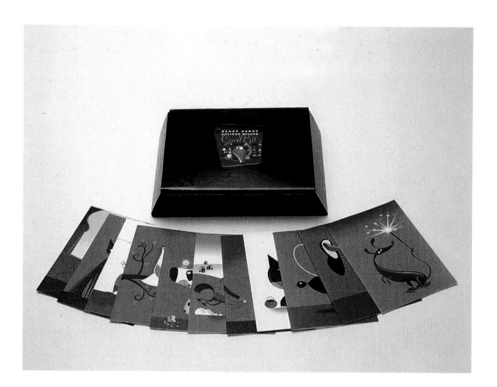

On the high end of the book paper scale, you can achieve absolutely beautiful printing results. These papers, sometimes referred to as *opaque*, have extremely smooth printing surfaces, hold solid images nicely, and handle halftones and screens very well. (Courtesy Paul Baker Printing, CMB Design, and Image Wise Packaging.)

Printing on Uncoated Paper

PRINTING AND HANDLING CHARACTERISTICS of uncoated papers on sheetfed presses are significantly different than those of coated papers. They require more time to dry, because more ink is required in comparison to coated paper, and the inks don't set as quickly due to the spongy nature of the sheet surfaces. As a result, turning uncoated sheets too quickly to print the other side can result in ink *picking off* onto the *impression cylinders* of the press. The printing image is transferred to the paper as the latter passes between the blanket cylinder that carries the image and the *impression cylinders*, which apply tremendous pressure. A build up of excess ink on any of these cylinders will create serious problems and force the pressman to halt the job for maintenance or additional drying time.

Coated Paper

AS A RULE, COATED PAPER IS THE BEST CHOICE for high-quality reproduction of heavy color and fine detail. Coated paper offers a smooth, ink-receptive surface and usually has excellent printing and handling characteristics.

Coated paper quickly absorbs the vehicle of ink, leaving the pigment on the surface. Because of this, coated papers require a much thinner ink application than do uncoated papers to achieve an even stronger density. Ink printed on coated paper can feel dry to the touch within a few minutes, and jobs can often be handled within a few hours of coming off the press. The ink vehicle may still be far from dry, but being absorbed into the fibers of the paper underneath the coating, this fluidity doesn't present a problem as long as the surface is dry enough to handle.

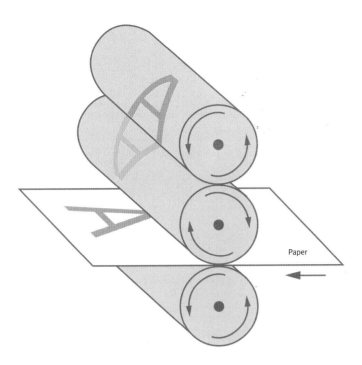

Paper

In this simplified illustration of offset printing, the top cylinder carries the printing plate and the middle blanket cylinder transfers the image to the paper. The impression cylinder is on the bottom. The relationship among these cylinders is critical, and settings are measured in thousandths of an inch. Buildup of ink residue from previously printed jobs, or from the backside of the current job, can create maintenance problems.

Multicolor sheetfed presses have devices that deposit a thin layer of vegetable-based powder across the surface of each sheet as it leaves the final printing unit to be deposited in a stack (usually referred to as the *pile*). The powder helps keep the sheets separated for the few moments required for the ink to begin setting. This powder is absorbed into the ink as it dries, and is seldom—if ever—noticed by the end user. Failure of the powdering device can cause the paper to stick together, which can ruin the job. Rigorous maintenance of these devices is a high priority for every press operator.

If the press applies more ink to the sheet than can be absorbed, the ink transfers to the next available location, which is usually the next sheet deposited in the delivery pile.

The result is called *setting-off*. Set-off can be caused by failure of the powdering device, or overinking, and is a common reason for spoilage and reprints.

Commercial web presses aren't subject to the same problems when using coated papers. On these machines, the job is printed on both sides as the continuous web of paper travels through the printing units, and through a superheated tunnel. This is followed by a series of *chill rollers* that cool the paper, set the ink, and send the web to the folding or cutting attachment at the delivery, or end, of the press.

Grades and Color Appearance on Coated Papers

ACCURATE COLOR REPRODUCTION is best achieved on coated stocks. The clay coating absorbs ink rapidly, leaving the color pigments and hardening agents on the surface with far greater fidelity than is possible with uncoated paper.

Grades of coated papers vary primarily in the amount of clay applied to the surfaces and the degree of polishing, or *buffing*, performed on the surface. Common grades of coated paper are three, two, one, premium, and cast coated. The three grades have the least amount of clay. Premium paper has a much higher clay content, with more buffing, to achieve a very smooth and consistent finish. Costs vary tremendously from lower to higher grades because of the manufacturing time and extra steps taken to achieve premium finishes.

Varnishes and Aqueous Coating— A Cheap Thrill

ADDING VARNISHES CAN ENHANCE and protect printed images. This is often a good idea when printing heavy color coverage on dull and matte coated stocks, as it offers protection from scratching and scuffing. Applying gloss varnish over four-color work printed on dull coated papers can make images pop. Dull varnishes are more subdued, and when used on gloss-coated paper can provide a great deal of contrast against the shiny surface of the paper. Depending on your printer, the cost of adding varnishes can be minimal, and it can pay to do some comparison shopping.

Flood and Spot Varnishing

PRESS OPERATORS CAN APPLY VARNISH to press sheets in two ways. *Flood varnishing* applies a coat of varnish over the entire sheet. Many printers do this allowing a heavy flow of varnish onto the inking rollers, which transfers to a blank plate, then onto the blanket and the paper as it passes through the press.

Spot varnishing requires the use of a plate exposed with the images to be varnished, in exactly the same fashion that ink is applied. As with inked images, the varnish images can be relatively complex to produce.

Printed images on uncoated paper have a much duller appearance than on coated paper because the spongy surface absorbs and scatters reflected light. Some printers have tried in vain to apply varnish to uncoated paper in an effort to achieve a glossy effect. While this is possible on highly calendared smooth finishes, the result is often so mottled that the idea is quickly scrapped. If you need a glossy appearance on uncoated stock, the best solution is a UV coating, which requires specialized equipment and involves an application of thick polymer coating that dries almost instantly under intense UV lamps. There are additional costs for the UV coating process, but this step provides a smooth and highly reflective surface.

Varnishing . . . Who Needs It?

ON SOME PRESSES, VARNISHING may require additional passes and add considerably to the job's cost. Many print shops with five- and six-color presses will bid the cost of four-color work competitively against other four-color presses. In these cases, the addition of a varnishing plate increases the cost of the job only by the plates and varnishes used. Many multithousand dollar printing jobs can be varnished for only a few hundred dollars more than the bid price.

Depending on the nature of your project and the paper stock it's to be printed on, your print rep may strongly encourage the addition of varnish for protecting the paper's finish. Printers sometimes add varnish at no cost to protect the interests of a reluctant client who doesn't think the job would be ruined in the binding and finishing processes. If your print rep insists, get another opinion from another rep. If they both insist, it would be wise to pay heed.

Aqueous Coating

MANY MULTICOLOR PRINTING PRESSES are manufactured with in-line aqueous coating units. These units apply coating in the same fashion as flood varnishing, with a layer of aqueous coating covering the entire sheet. Some manufacturers have developed systems for applying spot aqueous coatings with specially manufactured blankets that transfer coating to the paper in specific areas.

As the name implies, aqueous coating is a water-based material and is manufactured in finishes ranging from dull to high gloss. Drying systems on these presses are incredibly efficient, and these coatings can feel dry to the touch within moments.

The five gray towers on this press are the printing units. The lower gray tower is the aqueous coating unit. (Courtesy Heidelberg USA, Inc.).

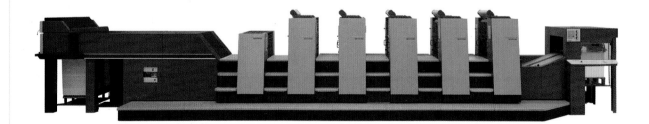

SUMMARY

PAPER CHOICES HAVE A HUGE IMPACT on the overall effect of your designs and can be instrumental in your client's reactions to the projects you design for them. Learning the printing characteristics of paper will enable you and your clients to make choices that will provide reliable results. You can also help your clientele make the most cost effective paper choices by understanding the variables of paper availability. This can help define your options, prevent last-minute disappointments, and goes a long way toward establishing that you have their best interests in mind. Ultimately, this knowledge helps build a foundation for enduring relationships.

7

WORKING WITH YOUR PRINTER

IF YOU'RE A PRINTER, IT'S IMPORTANT to establish a strong working relationship with the graphic design community. If you're a designer, it's equally important to keep this relationship open and harmonious. A mutual alliance can make a world of difference not only to your clients but also to your design career. For most print professionals, there's no such thing as a dumb question, and when it comes to color, there are plenty of questions to be asked. Specialists involved in printing can be terrific sources of information. The more you learn, the more quickly you'll realize that printers are always impressed by designers who know their stuff.

This chapter serves as a designer's introduction to selecting and working with a printer. It describes typical print facilities, the services and technologies available, guidelines for color press checks, and how to avoid nightmare scenarios. Working with color, from design to print, can be intimidating, especially when it comes time to do proofs and press checks. All successful color designers have learned from their printer and have a savvy understanding of the evolution of their color projects.

Choosing Your Printer Wisely

HOW DO YOU SELECT A RELIABLE printer for your color work? Many medium-to-large printers don't feel a need to invest in splashy advertising in the telephone directory because they don't rely on walk-in or call-in business. One of the best ways to find out about printers is to call other experienced graphic designers and ask whom they are using. Don't be afraid to also ask whom they're *not* using. With several telephone calls, you'll probably notice a pattern of printers who get a lot of repeat business and probably a few who don't. Once you've developed a list of potential printers, a few phone calls will probably result in a minor stampede of print sales reps. One benefit of new print technologies is that they are rapidly closing gaps in the quality of work that printers are capable of producing, and competition for your business is increasing at the same pace.

Printing Sales Reps

MOST MEDIUM-SIZE PRINTING companies, and virtually all of the large ones, maintain a staff of full-time *print reps*. The technical knowledge and experience of sales reps ranges from those who have degrees in graphic arts, to those who have spent years in the trade as press operators and prepress technicians to those who were selling shoes last week. Good sales reps have one thing in common: If they don't know the answers to your questions off the tops of their heads, they'll get answers for you—and quickly. Modern print production is complicated and rapidly changing, and while it may be unrealistic to expect someone to have a practical answer to every query, it's not unrealistic to expect a timely response.

Working with Your Print Rep

THE RELATIONSHIP BETWEEN designer and print rep begins with clear communication. At the root of this association is establishing responsibility and rapport. From day one, it's important that you and your print rep scrutinize the project and discuss all aspects regarding color, specifications, and submissions. The time to deal with problems involving color is at the beginning, because a concern that isn't brought up before production begins can lead to major charges in a hurry. Color is an expensive endeavor and changes can be costly.

Questions to ask a potential printer and/or print rep:

1. Do you offer tours of your printing facility?
2. Are you amenable to press checks?
3. Can I have contact with your prepress department?
4. How is your financing handled?
5. What proofing systems do you use?
6. What types of presses do you run?
7. How much, if any, of your work do you contract out?
8. If you do farm out work, do you notify your clients beforehand?
9. Can you provide imposition dummies that fit your formats for multiple-page projects?
10. Have you printed jobs identical to, or similar to, mine?
11. Can you provide samples and proofs of those projects?
12. How do you handle change orders and extra charges?
13. How do you handle paper problems that cause printing deficiencies?
14. What are your policies for reprinting jobs that are unacceptable to me?
15. Do you keep to your deadlines?
16. How do you handle shipping and delivery?
17. Do you charge for delivery?
18. What do you expect from a designer?

What Is A Wetland?

Before undertaking any activity that may impact a wetland, you should have some understanding of basic wetland principles. Wetlands are considered transition zones between open water and uplands. Wetlands types in Montana include sloughs, margins around lakes, ponds and streams, wet meadows, fens, and potholes. Even so, many folks have separate ideas of what constitutes these areas and as a result they have different definitions of wetlands.

Wetland: A Legal Definition

Government agencies have adopted a consistent wetland definition developed jointly by the Army Corps of Engineers (ACOE) and Environmental Protection Agency (EPA), in 'The Wetlands Delineation Manual of 1987':

Wetlands are those areas that are inundated or saturated by surface or groundwater at a frequency and duration sufficient to support, and that under normal circumstances do support, a prevalence of vegetation typically adapted for life in saturated soil conditions. Wetlands generally include swamps, marshes, bogs, and similar areas.

This wetland definition is based on hydrology, hydric soils and hydrophytic vegetation. Only areas that meet all three criteria are considered wetlands subject to federal regulation.

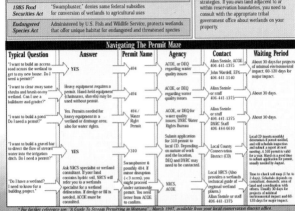

Key Federal Laws Affecting Wetlands

Clean Water Act (CWA) 1972 Preamble is administered by the Environmental Protection Agency, the Army Corps of Engineers, and state agencies.

Section 401 requires that states review and certify permits that may result in pollution discharges into surface waters and wetlands	Section 402 established a permit system required for any discharge of pollutants from a point source into navigable waters	Section 404 jointly administered by the ACOE and EPA, governs dredging and filling of land

National Environmental Policy Act	NEPA requires federal agencies to take action to minimize the destruction, loss or degradation of wetlands and to preserve the natural values of wetlands on federal lands
Executive Order 11990	Requires federal agencies take action to minimize destruction, loss or degradation of wetlands and to preserve natural values of wetlands on federal lands
Rivers and Harbors Act	Gives authority to the ACOE to prohibit discharge of solids or construction into tidal and navigable or adjacent waters
1985 Food Securities Act	"Swampbuster," denies some federal subsidies for conversion of wetlands to agricultural uses
Endangered Species Act	Administered by U.S. Fish and Wildlife Service, protects wetlands that offer unique habitat for endangered and threatened species

State Laws Affecting Wetlands

The Montana Environmental Policy Act and two Montana Administrative Rules regulate activities that may affect wetlands.

Tribal Laws Affecting Wetlands

Tribal governments in Montana safeguard the health, welfare, and economic security of their people. They protect aquatic resources—including wetlands—that are critical for water quality, fisheries and wildlife. The Confederated Salish and Kootenai Tribe and Blackfeet Nation currently have regulations and ordinances in place. Tribes on the other five Montana reservations are also developing wetland programs and strategies. If you own land adjacent to or within reservation boundaries, you need to consult with the appropriate tribal government office about wetlands on your property.

Navigating The Permit Maze

Typical Question	Answer	Permit Name	Agency	Contact	Waiting Period
"I want to build an access road across the wetland to get to my new home. Do I need a permit?"	YES	404	ACOE, or DEQ regarding water quality issues	Allan Steinle, ACOE 406-441-1375 — John Wardell, EPA, 406-441-1140	About 30 days for projects of minimal environmental impact; 60-120 days for major impact.
"I want to clear away some shrubs and brush on my wetland. Can I use a bulldozer and grader?"	Heavy equipment requires a permit. Hand-held equipment (chainsaws, shovels) may be used without permit.	404	ACOE, or DEQ regarding water quality issues	Allan Steinle or staff 406-441-1375	About 30 days.
"I want to build a pond. Do I need a permit?"	Yes. Permits needed for heavy equipment in a wetland or drainage area. Also for water rights.	404 / Water Right Permit	ACOE, or DEQ for water quality issues; DNRC Water Rights Bureau	Allan Steinle 406-441-1375 — DNRC Staff 406-444-6610	About 30 days.
"I want to build a gravel bar to direct the flow of stream water into the irrigation ditch. Do I need a permit?"	YES	310	Submit application for 310 permit to local CD. Depending on nature of work and the location, DEQ and DNRC may need to be contacted.	Local County Conservation District (CD)	Local CD (meets monthly) determines if permit needed, and will schedule inspection and submit a report at next meeting. A 310 permit is valid for a year. March is a good time to submit application for permit, usually needed by August.
"Do I have a wetland? I need to know for a building project."	Ask NRCS specialist or wetland consultant. If your land contains hydric soil, NRCS will refer you to a wetlands specialist for a wetland delineation. If dredge or fill is needed, ACOE must be consulted.	Swampbuster & possibly 404. If minor disruption (<3 acres), you might proceed under nationwide permit. You need letter from ACOE to confirm.	NRCS, ACOE	Local NRCS (Also provides a wetlands technical guide of regional wetland plants.) Allan Steinle or staff 406-441-1375	Time to check soil map (1 hr. to 2 days). Schedule depends on consultant, demands, area of land and coordination with others. Usually 30 days for projects of minimal environmental impact and 60-120 days for major impact.

For further reference see: "A Guide To Stream Permitting in Montana", March 1997, available from your local conservation district office.

Why Are Wetlands Important?

For decades, we were unaware of the critical functions wetlands perform. In this new century, we understand the importance of keeping natural wetland systems healthy. Montana's remaining wetlands are essential to waterfowl, shorebirds, and other wildlife, water quality, and for providing flood control.

What About Artificial Wetlands?

The Natural Resources Conservation Service (NRCS) defines an artificial wetland as land that was not a wetland under natural conditions, but now exhibits wetland characteristics due to human activities. Human-induced wetlands, like those under irrigation, may meet the requirements of wetlands by water, soils, and vegetation.

It is possible that artificial wetlands may not be subject to provisions of the NRCS Swampbuster Program, but be regulated by the ACOE under Section 404 of the Clean Water Act. The ACOE decides, on a case by case basis, if a human-induced wetland is subject to protection.

Wetlands And Water Rights

Although you may desire an artificial wetland, will you have a water right for the water in that wetland? Unless you have a valid water right, your use of water for that wetland may not be protected against others who desire the use of that water. A water right gives you a property right (and a priority date) that is valid in state Water Court. The Montana Department of Natural Resources and Conservation (DNRC) has

jurisdiction over the issuance of new water use permits, as well as changes of existing water rights to new uses. To find out more about water rights, and whether you have, or can obtain, a water right for an artificial wetland, contact your nearest DNRC Regional Office.

For More Information

Or to request additional materials on wetlands and wetland-related programs available in the state, contact the Montana Watercourse at 406-994-6671.

You may reproduce or copy any portion of this brochure by notifying the Montana Watercourse at the above number. Please acknowledge this publication as the source.

printed on recycled paper

Produced By

Montana Watercourse
P.O. Box 170575
Montana State University
Bozeman, MT 59717
406-994-6671

Funding was provided by the Environmental Protection Agency, Wetlands Grant Program of the Montana Dept. of Environmental Quality.

Copyright. All rights reserved. Printed in the United States of America, August 2000.

Design by Elisha Rocke, Bozeman MT

WETLAND LAWS, PERMITS AND REGULATIONS

Navigating The Maze

Often seen as wastelands, an estimated 25% of Montana's wetlands have vanished in the last century and a half. We now realize that wetlands are critical natural resources.

As our appreciation of wetland functions and values has increased, so has society's commitment to protecting them. Our laws express that commitment, and government regulations help us to implement the laws. This brochure describes wetland protection laws and provides a chart to help you find your way through the sometimes-complicated wetland permitting process. By working together, perhaps we can build a legacy of wetland gains to correct our historic losses.

Wetlands Losses (1780 - 1980)

Data from: Dahl, T.E. 1990. Wetlands Losses in the United States: 1780s to 1980s. US Dept. of Interior, Fish & Wildlife Service, Washington D.C.

The key to any successful color project is communication between designer and printer. When discussing a project, such as this two-sided brochure, the designer and print rep should evaluate it carefully to determine that it is an appropriate job for this printing company.

A laska is famous for the rugged beauty of its mountains, rivers, and coastlines, as well as for the distinctive arts and crafts produced by Alaskan Native artisans. If you are considering purchasing a Native-made art or craft item, it's smart to invest a little time learning about the processes and materials Alaskan Natives use to make these unique and beautiful objects.

Identifying Arts and Crafts Made by Alaskan Natives

Any item produced after 1935 that is marketed with terms like *"Indian," "Native American"* or *"Alaska Native"* must have been made by a member of a state or federally-recognized tribe or a certified Indian artisan. That's the law.

A certified Indian artisan is an individual certified by the governing body of the tribe of their descent as a non-member Indian artisan. For example, it would violate the law to advertise products as *"Inupiaq Carvings"* if the products were produced by someone who isn't a member of the Inupiaq tribe or certified by the tribal governing body as a non-member Alaskan Native artisan of the Inupiaq people.

Qualifiers like *"ancestry," "descent"* and *"heritage"* – used in connection with the terms *"Indian,"* or *"Alaskan Native"* or the name of a particular Indian tribe – don't mean that the craftsperson is a member of an Indian tribe or certified by a tribe. For example, *"Native American heritage"* or *"Yupik descent"* would mean that the artisan is of descent, heritage or ancestry of the tribe. These terms may be used only if they are truthful.

Buying Tips

Alaskan Native arts and crafts are sold through many outlets, including tourist stores, gift shops, art galleries, museums, culture centers, and the Internet. Here are some tips to help you shop wisely:

- Get written proof of any claims the seller makes for the authenticity of the art or craft item you're purchasing.

- Ask if your item comes with a certification tag. Not all authentic Alaskan Native arts and crafts items carry a tag. Those that do may display a *Silver Hand* symbol. This label features a silver hand and the words, *"Authentic Native Handicraft from Alaska."* The *Made in Alaska* emblem is another symbol you may find on some Alaskan-made products. This emblem certifies that the article *"was made in Alaska,"* though not necessarily by an Alaskan Native.

- Get a receipt that includes all the vital information about the value of your purchase, including any oral representations. For example, if a salesperson tells you that the basket you're buying is made of baleen and ivory and was handmade by an Inupiaq artisan, insist that the information is on your receipt.

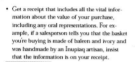

It can be difficult to distinguish arts and crafts produced by Alaskan Natives from items that are imitations: Price, materials and appearance are important clues to provenance.

- **Price** – The price of a genuine Alaskan Native art or craft item should reflect the quality of craftsmanship, the harmony of the design and the background of the artisan. Genuine pieces produced by skilled Alaskan Native artisans can be expensive.

- **Type of materials** – Materials often used by Alaskan Native artisans include walrus ivory, soapstone, argillite, bone, alabaster, animal furs and skin, baleen and other marine mammal materials.

- **Appearance** – Try to pick up and examine a piece before purchasing it. Some items that appear to be soapstone carvings actually may be made of resin. Real stone is cool to the touch; plastic is warm. Stone also tends to be

heavier than plastic. And a figure that is presented as hand-carved probably isn't if you see or can order 10 more like it that are perfectly uniform or lack surface variations.

Alaskan Native Carvings

Sculptures and carvings by Alaskan Natives vary in size, and usually portray animals or Alaskan people. Before you buy a carved figure, learn about the different mediums that are commonly used. It can help you spot a fake.

Walrus Ivory is one of the more popular and expensive mediums used in Alaskan sculptures. In carvings, *new ivory* often has "breathing cracks," or thin black lines that occur naturally and should add to the beauty of the piece. These lines are caused by abrupt changes in temperatures that the walrus experiences when moving from warm rock "haul-outs" to the icy waters of the Arctic region. By law, new walrus ivory may be carved only by an Alaskan Native and it may be sold only after it has been carved. *Old ivory* can be carved by non-Natives. *Fossil Ivory* also may be used, though it is both more rare and more expensive. Because of the differences in the fossilized ivory, no two carvings have the same design or color.

Soapstone is a soft rock with a soapy feel. It's popular with Alaskan Native artists because it's widely available and easy to carve. Soapstone ranges in color from gray to green, and while it scratches easily, it also resists acids, chemicals and heat.

Argillite is a compact rock used primarily by the Haida people of Alaska. It usually has a grayish-brown color and is smooth to the touch.

Bone, usually from whales and other marine animals, is used to create carvings and masks. Bone masks are made from the vertebrae or disk of the Bowhead whale. The color of bone masks ranges from light tan to dark brown. Bone carvings also are used as a way to express the Alaskan Native "way of life." Bone items resemble ivory, but are less expensive.

Alabaster, often a white or translucent stone, also is used as a sculpture medium by Alaskan Natives. Alabaster used in Alaska is imported.

Beyond Carvings

Alaskan Native artisans also produce baskets, dolls, drums, masks, prints, and etchings.

Baleen, also called whalebone, is a flexible material from the jaw of baleen whales. It is used to weave baskets and make etchings. Alaskan Native etchings often portray stories from the artist's unique culture; they're done in a style similar to the scrimshaw technique Boston whalers used in the 1800's.

Alaskan dolls are handcrafted by many Alaskan Native women and reflect unique styles. Dolls often portray the activities of the artist's people. Typically, a doll's clothes and body are made from calf skin (calf skin has taken the place of caribou/reindeer hide materials and is not native to the area), mink, badger, sea otter, arctic rabbit, seal, or beaver. In many dolls, dried marine mammal intestine (which sometimes is bleached naturally in cold temperatures and sun so that it is very white, or has a slight yellowed wax paper look to it) is used for clothing. The hair often is made from musk oxen, and some artists use baleen or ivory for the eyes.

Alaskan Native prints are produced using a variety of techniques. *Serigraphy,* also called *screen printing* or *silk screening,* involves printing through a surface, similar to a stencil technique. *Relief print making* is done from a raised surface, like a cut stone or wood block; *intaglio print making* is created using the recessed image from the surface of etchings or engravings on metal plates of copper and tin. *Lithography* involves the artist using a grease-water technique to apply a variety of colors to the etched design on stone or metal plates.

For More Information

To learn more about Alaskan Native arts and crafts, contact:

Alaska State Council on the Arts
411 West 4ᵗʰ Avenue, Suite 1E
Anchorage, AK 99501-2343
907-269-6610; fax: 907-269-6601
Toll-free: 1-888-278-7424
www.aksca.org

Where to Complain

The FTC works for the consumer to prevent fraudulent, deceptive and unfair business practices in the marketplace and to provide information to help consumers spot, stop and avoid them. To file a complaint or to get free information on consumer issues, call toll-free, 1-877-FTC-HELP (1-877-382-4357), or use the complaint form at **www.ftc.gov.** The FTC enters Internet, telemarketing, identity theft and other fraud-related complaints into Consumer Sentinel, a secure, online database available to hundreds of civil and criminal law enforcement agencies in the U.S. and abroad.

The **Indian Arts and Crafts Board** refers valid complaints about violations of the Indian Arts and

Crafts Act of 1990 to the FBI for investigation and to the Department of Justice for legal action. To file a complaint under the Act, or to get free information about the Act, contact the Indian Arts and Crafts Board, U.S. Department of the Interior, 1849 C Street, N.W., MS 4004-M1B, Washington, D.C. 20240; 202-208-3773; www.iacb.doi.gov.

Complaints to the IACB must be in writing and include the following information:

- The name, address and telephone number of the seller.
- A description of the art or craft item.
- How the item was offered for sale.
- What representations were made about the item, including any claims that the item was made by a member of a particular tribe or statements about its authenticity.
- Any other documentation, such as advertisements, catalogs, business cards, photos, or brochures. Include copies (NOT originals) of documents that support your position.

The **Alaska Attorney General's Office** investigates unfair and deceptive marketing and sales practices in Alaska. To obtain a complaint form, contact the Office of the Attorney General, Consumer Protection Unit, 1031 West 4th Avenue, Suite 200. Anchorage, AK 99501; 907-269-5100; or use the complaint form at www.law.state.ak.us/consumer/index.html.

The Alaska State Council on the Arts, the Federal Trade Commission, the U.S. Department of Interior's Indian Arts and Crafts Board, and the Alaska Attorney General's Office have prepared this brochure to help enhance your appreciation for Alaskan Native arts and crafts.

Alaskan Native Art

March 2002

Your print rep should be able to provide you with samples of work that are comparable to the projects you produce. If you're producing a brochure, you'll want representative samples like these. Bear in mind that print reps will probably only show you samples of their best work.

There to Help You

Print reps are there to help you—not avoid you. If you find that your rep is unresponsive, or doesn't answer your questions to your satisfaction, you should never be afraid to ask for a new one.

As with most professions, communication between buyers and vendors translates to time and money. The printing and design business is no different, especially considering the symbiotic relationship shared between the two fields. The best approach is an open and honest one, where all parties involved—client, designer, and print rep—are free to voice questions, concerns, financial arrangements, and everything in between. The printing process is both complex and specific, and the communication should cover all aspects of a project before, during, and after its completion. Addressing all issues up front—from design to financing, printing, and delivery—is vital, as it can help alleviate potential disasters down the line.

Samples

IF YOU'RE WORKING WITH a new printer, it's important and appropriate to ask for samples and proofs of those samples that are similar to the work that you're doing. Most print reps carry a collection of work that they've done, but those samples may not be appropriate to the nature of your project. Print reps are accustomed to clients requesting samples and there's no shame in asking. If they're resistant, you'd better look for a new printer.

It's not unreasonable to ask for a few samples along with the proofs that were used to print them. While the printer will certainly want proofs returned to their files, you should be able to inspect them, either in your office or during a tour of the plant.

GARGOYLE
monthly

$5.95

...ding Gargoyle Fanatic

Industry Standards

Always insist that any change orders be faxed directly to you and that you sign off on them before the printer takes any action. This may not prevent holdups should problems arise, but demonstrating that you understand the concept will serve notice that you're not easily duped. Good printers can rightfully expect you to pay for lost time and material, but they don't try to make a profit from your mistakes.

THE PRINTING INDUSTRY HAS traditionally been entrepreneurial, competitive, and resistant to standardization. The term *industry standards* gets tossed around and misused in numerous ways. You may hear that industry standards allow for 10 to 15 percent additional charges for overruns, that 10 percent shortages are acceptable, or that color variations of impossibly vague degrees are normal. Most printing companies are independently owned, and many regard the concept of industry standardization largely as a means to a competitive edge, rather than making any genuine effort to standardize. In the real world, you and your printer are the ones who set acceptable standards.

Accountability and Responsibility

IT'S NO SECRET THAT PRINTERS, because they're last in line to produce a project, occasionally get blamed when problems occur. The nature of the problem is the key to determining who is ultimately responsible. Although printing errors do happen, it's not always the printer's fault. Errors can slip past the proofing stage, specially ordered paper may get sidetracked in transit, outsource vendors may botch up their end of the job, or the low-rate ground delivery service may lose the shipment. Making assumptions about responsibility can be a mistake if problems arise, and the best way to avoid finger-pointing is to communicate all of your concerns.

Change Orders

IT'S NEVER TOO SOON to discuss *change orders* and their ramifications with your print rep. Some printers will intentionally lowball a printing bid with the expectation of making money on change orders, charging the client for every extra step they take in the production process. Be specific about your concerns, and get specific answers. For example, a client may think the printer is responsible for delivery to multiple local destinations, but this usually isn't the case. And if there's a relatively simple error in one color on a single image, some printers will insist on charging hefty fees for reproofing the entire job. You can ask for a simple spot proof of the correction, but make sure the printer's policy allows for it.

Change Order

Client:					Job No:			
Project:								

Date:	AA/HE:	By(Init.)	Description	Amount of Time Spent:	Date:	By(Init.)	Price:

Faxed to Client:	Date:	Time:	Original Price:
Faxed By:			Total Additional Charges Itemized:
CLIENT SIGNATURE:			TOTAL AS OF THIS C.O. FORM:
(Please Sign and Fax back as soon as possible)			

Prepress and Proofing Sources and Standards

MOST PRINTERS TRY HARD to project the image that they produce superior work, and this is often evident in their presentation of proofs and the types of proofing systems they use. Printers are generally committed to one brand or type of proofing system, particularly with the onset of direct-to-plate technology. The capital outlay for proofing systems is significant when coupled with the hardware required for outputting plates with the same systems. The benefit to the print buyer is that printers generally make every effort to establish that the systems they use produce good color results.

Service Bureaus and Color Houses

A NUMBER OF SMALL TO MEDIUM-sized printing companies still rely on *service bureaus* to handle their scanning and prepress production. These prepress houses serve a wide variety of clients with the variable of not knowing the final application or limitations of the printing equipment. Most prepress houses use working parameters and ranges for acceptable results in the finished product. This is one reason why it's important to ask for samples of printed material *and* proofs of samples. Because of press variables outside the service bureau's control, it's possible to generate a proof that can't reasonably be reproduced by the equipment on which the job will be printed. As the designer, you deserve to know the source of your proofs, with assurances that they can be reasonably duplicated on press.

Service Bureaus and the Future

MOST PRINTING COMPANIES strive to develop consistent protocols resulting in final proofs that can be reasonably matched on the shop's printing equipment. This is a key element of customer confidence and business survival for multicolor printers. It's also one of many reasons that traditional prepress houses are falling on hard times.

In years past, prepress houses provided a valuable service to designers and printing companies. Scanning devices were frightfully expensive and required full-time production to justify the cost, which was well beyond the scope of most medium-sized printers. With well over half of all commercial printing companies considered medium sized, this presented a huge market. Economically, it made sense to send electronic files out to specialists for preparation and proofing, while focusing capital investments on printing presses and bindery equipment—a daunting fiscal challenge in itself.

These figures illustrate an example of an excellent proof outsourced by a printer to a service bureau and then reproduced poorly on the printer's ailing press. This is an unfortunate case where the proofing source exceeded the printer's capacity.

Prepress houses and service bureaus with a solid clientele are still investing in high-end drum scanning equipment and sophisticated color-management systems. Here, a technician prepares transparencies for scanning. (Courtesy Heidelberg USA, Inc.

A scanner operator makes adjustments using an integrated color-management system. (Courtesy Heidelberg USA, Inc.)

Direct-to-plate technology has also had a huge impact on prepress houses. Virtually all printers who have invested in direct-to-plate systems have also invested in direct proofing systems that accurately reflect the reproduction capabilities of their presses.

Increasingly computer-savvy designers have also taken a bite out of the specialized prepress market. Good software and color-management systems are available, and designers who once outsourced medium-quality scanning to prepress houses can now do so themselves using desktop hardware.

Prepress houses are still operating successfully, and provide valuable services to designers and printers. For designers, a relationship with prepress services can enhance design quality, and allow the designer to finalize color files before choosing printers. This can be particularly advantageous for projects that may go to press some distance from the design agency. For the smaller printers that haven't established in-house output systems, prepress providers are the critical link to working with electronic files.

Service bureaus and prepress houses lie in the path of technology that is forcing reevaluations and new directions. Some have successfully made a transition to direct-to-press color printing, while maintaining more traditional magazine and quality-conscious advertising agency clientele.

Color Scanning:
DO IT YOURSELF OR SEND IT OUT?

THE CAPABILITIES OF TABLETOP and low-profile flatbed scanners have increased dramatically in the past few years, but for the highest-quality four-color scanning, high-end drum scanners still reign thanks to their definition, resolution, and color fidelity. This is due in part to the almost infinite color adjustments permitted by high-end color management systems. For medium-quality color work, you can get good results on many relatively inexpensive tabletop scanners. But high-quality work requires the sophisticated equipment that printers and service bureaus have invested in. By experimenting with in-house scanning equipment and sending the files out for gang proofing, good designers will quickly recognize their in-house limitations, and send out for scans on the appropriate jobs.

Sophisticated tabletop scanners, such as the model shown here, are now within the budgets of many designers. Instead of relying on your imaging service, you can use these products perform much of your scanning in-house. However, if quality expectations are high, you'll still get the best results by farming the work to a service bureau equipped with costly drum scanners. (Courtesy Heidelberg USA, Inc.)

Facility Tours

A few printers have one basic rule of quality control: Give me twenty-five good samples for the client, and ship the rest to the mailing house. Bad print jobs are sent out every day, and it behooves you to ensure that yours won't be one of them.

AS A DESIGNER, you should not hesitate to ask your print rep about touring the printing facility. Good printers are usually proud of the shops they keep, and any reluctance to permit visits should raise a big red flag. Some printing conglomerates hire sales reps to work specific geographic areas and send print jobs through hubs to any of several facilities. If your projects don't require press checking and close oversight, these resources may have financial benefits. The major risk is that your only proof of a successfully completed project is the handful of samples your print rep gives you—and you can bet that they were handpicked.

You can learn quite a bit about a printer's capabilities and attention to detail by the condition of the shop. Your print rep may be decked out in a three-piece Armani suit, but warning bells should be sounding if he takes you on a tour of a messy plant. This is also a good opportunity to meet with the sales manager. Establishing a relationship with the manager puts you in a much stronger position should communication problems arise with your rep.

Busy print shops work with thousands of pieces of paper every day, and sooner or later an unruly sheet hits the floor. Whether it stays there or not is the responsibility of the crew and the shop management. Clean walkways, good lighting, and a friendly crew are signs of a well-run operation that will probably have a designer's best interests in mind. (Courtesy Heidelberg USA, Inc.)

On your tour of the plant, note the press carts stacked with freshly printed sheets. Are they neat and orderly as illustrated here? Attention to these details will be reflected in the attention paid to your project. (Courtesy Heidelberg USA, Inc.)

A Well-Adjusted Press

FOR ANY PRINTING PRESS to achieve its maximum color gamut, it must be well maintained, properly adjusted, and operated with the discerning eye of an experienced press operator. Many of the printing industry's technological advances are focused on streamlining the front end. Printing presses themselves have undergone massive changes and improvements, but their essential function is little changed from what they were designed to do years ago: Apply a few micrometers of ink to a whisker-thin piece of paper with as little harm as possible to the original image.

Printing presses represent some of the most enduring machinery that's still used, and equipment manufactured in the 1960s is bought, sold, and operated every day. One of our favorite printers recently upgraded his shop with two acquisitions: A new film-output system, and a two-color 40-inch press manufactured in 1964. Good press reproduction often defies dating, and we've seen several jobs printed on this thirty-nine-year-old machine that easily compare with work done on the most modern equipment.

The essential ingredient in this process is the operator and/or pressroom manager who understands the subtleties of any given press. These nuances often appear in the visual and mechanical information the operator receives with each press sheet pulled and inspected from the delivery pile. Experienced operators know how to read ink densities, interpret color bars, and spot telltale signs of impending trouble, and they can ward off problems before they occur. Many press operators even *listen* for signals, and can tell that all is well by the sound of a smoothly running press.

Digital Imaging

DIGITAL THERMAL- AND LASER-IMAGING equipment has advanced tremendously in speed, quality, and value. Digital imagers can produce bound booklets—with photo-quality, 600-dpi, four-color images; tab inserts; and variable data for personalizing and mailing addresses—directly from electronic files. This technology is feeding the print-on-demand market with exceptional imagery and resolution.

On-demand printing systems, such as Heidelberg's black-and-white Digimaster, can streamline the production process by generating bound booklets directly from electronic files. Going direct to press with these systems lets you produce exactly the number of copies needed, and you can easily make copy changes on subsequent runs. (Courtesy Heidelberg USA, Inc.)

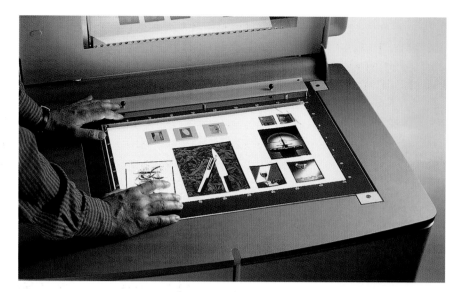

Heidelberg's Nexpress is a more advanced color digital-imaging system that produces bound booklets, with tab inserts, and 600-dpi photo-quality images directly from electronic files. (Courtesy Heidelberg USA, Inc.)

Graphic Designer's Print and Color Handbook

Computer-to-Press Printing

THE CONCEPTS OF computer-to-press (CTP) printing are changing rapidly as technologically advanced equipment comes to market. Virtually all printing done today is digital in some form. Most design work is produced with computer software, jobs can be processed for laser printing, film output, and direct-to-plate or computer-to-press output. With this in mind, it's extremely important for designers to understand the CTP process.

Direct-imaging technology for printing presses is based on the same processes used to image film. From relatively humble beginnings in the late 1980s, to the first commercially available direct-imaging press introduced by Heidelberg in 1991, this technology is filling a huge demand for short-run, good-quality multicolor printing.

Designed for press runs as low as five hundred, this technology allows you to cost-effectively produce four-color work in lower quantities than you can with conventional prepress and printing processes.

In a way, we've come full circle: These presses represent an early form of direct-to-press technology. The presses were prepared with hand-set type and wood blocks, and inked up for a press proof. With the proof okayed, the press was ready to run. In two weeks, this machine could produce the volume of work that would take modern direct-imaging equipment about fifteen minutes. (Courtesy Heidelberg USA, Inc.)

Proofing mechanisms for CTP presses, while not accurate for critical color matching, lets you proof content before initializing the imaging systems. Once the proofs are approved, you can burn images from the electronic file directly to the plate cylinders on press, and print the first sheets for inspection in less than ten minutes. The technology permits these fast setup times in part because images are burned into the plates in nearly perfect registration. Such variables as developing and hanging plates on the press as a separate step have been eliminated.

CTP presses operate in a similar fashion to conventional presses, with a series of printing units applying ink in conventional CMYK sequences. These presses use inks that are comparable in pigment composition to standard offset printing inks, and printed sheets appear similar.

The print quality of these systems can range from medium, at 1,250 dpi, to very good, at 2,400 dpi with 150-line screens, and approaches the quality levels possible on conventional offset presses. Press sizes range from models that can handle 13 x 18 inch sheets, up to a full-size 40-inch press.

As with conventional offset presses, CTP presses have printing units for each of the four process colors. The Heidelberg press illustrated has a compact design, with all four color-printing units configured in a semicircle around a single common impression cylinder. One of the real innovations in this technology is the plate-imaging system, consisting of a spool of silicon-coated printing surfaces that can produce about three dozen separate plates on each unit. These plates are automatically fed and clamped around the printing cylinder, and the printing image is burned onto each through a laser array in a process similar that used by laser recorders that produce film for printing. The silicon layer repels ink and the burned images accept ink, making the process waterless. With the images burned, the press is ready for inking and printing the first set of makeready sheets. Final adjustments are made via computer, and the job is ready to run.

This cutaway side view shows how the four process-color printing units surround a single common-impression cylinder. One benefit of this design is that misregistration is nearly eliminated. (Courtesy Heidelberg USA, Inc.)

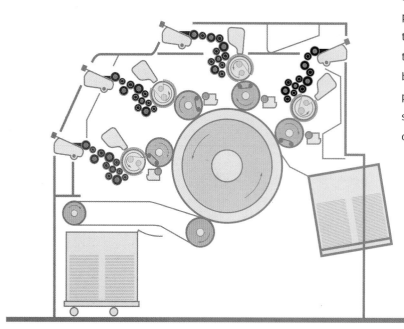

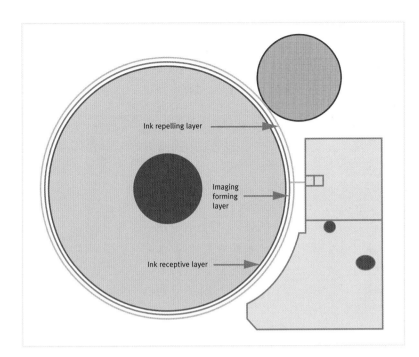

Ink repelling layer

Imaging forming layer

Ink receptive layer

In a computer-to-press system, plates on spools are automatically fed and clamped around a printing cylinder. The image to be printed is burned to the plate directly from digital files. (Courtesy Heidelberg USA, Inc.)

Laser-imaging arrays in a CTP system, as shown in this diagram, are similar to those used in laser recorders that produce film. (Courtesy Heidelberg USA, Inc.)

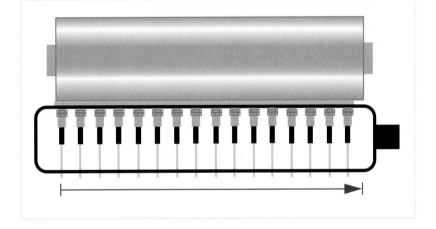

In a CTP system, ink is repelled by the plate's silicon layer, but adheres to the area of the plate burned by the laser. (Courtesy Heidelberg USA, Inc.)

From one end to the other, computer-to-press systems offer the same features as their big brothers in amazingly compact units. These presses can print affordable, high-quality four-color work, and have opened opportunities for designers in the growing marketplace for short-run, on-demand printing. (Courtesy Heidelberg USA, Inc.)

A CTP system uses CMYK inks similar in pigment composition to standard offset printing inks. Magenta and cyan inking units are shown here. (Courtesy Heidelberg USA, Inc.)

Print on Demand and a Portent of Things to Come

BEFORE THE ADVENT of direct-imaging presses, the costs for printing good-quality four-color work in short runs of five hundred copies or so was often prohibitive. Whether the press run was five hundred or five hundred thousand, the cost of preparing files was exactly the same. For short runs, the cost of file preparation could actually exceed the cost of printing. When producing low-volume projects, print buyers often simplified their designs to one or two colors that could be printed at reasonable costs on small offset duplicators, thus avoiding the additional expenses of preparing four-color files, proofs, and plates.

With computer-to-press imaging, files can be prepared for a short press run to fill a current need, and saved for low-cost reprints if the customer requires additional copies in the future. With conventional processes, uncertainty about the number of copies needed often leads to print overruns. Because the cost of file preparation and press setup has already been incurred, the only costs for overruns are paper, press time, and storage. For projects with guaranteed overrun requirements, this approach makes economic sense. Without guarantees, it can be a costly gamble.

Print on demand, while still in relative infancy, is a growing market, and press manufacturers and printers will likely be moving more in this direction.

Submitting Color Projects to Your Printer

CLEAR JOB SPECIFICATIONS ARE essential when communicating your expectations to the printer. Some printers prefer that you use their own specification sheets, while others are happy to use yours. Establishing your own checklist is the safest way to ensure that your bases are covered. Your specific needs may vary slightly, but this list describes the minimum specifications you should provide. Once you have mastered this submission process, it will be invaluable to your time and reputation.

Designers, printers, and others involved in the project should always discuss any issues that might arise, such as job specifications and change orders. Where appropriate, designers should issue copies to all concerned parties in writing so that everyone is clear on how the project will be handled from start to finish.

When submitting a project to the printer, here is the information and material that you should provide:

- Contact (name and telephone number)
- Proofing contact (name and telephone number)
- Change order contact (name and telephone number)
- Job description
- Quantity
- Minimum quantity acceptable (no shortages)
- Overruns acceptable (billable)
- Paper
- Ink colors (CMYK, Pantone colors, special mixes, metallics)
- Ink drawdowns required (for critical specially mixed colors that must match sample swatches accurately)
- Varnishes (gloss, matte, dull)
- Letterpress (scoring, foiling, die-cutting)

- Trim size (finished size, flat size)
- Binding (folding, saddle stitching, perfect binding)
- Page count
- Bleeds
- Built-in blank pages
- CDs or disks containing clearly marked files
- Printout of the window or file directory showing disk contents
- Clear separated laser printouts of each page (one composite and one laser for each color CMYK plus additional colors)
- A copy of the print estimate to ensure that the printer is working with the correct cost data. Print estimates are often recalculated, so this keeps the designer and printer on the same page.

The Electronic Prepress Department

A DESIGNER'S BEST ALLIES IN PRODUCING high-quality work are usually chained to a computer in the heart of the print facility, nose-to-nose with their monitors. These folks comprise the electronic prepress department and they are your key contacts. Print reps are usually happy to direct you to the prepress department so you can question these specialists in-depth about specifications ranging from PDF settings, to hard-copy submissions, to registration and crop marks—just about any concern or question you might have. They will always help you, because in doing so, it makes their job easier. If you submit a clean job, they don't have to chase down missing fonts, corrupt images, or improperly saved files, and they won't have to redo anything because of incorrect specifications. They are the link between you and a clean, trouble-free printing experience, so take the time to get to know them.

Press Checks

IT'S IMPORTANT TO FIND OUT IF THE printer is amenable to certain procedures, such as press checks. Good printers will encourage press checks because they appreciate the benefits of permitting a client to make final approvals before the press run begins. However, some printers are hesitant to allow press checks, either because they feel that the client may create confusion on press, or because they are mindful of lost production time while clients make last-minute decisions. While production time is a reasonable concern for the printer, you are better off taking your business to those who appreciate your needs—and your final approval—on press.

Before the Press Check

- Discuss press check expectations and limitations carefully with your print rep.

- Be sure that you have allotted ample warning and travel time for scheduled press checks.

- Before you arrive, ensure that your printer has all the elements needed for your press check, such as swatches of specific colors, or samples of previously printed jobs to match.

- In addition to allowing for travel, be sure to schedule ample time for the press check itself. Many factors can play havoc with a printer's schedule: The job just before yours could go haywire and cause unexpected downtime; plates for your project could be faulty and require reimaging; or the power could go out. You name it, it's happened.

- If time is really tight, ask that your project be the first one run in the morning, or that it goes to press at night when you aren't occupied by other matters.

The most important thing every designer needs to bring to a press check is a Sharpie, or a similar felt-tipped pen. These are ideal for marking up press sheets, particularly on coated paper, because of their high visibility. Use a ball-point pen and you might find yourself spending extra time hunting for all your notations.

It is highly recommended that all designers working with color invest in a good-quality loupe so they can review registration on proofs and press sheets during a press check. The magnifier can be adjusted to an individual's visual preferences.

Fourth Annual

ROSE FESTIVAL

2002 Catalog

In the first color press proof, you can see that the targets are in registration, but the reversed type in the image is off. In the second press proof, the image has been adjusted to register and the targets become unimportant.

Fourth Annual

ROSE FESTIVAL

2002 Catalog

Going to a Press Check

IF YOU ARE CONFIDENT that all bases have been covered, seeing your work in progress and being produced correctly will be a relief, and almost a formality. Good designers will come armed with either a written or mental list of elements to check on the proof.

A press check can be a terrifying experience for junior-level designers, who sometimes avoid signing off on press sheets for fear they will miss something that invokes wrath and shame when they return to the office. A press check is no place for a neophyte whose job may depend on making logical printing decisions. If you're working with a novice, do some handholding until they've gone to a few press checks with experienced designers. If *you* don't have much experience with press checks, tell your print rep. You can't fake it, and the first time you hold a solid-based magnifier, or *loupe*, upside down to inspect dots, every eye in the pressroom will roll. A good print rep or pressroom manager will guide you through the process, saving time for you and them. When creating a checklist, be sure to include the following:

1. Take out your Sharpie, and prepare to make notes—right on the press sheet.

2. Feel the paper first. Does it seem like the right weight? Then ask if the paper is what you specified. If you're the slightest bit concerned, or if the paper doesn't feel right, ask for the stock label. All paper comes labeled, whether it's in cartons or stacked on skids. Printers occasionally make human errors and load the wrong job stock for a press run. Make sure you're comfortable with the paper before proceeding.

3. Inspect the press sheet for overall appearance and color evenness. Look for hickeys, pinholes, and other blemishes.

4. Check for registration before looking through a loupe. Misregistration is usually noticeable first to the naked eye as off-color halos or rows of dots, particularly next to what should be crisp lines in images. Double-check questionable registration using the loupe.

5. Inspect the register *targets* on the press sheet for registration. Targets are just that—markings that let the press operator make registration adjustments before inspecting the images themselves for registration. Bear in mind that targets are often burned separately from other images, and due to minute variations in positioning the film against the plates, targets may be slightly off-register even though the images are dead on. By the same token, the targets can be registered perfectly, and the images may be off. Targets are a visual reference only.

6. Check for matches of specially mixed colors against your sample swatches or color guide.

7. Scan the press sheet for content, missing images, anything that doesn't look right.

8. Next, compare the proofs for each individual page to the corresponding press sheets for color breaks and color accuracy, and to ensure that any changes you requested in the proofing stage have been made.

9. When you're done, ask the press operator if they've had a press sheet *ruled up*. Here, the operator uses a T-square on a light table to draw lines connecting the trim marks, ensuring that the trims don't cut off critical elements. If this hasn't been done, you're within your rights to ask for it.

10. Pick a convenient corner of the press sheet you just marked up and label it "1."

11. Discuss any needed adjustments with the press operator or pressroom manager. Unless you see something that is clearly out of whack, such as a missing image, go over your adjustments all at once. You'll drive the press operator crazy if you ask for a dozen changes to be made one at a time, each requiring a separate press startup.

12. From this point on, you'll be whittling down your concerns to acceptable levels through a successive series of adjustments. Good print quality is extremely subjective, and you may ask the press operator to make a half-dozen series of corrections before you're satisfied that what you see on the sheet is as good as it will get.

13. When you are satisfied that the job is satisfactory, and that your client will accept it, sign and date the sheet and ask for two or three press sheets from the same pull.

Press sheets on the press
table and ready for inspection.
Here's where your Sharpie
comes in handy for making
notations directly onto
the sheet.

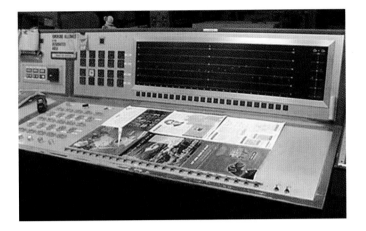

Pressrooms can be filled with
activity, noise, and fast-moving
machinery, which can add to
the anxiety of a press check for
the novice. Experienced help is
the best cure.

At press checks, you should
view press sheets with
corrected lighting, either on
a press table or in a viewing
booth, such as the one
shown here.

Here, the press operator adjusts color and registration with electronic push pads connected to the press.

A loupe provides a clear and accurate view of registration. It can be a worthwhile investment for designers who frequently attend press checks.

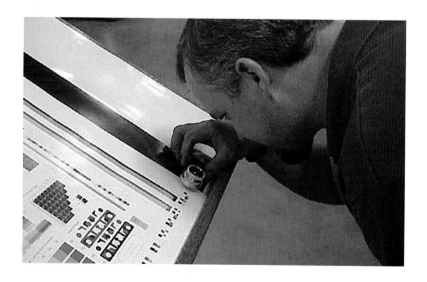

Knowing When to Say When

EXPERIENCE CAN'T BE TAUGHT. If you've established a reasonable rapport with your print rep, have faith in your choice of printers, and believe they are doing everything they can to make your job look as good as possible, you should be comfortable following their lead and accepting their advice during press checks. At times, you'll be asked to sign off on a press sheet with assurances that your adjustments will be made before the press run begins.

Presses are more sensitive to operating conditions than many people realize. Most require a few minutes running time to stabilize ink/water balances, to achieve optimum operating temperatures, and for ink tack to stabilize through the roller systems. A press operator's nightmare is a job that must be started and stopped repeatedly, but this is the condition under which press checks are conducted. The operator may tell you that they have to get the press running to stabilize the process, or need to perform some time-consuming maintenance procedure before the job can begin. If you've chosen your printer with care, and trust your own judgment, take them at their word and let them do their job.

If you've given your work to a printer who low-balled the bid, they may want to get you out the door as quickly as possible so they can run the press and make up for some of the low bid price. As a ploy to get you to sign off, they may also tell you that they've got to get the press running, but first need to perform maintenance procedures. If you don't quite believe them, sign off on the press sheet with a note about conditions that they've promised to correct, and ask for extra samples.

Avoiding Nightmare Scenarios

AT ONE TIME OR ANOTHER, every graphic designer will have—or hear about—a color printing nightmare. To keep these to a minimum, good designers carefully select their printer, clearly communicate their needs and concerns, and pay attention to detail. Many printing jobs cost as much as new car, but some designers spend more time on the auto lot than they do shopping for a good printer.

One way to avoid color conflict is to run sample proofs of your images. In this example, a designer thought this photo was the correct shade of burgundy. After seeing the printer's press proof, they realized that what appeared to be burgundy on the computer screen was extremely pink in print. The image and press proof had to be redone.

Dust and scratches in the sky didn't raise red flags at the proofing stage, and were exaggerated even more on press. It was a costly error: Because the image was critical to the client's brochure, the job was pulled from press and the photo retouched.

Color variations on a press run can result in varying samples as shown by these images. It's usually a judgment call, but in this case, the image was not critical enough to warrant a reprint.

Eight Steps toward Trouble-free Printing

Value is seldom reflected in the lowest bid, and an extremely low bid on a complicated project should trigger a warning. Investigate low bids thoroughly before committing your project. Hidden costs in the form of change orders can bite you, or your high-end annual report could be farmed out to a low-quality printer in Timbuktu. Make certain that your print reps are quoting on the same specifications. Some printers have been known to print a portion of sample-quality material on the premium stock specified, and run the balance of the job on a lower-grade paper. Check your printer's references. What follows are a few reminders of what you need to remember to avoid turning a dream job into a nightmare.

1. **SPECIFICATIONS**

   Make certain your specifications are clear and concise and that your print rep understands them completely. Ask questions: Will it need scoring? Should it be varnished to avoid scuffing? Is the specified paper a good choice for the project?

2. **COLOR MATCHING**

   If specially mixed ink colors *must* accurately match a color swatch or sample, you should make this clear in your specifications and to your print rep. You can request ink draw down samples on the same paper as your job specifies. Remember that color guides will fade with age and that minor variations occur from one guide to another.

3. **PRESS CHECKS**

   If you want to see your job on press, make sure you have that option. In some print shops, you can ensure a higher standard of work if they know the job will be press checked and that you will have a copy of the signed-off press sheet when samples are delivered.

4. **PRESS PROOFS**

   If you've signed off on an initial press check and are comfortable having the printer handle the remainder, ask that the pressroom manager or sales rep sign off on the runs. Ask for sample press sheets of each run.

5. **PAPER**

   When press checking, always verify that the paper used for the press check and press run is the stock you specified. If you sign off on a press sheet and the stock is not the right weight or grade, some printers will insist that it's your fault for okaying the wrong paper. It's not unreasonable to ask for verification of stock at the press check.

6. **SAMPLES**

   Always ask for samples. Many ask for ten to twenty samples, which are easy to handpick out of the run. Some print buyers ask for fifty samples, which are much more difficult to pick out of an erratic press run. If you have the slightest concerns about the printer you're using for a project, ask for fifty on your specification sheet. This number will probably count as part of the overall delivery quantity on the job, but it gives you a better reflection of the quality of the run.

7. **PAPER AND REGISTRATION ON PRESS**

   Printing on a large press with heavy ink coverage and small reversed images on light paper can often result in a disappointing finished product. Good registration is a key to good presswork, but there are inherent limitations when you have a flimsy 38-inch wide sheet of paper traveling through six units of a multicolor printing press.

   If you're planning a potentially difficult project, grill your print rep about their press capacities. Direct-to-plate printing provides more-accurate registration from color to color because the variables of film—and the steps required to expose printing plates—have been eliminated. Film isn't as stable as the aluminum compounds used to make a plate, and the latter's stability generally enables more accurate registration. This is a good point to remember when you're going out for bids.

8. **FINANCIAL IMPLICATIONS OF COLOR MISTAKES**

   This is a touchy subject that all printers and designers have to endure at some point in their career. Plainly said, color mistakes are costly. The best way to avoid color mistakes is awareness. Run a color sample with your printer and show it to your client. If there are any changes to be made, now is the time to do it—not after the job has printed.

Printing through the Ages

Printing became a "high-volume" industry in the fifteenth century with Johannes Gutenberg's introduction of moveable type. This woodcut illustrates the same basic principles we use today. On the left foreground, the typesetter is at work, with the proofreader next to him. In the center foreground, the printer's devil, usually a young boy, is stacking freshly printed sheets, while the printer pulls the screw handle to create an impression on the wooden press. Behind the printer, a woman sews the binding on finished books, and in the background, the deliveryman is on the way out the door. And of course, on the far right is the shop owner, probably asking why this is all taking so long. A full day's work in this era would produce about three hundred printed sheets.

In another fifteenth century woodcut, the printer in the background on the left is holding a leather-covered inkpad, which is used to tap ink onto the type. This was the earliest form of ink-density control, and took years to master. The printer's helper uses a long handle on the vise screw to press the impression block onto a sheet of paper. On the left, a typesetter uses an opened book as copy to set type.

Like modern printing presses, early models were built with massive beams to distribute the pressures required to print a single sheet of paper. This press has an advanced design for its time, with metal screw vise and leverage handle for applying printing pressure by hand.

SUMMARY

THE VALUE OF HELPING CLIENTELE make good printer choices should never be underestimated. Understanding the printing options that are available today, and knowing the processes that your printers use can quickly lead you to the most effective vendors, and result in a final product that will meet your expectations. Digital imaging and direct-to-press processes have created many opportunities for short press runs that would be cost prohibitive using traditional lithographic techniques. This is a growing market and is ripe for designers who guide their clientele into taking full advantage of new technologies.

8

COLORFUL WORDS FROM THE PRESSROOM

DESIGNERS AND PRINT PROFESSIONALS HAVE A SYMBIOTIC RELATIONSHIP. Each expects the other to hold to the highest standards, and each knows that their success hinges on the other. It's an important concept to understand when working through the color process.

Any designer fortunate enough to establish a solid working relationship with their printer often becomes privy to the facility's inner workings. A personal tour of the press and prepress areas is an invaluable experience, and all designers should try it at least once in their careers. In addition to giving you a better understanding of color mechanics, it also provides insight into how colors work together on screen and on press. The color brochure concept that you sketched out on a notepad will suddenly become very real as a press operator pulls a sheet off the press and hands it you. with this in mind, you should strive to understand the realities of print production.

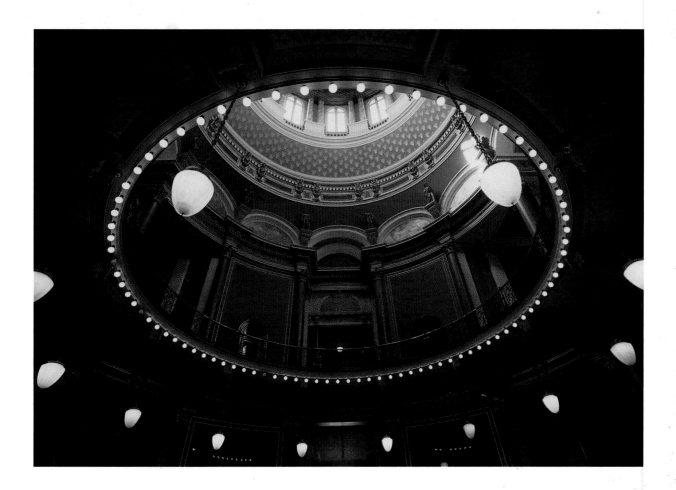

What Printers Look for in Color Submissions

IN CHAPTER 7, WE DISCUSSED THE information and materials that designers should submit along with their print jobs. Here, we'll delve into the practical aspects of offset print production by covering situations that often arise on the press floor. Many of these situations have the potential to affect your designs, and understanding them will help to clarify the limitations of print production.

One of the most common mistakes that designers make when submitting art is failing to convert all images from RGB to CMYK. If you don't do it, your printer may not be able to, and the images probably won't print.

Common Mistakes

EVERYONE MAKES MISTAKES, and designers and printers are no exception. However, when the errors add up, a seemingly simple job can quickly turn into a nightmare. Ask a printer about the common mistakes made by designers, and they'll probably cite unconverted RGB images, missing fonts and files, and miscommunication. Avoiding these mistakes is especially important when color is involved because the stakes are much higher. Color corrections at press are costly and time-consuming, and they tend to make everyone crabby.

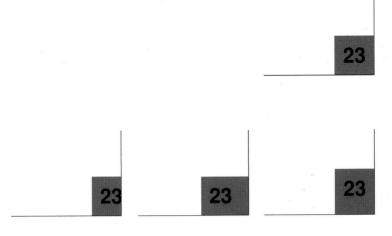

Extremely tight trimming requirements often pose problems, and can be difficult to overcome. It's relatively easy to design an element—such as the folio on top—that depends on precise trimming. The next three figures show how page layout, press registration, folding, and trimming can cause unwanted variations.

The best way to avoid mistakes is to communicate effectively with your printer. If you ask all the necessary color questions and run sample proofs early in the project, you will avoid conflict later. Don't ever be afraid to ask questions, no matter how inane they may sound. When working with color, leave no stone unturned. You don't want to risk losing a client because of poor color performance.

Common mistakes:

- Wrong, missing, or corrupt fonts
- Missing images and files
- Renaming TIF or EPS files, which will break the link with the page layout file
- Images and files improperly saved
- RGB or indexed color files not converted to CMYK
- Text or images too close to the trim
- Position-only images still in the final file
- Missing or incorrect lasers copies
- Corrupt files
- Missing contact information
- Incorrect trim size
- Incorrect imposition

When Things Go Horribly Pink

PRINTING CONSIDERATIONS loom large from the moment you begin designing a color project. You can spend all day tweaking your colors, but the effort will be useless if they don't translate on press. Never hesitate to run proofs, especially if the images are questionable. It takes only one bad image to spoil a project.

A good printer will alert you about poor color choices. You might be tempted to disagree, but printers have the best understanding of how the colors will translate into a finished product. If the printer thinks your choices are wrong, and you're inclined to stick to your guns, get a second opinion from a comparable source.

Quadtones can add depth to flat black-and-white images, as seen in these photos of a gravy boat.

Duotone Effects and Expectations

IF YOUR COLOR PROJECT includes black-and-white photos, you might consider dressing them up by converting them to *duotones*, *tritones*, or *quadtones*. Here, the photo is reproduced using two, three, or four colors respectively, adding depth and vibrance to an otherwise lackluster image. Many variables come into play when producing such images, and printers often prefer scanning them inhouse. Printers usually have common protocols for multitone production that work well with their systems.

Because quadtones are reproduced in all four process colors, they will reflect any color shifts on press. If you're running them with four-color images that are being pushed in a certain color direction—such as by adding cyan or magenta—the quadtones will reflect the same color cast. However, with many images, this can be pleasing to the eye, and shouldn't be cause for alarm.

Roll the Presses

NUMEROUS PHYSICAL and mechanical considerations affect every job on press. Some are out of your control, with one possible exception: Your choice of printers. Still, designers who understand such elements as ink density, sheet layouts, and signature formats will develop a knack for envisioning the project as it will appear on the press sheet.

Pressroom Controls

ALTHOUGH THERE ARE FEW industry standards that compel individual printing companies to perform in a predetermined fashion, manufacturers of proofing and control systems offer equipment that is carefully evaluated to meet industry expectations. Offset presses, as massive and ominous-looking as they may be, are relatively sensitive machines that operate with incredibly close tolerances. Settings that are off by a few thousandths of an inch can have detrimental effects on print quality. No two presses operate exactly alike. Regular maintenance, the use of *test forms*, and proper understanding of color bars and densitometer readings are essential when producing high-quality color.

Duotones are often used in two-color print projects, providing an inexpensive way to add color to black-and-white images.

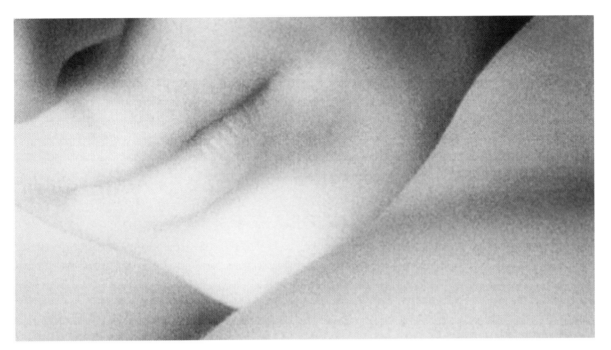

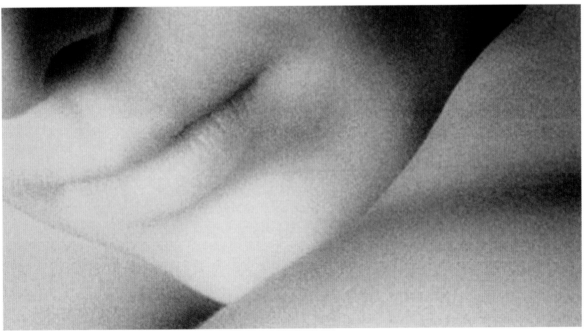

Tritones, like quadtones, can add color and warmth to the page. This tritone consists of a full black-and-white halftone with small percentages of cyan and magenta added to midtones and highlights.

Handheld reflection densitometers are invaluable for monitoring press runs and maintaining press calibrations. Designers should be aware of this procedure when working with press operators. (Courtesy Heidelberg USA, Inc.)

Densitometers

A *DENSITOMETER* IS (usually) a hand-held electronic device that measures ink density, dot size, dot gain, *ink trap* (the ability of one ink color to print, or *trap*, over another), and hue error and grayness. Transmission densitometers are designed to read through transparent material, such as film. However, most pressrooms use reflection densitometers, which bounce a light beam from the surface of a sheet and electronically calculate the result. In most color jobs, these measurements are taken on color bars printed outside the image area.

Ink Density

INK DENSITY REFERS to the amount of each ink color applied to the press sheet. More ink results in higher densities and a corresponding increase in the depth of color. When you tell the press operator you would like to see more blue in a particular image, they increase the cyan ink flow with electronic or manual adjustments, then pull another set of press sheets for your inspection. Invariably, they will check ink density with a densitometer before and after making the adjustment, the latter to ensure that you haven't exceeded optimal levels or thrown overall color out of balance.

In the first illustration, the sky looks a little washed out. Adding cyan on press will make the sky bluer and brighter, but it also increases the blue in the entire image. Unlike photo-editing programs, such as Adobe Photoshop, offset presses cannot make selective adjustments within the confines of an image.

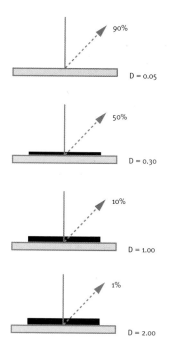

90% D = 0.05

50% D = 0.30

10% D = 1.00

1% D = 2.00

How Densitometers Work—
A Short Primer

A REFLECTION DENSITOMETER, as noted earlier, bounces light from a controlled internal source to the surface of a printed sheet, and back into a series of filters and monitors that translate the reflection into numeric values. An increase in ink results in a correspondingly higher reading. The readings of each process color, taken from the color bar on your approved press sheet, will help the press operator maintain optimal settings throughout the print run. This can be a balancing act. Overly light density will increase the number of hickeys, because thinner ink is also sticky. If the density is too high, you'll see increased dot gain, plugged shadows, and perhaps set-off onto subsequent press sheets. Between these extremes, the operator can use ink adjustments to create wide variations in color output.

You can use your eye to evaluate ink density, but you'll get more accurate results using a reflection densitometer. This device can detect slight variations in ink density and helps the press operator log and maintain the densities that you approved.

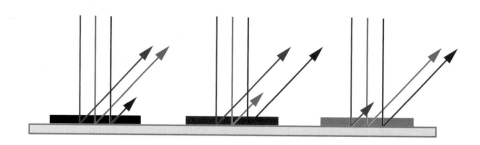

This illustration shows a simplified view of the inner workings of a reflection densitometer. Light is reflected from ink and paper into a series of filters and sensors that translate the signal into numeric values.

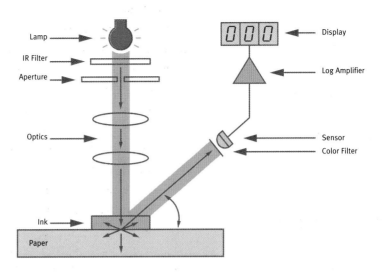

Components of a Reflection Densitometer

Reflection densitometers are sensitive to such subtleties as the shadow the ink dot casts inside the paper. Minute variations can be measured, notated, and stored to allow repeatable results on reprints.

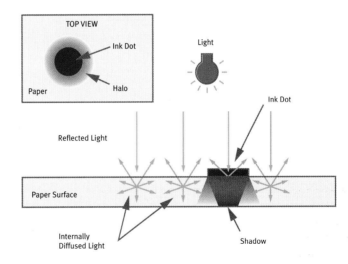

The Effect of Light Scattering Properties

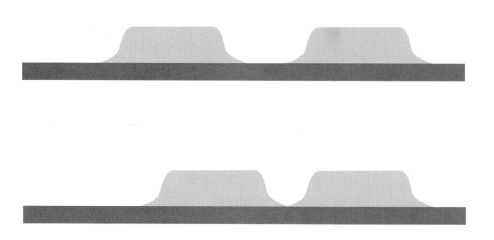

Handheld reflection densitometers, as seen in this exploded view of spreading dots, can detect changes in screen values more accurately than the naked eye.

Densitometers and Screen Values

DENSITOMETERS ALSO TRANSLATE screen values numerically. By monitoring the screen values in color bars, the press operator can detect variations that may affect the system's operating balances. With ink densities on the high side, shadows may gradually begin to fill in, creating unacceptable dot gain. Changes in ink/water balance will also affect screen values.

Densitometers and Ink Trap

THE TERM *TRAP* SERVES DUAL purposes in the pressroom. "Image trapping" refers to how images are overlaid on the press sheet. "Ink trapping" refers to printing one color of ink over another; bad trapping results in poor dot reproduction and lost color gamut. Under ideal conditions, with proper ink tacks and ink/water balances, colors will smoothly print over each other. With improperly tacked inks or other problems, overprinting can become mottled and uneven. Good ink trap is imperative for high-quality printing. The illustration shows blocks of solid ink overprint that are large enough to see, but the same thing is happening to the tiny dots in your four-color job.

This series of color blocks depicts ink that is trapping (overprinting) as it should be, and the effect is a smooth color. The combination of 100 percent yellow and 100 percent red looks just like it was intended—solid red. In the green block, 100 percent cyan overprinted by 100 percent yellow produces a smooth green. Good ink trapping is a key to good printing.

These blocks illustrate the effects of poor ink trap. The yellow is not trapping over the red properly, producing a mottled-looking green. And it's not trapping well over the cyan, with similar results. All of these blocks represent poor ink trap. The cure is to adjust press balances or ink tacks.

Good color printers invest in high-quality equipment, rigorous maintenance programs, and quality materials that add up to excellent reproduction, as seen in the first image. The second image shows what you can expect from an inexpensive facility with poorly maintained equipment.

Why Bad Traps Happen on Good Presses

THE WHY'S AND HOW'S of ink trapping could probably fill a book. What follows is a practical overview.

Ink Quality

INK QUALITY PLAYS A ROLE in trapping problems. Cheap inks can be overly sensitive to press variations and can fluctuate radically during a print run.

Good-quality ink handles the printing process with relative ease. High-end printers tend to buy grades of ink that offer consistent handling characteristics on press.

Press Roller Systems—A Major Player

INKING SYSTEMS ON PRINTING presses are designed to distribute ink smoothly and evenly to the plate, and from there to the blanket and onto your press sheet. Inking rollers are made of steel cores covered with specially formulated rubber compounds that are ground to specific diameters. When the rubber rollers are new, they have a soft velvety surface that is ideal for transferring thin ink films. As rollers age, the surfaces tend to swell and harden, and sometimes develop cracks and pits. Their ability to transfer ink diminishes, and print quality suffers. Effective press roller life can range from two to six months, depending on the chemicals used to clean them, roller adjustments, and shop environment.

Just as car tires can be retreaded, press rollers can be recovered with new rubber and given new life. This is a common practice, and several companies specialize in remanufacturing printing rollers. Many printers maintain a regular roller exchange program, but unfortunately, some don't.

At rest, press-inking rollers are raised from the plate cylinder, as shown at the top in this cutaway side view. When the press is turned on and printing, rollers are mechanically lowered onto the plate.

Keeping New Rubber on the Press

MAINTAINING A REGULAR ROLLER exchange program is expensive and can be a significant part of a shop's overhead. The best printers adhere to a regular exchange of press rollers and factor this into their production costs. Others put off exchanging rollers as long as possible. This can be reflected in lower costs, but is also reflected in lower-quality color work.

How Important Can Rollers Really Be?

A THIRTY-YEAR-OLD PRINTING PRESS in reasonable condition with good press rollers will print better than a year-old press with aged rollers. Many printing problems attributed to mechanical glitches have been cured with roller replacements.

Press *form rollers*, which physically contact the plate, can be lowered by hand to reveal the stripes on the printing plate. This figure illustrates the proper appearance of stripes in a press's magenta printing unit. These stripes can be measured, and their widths adjusted to the press manufacturer's specifications.

This figure illustrates ink stripes of aged, poorly adjusted press rollers. The stripe at the top results from a form roller adjusted too tightly to the plate cylinder. The second stripe shows the effect of a roller swollen in the center. The third stripe is unevenly adjusted from one side to the other. The bottom stripe is adjusted too lightly to the plate cylinder. These problems indicate poor adjustments, poor roller condition, or a combination of the two. All will lead to poor print reproduction.

Smooth Solids on Press

PRINTING SMOOTH SOLIDS ON offset presses is one of a press operator's greatest challenges. Good inking rollers, coupled with a high-end press, make solid reproduction a relatively trouble-free operation. Poor inking rollers, and often the less expensive presses on the market, can turn solids into an operator's nightmare. Great solids don't come cheap, and if you've got solids in your design, you'll want to take a close look at the capacities of your low bidders.

A proof should give you a good representation of the image you'll see on press, as illustrated here.

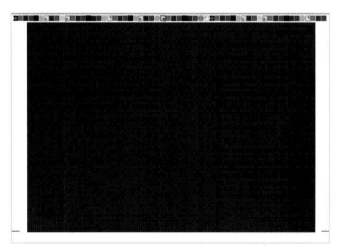

Mechanical Ghosting

MECHANICAL GHOSTING REFERS TO artifacts that appear when solid or screened images are disrupted by design elements that break the even distribution of ink. This always occurs in the direction the sheet travels. You end up with slight variations in ink density in areas where you want even coverage. Mechanical ghosting is a fact of life to some degree. Projects with a high likelihood of mechanical ghosting are best printed on high-quality presses in good operating condition.

Here are two examples of solids you'll see reproduced on low-end presses, or expensive models with aging, misadjusted rollers.

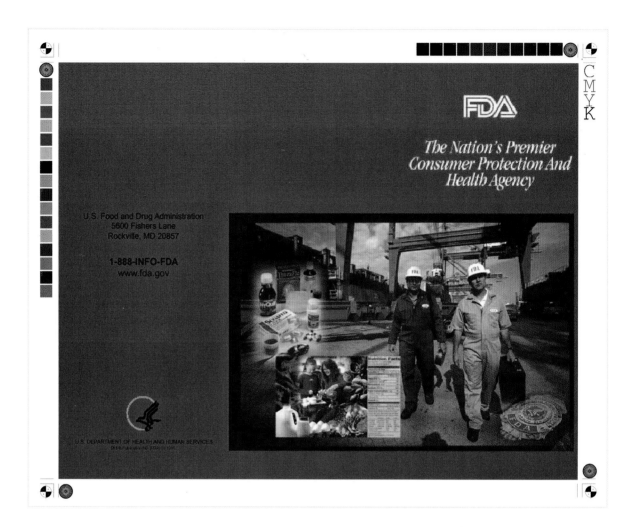

These images show the effect of mechanical ghosting. The first image, a proof with an even, solid background, shows no ghosting. The second image illustrates mechanical ghosting on an inexpensive press, with a noticeable difference in ink density following the edges of images that break up the solid coverage. The third image is printed on a high-end press designed for demanding jobs.

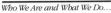

Who We Are and What We Do…

We are a team of 9,000 dedicated public health employees that includes physicians, nurses, consumer safety officers, lawyers, and scientists, with specialties ranging from biomaterials engineering to pharmacology. Decisions made by FDA affect every American every day. In 2000, consumers spent $1 trillion — more than 20 percent of their income — on hundreds of thousands of products whose safety and effectiveness is our responsibility. Yet, the per capita cost of all FDA services is less than 2 cents a day!

The public trusts FDA to ensure that:

1. Foods are safe, wholesome and truthfully labeled
2. Drugs for both humans and animals, and vaccines for humans are safe and effective
3. Blood used for transfusions is safe and in adequate supply
4. Medical devices, from scalpels to CT scanners, are safe and effective
5. Transplanted tissues are safe and effective
6. Equipment that uses radiant energy, such as X-ray machines and microwave ovens, is safe
7. Cosmetics are safe and properly labeled

Our Priorities For The Future

FDA has identified the following four strategic priorities for FY2001 and beyond. Each priority reinforces the importance of prevention as the agency's primary response to the nation's health and safety concerns.

Assuring a Safe Food Supply: FDA is responsible for assuring the safety of 80 percent of the U.S. food supply and annually monitors more than 4 million food import entries into the United States. That includes half of all seafood and more

than 20 percent of the fresh fruits and vegetables consumed by Americans. FDA is working with partners to significantly reduce foodborne illnesses and deaths. Prevention strategies based on strong scientific research and risk assessment are implemented through a nationwide inspection program in partnership with the states.

Assuring Medical Product Safety: FDA will continue to ensure that drugs, vaccines, and medical devices are safe by conducting more than 15,000 inspections each year to make certain that these products are properly manufactured and distributed, and by monitoring their safe performance and use.

Managing Emerging Hazards: FDA must be vigilant in assessing, and then quickly and effectively reducing risks associated with unexpected health and safety threats to Americans such as bioterrorism, AIDS and Bovine Spongiform Encephalopathy (BSE), also called "mad cow disease." FDA's approach has been to counter these hazards through a regulatory framework and the agency's scientific expertise.

Bringing New Technologies to Market: FDA ensures that the products of new technologies are available to U.S consumers. Because of the agency's timely, science-based decisions, millions of Americans can get the medicines, biologics, and medical devices they need and be assured of their safety and effectiveness.

Principles

To effectively carry out these priorities, FDA adheres to fundamental principles that frame its

actions and lead to more effective public health results. These principles include:

- Use state-of-the-art science to make accurate and timely decisions about the safety of products and processes.
- Think and act in a global context as we regulate products that are marketed worldwide.
- Make decisions that consider the total product life cycle from premarket development stages to postmarket monitoring and surveillance of product safety.
- Work with partners in all sectors to strengthen the FDA's prevention efforts.

Did You Know…

- FDA approves new drugs in the United States as fast as, or faster than, anywhere else in the world.
- FDA helps select the flu strains to be included in each year's flu vaccine and participates in the development of flu and other vaccines.
- FDA scientists have developed an inexpensive seafood freshness indicator called "Fresh Tag" that changes color to indicate when the product has spoiled.
- FDA tests home-style meals prepared from ingredients purchased in grocery stores nationwide to check for pesticide residues and other food contaminants.

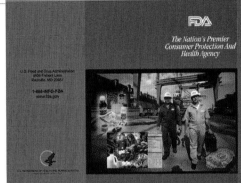

FDA

The Nation's Premier Consumer Protection And Health Agency

U.S. Food and Drug Administration
5600 Fishers Lane
Rockville, MD 20857

1-888-INFO-FDA
www.fda.gov

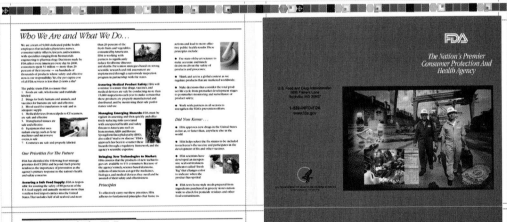

Duplicator presses are common in small and quick print shops. These machines can handle sheet sizes up to 11 x 17 inches and do an excellent job of reproducing relatively simple color projects. Most have only two inking form rollers, as shown in this illustration, and are not designed to handle large, solid images.

Small duplicating presses are not designed to print the heavy solids seen here. The arrow shows the direction of sheet traveling through the press.

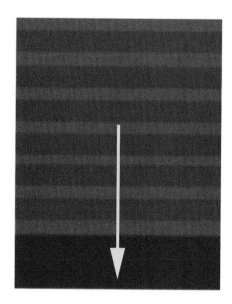

Test Forms for Offset Printing

GOOD PRINTERS FREQUENTLY RUN TEST FORMS—such as those provided by the Graphic Arts Technical Foundation (GATF)—to monitor print quality of the presses they operate. These exacting forms offer common reference points for evaluating virtually every aspect of offset printing, including dot gain, ink trapping, color fidelity, color gamut, and the accuracy of *print length*. Print length is a measurement of the printed image from the leading edge to the tail edge of the press sheet.

By printing the test forms from digital files and then submitting them to the GATF for evaluation, printers gain a valuable means of maintaining quality control on their equipment. If your printer uses these forms, or similarly rigorous process controls, it's a good sign that they take their work seriously. Many printers simply wing it, hope for the best, and then blame any quality problems that arise on everything except their process controls.

GATF Test Forms

WE HAVE INCLUDED ON THE FOLLOWING PAGES a series of test form elements provided by the GATF. These forms and their results tend to stay tucked away within the printing industry, but they are highly informative and deserve recognition for the positive impact they have on the quality control of high end color reproduction.

Elements of these test forms are appropriate to the digital printing process, and will give you an idea of the demanding definition and color fidelity that high quality printers are striving to achieve.

THE GATF TEST FORMS shown here illustrate the steps that better printing companies take to ensure quality. Each form presents difficult challenges for offset reproduction, pushing the presses to their limits.

Low-key images

The red couch photograph is referred to as a *low-key* image because of the predominance of dark hues in the midtone to shadow portions. This photograph also presents a challenge in its high level of resolved detail. (Courtesy GATF)

High-key images

The wedding photograph is referred to as *high key* because the dominant tones are light pastels and whites, which fall in the highlight to midtone areas. (Courtesy GATF)

Realistic skin tones

In the painting kids photograph, the challenge is to reproduce all five skin tones equally well. (Courtesy GATF)

Capturing tonal differences

In this portrait, close attention is required to capture tonal differences in the face, chest, arms, and hands, as well as more subtle transitions from the forehead, cheeks, nose, and chin. (Courtesy GATF)

Measuring color cast

This photo, dominated by tones approximating neutral grays, provides a good measure of color cast. The image is also low key due to the preponderance of dark tones and relatively few highlights. (Courtesy GATF)

Broad color gamuts

This photo provides a broad color gamut. The fruit and fabrics were selected for their variety of saturated hues, pushing the limits of transparency film. Reproduction of these hues is particularly difficult. (Courtesy GATF)

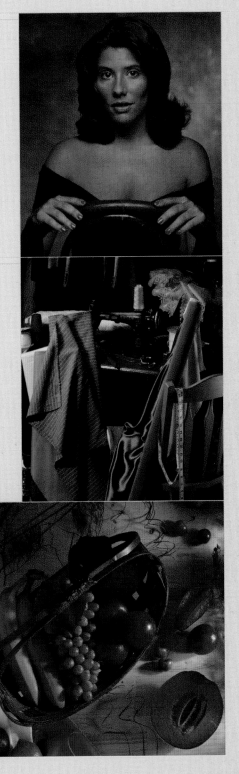

This photo of a covered bridge demonstrates the reproduction of *memory colors*. As the name implies, these are colors, such as green grass and blue sky, that the viewer subconsciously compares with their own expectations based on what they've seen before. (Courtesy GATF)

Twenty-two step tone scales show each process color, plus blue, green, red, and an even mix of cyan, magenta, and yellow. (Courtesy GATF)

	C	M	Y	K	R	G	B	3C
5								
10								
15								
20								
25								
30								
35								
40								
45								
50								
55								
60								
65								
70								
75								
80								
85								
90								
95								
S								

Star targets indicate the resolution and directional bias of an imaging system. Systems capable of higher resolution will come closer to presenting the center of the star as a single point. (Courtesy GATF)

The line-resolution target shows the system's ability to handle positive and reversed line elements and a variety of orientations. (Courtesy GATF)

Vignettes for each process color show smooth transitions from highlight to shadow. The tonal transitions of different colors should be the same. (Courtesy GATF)

This test chart is used to evaluate highlight and shadow reproduction. (Courtesy GATF)

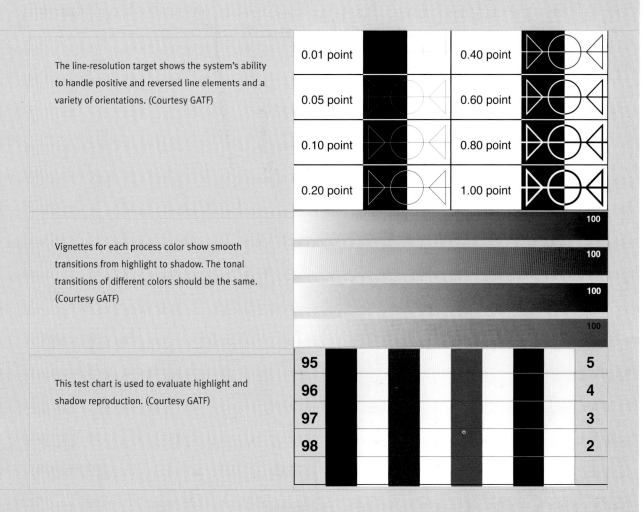

These gray values are recommended for reproducing neutrals with typical magazine production techniques and materials. (Courtesy GATF)

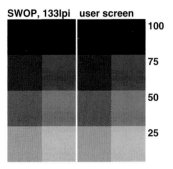

These pixel line patterns are sensitive targets for high-exposure imaging systems. (Courtesy GATF)

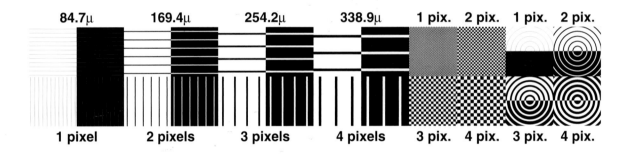

The image fit target is used to evaluate the register accuracy of any output device. Elements are placed with no trapping between colors. (Courtesy GATF)

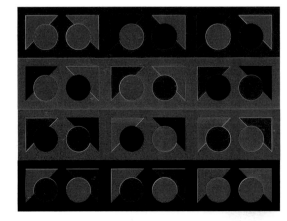

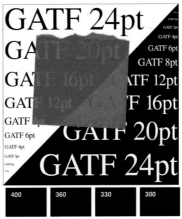

Type Resolution Target / D-Max Patches

The type resolution target has samples of type ranging from 24 points to one point in positive and reversed formats. Most systems do not resolve positive and negative one-point type successfully. (Courtesy GATF)

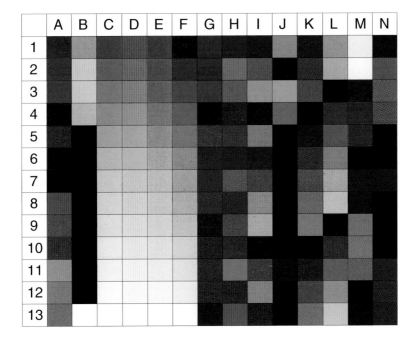

The colors in this data set were chosen to demonstrate the color gamut of the imaging system. (Courtesy GATF)

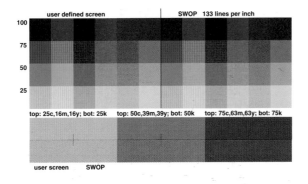

The GCA/GATF digital proof comparator contains 25, 50, 75, and 100 percent tone values to show how the system reproduces process colors, plus blue, green, and red. The black tone patches provide a visual reference against which you can compare the neutrality of the three-color patches. (Courtesy GATF)

Tones in these opposed line
targets should be uniform,
with no differences between
tones formed by the horizontal
and vertical lines.
(Courtesy GATF)

The color control bar consists
of a sequence of 100, 75, 50,
and 25 percent tone patches in
cyan, magenta, yellow, black,
blue, green, and red. This con-
firms that the imaging system
is producing consistent color
and tone from page to page.
(Courtesy GATF)

This photo presents significant
areas of highly saturated blue,
red, and green that help define
the saturation limits of the
reproduction system. Also, the
slightly off-neutral hues of the
pencil tips are highly susceptible to color variations.
(Courtesy GATF)

The gray balance charts help determine the best combination of cyan, magenta, and yellow needed to reproduce a neutral scale. Operators usually evaluate gray visually and must do so under standard viewing conditions. (Courtesy GATF)

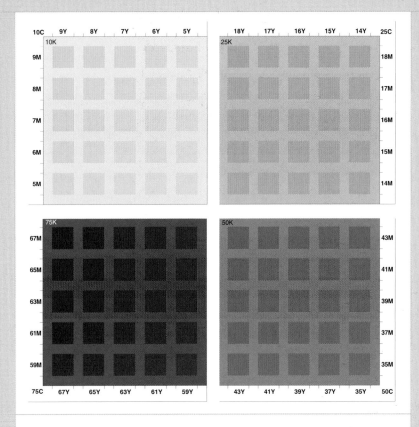

The process color tint blocks are used to evaluate the uniformity of an even dot pattern. Additionally, the tint patches will also change value if dot gain is adjusted. (Courtesy GATF)

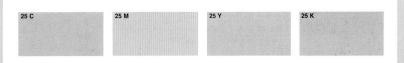

This portrait of a young woman in front of an abstract colored background provides a human image to evaluate. Because fleshtones are so familiar to us, we're very critical of how hue and contrast are reproduced. (Courtesy GATF)

Press Sheet Configurations

PRESS SHEETS ARE SET UP TO RUN on a variety of press sizes. Small duplicating presses are generally built to handle 8 ½ x 11 to 12 x 18-inch sheet sizes. The next size up is 14 x 20 inches. Half-size presses fall in the 20 x 26-inch range. The next most common size press handles a 28 x 40-inch sheet. While press sizes can go up to a whopping 70 inches, the vast majority fall into these ranges.

Signature Sizes

PRESSES ALSO HANDLE A RANGE of potential *signature* sizes. A signature is a printed press sheet designed to fold at least once to become part of a publication. Signatures are generally multiples of four pages—one sheet folded in half—and signature page counts rise in four-page increments. Trim sizes for finished publications run a wide range, from tiny 3 x 5's up to 11 x 14 and larger. Most common publications fall within the 5 ½ x 8 ½ to 8 ½ x 11-inch sizes.

These images show the sheet direction through an offset press. Duplicating presses feed an 8 ½ x 11-inch sheet on the 8 ½-inch side. Larger presses invariably feed paper on the long side, as illustrated here with a 19 x 25-inch sheet and a 25 x 38-inch sheet.

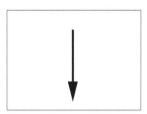
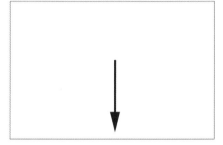

All sheetfed presses require a gripper edge and set-back, which constitute a no-print zone before the printing image begins. (This no-print zone is usually minimum of a ½ inch.)

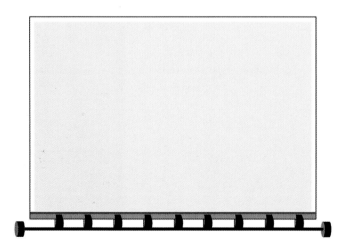

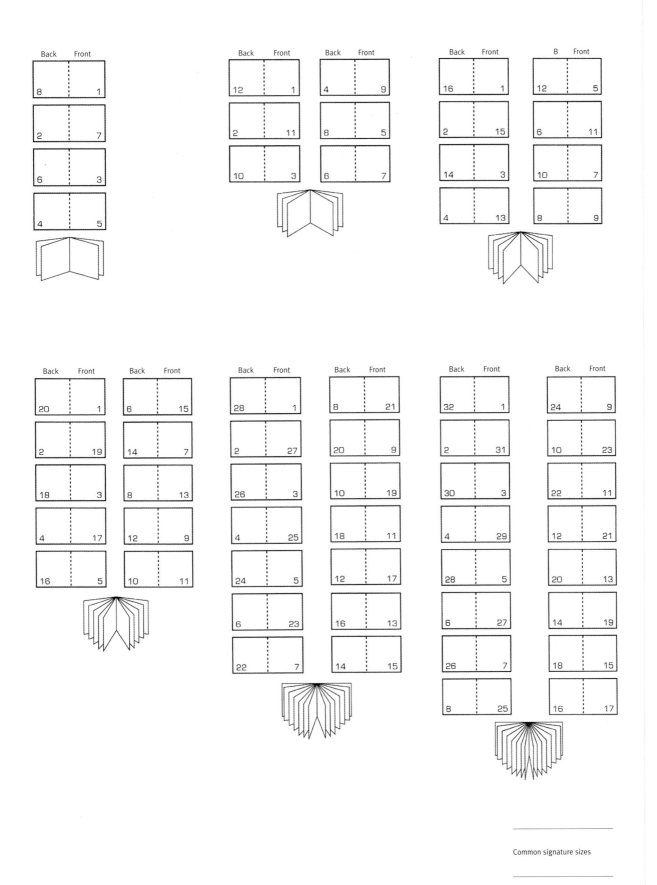

Common signature sizes

Layouts and Imposition Dummies

UNDERSTANDING IMPOSITION and layout dummies is a key to effective design and predictable output. These are often nothing more than a piece of letter-sized paper folded in half for a four-page dummy, in quarters for an eight-page dummy, or in eighths for a sixteen-page dummy. With page numbers noted consecutively, the sheet can be unfolded to reveal the pages that will fall on each side of a press sheet. These *printer spreads* are much different from *reader spreads*, and they will vary from printer to printer depending on press sizes and how their bindery equipment is configured for folding.

Seeing a dummy layout of your job can greatly help in making color decisions. If you are running a variety of Pantone spot colors, you can set them up to print on pages on one side of the press sheet, thus avoiding extra passes through the press, extra plates, and extra press washes to change colors.

Dummy layouts can also help you anticipate potential problems, such as mechanical ghosting, and they let you see the placement of critical color images that you may need to adjust on press.

Your print rep should be able to supply you with a variety of imposition dummies and press sheet layout configurations as illustrated. Imposition dummies can vary from shop to shop, depending on press sizes and folding equipment.

This illustration shows a typical four-page layout dummy, followed by an example of how it would appear on press. The blue lines represent non-printing trim lines, while the red line represents the non-printing fold line.

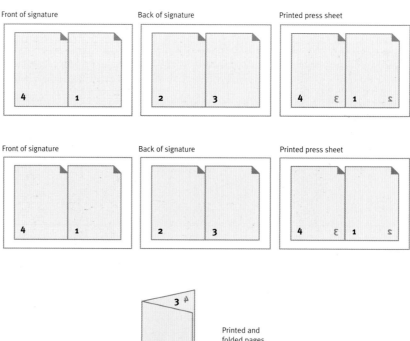

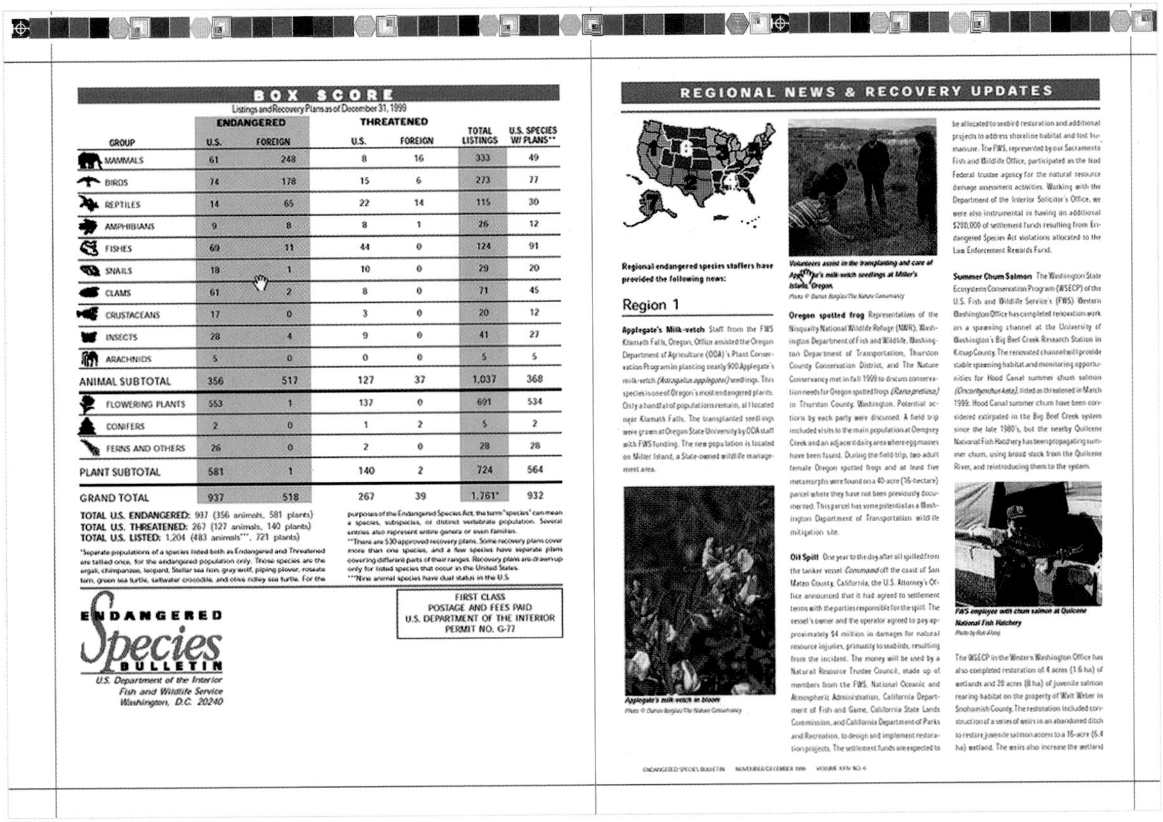

BOX SCORE

Listings and Recovery Plans as of December 31, 1999

GROUP	ENDANGERED U.S.	ENDANGERED FOREIGN	THREATENED U.S.	THREATENED FOREIGN	TOTAL LISTINGS	U.S. SPECIES W/ PLANS**
MAMMALS	61	248	8	16	333	49
BIRDS	74	178	15	6	273	77
REPTILES	14	65	22	14	115	30
AMPHIBIANS	9	8	8	1	26	12
FISHES	69	11	44	0	124	91
SNAILS	18	1	10	0	29	20
CLAMS	61	2	8	0	71	45
CRUSTACEANS	17	0	3	0	20	12
INSECTS	28	4	9	0	41	27
ARACHNIDS	5	0	0	0	5	5
ANIMAL SUBTOTAL	356	517	127	37	1,037	368
FLOWERING PLANTS	553	1	137	0	691	534
CONIFERS	2	0	1	2	5	2
FERNS AND OTHERS	26	0	2	0	28	28
PLANT SUBTOTAL	581	1	140	2	724	564
GRAND TOTAL	937	518	267	39	1,761*	932

TOTAL U.S. ENDANGERED: 937 (356 animals, 581 plants)
TOTAL U.S. THREATENED: 267 (127 animals, 140 plants)
TOTAL U.S. LISTED: 1,204 (483 animals***, 721 plants)

*Separate populations of a species listed both as Endangered and Threatened are tallied once, for the endangered population only. Those species are the argali, chimpanzee, leopard, Stellar sea lion, gray wolf, piping plover, roseate tern, green sea turtle, saltwater crocodile, and olive ridley sea turtle. For the purposes of the Endangered Species Act, the term "species" can mean a species, subspecies, or distinct vertebrate population. Several entries also represent entire genera or even families.

**There are 530 approved recovery plans. Some recovery plans cover more than one species, and a few species have separate plans covering different parts of their ranges. Recovery plans are drawn up only for listed species that occur in the United States.

***Nine animal species have dual status in the U.S.

ENDANGERED
Species
BULLETIN

U.S. Department of the Interior
Fish and Wildlife Service
Washington, D.C. 20240

FIRST CLASS
POSTAGE AND FEES PAID
U.S. DEPARTMENT OF THE INTERIOR
PERMIT NO. G-77

REGIONAL NEWS & RECOVERY UPDATES

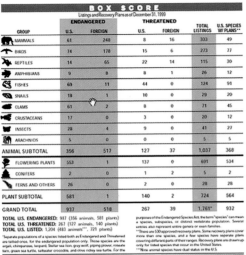

Applegate's milk-vetch in bloom
Photo by Darien Borgias/The Nature Conservancy

Volunteers assist in the transplanting and care of Applegate's milk-vetch seedlings at Miller's Island, Oregon.
Photo by Darien Borgias/The Nature Conservancy

Regional endangered species staffers have provided the following news:

Region 1

Applegate's Milk-vetch Staff from the FWS Klamath Falls, Oregon, Office and the Oregon Department of Agriculture (ODA)'s Plant Conservation Program in planting nearly 900 Applegate's milk-vetch *(Astragalus applegatei)* seedlings. This species is one of Oregon's most endangered plants. Only a handful of populations remain, all located near Klamath Falls. The transplanted seedlings were grown at Oregon State University by ODA staff with FWS funding. The new population is located on Miller Island, a State-owned wildlife management area.

Oil Spill One year to the day after oil spilled from the tanker vessel *Command* off the coast of San Mateo County, California, the U.S. Attorney's Office announced that it had agreed to settlement terms with the parties responsible for the spill. The vessel's owner and the operator agreed to pay approximately $4 million in damages for natural resource injuries, primarily to seabirds, resulting from the incident. The money will be used by a Natural Resource Trustee Council, made up of members from the FWS, National Oceanic and Atmospheric Administration, California Department of Fish and Game, California State Lands Commission, and California Department of Parks and Recreation, to design and implement restoration projects. The settlement funds are expected to

Oregon spotted frog Representatives of the Nisqually National Wildlife Refuge (NWR), Washington Department of Fish and Wildlife, Washington Department of Transportation, Thurston County Conservation District, and The Nature Conservancy met in fall 1999 to discuss conservation needs for Oregon spotted frogs *(Rana pretiosa)* in Thurston County, Washington. Potential actions by each party were discussed. A field trip included visits to the main population and to Dempsey Creek and an adjacent dairy area where egg masses have been found. During the field trip, two adult female Oregon spotted frogs and at least five metamorphs were found on a 40-acre (16-hectare) parcel where they have not been previously documented. This parcel has some potential as a Washington Department of Transportation wildlife mitigation site.

Summer Chum Salmon The Washington State Ecosystems Conservation Program (WSECP) of the U.S. Fish and Wildlife Service's (FWS) Western Washington Office has completed restoration work on a spawning channel at the University of Washington's Big Beef Creek Research Station in Kitsap County. The renovated channel will provide stable spawning habitat and monitoring opportunities for Hood Canal summer chum salmon *(Oncorhynchus keta)*, listed as threatened in March 1999. Hood Canal summer chum have been considered extirpated in the Big Beef Creek system since the late 1980's, but the nearby Quilcene National Fish Hatchery has been propagating summer chum, using brood stock from the Quilcene River, and reintroducing them to the system.

FWS employee with chum salmon at Quilcene National Fish Hatchery
Photo by Ron Wong

The WSECP in the Western Washington Office has also completed restoration of 4 acres (1.6 ha) of wetlands and 20 acres (8 ha) of juvenile salmon rearing habitat on the property of Walt Weber in Snohomish County. The restoration included construction of a series of weirs in an abandoned ditch to restore juvenile salmon access to a 16-acre (6.4 ha) wetland. The weirs also increase the wetland

REGIONAL NEWS & RECOVERY UPDATES

Bald eagle
Corel Corp. photo

Region 5

Endangered Bats The FWS West Virginia Field Office, Canaan Valley NWR, and West Virginia Division of Natural Resources have joined to construct a large single-iron gate at the entrance of Schoolhouse Cave in Germany Valley, Pendleton County, West Virginia. The gate, which is the largest of its kind in the world, will permanently protect a large summer and winter colony of the endangered Virginia big-eared bat *(Corynorhinus townsendii virginianus)*. A small number of Indiana bats *(Myotis sodalis)* and two species of concern, the Eastern woodrat *(Neotoma floridana)* and the small-footed bat *(Myotis subulatus)*, will also be protected by the gate.

acreage by 4 acres. The wetland and a 50-foot (15-meter) buffer on both sides of the ditch will be replanted with a mixture of native conifers and wetland shrubs in spring 2000. Project partners include the landowner, Adopt-a-Stream Foundation, Stilli-Snohomish Fisheries Enhancement Task Force, Stillaguamish Tribe, and Snohomish Conservation District.

Bald Eagle *(Haliaeetus leucocephalus)* The gating project was partially funded by the FWS staff biologist Doug Loye assisted the fire crew from the Klamath Basin NWR Complex with the bird prescribed fires in almost a decade at Bear Valley NWR in Oregon. This refuge was designated specifically for its value as a winter roost for bald eagles and is host to hundreds of bald eagles in the winter and early spring. A total of 40 acres (16 ha) were under-burned in an area that had been thinned by timber operations last year. The thinning was designed specifically to benefit the growth and maintenance of large trees used by the eagles for roosting and nesting.

Reported by LaRee Brosseau of the FWS Portland, Oregon, Regional Office.

Bat gate at Schoolhouse Cave
USFWS photo

Chesapeake Bay/Susquehanna River Ecosystem program. Our West Virginia Field Office contracted with Roy Powers of the American Cave Conservation Association to design and direct the construction. Other FWS personnel key to completion of the project came from the Ohio River Islands NWR, FWS Pennsylvania Field Office, and Patuxent NWR. Participants in the project also included The Nature Conservancy, U.S. Forest Service, and National Speleological Society chapters (or Grottoes) from Ohio, Virginia, West Virginia, and Maryland. Forty-six people participated in the effort.

Reported by William A. Tolin, Endangered Species Specialist in the FWS West Virginia Field Office in Elkins.

ON THE WEB

The Fish and Wildlife Service's Endangered Species Homepage provides a wealth of information on our Endangered Species Program:

Listing Web Page
http://endangered.fws.gov/listing

View or download recent listing notices or actions published in the *Federal Register*, find out which animals and plants are protected by viewing species lists; visit the frequently asked questions to learn more about the listing process, petition management, listing candidates, "candidate conservation agreements with assurances" for private property owners, and critical habitat designations.

Habitat Conservation Planning Web Page
http://endangered.fws.gov/hcp

Go to this website for details on the habitat conservation planning process, download the HCP Handbook, and view a list of HCPs and the species they address.

Recovery Web Page
http://endangered.fws.gov/recovery

An overview of the recovery program and reclassification and delisting activities and more is provided on the recovery program's web page. Recovery plans approved during 1994-1998 are available online at http://endangered.fws.gov/recovery/recplans/.

Law Enforcement
http://www.le.fws.gov/

Learn about our nation's wildlife laws and take a virtual tour of the National Fish and Wildlife Forensics Laboratory. Information on wildlife permits is also available.

Listing Actions
http://endangered.fws.gov/frpubs/00fedreg.htm

View or download new listing notices, policies, and other announcements as published in the *Federal Register*.

Prepared by Julia Bumbaca of the FWS Division of Endangered Species, Branch of Information Management, at the Service's Arlington, Virginia, headquarters office.

LISTING ACTIONS

During August and September 1999, the Fish and Wildlife Service and National Marine Fisheries Service (NMFS) published the following **Endangered Species Act (ESA)** listing actions in the *Federal Register*. The full text of each proposed and final rule can be accessed through our website:
http://endangered.fws.gov.

Proposed Rules

Aleutian Canada Goose *(Branta canadensis leucopareia)* This unique subspecies nests only on a few of Alaska's remote Aleutian Islands and winters in areas of California and Oregon. Historically, the populations are small, and were rare on privately owned lands vulnerable to draining, development, mining, fire suppression, and a variety of other changes in habitat management. On August 16, we proposed to list this rare plant as endangered. We are also working with the State of North Carolina (which already considers the plant endangered), The Nature Conservancy, and landowners on cooperative protection and management plans.

Aleutian Canada goose
Photo by Glen Smart/USFWS

For the past several decades, biologists have worked intensively to remove the non-native foxes, reintroduce geese back onto the fox-free islands, research migration routes, and protect wintering habitat. Today, we estimate that the Aleutian Canada goose numbers more than 32,000 birds and is no longer in danger of extinction. On August 3, we proposed to recognize the bird's recovery by removing it from the list of threatened and endangered species. (See "A Spectacular Summer for Birds" in *Bulletin* Vol. XXIV, No. 4.)

Golden Sedge *(Carex lutea)* A perennial in the family Cyperaceae, the golden sedge has yellowish-green, grass-like leaves and produces stems that may reach 3 feet (0.9 meter) or more with many flowers. This plant is native to the coastal plains of North Carolina, where it is associated with wet pine savannas on sites underlain with calcareous (chalky) deposits. Historically, its open habitat was maintained by periodic wildfires.

The golden sedge currently is known only from eight populations in Pender and Onslow counties. Most of the populations are small, and several are on privately owned lands vulnerable to draining, development, mining, fire suppression, and a variety of other changes in habitat management. On August 16, we proposed to list this rare plant as endangered.

Scaleshell mussel
USFWS photo

Scaleshell Mussel *(Leptodea leptodon)* A freshwater mollusk, the scaleshell mussel has a thin, fragile shell that measures up to about 4 inches (10 centimeters) in width and is marked with faint green rays. It once inhabited 53 rivers or streams throughout most of the eastern United States, with populations found as far west as Oklahoma. Like many other native mussels, however, the scaleshell has declined drastically in range and numbers. Today, populations of this species are known in only 13 rivers in Missouri, Arkansas, and Oklahoma, and we believe 10 of these populations are continuing to decline. Accordingly, on August 13, we proposed to list the scaleshell as endangered.

Threats to the scaleshell, as with many other mussels species, include degraded water quality due to pollution and sedimentation; alteration of habitat through the damming, dredging, or channelizing of waterways; and competition with non-native species like the zebra mussel *(Dreissena polymorpha)*. Because the range of the scaleshell overlaps those of several other endangered or threatened mussel species, we do not expect that a decision to list the scaleshell would have any significant additional impacts on river use.

Critical Habitat On August 3, we proposed to designate Critical Habitat in parts of Orange and San Diego counties, California, for the tidewater goby *(Eucyclogobius newberryi)*, a small endangered fish. Such a designation requires Federal agencies to ensure that any actions they fund, authorize, or carry out are not likely to adversely modify the Critical Habitat. Descriptions and maps of the proposed Critical Habitat areas were published as part of the proposal.

Final Rules

Ten Hawaiian Plants The following plant taxa native to the Maui Nui group of Hawaiian islands (Maui, Moloka'i, Lana'i, and Kaho'olawe) were listed on September 3 as endangered:

- *Clermontia samuelii* or (in Hawaiian) 'oha wai, a shrub in the bellflower family (Campanulaceae);
- *Cyanea copelandii* ssp. *haleakalaensis* or haha, a vine-like shrub in the bellflower family;
- *Cyanea glabra* or haha, a branched shrub;
- *Cyanea hamatiflora* ssp. *hamatiflora* or haha, a palm-like tree;
- *Dubautia plantaginea* ssp. *humilis*, or na niu e, a dwarfed shrub in the sunflower family (Asteraceae);
- *Hedyotis schlechtendahliana* var. *remyi* or kopa, a subshrub in the coffee family (Rubiaceae);
- *Kanaloa kahoolawensis*, a densely branched shrub in the legume family (Fabaceae);
- *Labordia tinifolia* var. *lanaiensis* or kamakahala, an erect shrub or small tree in the logan family (Loganiaceae);
- *Labordia triflora* or kamakahala, a climbing plant; and
- *Melicope munroi* or alani, a sprawling shrub in the citrus family (Rutaceae).

These figures illustrate the imposition of an eight-page layout, with folding dummies, and examples of the front and back of an eight-page signature. The blue and red lines represent folding and trimming lines.

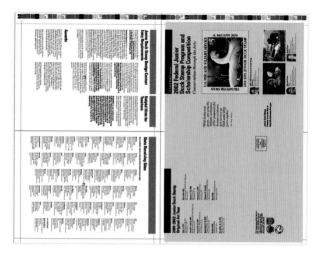

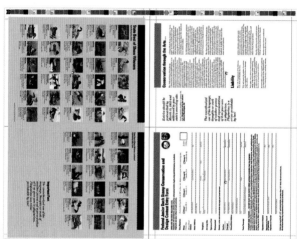

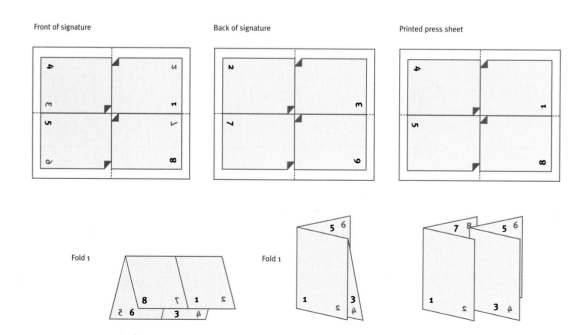

Front of signature

Back of signature

Printed press sheet

Fold 1

Fold 1

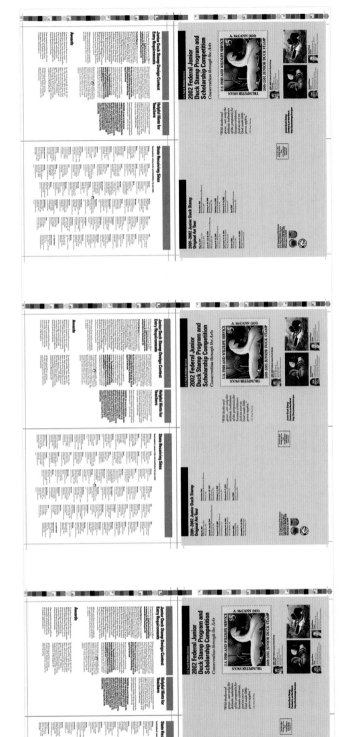

The same brochure is illustrated here being printed on a continuous roll of paper on a web press. Large press runs justify the costs of setting up and running this high-speed printing equipment.

An imposition-folding dummy shows exactly how this sixteen-page signature will be laid out on press. You can use it to evaluate the positioning of design elements before sending the project to the printer.

Front of signature

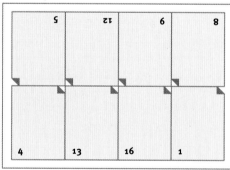

Back of signature

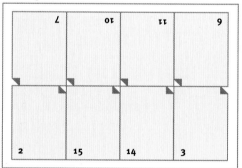

Printed press sheet

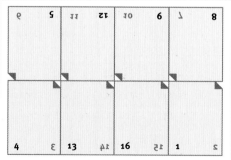

First fold

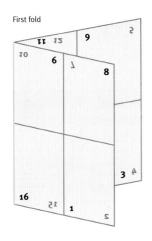

Second fold

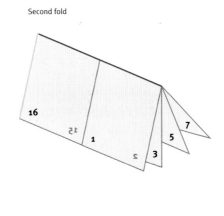

Third fold

.... Fold 1
———— Fold 2
.... Fold 3

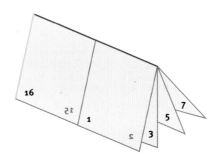

The Sheet Size on Press

PRESS SHEET SIZES AND LAYOUTS can affect the operator's ability to make press adjustments. Control panels allow operators to make incremental ink-flow adjustments about 1 inch apart. These adjustments control ink density from the sheet's leading edge to its trailing edge as it passes through the press. This can be a significant factor in layout, especially when critical color images are positioned one behind the other. Tweaking color densities to improve one image can have detrimental effects on the image that follows it on the sheet.

These figures illustrate the direction of ink adjustments on the press. All adjustments affect the sheet from the leading edge toward the trailing edge, as the arrows show.

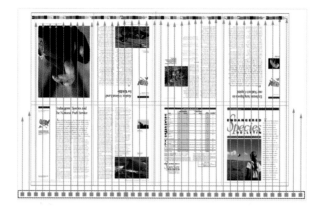

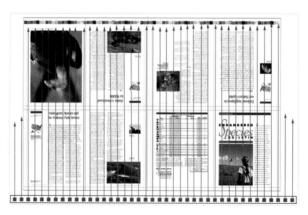

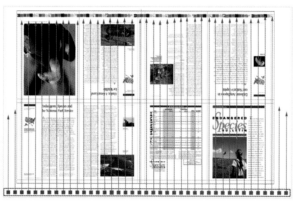

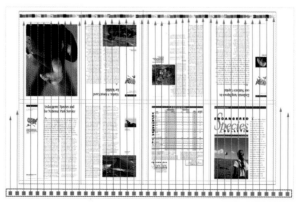

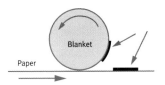

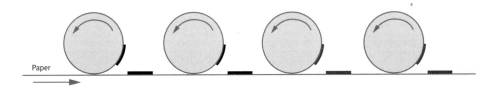

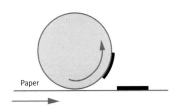

Offset presses, whether sheetfed or web, have the same ink flow characteristics from the lead to trailing edge of the plate. This figure shows a cutaway view of paper traveling through a sheetfed printer.

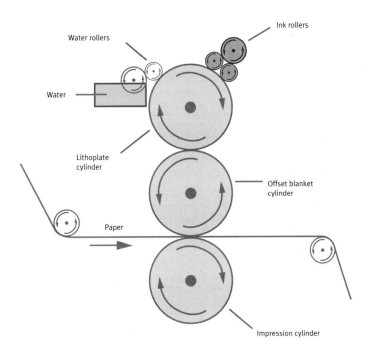

A similar view of the web process shows paper traveling from a continuous roll of paper.

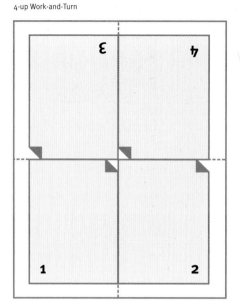
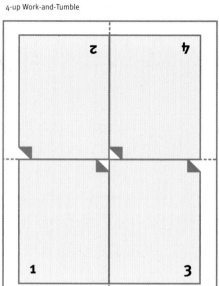

Work and turns are staples of the printing process. Work and tumbles, though less common, are also effective for jobs that don't require precise image placement. In both cases, you print both sides of a press sheet with the same set of plates. In a work and turn, the gripper edge is the same in both passes, enabling precise placement. In a work and tumble, the gripper edge on the first pass becomes the trailing edge on the second.

Work and Turns

ONE OF THE COMMONLY MISUNDER-STOOD concepts in print production work is the *work and turn*. A work and turn job is laid out so that both sides of a job can be printed with one set of plates. The front side of the job is imaged on one half of the plate, with the back side imaged on the other. You can run sheets through the press, and then turn them over and run them again with the same plates, with the images backing up in perfect imposition. An eight-page signature for an 8 ½ x 11-inch publication can be run as a sixteen-page work and turn on a 40-inch press. For very long runs, an 8 ½ x 11-inch brochure can be printed on a 40-inch press as a work and turn, yielding sixteen finished pieces per *sheet*—with one set of plates. Printers who use work and turns effectively can save a great deal of setup and press time, and a lot of money.

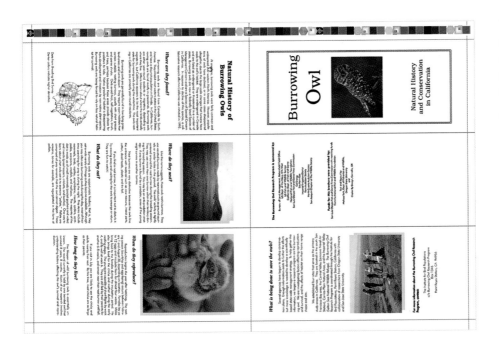

This brochure can be printed effectively as a work and turn on a 12 ½ x 19-inch press sheet.

In this configuration of a work and turn, you're getting twice the value. This is a good option for longer runs and requires only a single set of plates.

Excellent color reproduction typically requires high-quality inks, premium-coated papers, and well-adjusted presses. Printing companies that offer these combinations may not offer the lowest prices, but they will give you the highest quality for your dollar.

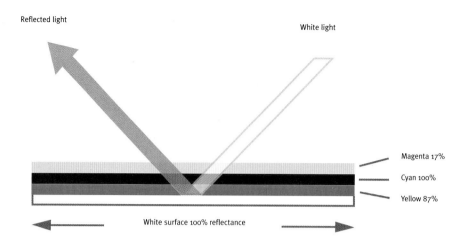

Reflected light

White light

Magenta 17%

Cyan 100%

Yellow 87%

White surface 100% reflectance

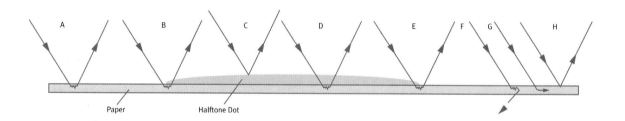

Paper

Halftone Dot

A,B,D,E: diffuse reflection

F: transmission

B,E: Yule-Nielsen effect

C,H: direct reflection

G: absorption by the paper

Light is reflected from—and absorbed by—proofs and printed sheets in a variety of ways. This illustration provides a simplified view of how light sources interact with images as they reflect back to your eyes. The pigments and substrates used in proofs are not identical to those used in offset printing, and minor variations are inevitable.

Press Register

MECHANICAL REGISTRATION ON PRESS refers to the precise positioning of the sheet's *lead edge* and *guide side*, which function as reference points to ensure that images print in exactly the same position on every sheet. This is sometimes overlooked on modern multicolor presses because all colors are printed in a single pass. The colors will be in register with each other, but the composite images may bounce around, resulting in slight variations in their position on each sheet. This can play havoc with the bindery process, because folding machines rely on consistent image placement from sheet to sheet to make multiple folds accurately.

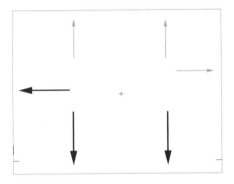 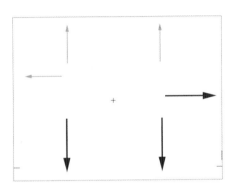

These figures illustrate a press sheet's lead edge and guide side, which provide reference points for precise positioning of images. The gray arrows point to the *wild* sides of the sheet opposite the lead edge and guide side. Minor variations in sheet sizes are inevitable, but as long as the lead edge and guide sides are registering, the wild sides won't influence the final trimming and binding processes.

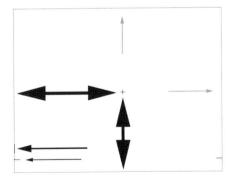

The two double-ended red arrows show the relationship of the lead edge and guide side. The next smaller arrow points to the *side guide* mark on the sheet's edge. The smallest red arrow points to the lead edge register marks. The gray arrows indicate the wild sides.

These figures illustrate the registration check of several successive sheets pulled as the press is running. Fanned out on the press table, they show the registration of the front and back sides of the job. Good press register shows the side guide mark in position on the edge of each sheet, and the lead edge registration marks form a straight line across the sheet edges.

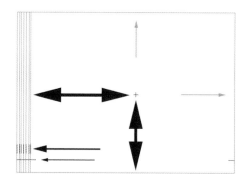 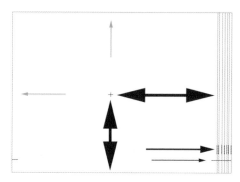

Misregistering guide sides will cause the side guide marks to move into, or completely off of the sheet edge. Again, the result is that the image moves out of position in relationship to the sheet's edge. This can be a common cause of trimming and binding problems that may go unnoticed by the print buyer.

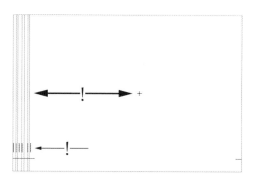 

It's a Colorful World

DESIGNERS WILL GIVE YOU A PORT-FOLIO full of reasons why they chose their profession. Whether those reasons are creative, technical, or financial pales in comparison to the ultimate reason—freedom. The design world, whether it's in print or cyberspace, is a vast and complex place where eccentricities and creative liberties allow individuals to flourish personally and professionally. As long as there's color in the world, there will always be designers, artists, and printers who combine their talents to bring those brilliant colors to life.

SUMMARY

COLOR REPRODUCTION IS A HIGHLY technical process that is subject to more variables than any other production industry. Virtually every print project is customized by designers as a unique product, and good understanding of the techniques and variables involved in the process can be used to your best advantage. Excellent quality in this industry is a moving target, and printers who provide consistent results make ongoing investments in maintaining high standards. Always remember that low bid prices may come at a high cost in quality.

Understanding press configurations and layouts can help you refine your designs and can ensure that you get the best possible value for your printing budget. This is the kind of knowledge that will provide you with consistent and beautifully reproduced designs, job after job.

9

DIGITAL PRINTERS

Some years ago, I was asked by a research firm to save every piece of direct mail that I received for one month. They asked me to sort it into three categories: pieces that I opened and acted upon; pieces that I opened but ultimately discarded; and pieces that I didn't even bother to open. They gave me three accordion folders in which to file my mail and told me I could get more folders as needed.

Within a week, I called to ask for another Category 3 folder for mail that I never opened. A week after that, I needed another folder for Category 3, and then another. By the end of the month, I had filled four Category 3 folders. I had put two pieces of mail into my Category 2 folder (looked at but did not buy); and nothing into my Category 1 folder (the category that should have been going, "Ding! Ding! Ding! You have hit the jackpot, Mr. Retailer. I am buying your product").

I carted all the mail down to the Post Office to be sent to the research firm. It weighed 40 pounds. All 40 of those pounds were destined for the Dumpster.

Some would see this as a problem. Savvy printers saw it as a solution. In the last two decades, as large printers began to consolidate into even larger printers, they realized that conventional printing would soon become a commodity rather than a craft. Technical advances were smoothing out the differences in quality that used to set one printer apart from another. Printers worried about how they could attract and keep print buyers in a market where customers perceived that all the printers provided about the same level of quality for roughly the same price. The one thing the printers wanted to avoid was a price war, but what else could they do?

While this trend was developing, another equally powerful trend was shaking corporate America. Customers were demanding to be treated like real people. They were spurred on by urban legends about a retail department store based in Seattle where clerks went out of their way to satisfy customers. Consumers who had been putting up with vendors treating them like no-tip diners in a New York eatery began expecting customized service. They wanted products that were tailored just to them.

A few innovative printers thought they could tie into consumers' desire for individuality and began offering a service they called selective binding. It combined a crude ink-jet printer that could be interfaced with a computer containing a database of names and addresses. As a pre-printed signature ran by the ink-jet station on the bindery, the computer would tell the printer to spew out the subscriber's name and a little message onto a blank space on the page.

The message was usually keyed to an ad that had been printed normally on press. Only the ink-jet-printed name and message changed as each copy of the signature passed by.

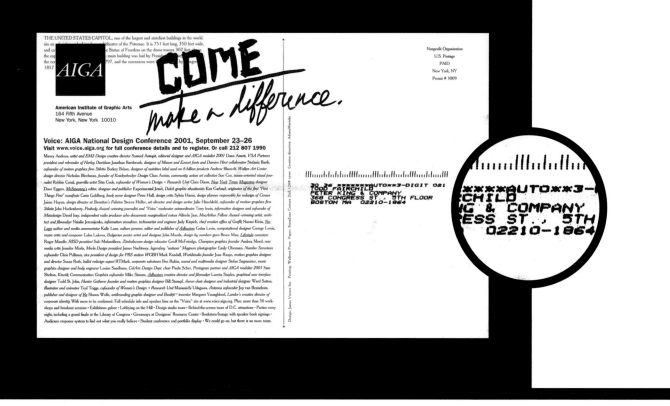

(ABOVE)

Selective binding is a way to marry mass-produced printing (like the above postcard) with individualized messages (such as a mailing address). Although the process combines the speed of conventional printing with the customization of ink-jet technology, the results are visually crude and the amount of customization is limited.

(FACING PAGE)

The fundamental difference between conventional printing and digital printing is the ability to print different images. With conventional printing, you create one plate and print multiple copies, all the same. Different images require new plates. With digital printing, you create one image at a time and print one image at a time. When you want to print another copy, you re-create it all over again and print it again. You can thus alter each new copy any way you want.

The message was sometimes almost comical in the way it tried to appear personal and unique: "Mr. Seidels, we have a great offer for you," said one that came to my house. Never mind the fact that I'm not a mister, nor is my name Seidels.

As the technology improved, however, the system became capable of assembling variable signatures into one book. So Mr. Seidels might get a magazine that included a piece about golf, while my neighbor might get the same magazine but with a piece about kayaking instead of golf.

Selective binding, coupled with ink-jet labeling, did something very important for large-run printers. It transmogrified a mass-production technology into a customized one. High-speed presses work best when they produce vast quantities of the same piece. Selective binding takes all those look-alike signatures and transforms them into personalized messages. So now, instead of getting direct-mail pieces that have nothing to do with your life, you can get offers on items that you might actually want.

Unfortunately, there's a worm in the apple of selective binding. In many ways, it's still a technology of mass production. Printers still have to print thousands of copies at once. Those copies must be either mass-distributed or inventoried. The system cannot truly produce an individualized piece, only a somewhat-customized one.

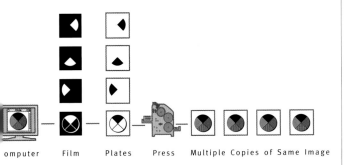

omputer   Film   Plates   Press   Multiple Copies of Same Image

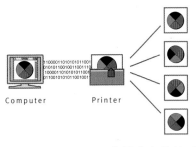

Computer   Printer

Multiple Individualized Copies

Digital printing has changed all that. For the first time in history, we have technology that can produce one-of-a-kind designs at commercially acceptable speeds.

Digital printing is fundamentally different from conventional printing. With conventional printing, the technology images one plate at a time. This plate is then used to produce many copies of the same design. By contrast, digital printers image one design at a time. This process is called variable-data printing.

Variable-data printing is the most powerful contribution that an all-digital process can make to your clients. With variable-data printing, you can individualize every single message that you print.

As each page goes through the printing process, a computer tells the printer how to output a given set of bits. Neither the computer nor the printing device cares what the bits look like. They could be the same bits for every copy, or they could be completely different bits for each copy.

Furthermore, because no physical image of the design exists until after each page is output, there is no make-ready needed. In a certain sense, the makeready happens each time the computer outputs a copy, as it tells the output device where to print each separate pixel. With all-digital printing, there are no plates to hang, no colors to balance, no ink fountains to twiddle.

The one-of-a-kind capability of digital printing gives it two powerful advantages:

Customization: You can print press runs that are completely customized to each recipient. The only limitations are the nature and quality of your database, and the slower speed of digital presses.

Short-run Color: You can print extremely short-run full-color jobs at a reasonable price, when you need them. By short-run I mean as few as one copy.

These custom invitations were mailed to people attending seminars on different days. Each recipient received an invitation appropriate to his or her schedule. With conventional printing, the four-color invitations would all be printed at once, and the black-and-white dateline imprinted separately later. With digital printing, each invitation could be printed completely finished, as needed. Last-minute schedule variations could be accommodated on demand.

Customization

One florist in southern California asks his new customers to fill out a short questionnaire when they first buy flowers. On the form are questions such as the name and birth date of a significant other. Sometimes people object to the intrusion, but the florist quickly explains.

"If you'd rather not fill out the form, that's fine," he says. "But if you've ever had trouble remembering your partner's birthday, your anniversary, or any other holiday, then we can help. We keep all this information on a computer that automatically generates a reminder card for all the holidays in your life. Or, if you prefer, you can just place a standing order. We'll take care of sending out flowers on the proper day, and we'll even include a card!"

When people perceive that the florist is really going to make their lives easier (no more last-minute rushes out the door because you "left your briefcase in the car, hah, hah"), they are thrilled to contribute to his vast database.

The florist combines his data management with on-demand printing to generate postcards, letters, special offers, and flyers, all customized to each consumer's needs. When a holiday rolls around, he prints out one-of-a-kind offers that he simply drops in the mail. None of his clients think of his designs as junk mail—they've come to look at these reminders as a kind of free service that saves them time and trouble. The florist even keeps track of clients' kids' ages, so he can send out reminders for *quinceaños* celebrations, confirmations, proms, and graduations.

Friday, May 25, 2001 — Santa Monica, California

Monday, May 28, 2001 — Chicago, Illinois

Wednesday, May 30, 2001 — New York, New York,

Short-Run Color

Five thousand physicists from the American Physical Society gathered in Seattle recently to view their colleagues' latest, most cutting-edge research. Only a few physicists among the thousands attending had won the right to present their research. Knowing how great this opportunity was—and how critical his colleagues could be—one local physicist decided that he would make a large-format color poster with graphics, instead of the usual bulletin board pinned with pages and pages of boring data. "Even physicists like to look at pictures," he said.

So he worked all week on the project, combining many different software programs, including Adobe Photoshop and PageMaker, a text language called TeX, and Microsoft PowerPoint. He took GIFs off his Web site and ran them through Adobe Acrobat to create PDF files. He captured text from previously published articles and imported it into his new file. He looked for stock photos from a CD to provide a colorful background.

Naturally, he wanted to keep working up to the last minute because he was a physicist, and physicists can always keep improving things just a little bit more. He knew that the large-format ink-jet digital press could output only 1.25 feet (46 cm) every 15 minutes. His poster was going to be 5 feet long, so he needed an hour to print it.

(ABOVE)

This super-sized poster (5 feet by 3 feet/1.5 meter by 1 meter) was printed on a digital ink-jet printer literally seconds before its physicist-designer made his presentation. It depicts a nano-scale imaging device capable of "seeing" the biological molecules held by the physicist's graduate students. No other technology could have produced this color poster in the time needed.

One hour and five minutes before he had to go to the conference, he was ready to print his poster, a 5-foot by 3-foot (1.5-meter by 1-meter) monster that would blow off his colleagues' rumpled socks.

The print operator was waiting, all the equipment primed and ready to go. He loaded up the professor's files, which crashed upon attempting to print the poster. All those different software programs had created an incompatibility. The machine couldn't RIP (raster image process) them all. The printer typed new commands into the computer. Crash. The printer and the professor split up. Each took over a terminal to try different strategies to overcome the RIPing problems.

Now the printing process became not only a race against time for the physicist and the printer, but also a race against each other's expertise. The printer tried one trick, the physicist another. Their fingers flew over their respective keyboards.

"Got it," said the printer, and paper started scrolling through the ink-jet device.

One hour later, the physicist flew out the door and managed to tack up his poster a full 30 seconds before his session began. No problem.

Both the florist and the physicist succeeded because digital printing gave them the power to print a design completely suited to their individual needs. No other form of printing can do that better, because no other form of printing is as flexible and as fast.

Part of the flexibility of digital printing comes from the fact that there are many different output devices on the market. The florist used laser printing to output his cards and brochures. The physicist used ink-jet printing to produce his poster. Both devices are controlled by a computer that outputs pixels, one page at a time. But the output technology differs widely, both in terms of mechanics and capabilities. To make digital printing work for you, you need to know what some of these differences are, and how they might apply to your particular designs. Here is a rundown of the most common devices on the market today and what they can do for you:

Digital Direct-to-Plate: Conventional Printing with a Digital Twist

Even conventional printing companies recognize the value of digital printers that can output any given set of pixels individually. Many have purchased digital platemaking systems that do essentially the same thing as your desktop laser printer: output one copy at a time, based on digitized prepress data input via computer. The only difference is, instead of outputting individual paper copies, these systems output individual printing plates.

The basic idea of digital direct-to-plate is that you give your file to the printer, ready for printing right away. The printer then RIPs your file directly to the printing plates, with no intermediate film steps. Typically the plates are

prepared by a laser ablation process, in which a digitally controlled laser burns away a top silicone layer that repels ink, to reveal an underlying layer that accepts ink.

Once the plates are made, they are then hung or mounted onto conventional offset, flexographic, or gravure presses that mass-produce thousands of paper copies made by the plates. The whole process from starting file to printed page can be as short as 10 minutes, sufficiently fast considering that proofing must be done digitally, on the printer's monitor, immediately before burning the plate.

It is important, therefore, that the color profile of your monitor matches the profile of your printer's monitor, and that the printer's monitor must be well-matched to the ink-and-paper

output. To avoid unpleasant color balance surprises, you need to talk to your vendor about calibrating monitor profiles before the final 10 minutes of production.

Digital direct-to-plate printing is the only option that offers you the full quality and speed of offset or gravure printing. This is because digital direct-to-plate is true offset or gravure printing. The only thing digital about it is the method by which the lithographic plates are produced. Thus, while conventional printing has incorporated some aspects of the digitized world, it remains at heart an assembly-line process whose main goal is to produce as many look-alike copies of a design as it can for the lowest possible price.

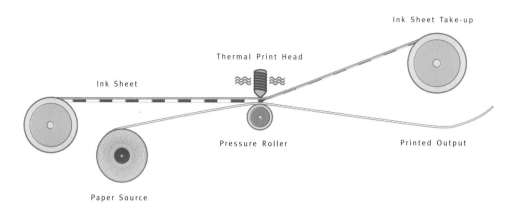

Ink Sheet Take-up

Thermal Print Head

Ink Sheet

Pressure Roller

Printed Output

Paper Source

Thermal-wax printing devices were one of the earliest digital printers. Controlled by computer commands, heated pins—or thermal print heads—melted waxes from colored ribbons onto paper.

Scan-Head Printing: Ink-Jet and Dye-Sublimation

If you have a print job that either is short-run or variable-data, digital direct-to-plate is usually not an option. Or perhaps you want to print your piece onto fabric, vinyl, or some other medium that a lithographic press will not accommodate. In this case, you should seriously consider using one of the two kinds of modern scan-head printers: ink-jet and dye-sublimation.

The ancestor of scan-head print technologies is the dot-matrix printer. This machine was hooked up to a computer and used a series of pins mounted in a printing head. As the printing head slid across a piece of paper, the computer would tell the printing head to strike with its pins in certain patterns.

The pins would strike against an ink ribbon and transfer dots to the paper, creating letter shapes. The resulting letters were crude—no fine serifs here, nor any halftones or line art. But the dot-matrix printer was capable of true digital output. As such, it made the boom in desktop systems possible.

Driven by market forces, the basic idea of scanning a print-head over paper has rapidly evolved in stages from dot-matrix printing to thermal-wax printing (heated pins melting waxy dyes) to the two scan-head technologies that dominate digital printing today: ink-jet and dye-sublimation printing.

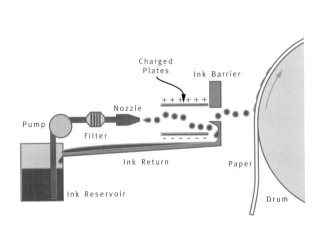

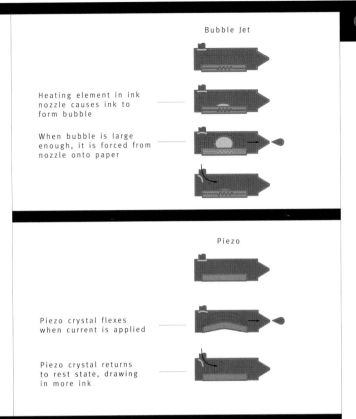

Bubble Jet

Heating element in ink
nozzle causes ink to
form bubble

When bubble is large
enough, it is forced from
nozzle onto paper

Piezo

Piezo crystal flexes
when current is applied

Piezo crystal returns
to rest state, drawing
in more ink

INK-JET TECHNOLOGY

With ink-jet printing, the clumsy mechanical impact of dot-matrix devices has been eliminated in favor of electronically controlled jets of ink, which squirt out of nozzles onto paper. There are many different ways that ink-jet companies have invented to squirt out the ink.

For example, the ink streams can be squirted in discrete pulses by various mechanical means (like a water pistol), or the ink can be pushed out by micro-bursts of steam (called "bubble-jet" printing). Alternatively, a continuous stream of drops can be electronically steered onto paper, or steered away from the paper and into a recycling reservoir.

Early ink-jet printers fell far short of the quality of offset-press printing. But in recent years, the technology has improved rapidly, to the point that resolutions equivalent to 1,400 dots per inch (dpi) are attainable by top-of-the-line machines, along with printing speeds of up to 500 feet (152 meters) per minute. However, no ink-jet press presently offers both highest quality and fastest speed; there is always a tradeoff between the two. This is where you need to consult with your vendor—you may have to shop around to find a vendor with the latest and greatest technology.

(ABOVE)

There are many ink-jet technologies on the market. All of them work by forcing droplets of ink onto a substrate (the surface on which printing is done), but they do it in different ways. In one system (above left), charged plates direct liquid ink onto the substrate, which is mounted on a drum. Excess ink not directed onto the substrate falls into a return system and flows back to a reservoir, to be used again. A bubble-jet system (above right, top) uses a heat source to make the ink form a bubble, which is then forced out of the nozzle onto the substrate. A piezo system (above right, bottom) uses electric current to flex a crystal and force ink out.

Color posters like this one are a perfect job for digital printers, including ink-jet and commercial web or sheetfed presses. Such printers can output high-quality color for one-of-a-kind jobs on large-format paper.

The quality of ink and paper is always a major concern with ink-jet printing. Persuading the tiny dots of ink to adhere to paper is not easy, and your vendor may not be able to combine the paper you prefer with the kind of ink you want. Printers are constrained to use inks and papers that are compatible with the ink-jet process.

Furthermore, many ink-jet inks are neither water-proof nor colorfast. Even under indoor fluorescent lights, some inks fade notably within a few months. Put outdoors under strong sunlight, they fade even faster. So if keeping a print colorfast for the long term is important to you, don't just get assurances from your ink-jet printer—get a guarantee.

Ink-jet printing is ideally suited to jobs like poster-making, for several reasons. Modern ink-jet printers can easily print widths of 5 feet (1.5 meters) or even more—it is just a matter of providing longer rails for the ink-jet head to slide upon. And posters are usually short run, so the typically slow speed of ink-jet printing is not a big liability. Finally, the vibrant colors available with modern ink-jet printers look great on posters.

DYE-SUBLIMINATION TECHNOLOGY

Besides ink-jet, the other main scan-head printing type is dye-sublimation. Dye-sublimation technology grew out of thermal-wax printing, in which dots of waxy dye were heated to melting temperature and fused with paper or plastic. Thermal-wax printing was limited in that the resulting printed pieces had a waxy feel combined with appreciable build-up of the dye.

To solve these problems, thermal wax manufacturers raised the operating temperature higher and higher, and developed more and more sophisticated dyes, to the point that the dyes began to be transferred by sublimation rather than by melting.

Sublimation is a technical term that means "the direct transformation from a solid to a gas, with no intervening liquid state." In a modern dye-sublimation printer, a scanning head heats special dyes embedded in a ribbon, which is interposed between the scan head and the paper. As the temperature passes 270 degrees Fahrenheit/ 132 degrees Celsius (which is well above the boiling point of water), the dye vaporizes and transfers to the paper or fabric. There is no intervening liquid state.

(BELOW)

Dye-sublimation printers apply high levels of heat to a roll of transfer dyes. The heat is so great that it forces the solid ink to turn into a gas, which is then bonded to the paper or fabric substrate.

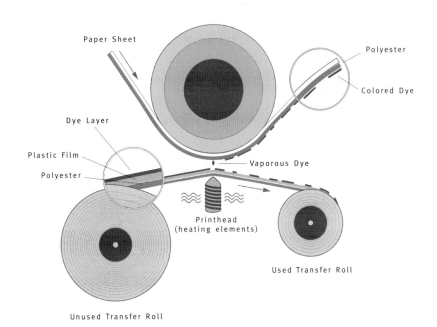

Paper Sheet

Polyester

Colored Dye

Dye Layer

Plastic Film

Polyester

Vaporous Dye

Printhead
(heating elements)

Used Transfer Roll

Unused Transfer Roll

Dye-sublimation printers are especially effective for printing on fabric because the high temperature of the process bonds the dyes directly into the fabric fibers. Because the process is digital, the registration problems inherent in conventional screen printing are nonexistent. The result is high-quality color art that is detailed and color-saturated.

If the paper or fabric contains polyester fibers, and the temperature is hot enough to soften the fibers (350 degrees Fahrenheit/176 degrees Celsius or more), then the dye-fiber bond is completely permanent and cannot be removed by washing or by any ordinary amount of heat. Other advantages are that there is no appreciable mechanical buildup of dye, and the dye colors achieve extraordinary brilliance through their bonding to the transparent fibers.

Dye-sublimation printing has one other big advantage: it is the only kind of commercial printing which can achieve truly continuous tones without resorting to halftone screens. This is accomplished by simply varying the heat applied to each element of the piece; more heat creates a more intense local color. Thus, a top-quality dye-sub print can show the same continuous color intensity as a Kodachrome 35mm slide. Not surprisingly, high-quality photo prints are one of the main uses of dye-sublimation printing.

These advantages of dye-sublimation prints did not escape the notice of ink-jet printer manufacturers. They swiftly realized that ordinary ink-jet printers could be loaded with sublimating dyes. Such dyes could be

printed onto special heat-resistant paper; the resulting paper could then be used to heat-transfer the dyes onto materials such as polyester fabrics.

Building on this idea, they found that consumer items such as coffee mugs can also be coated with a thin layer of polyester robust enough to survive repeated wash cycles. Thus, nowadays there is growing overlap between the use of ink-jet and dye-sublimation technologies.

The main limitation of ink-jet and dye-sublimation technologies is the inherently slow speed of the scan-head. Companies are continuously engineering their way around this obstacle by building larger and larger arrays of ink-jets, combined with faster and faster steering of the jets of inks. Because ink-jet and dye-sublimation technologies are evolving so rapidly, you need to check with your vendors to see how nearly they can meet your needs for speed, resolution, paper quality, color-fastness, and water fastness.

(ABOVE)
Thermal-wax printers apply ink by using heated pins to melt a waxy dye onto paper.

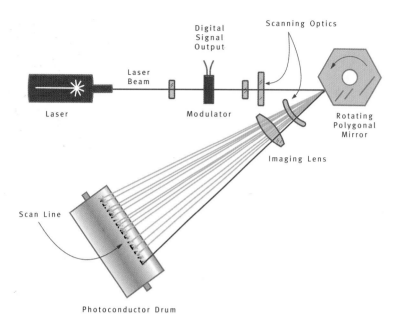

Laser

Laser Beam

Digital Signal Output

Modulator

Scanning Optics

Rotating Polygonal Mirror

Imaging Lens

Scan Line

Photoconductor Drum

Xerography and laser-printing systems work with essentially the same technology: A plate or drum is statically charged, and light shines where ink is to be repelled. Toner particles are then attracted to the charged areas of the plate or drum. These particles are transferred to paper and fused onto the paper surface with heat. Xerography printed its images by projecting an original image onto the drum. Laser printers accomplish the same thing by synthesizing the image digitally.

Xerographic Processes: Laser Printers, Digital Web Presses, Digital Sheetfed Presses

Let's suppose you have a job that truly requires variable-data printing, thus eliminating digital direct-to-plate. Furthermore, it requires more speed or a different ink-paper combination than your local ink-jet vendors can supply. Now it is time to consider xerographic processes.

The idea behind xerography grew out of the oldest idea in printing: Put the ink on a plate, press the paper onto the inked plate. Conventional non-digital printer technologies put the ink variously into hollowed-out areas (gravure or intaglio printing), relief areas (letterpress printing), or greasy areas (lithographic printing).

The trouble is, none of the above methods are suitable for variable-data printing because none of them allow the printing plates to be swiftly erased and re-created. What was needed was a printing plate that could be erased and re-created an indefinite number of times.

Out of this need grew the concept of xerography, which is at heart nothing more than the familiar method of lithographic printing—but with an erasable charge of static electricity instead of grease serving to stick ink to the plate.

The process was invented in 1938 by Chester Carlson and remains basically unaltered to the present day. A specially made drum or plate is sprayed with a uniform electric charge. This can be accomplished in a fraction of a second. Then light is shined upon

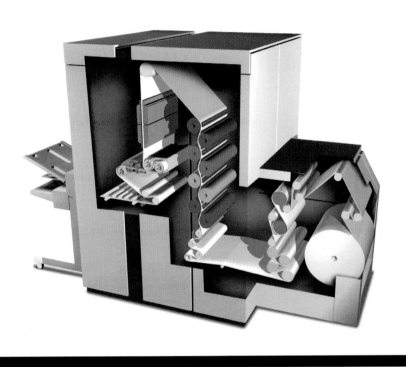

areas of the plate where ink is not desired. This eliminates the charge in all the areas upon which the light shines. Finally, the drum is coated with a "toner" consisting of tiny particles of dye. The toner particles stick only to the parts of the drum that are still statically charged. The drum now holds an image consisting of toner particles; they are transferred to paper and fused there, typically by heat. During the 1950s, the Xerox Corporation's pioneer xerographic machines carried through this process with no digital assistance: An image of a page to be duplicated was projected directly upon a rotating drum, and the resulting copies were produced without alteration. Then, during the 1980s,

Apple Computer produced the LaserWriter, which revolutionized digital printing. The LaserWriter was a consumer-priced xerographic printer in which the electrically charged image was synthesized digitally. Suddenly, any image that could be stored in a computer could be directly transferred to a printed page.

The original LaserWriter had its limitations. It printed only in black-and-white; it achieved a resolution of only 300 dots per inch; and it was not very fast—it could print, at the very most, less than ten pages per minute. In contrast, modern xerographic printers, like those produced by Xeikon and Indigo, can achieve 1,200 dpi or more of resolution, at print speeds of up to 240 feet (73 meters) per minute, using up to seven simultaneous process colors.

A Xeikon printer applies toner using electro-magnets to charge drums that can then transfer the toner to paper. Xeikon printers can print multiple colors on web paper at speeds that approach conventional sheetfed printing. Unlike conventional printing, however, Xeikons can print unique versions of any design.

Because the Xeikon printer uses web paper, it can print large-format designs such as posters. The size is limited by the width of paper, not the length.

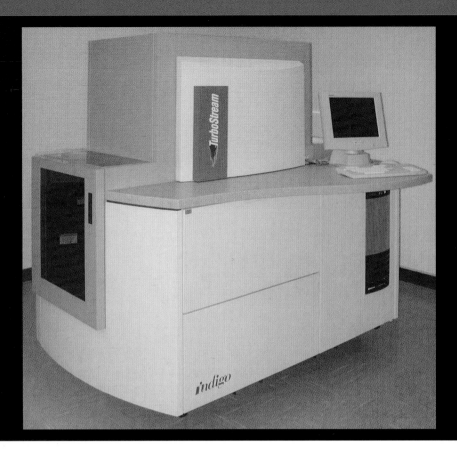

Today's top-end Xeikon and Indigo printers exemplify the two main options in high-end xerographic printing, dry toners (Xeikon) and wet toners (Indigo). The relative merits of the two kinds of toner are vigorously debated, and all the xerographic print technology companies are continuously updating their product lines.

The different companies also employ different strategies for feeding paper through their machines. Some use continuous-roll web paper. So while the width of the printed piece is limited by the width of the machine itself, the length can be almost anything. Other companies use only sheetfed paper, which limits the cutoff size of the final printed piece but also allows for a wider choice of papers.

Xeikon and Indigo occupy a very dynamic niche within the printing industry. At the low end, their digital presses must compete with desktop ink-jet and laser printers, which keep getting faster and can deliver better and better quality. Digital presses are also being squeezed by so-called "enterprise printing" systems. These are basically in-house corporate publishing machines manufactured by business-oriented companies like IBM and Xerox. Originally these enterprise printers were capable of making only xerographic copies. Recently, however, new models can either make copies or print out designs directly from a desktop computer.

At the high end, digital presses must compete with traditional high-volume lithographic print processes. These presses keep getting more efficient with their makeready, so that they become cost-effective at lower and lower quantities of press run. As a result, every year we can expect to see new xerographic print engines of ever-higher quality, color range, and speed.

In day-to-day production, however, only a small fraction of all jobs are printed on state-of-the-art machines. More commonly, your vendors will print your job on machines that they have had for several years and with which they are intimately familiar. It is important to appreciate your vendor's expertise and the stability of his hardware and software. That combination can be far more valuable to you than access to this year's state-of-the-art hardware.

(FACING PAGE)

This Indigo TurboStream digital printer is a commercial sheet-fed printer that can print six colors (CMYK plus two spot colors) at one pass, at a rate of 2,000 pages per hour. It can completely customize each copy it makes, and it can also print a single full-color copy of a design for an economical price.

(ABOVE)

Digital commercial printers such as Xeikon and Indigo can print short-run, multiple-page, full-color brochures economically because they can treat each signature of the brochure as a customized copy. After the printer prints a page, it erases the image on its printing drum and creates a new one. So each page it prints can be the same as the one before, or completely different.

WHAT TO DO?

If you have a short-run or variable-data job that must approach the quality of traditional offset printing, ask to see similar jobs which have been printed by a prospective vendor. Look for designs that are printed on similar paper, with similar inks and in similar quantities. Pay attention also to the color range of the jobs in the printer's portfolio. In a sense, picking out a printer is like selecting a surgeon: You want the guy who has performed thousands of similar operations, not the one who's doing it for the first time.

Once you find a technology and a printer that produce designs similar to yours, you should use the same software and color-matching scheme that the successful jobs used. Particularly if digital printing is a new experience for you, you can't go wrong sticking as closely as possible to a vendor/software/print technology package that has been proven to work well for jobs similar to yours.

For short-run jobs, most printers do not expect you to sign a formal contract. Instead they run the jobs with a simple purchase order-type arrangement. For complicated or long-run jobs, you might want to solicit bids from competing printers. The bidding spec sheet can then serve as the basis for a formal contract. Whether you use a P.O. or a contract, however, the printer needs to know some basic data:

- NAME OF JOB

- CONTACT NAME AND ADDRESS

- DESCRIPTION OF JOB

- QUANTITY

- TRIM SIZE

- BLEED SIZE *(if any)*

- TOTAL PAGE COUNT

- PRINTED ONE SIDE OR TWO

- BINDING METHOD *(if multiple pages)*

- FOLDING *(if necessary)*

- PAPER STOCK

- INK

- FURNISHED MATERIALS *(including all software programs used to assemble the prepress)*

- PROOFS NEEDED, OR FURNISHED?

- VARIABLE DATA REQUIREMENTS

- VARIABLE DATA SOFTWARE PROGRAM(S) USED

- DELIVERY METHOD

- DELIVERY DATE

In this era of digital production, the item "furnished materials" can be complex. Submit a list of the applications you used to create your design, organized around a toolbox idea (for more information on such applications, see the chapter on workflow). Such a list might consist of the following:

- TYPE
  Fonts used (include all font software)

- LAYOUT APPLICATIONS
  (usually Adobe Pagemaker or QuarkXPpress)

- OBJECT-ORIENTED GRAPHICS APPLICATIONS *(such as Adobe Illustrator)*

- BITMAP GRAPHICS APPLICATIONS *(such as Adobe Photoshop)*

- COMPRESSION APPLICATIONS: *JPEG, TIFF, GIF, etc. (also note links between your low-resolution "for position only" artwork and your high-resolution final versions)*

- TRAPPING APPLICATIONS *(such as Adobe Acrobat InProduction)*

- IMPOSITION APPLICATIONS, IF ANY *(note whether you use a simple book-it function in a layout application, or whether you've used a separate plug-in)*

- SEPARATION AND OUTPUT APPLICATIONS *(note how you convert RGB to CMYK or spot color)*

- PDF APPLICATIONS USED TO COMPRESS THE FINAL OUTPUT OR MAKE IT PLATFORM-INDEPENDENT *(software might be Adobe Acrobat or a third-party PDF-creation utility)*

- PREFLIGHT APPLICATIONS *(note the software you used; at least in that application, everything embedded in your design should RIP)*

- WORKFLOW AUTOMATION APPLICATIONS *(some applications can automate corrections found in preflights; note if and when you employ these)*

design company COMMUNICATION DESIGN

REQUEST FOR QUOTE

DIGITAL PRINTING

PAGE 1 ___ OF ___

DATE:	ESTIMATE DUE:	
FROM:		
PHONE:	FAX:	

JOB NAME:

DESCRIPTION:

SCHEDULE	Files in:		Material arrives:
QUANTITIES	1.	2.	3.
SIZE	Finished Size:	Flat Size:	# of Pages:
STOCK	Cover:		
	Text:		
	Other:		
INK	Side 1 Cover:	☐ Bleeds	Side 1 Text: ☐ Bleeds
	Side 2 Cover:	☐ Bleeds	Side 2 Text: ☐ Bleeds
	Other:		
ARTWORK	☐ Electronic Files	☐ Live Art	☐ FPO Scans ☐ Links to Images
SOFTWARE			
FONTS			
PROOFS	☐ Loose Proofs	☐ Dummy	☐ On Actual Stock ☐ Press Check
VARIABLE DATA	Description:		
	Software:		
FINISHING	☐ Fold	☐ Trim	☐ Perfect Binding ☐ Drill
	☐ Score	☐ Pad:	☐ Plastic Binding ☐ # Holes
	☐ Perforate	☐ Collate	☐ Saddle Stich ☐ Size Holes
SPECIAL			
SHIPPING			
PACKAGING	☐ Shrink Wrap:		☐ Band:
	☐ Carton Pack	☐ Labeling:	
	Samples:		To:
	Other:		

10

COLOR ON THE WEB

The CMYK process reigns
supreme in print media. But on
the World Wide Web, RGB is
king, with colors composed
from combinations of red,
green, and blue.

When red, green, and blue are combined at full intensity, the monitor displays white, as shown in this screen shot. You can verify this on your own monitor with a 10x magnifying glass or loupe.

Seeing Red, Green, and Blue

FOR MOST OF THIS BOOK, we've concentrated on the use of color in print production. But the discussion wouldn't be complete without exploring the options available to designers targeting the World Wide Web.

Designing for the Web requires instinct, luck, and retraining your discerning eye. In the world of CMYK print production, a designer who errantly submits an RGB file will suffer repercussions. By contrast, the Web embraces RGB.

As noted in Chapter 3, the RGB color model is additive. When you combine red, green, and blue at their full intensity, you see white on the monitor. When RGB intensity is zero, you see black. By combining RGB in various percentages, you can generate the 16.7 million colors available on a 24-bit display.

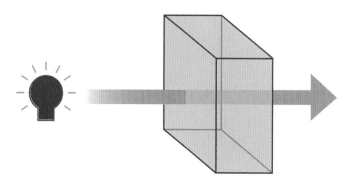

The simplified cutaway view of a computer monitor shows the electron gun firing at full intensity through a single color pixel. The figure on the facing page illustrates a surface printed in CMYK, which depends on the reflection of ambient light.

Specifying Color for the Web

SAVVY WEB DESIGNERS are well versed in RGB, but for novices, it helps to begin from scratch and learn how these colors are created. RGB colors are specified by numeric values between 0 and 255 that determine the intensity of red, green, and blue. Higher numbers equal greater intensity. For example, values of 255 red, 255 green, and 255 blue generate white. Values of 0 red, 0 green, and 0 blue generate black. Values of 0 red, 0 green, and 255 blue generate a pure RGB blue.

In theory, an RGB monitor can show up to 16.7 million colors. But in practice, this number is limited by several factors, most importantly the file format you're using and the maximum *bit depth* of your computer display.

Each pixel you see on a computer screen is described internally as a series of zeroes and ones, the bits—short for binary digits—that represent the fundamental building blocks of all computer data. The number of bits used to describe each pixel determines how many colors the computer can display. For example, in an 8-bit image, each pixel is defined by a combination of eight zeroes or ones. The image is thus limited to 256 colors, because there are only 256 possible combinations of bits: 00000000, 00000001, 00000010, 00000011, and so on, up to 11111111. A 24-bit image uses 24 zeroes or ones to describe each pixel, and can thus display up to 16.7 million (256 x 256 x 256) colors. A 16-bit image can show up to 65,536 (256 x 256) colors.

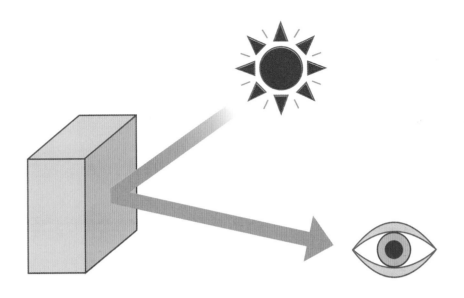

Thus, if you specify color values of 133 red, 96 green, and 168 blue, the computer translates them internally into their binary equivalents: 10000101 for red, 01100000 for green, and 10101000 for blue. The result is a light violet—as long as you have a 24-bit monitor. Although 24-bit displays are increasingly common, many older computer systems are limited to eight or 16 bits (this is actually a limitation of the graphics adapter that drives the display—almost all color monitors are 24-bit capable). If you try to display a 24-bit image on one of these computers, the system uses a technique known as *color reduction* to translate any colors it can't show into their nearest neighbors from the smaller system palette. In many images, especially photos, this color reduction causes banding in areas that should have smooth color gradations.

It's important to keep these points in mind when you're preparing Web graphics, because you generally want your designs to be viewable on the widest possible range of computers.

Additionally, the popular Graphics Interchange Format (GIF)—commonly used to produce stylized type treatments, line art, animated banner ads, and other design elements that require sharp detail—is limited to a maximum of 8 bits, or 256 colors. To reduce the size of these files, experienced Web designers often use software-based color-reduction techniques to further limit the color palette. Leading image-editing programs, such as Adobe Photoshop and Macromedia Fireworks, include features that let you see the effects of GIF color reduction, so you can achieve an optimal balance between image quality and file size. Effectively

making such trade-offs is a major challenge of Web design. For example, it's often wise to apply *antialiasing* when you're creating type treatments that will be saved as GIF files. Antialiasing smoothes jagged edges in type and line art by slightly blurring pixels along the edges, but it also increases the number of colors.

The Joint Photographic Experts Group (JPEG) format, generally used to reproduce photographs and fine art, employs the full 24-bit RGB palette. Here, you reduce file sizes by applying greater or lesser levels of compression. A high degree of compression tends to reduce the image's sharpness, but has little or no effect on the range of colors.

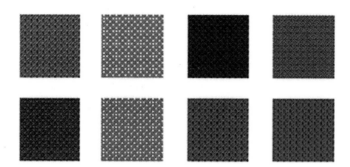

Venturing outside the original Web-safe color palette can create unsightly dithering patterns when images are viewed on 8-bit displays. These blocks illustrate the effect of dithering on different colors.

The Web-Safe Palette

WEB DESIGNERS ARE ACCUSTOMED to working with the 216 colors that comprise the *Web-safe palette*. Colors in this palette can be shown on any Mac or PC monitor, even if it's limited to a maximum of 256 colors. The number of colors is less than 256 due to differences between the Mac and Windows system palettes.

If you specify a color outside the Web-safe palette, it will likely be *dithered* when seen on an 8-bit monitor. Much like a printed halftone, dithering simulates colors that cannot otherwise be displayed by arranging some of the 256 available colors into patterns. Unfortunately, whereas color halftones do a reasonably good job of simulating real-world colors, dithering often produces unsightly arrangements of pixels.

It's important to remember that dithering appears only when you view colors on an 8-bit monitor; almost all computer systems sold these days sport 16- or 24-bit displays. But if you want to ensure that your designs are viewable without dithering on the widest range of computers, you should stick with the 216 Web-safe colors. Many graphics programs include a built-in Web-safe palette as an option. You can either specify Web-safe colors as you're creating a design, or use color-reduction tools to convert existing designs into a Web-safe format.

This palette applies primarily when you're creating GIF files, or specifying color elements within an HTML-authoring program, such as Adobe GoLive or Macromedia Dreamweaver. JPEG images, as we noted above, use a full 24-bit color palette that can't be reduced.

Testing for Variation

VARIATIONS AMONG BROWSERS, displays, and operating systems make it virtually impossible to ensure the absolute accuracy of colors on the Web. In addition to considering different display capabilities, designers need to account for differences in the way Macintosh and Windows systems show color. By default, images displayed on Windows systems are slightly darker than those displayed on the Mac. Additionally, Microsoft's Internet Explorer and Netscape Navigator have subtle variations in the way they render graphics. It's thus important to test your Web designs as they'll be seen on a variety of monitors, platforms, and browsers. You can simulate these variations to some degree by setting your display to a lower bit-depth, or by adjusting the monitor brightness. For example, the Macintosh operating system includes a monitor-calibration utility that lets you reset the display *gamma*—a technical term for overall brightness and contrast—to match that of a Windows PC.

Extensive testing improves the odds that your creation will be displayed with predictable results on the system your client is using—and just as importantly, on the systems *their* clients are using.

Color is tricky business on the Web. Warm and cool colors can be vibrant on some systems and muted on others. These variations can be difficult to track, as most designers don't have all platforms on their desks. You're best bet is to stick with Web-safe colors until you're comfortable creating new customized palettes, especially on crucial color-dependent projects.

RGB images, as you can see from this photo, will vary from one computer system or browser to another. In this case, the differences are noticeable, but don't detract from the quality of the image.

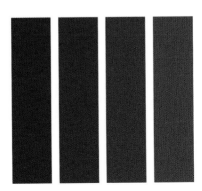 

Effective Web Presentations

THE WEB PRESENTS A NEW SET OF challenges for designers accustomed to working in print. For example, the feel of a printed piece often has a direct effect on how it's perceived. The Web, in contrast, is a more purely visual medium, while adding a degree of interaction that isn't possible in print. Due to the fundamental differences between the CMYK and RGB color models, many colors, such as pastels, muted hues, and neutral shades, change drastically when transferred to the Web. It can't be overstated that learning the Web color process requires practice and some diligent research.

Despite the many differences between print and Web design, it's important to stick to your color roots, as most of the same rules apply. Even if you're using the Web-safe palette, you can choose from plenty of warm, cool, and rich colors, as well as a few muted ones. Depending on your project and audience, you still want to assess appearance and marketability as you would for any print job.

Keep It Simple

USER-FRIENDLINESS AND CLARITY are crucial to effective color communication on the Web. While black-and-white copy offers the greatest contrast and easiest readability on a monitor, it's not very appealing to the average Web surfer. You may have a limited number of colors to work with, but it doesn't mean that you have to abandon your classy or flashy designs. Web designs can use any number of visually exciting color combinations that offer easy readability.

Color is particularly important in regard to navigation. If navigation bars and icons are logically placed and/or highlighted with color, navigating the Web page can be effortless. However, nothing will frustrate a viewer as much as running the cursor over an item that appears to be a navigation tool, only to find out that it's simply highlighted text.

The example here provides a good example of a clean site that's easy to read and navigate. Above all, it doesn't sacrifice anything in terms of color usage.

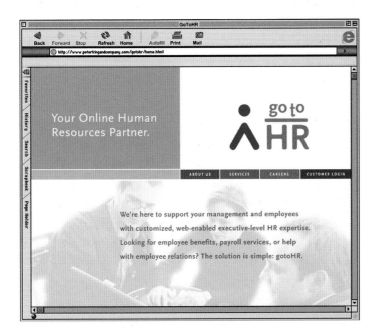

Clean design, effective use of complementary colors, and simple navigation tools help make these user-friendly Web sites. The logos are easily visible and navigation buttons are colorful and interesting. (Courtesy Paul Baker Printing, Inc. and Peter King and Company, Inc.)

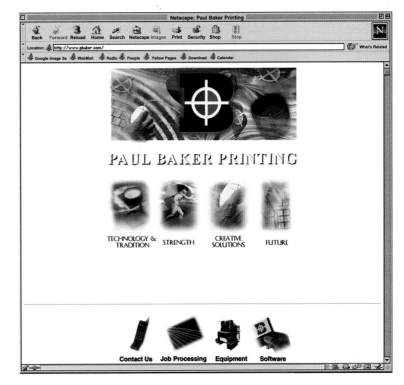

Simplicity in color and style creates harmony on these pages. The logo appears throughout the site without being overbearing, navigation photos are easily recognizable, and concise text makes it very readable. (Courtesy Paul Baker Printing, Inc.)

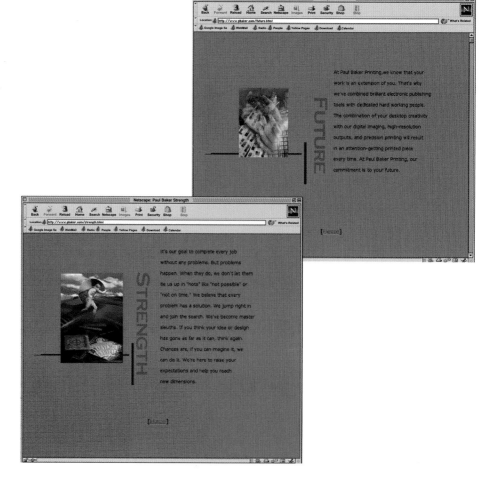

Both of these pages make a powerful statement by using a strong background color that complements the bold images. The design and coordinating colors are simple and elegant. (Courtesy Paul Baker Printing, Inc.)

Because of the freedom the Web affords, it's easy to throw caution to the wind, overdesign your elements, and splash too much color onto a Web page. Cramming too much information and using a wild variety of colors can cause a cluttered look that many will find confusing and frustrating. These sites can trigger disconcerting color responses.

Think about sites you've visited and make mental notes of what you've seen. We've all surfed obnoxious sites flooded with blinding backgrounds, Day-Glo fonts, and animated critters doing the samba, but can you recall what the site was about? If there's a lesson, it's that nothing is wrong with keeping things simple.

Scanning for the Web

THE EXPENSE OF BUILDING AND maintaining Web pages often justifies the use of professionally scanned images. While you may consider an inexpensive desktop scanner to be "good enough," the difference in the final page will be noticeable. Because images on the Web are 72 dpi, your prepress house can *scan to disk* for nominal fees. These scans are usually provided without hard proofs, which most designers find unnecessary if the scans are from a good source. Once you have the disk, you can *soft proof* the images by viewing and adjusting them on your monitor. If you are producing images simultaneously for print and Web, your prepress house can scan at a higher resolution suitable for CMYK production and then down-sample the images to a lower resolution for use on the Web.

Overuse of bright colors can have your audience literally seeing spots. If you stare at the center of the green square for thirty seconds without wavering, and then quickly shift your view to the center of the white square, you'll see red.

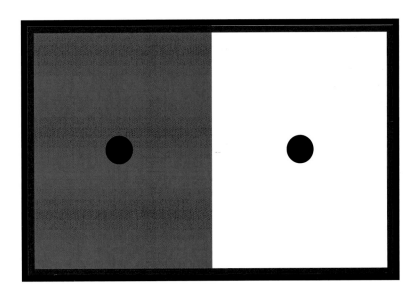

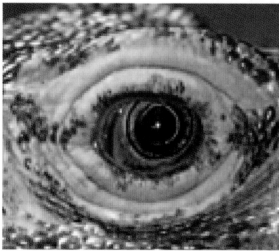

Images scanned at 72 dpi are generally unsuitable for traditional CMYK reproduction but look fine on the Web.

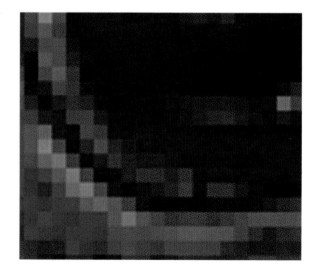

Color and Contrast

TEXT PLACED OVER COLOR elements provides good contrast and can be highly readable. Remember that about one out of twelve males has some degree of color blindness. If you've used sufficient contrast between background and text, most of your audience will receive your message without difficulty, even if the colors are a little skewed for their individual visual interpretations.

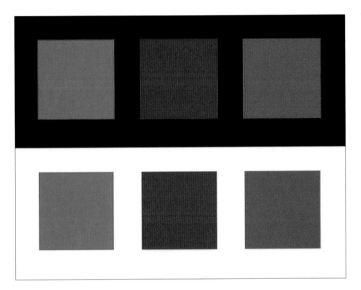

The phenomenon known as simultaneous contrast can create optical illusions. In this illustration, colors within the black box appear to be larger and lighter than the same color blocks duplicated below.

Good contrast results in a pleasing and readable appearance. Too little contrast can make the text virtually unreadable. Too much contrast in complementary colors can make them visually jarring.

Thematic Use of Color

BEYOND THE USE OF A WEB-SAFE or custom palette, you can establish harmonious color themes by sampling colors from photographs or other images on a Web page.

Each of the following images expresses a different theme, and each can be used as a sample for planning a color scheme. Many designers have made this a permanent part of their color regime, and do so automatically when a new job lands on the desk. The frames that surround each image often set the tone of the color scheme, whether it's warm, cool, rich, muted, elegant, or playful. The accompanying color blocks are sampled from the photo. The more you experiment with various frames and blocks, the more surprised you'll be at which colors ultimately serve the your purpose. Over time, you'll develop an eye for which colors work best, and you'll be able to create a secure and stable Web-color repertoire.

Warm colors

The red frame in this sample, along with the accompanying swatches, exudes warmth. Cool colors can provide contrast to these images but should be used sparingly. Warm colors are comfortable and passionate and usually add appeal to anything they surround. Even the dark chocolate colors provide depth and richness.

Neutrals

Neutrals, muted colors, and earthtones can be challenging to replicate on the Web. In this case, running a sample is advisable. The neutral colors shown here mix and match well with most designs, and provide a calming effect.

Vibrant colors

Vibrant blues, reds, greens, yellows, and pinks work well in contrast with calmer colors but also combine well with each other. This parrot shows how a palette full of screaming color can bring balance, boldness, and fun to a design.

Metallics

Metallics are as difficult to match as glassware, but you can always fall back on an elegant color scheme. In addition to the gray and silver hues, you'll easily find success in deep, rich burgundy, purple, royal blue, and hunter green. For contrast, yellow, white, and lighter pastels will punch out of the darker tones without interrupting the feel of your design.

Food images

Designs involving food or other consumer products can be tricky but certainly not impossible. If you have a strong image, such as this sandwich, it's best to let the ingredients speak for themselves. The strong frame is matched to the olives and sets the tone for the scheme. The yellow, green, white, red, and brown are all vibrant, so to avoid overwhelming the viewer, you should use them sparingly.

Cool Colors

The deep blue hues coupled with bright yellow add to the chill of this image. This is a case where cooler is better. Adding reds, oranges, or magentas would spoil the rugged appeal.

Glass Images

Designs involving glassware are always a challenge, and many designers are frustrated by the lack of available color. But take another look—reflections and accessories offer color depth that can be drawn into the body of a design. In this case, the last color you would think to match, lime green, affords the best flexibility. Images with rough textured backgrounds also offer a range of colors, as seen in this photo.

Busy Images

Designers often find themselves frustrated with busy images that contain too much color. For these designs, swatches are paramount. Here, the yellow frame helps center and lighten the image without washing out the metallic golds. What may seem a daunting task is made easier when you pull the lesser colors into the swatches. Any of the red, blues, or browns could easily be used as highlight colors. But remember, with a busy image, a little goes a long way.

Bold Colored Objects

Images with bold colored elements and muted backgrounds can be deceptively difficult to sample for color themes. The red and yellow are eye-catching, but they fail as dominant colors. The surrounding green and brownstone cause the image to fall flat. Your best bet is to search for a small highlight color to pull the scheme together. In this case, the blue from her skirt was the best option.

Minimal Color Schemes

This image is a perfect example of how to build a color scheme around shades and hues of only two colors. The deep teals and purples add to the mystery and aura of the image. Modern or abstract designs can generally handle all types of color schemes, from bold to subtle.

Subjects with Contrast

Images that contain many contrasting and colored elements are difficult under any circumstances. In this image, setting up a color scheme is made infinitely more challenging by the falling water, bright green/yellow turf, and red shadows cast by the umbrella. When none of the colors in an image match in combination, the best approach is to use a darker shade of the most offending color. The brightness of the turf matched with a dark green helps contain the other colors, making the image easier to work with.

11

TYPE

Years ago, San Francisco–based designer Dugald Stermer worked for a
boss who invited him out to lunch regularly. It was no treat. Stermer's
boss held a contest to see who had to pay for the meal. Each day, he
would suggest that both men draw a letter of the alphabet in a specific
typeface and point size. The one who drew it best ate for free. "He
would say, 'Draw me a 144-point Bodoni capital B,' or 'Let's see a
72-point Caslon lower-case M,' and we would sketch it on a napkin,"
recalled Stermer. Stermer said he paid for a lot of lunches before he
learned how to draw type.

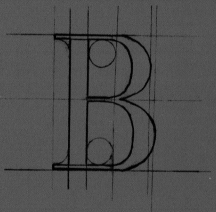

Why was it important for designers to know how to draw type? Back in the days before desktop systems and digital type, if designers wanted to see how a design might look, they had to submit handwritten instructions to their typesetting houses. These specifications (type specs) told the typesetter what typeface and point size to use, as well as the alignment, letter spacing, word spacing, and line spacing. The typesetter would go to his type case and pull open drawers that contained individually cast metal dies, each with one letter on it. The capital letters were stored in the upper half of the case (upper case); the lowercase letters were in the lower half of the case. The typesetter would pull out the dies, letter by letter, and line them up on a plate.

Between the lines, he would insert slugs of lead to create the desired amount of space (leading). Then he would print a proof of the type by inking the surfaces of the dies and pressing a piece of paper on top to transfer the ink to the paper (letterpress).

When he was all done, the typesetter would call for a messenger to run the proof over to the designer. If the designer hated the design, he would have to start all over again from scratch.

(ABOVE)

Setting type for letterpress printing has always been slow and expensive. Each metal character must be placed by hand onto a plate, which is then inked and pressed against paper. For display type such as this, typesetters charge by the letter.

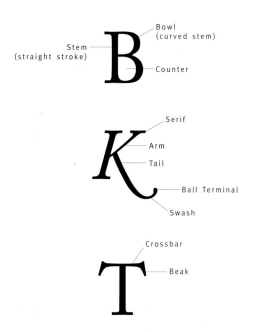

Garamond

Bodoni

Each portion of the letter has a specific name.

Old-fashioned designers who could draw their own type knew intimately the letterforms of the fonts they used and could capitalize on the subtleties of design. Notice the difference in formality between the Bodoni "T" and Garamond "T."

Because letterpress and Linotype designers fashioned totally different fonts for italic and roman typefaces, they could alter design to make each look similar and natural. Notice here how the italic "a" is completely different from the roman "a." Note also how the baseline serifs of the roman letterforms do not appear on the italic version, making the italic letters look more like cursive writing.

Not only was the process slow, it was expensive. Typesetters charged as much as fifty cents per letter for display type. Thus, designers who could sketch their own displays had a real competitive advantage, both in terms of money and time. If this system seems medieval to you, Stermer thought it was great. He says knowing how to draw type forced designers to learn crucial aesthetic lessons, such as the importance of proportion between strokes (straight edges of a letter) and counters (round edges). The very slowness of the process gave designers time to consider the subliminal messages that different type styles can convey, especially through small differences in type design.

A Garamond T and a Bodoni T both have serifs, for example, but look how the Garamond T sticks up above the straight horizontal of the letter, unlike the Bodoni, which is flat.

The downstrokes of the Garamond serifs curve a little, while those of Bodoni have straight edges. The net effect is that Garamond looks more like calligraphy while Bodoni looks more carved. The difference in feel is obvious to anyone who has had to draw them.

Stermer also liked the fact that typefaces were difficult to manufacture. Each letter at each point size had to be carved by hand before the dies could be cast to create a useable alphabet. That meant that a type designer could control all aspects of proportion when it came to changing point sizes. At very large point

Washington

Times Roman

Washington

Times Roman Italic

sizes, for example, a type designer might fatten up thin strokes of a letter so that they were in better proportion with the thick strokes of that letter.

Within a type family, italic and bold faces were all designed and carved separately, giving the type designer enormous control to design faces that carried the feel of the roman face but were subtly modified to look good on their own.

(ABOVE RIGHT)
Notice how much better the scaled "W" is designed compared to the enlarged "W" above it.

(RIGHT)
Letterpress type and Linotype type was manufactured with metal dies (with type either raised or inlaid). Each die was painstakingly carved by hand, so type designers paid a lot of attention to proportion when making different sizes of the same font.

W
Regular Minion (12pt.)

Regular Minion (scaled to 144pt.)

Display Minion (144pt.)

(ABOVE)

Phototype like this revolutionized graphic design. For the first time, typesetting was cheap and fast. An additional benefit was that, because phototype could be letter-fitted photographically, designers could kern letters as tightly as they wished, even to the point of overlap. Letterpress type, by contrast, was carried on a physical die that gave each letter a border so kerning was limited to the size of the metal border around each letter. Printers could physically cut away part of the metallic border to kern letters more tightly, but that was prohibitively expensive.

Of course, Stermer's gain was a typesetter's pain. Acquiring type fonts, with all the point sizes and typeface variations required, was expensive. Heavy, too; the metal letters of a typeface weighed several pounds. You couldn't just download a new font — you had to pay dearly for shipping. Typesetters usually limited themselves to a few faces in a small number of point sizes.

Those limitations spurred the invention of the Linotype machine by Ottmar Merganthaler in 1886. A Linotype machine was a combination of a typewriter-like keyboard and a molten-metal foundry. An operator would type in a line, causing metal dies to line up in a holder. When the line was set, the operator would press a key to cause molten lead to flow into the dies. The lead solidified quickly, forming a line of type. This system had the advantage of speed, since the operator could type faster than it took to pick out individual letters from cases.

Unfortunately, the printing process was still slow and the resulting printing plates were heavy. Printers began experimenting with thin, photo-reactive plates that could be wrapped around printing cylinders. Because the press cylinders rotated, printers could run a continuous stream or web of paper through the press at high speed.

The idea of producing type and print photographically, coupled with the advent of computers, led to a major advance in typesetting called

```
Cell[BoxData[
    FormBox[
      RowBox[{"\t",
        RowBox[{"\[ScriptCapitalG]", "=",
          RowBox[{
            RowBox[{"\[Chi]", "(", "0", ")"}], "=",
            FractionBox[
              RowBox[{
                SqrtBox["\[ScriptCapitalR]"], "+", "1"}],
              RowBox[{"1", "-",
                SqrtBox["\[ScriptCapitalR]"]}]}]}]}]}],
TraditionalForm]], "Text"]
```

$$\mathcal{G} = \chi(0) = \frac{\sqrt{\mathcal{R}} + 1}{1 - \sqrt{\mathcal{R}}}$$

phototypesetting. Instead of using metal letters, typesetters bought photo-templates of typefaces that could be mounted in a machine that exposed film to produce letters.

Acquiring new typefaces became much cheaper, and back strain as an occupational hazard for typesetters became a thing of the past.

The only problem was, how would a typesetter tell the computer how to use the right letter at the right point size and in the right typeface? Programmers came up with computer languages that did the job, using codes that could be input with a keyboard. In one system, for example, a $ was used as the symbol that would tell the computer that a directive was

coming. So an operator might type in Gr$p8$l9$y20$u, followed by the text. That would tell the computer to typeset the text in Garamond roman, in a point size of 8 with 9 points of leading at a line length of 20 picas, justified. This kind of language is called a markup language and is still used today by academics who typeset journals and textbooks in a markup language called TeX. It's also used in Web design: HTML stands for hypertext markup language.

Markup languages give the user enormous power to control every aspect of typesetting, but they have two severe drawbacks. They are a pain to learn, and you can't see what you're getting until you output your codes.

These problems were tackled when Microsoft and Apple introduced operating systems for desktop computers that employed the idea of WYSIWYG, what you see is what you get. For the first time, designers could specify typefaces, styles, and point sizes and instantly see what they were getting. Modern digital type was born.

The Advantages of WYSIWYG Digital Type Are Enormous

SPEED

By merely pointing and clicking on a menu, designers can call up a vast array of typefaces, limited only by your computer's memory and your willingness to download more, more, more. If you design something you don't like, you can instantly change it. No more waiting for a messenger to show up with your typesetter's proofs. No more begging your typesetter to please bump someone else's job and do yours first because your client is coming in this afternoon and you really, really need your type.

CONTROL

Having the power to alter virtually every aspect of design, at will, allows designers to do what they do best: see their creativity. In the past, when designers were limited by time and money, they could select very few variations of their designs. When I was a production manager in the old days, for example, I limited my designers to three variations of headline type.

Anything more was simply too expensive. Designers had to hope that one of their choices would look the way they imagined it should. If not (and this was frequent), they either had to convince a penny-pinching production manager to ease up for God's sake, or they had to accept an imperfect design that just didn't look right. Neither prospect was very appealing.

COST

Setting digital type can seem almost free. No one charges you by the letter anymore. Production managers no longer yell at you when you change your mind about your headlines. No one dings you to correct typos. Of course, digital type isn't free. You have to acquire typefaces and page-layout programs. And you have to factor in the cost of your seat-time, as you play around with designs on your monitor. But if you exercise a little self-control and limit your play, digital type is ridiculously cheap, at least in terms of money.

The real price of digital type, however, comes not in coin but in accountability: Who is responsible for quality? In the past, you could literally send out a wadded-up piece of paper with handwritten instructions scrawled all over it, and your supplier had to spin that pile of straw into gold. Now you're the one who has to do it.

To do this well, you have to know a lot more than the principles of good design. You also have to know the principles of typography so that your designs are readable. And you have to know production so that your designs will print.

All this can seem intimidating, especially because software manufacturers like to change their programs often. Just when you feel that you really understand Adobe PageMaker 6.5, for example, along comes Adobe InDesign to put you back into kindergarten.

Digital type is frequently frustrating, too. None of the manuals seem to tell you what you need to know—just try setting a title in boldface followed by leader dots in roman, and you'll see what I mean. The frustration can escalate when you think you've preflighted every possible thing that might go wrong, and then your service bureau calls to say your job won't RIP and what the heck did you embed?

But whenever you feel the urge to open your eighth-story window and fling out your monitor in a magnificent gesture of freedom, remember this. Suppliers want you to succeed. They really do.

The ease of WYSIWYG type allows you to create an image in a matter of minutes using vector-based programs such as Adobe® Illustrator.

(ABOVE)

Setting type in a curve like this one is almost impossible in markup languages such as HTML. By contrast, WYSIWYG applications such as Adobe Illustrator have the mathematics built in to allow you to drag type and art by using "handle" points. The result is faster and better.

(RIGHT)

Placing images within asymmetrical outlines is also nearly impossible for markup languages. WYSIWYG applications like QuarkXPress can do it in mere seconds.

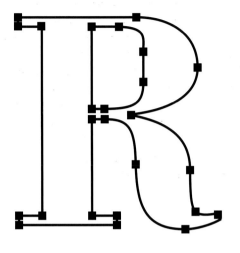

Graphic Designer's Print and Color Handbook

The advantage of object-oriented type is that you can grab onto any of the points defining a letter, and use it to move that portion of the letter around. You can enlarge, reduce, fatten, condense, tilt, or otherwise distort the type without affecting its clarity or resolution.

With that in mind, here are some issues that you need to address in order to make digital type work for you:

Fonts

Back in the days when Microsoft and Adobe were at war with each other, they each assigned programmers to figure out how to tell a computer how to draw type. These programmers devised mathematical equations to draw the curves and straight edges that make up our fonts today. Of course, both companies wanted to keep their mathematically described font outlines to themselves because they were unique. And that was just the problem. Their very uniqueness meant that users could not interchange fonts. Microsoft's TrueType equations did not compute with Adobe's PostScript Type 1 equations.

From the software companies' point of view, that was not bad. It meant that customers had to buy more of each company's products. But from the user's point of view, it was a pain. Many of us visually oriented users flocked to WYSIWYG precisely because we didn't want to deal with complicated coding or, heaven forbid, the math we thought we'd left behind in high school. We didn't care what the equations were, we just wanted to see typefaces that looked good and didn't cause our computers to freeze up.

OUTPUT DEVICE LANGUAGE

In an attempt to capture their market share, Adobe and Microsoft competed in another area: output device language. Each company tried to convince users to accept either one language or the other as an industry standard.

Unfortunately for Microsoft, Adobe's PostScript programming language hit the street before Microsoft's, and it caught on with the companies who made output devices such as laser printers and imagesetters. The way that PostScript handles type is the same way that illustration programs handle art: with object-oriented curves (as opposed to bitmap images; see page 120). Object-oriented curves are called vector or Bézier curves and are mathematical formulas that can be used to make up straight lines, fixed angles, and complex curved shapes called paths. Using vector curves, you can draw letterforms, diagrams, illustrations, maps, etc.

The way it works is like this: Objects in these software systems are defined by a set of control points that you can input. The points can be manipulated and moved using "handles" that you can attach to the control points (see diagram below). As you move the points around, you can reshape the curves and angles that the points define. As you do so, the computer alters the mathematics of the curves automatically. What you see on your monitor are new shapes that you can change, fill in, rotate, and stretch.

Object-oriented software languages don't care if the objects are letterforms or illustrations. The main difference is that the control points of type fonts are set by the type supplier. You don't have to worry about them, unless you want to alter the type in some way. You can customize PostScript type fonts by grabbing their control points with handles. Then you can stretch it, condense it, fatten it, rotate it, swoosh it, or deform it in any way that you desire.

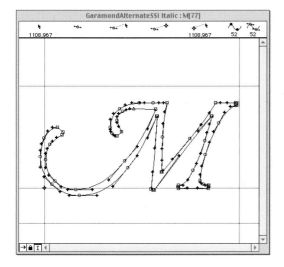

TrueType

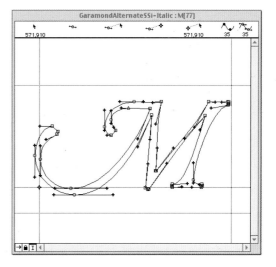

PostScript

(ABOVE)

Both TrueType and PostScript are object-oriented languages, meaning that each letter is defined with a series of mathematically placed points. The problem is that the mathematical formulas for each language are completely different. It's like the difference between Adobe PageMaker and QuarkXPress: Both software applications are layout programs, but their underlying programming is different, and they can't talk to each other.

The overall clarity of the type is not affected in any technical sense (although aesthetically you may end up with type so ugly that no family newspaper would be able to describe it adequately). The reason that clarity remains pure is because the computer makes all your adjustments mathematically. It writes new formulas for each new look.

The most important consequence of this characteristic is that you can resize object-oriented type and art without any loss in quality, whether you make things bigger or smaller. This is the opposite of bitmap resizing (see chapter 5), where pixels are added or subtracted.

Object-oriented designs must be converted into bitmaps, however, so that they can be printed with dots on paper or film. This conversion process is called rasterizing. The machine that performs it is called the Raster Image Processor, or RIP. A RIPing device, such as an imagesetter, converts all imported data (whether in the form of object-oriented type and art or bitmapped layouts and photos) into an output with a given resolution. Once this is done, you can no longer resize your type or art without changing the resolution.

Sometimes the RIPing process causes machines to freeze up. Often this can happen with older imagesetters that can't integrate all the rival font outline

languages. One result of the Microsoft/Adobe font wars is the megillah we still wrestle with today. Newer output devices have tried to incorporate software that will read both font outline languages. But the older, PostScript-only devices are still around. That's because people in the print business tend to be conservative. We don't really like to throw anything away, especially anything that continues to work. After all, old letterpresses can still be found churning out flyers. Even woodblock artisans still produce art prints. So it should be no surprise that printers have a hard time believing that an imagesetter that they've owned for only three years and that they're still making loan payments on could be obsolete.

People in the print business tend to be conservative. We don't really like to throw anything away, especially anything that continues to work. After all, old letterpresses can still be found churning out flyers. Even woodblock artisans still produce art prints.

Why should you care about this issue? The fact is, older PostScript-only imagesetters cannot reliably output TrueType. Sometimes they do fine; others times, not. The trouble is, you can't predict when your job will work fine and when it won't output at all.

Because of these factors, there are two things you should check early in the design process: Are your fonts PostScript Type 1 or TrueType? And, can your printer and/or service bureau handle them? In fact, can your printer and/or service bureau handle all of the software programs you have used to create your design? If your print suppliers say they're going to have problems, believe them—and make appropriate changes. You have two choices: either find a supplier who can handle your work, or change your work.

Neither choice is very palatable. Changing suppliers involves establishing new lines of communication, new personnel relationships, new procedures—and new glitches. Start the process early.

Changing your work may be even worse. This is because the typefaces designed by TrueType artists look different from the typefaces designed by Adobe artists. Even a standard typeface such as Times Roman has subtle differences. Some typefaces aren't duplicated at all by the rivals.

This problem came up for me last year when my book designer specified Arial and had to settle for Futura. At first she was very unhappy. Later she became reconciled after working with Futura for awhile. But if I had to put a number on her satisfaction level, I would say the happiest she ever got was about 85 percent. For a production person like me, 85 percent is great. But artists, I've found, are 100 percent-type people. Every few weeks, my designer would kvetch about the type. The book has been out now for seven months, and she still comments on the type now and then. But at least the book did come out. It wouldn't have RIPed at all if we had stuck with the original type specs.

OPENTYPE OUTLINE LANGUAGE

To address these nagging problems, recently Adobe and Microsoft decided to establish détente. They cooperated to create OpenType outline language. Mathematically OpenType attempts to reconcile the differences between the older font outline languages. So a font designed in an OpenType language should work on anybody's system, no matter what.

Of course, that means everyone needs to have upgraded to applications software than can read OpenType and take advantage of its features. That software will come, but you will still need to be careful. Software is not a two-way street. Newer upgrades almost always can handle older software—this is called backward compatibility. But older software cannot read newer upgrades. Once again, you need to check early with your suppliers to make sure that they can handle your fonts.

BOOTLEGGED FONTS

Another pitfall that you must avoid is buying or downloading poorly conceived font outline language. Bootlegged fonts are almost always short on mathematics. In many cases, a bootlegger simply scans someone else's font and then applies simple mathematical equations to describe the gross outlines. The font may look right, and it may even function to some extent. But using it would be like directing a blindfolded mountain climber to cross a narrow ice bridge. "Okay, now you move your right foot 5 inches to the right, and then you take your left foot and move it . . . Ahhhh." Say goodbye to your client.

The main trouble with bootlegged or free fonts is that you don't really know what you're getting. By the time you find out that you have a problem, it's usually late in the production schedule. That's because WYSIWYG is really a bit of a myth. What you see on your monitor is kind of what you get from your output device, but not exactly. Something may look fine on

your monitor but not compute at all in your digital printer's markup language. Or it may not RIP at all on an image-setter. Or it may RIP but come out looking different. If you discover a glitch like this at the last minute, it's usually going to cost you big to fix.

Of course, when you spend a lot of money to buy fonts from a reputable type foundry, you don't really know what you're getting, either. You do know, however, that these companies stand behind their work. For most of us, that's all we really want to know. My advice is, spend the money to buy high-quality fonts. The quality assurance you gain is well worth the price you pay.

If you decide that you simply must save a few bucks by taking the risk of downloading free type fonts, do so early in the production cycle so you have enough time to ask all your suppliers to run tests with them. At least then you'll know what kind of crevice you're going to fall into and maybe you'll even be able to determine how to crawl out again.

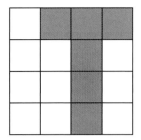

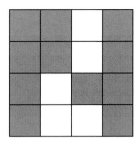

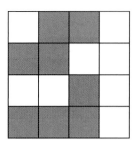

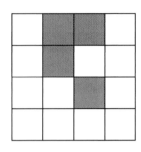

Hints for Working with Digital Type

In the old days of photographic type, no one had to worry about whether the edges of a letter would print smoothly. If the photo negative was unscratched, the letters would print cleanly. The process was a physical one: light shined through a negative exposed light-sensitive paper, film, or plate and made a letter with perfectly smooth curves and perfectly straight edges.

Digital type is completely different. Digital type does not exist physically until it is output. It exists as a mathematical formula inside a computer program. When you tell the computer to output digital type, the computer has to think how it can draw a letter onto paper, film, or your monitor screen. The tools it uses to make the drawings are called screen pixels (if output

is on your computer monitor), or dots (if output is on paper or film). Screen pixels are little squares that can be turned on or off at various intensities on your screen; dots can be printed or not printed on paper or film.

The more screen pixels or dots a computer has to work with, the more detail it can show. Think of it this way. Let's say a computer has sixteen screen pixels to work with, four across and four down. How would the computer draw the letter T?

With sixteen screen pixels, the computer can draw any letter with perpendicular or horizontal straight lines. But how can the computer draw a letter with a diagonal, such as N? Even more difficult are letters with curves, such as S. If letters are designed with small details, such as serifs, the computer is completely baffled.

To solve this problem, manufacturers of output devices realized they would need many, many pixels and dots to allow computers to draw details, curves and diagonals. Over time, they settled on widely accepted norms: seventy-two pixels per inch for computer screens; 300 dots per inch for low-quality paper output and up to 1,200 or 2,400 dpi for high-quality paper output (for further discussion of pixels and dots see Chapter 5).

At these high-end levels, most typefaces look smooth, with crisp details and fully rounded curves. Problems can develop, however, when point sizes are very small or when the number of dots per inch falls below 300. The problem is acute with computer-screen type because only seventy-two screen pixels per inch are used. See for yourself. Take a loupe and look at some type on your computer screen.

HINTING

One way that typeface designers have attempted to make digital type more legible is a process called hinting. When a computer draws type, it has to decide which pixels to turn on or off. As an entity with very little brain, a computer uses general equations to make these decisions. A human artist, given the same problem, would exercise artistic judgment when choosing which pixels to use. A human's choices might not always be consistent, mathematically. A computer's choices always are.

Hints are mathematical algorithms that tell a computer how and when to exercise a little more choice about when to use its pixels. The more sophisticated and particular the hints are, the more discretion a computer has to apply itself to pixel problems in different situations. For example, to draw an M at a small point size, a computer might realize that turning on a pixel too far to the left of the center of the diagonal would make the stroke of the letter look bumpy (see below).

But at a large point size, turning on pixels in that same area of the letter M might help make the stroke look smoother.

Programmers can spend a lot of time writing hinting codes. However, the more hints they use, the better the typeface looks. This is one of the main reasons why you should be very careful about downloading bootlegged or free fonts. Such fonts are almost always short on mathematical hints. In many cases, a bootlegger simply scans someone else's font and then applies simple mathematical equations to describe the gross outlines.

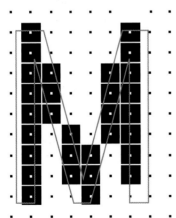

(ABOVE)

An outline that hasn't been grid-fitted. Note how poorly the outline corresponds to the pixel pattern and, above all, how awkward the bitmap of the M is.

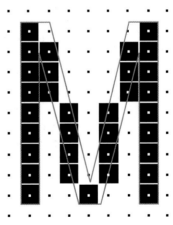

(ABOVE)

The same outline grid-fitted. Now the outline has been adjusted to fit snugly around each pixel, ensuring that the correct pixels are turned on.

Toyota

abode

Our Roman alphabet looks great when all the letters in a word have similar shapes, such as these round letters in the word "abode." But look how our eyes struggle with the letter-spacing when diagonal strokes are positioned next to circles, and skinny letters appear next to fat ones (above far right). Kerning individual letter-pairs helps overcome this optical difficulty.

Kerning

There's no doubt that when the early Phoenicians designed the letters of what later became our alphabet, they made a great technical advance in the science of written communication. The designers, however, must have been engineers. Any artist would have come up with a design that aesthetically was easier to work with.

The design works fine when you're using compatibly shaped letters of equal width.

Unfortunately, most of the letter combinations in our language present a concatenation of diagonal lines next to straight ones, curves next to diagonals, square shapes next to diamond shapes, and so on.

Word shapes that have too many uneven amounts of solids and white spaces can be hard to read.

To solve this problem, typeface programmers use kerning. Kerning is the removal of excess white space between pairs of letters to create the optical illusion of even spacing.

During the font wars of the 1980s, type programmers competed against each other to see who could supply fonts with the greatest number of kerned pairs. How many? Consider that the English alphabet has twenty-six letters, each with an uppercase and lowercase.

Yo We To Tr Ta Wo
Tu Tw Ya Te P. Ty Wa
yo we T. Y. TA PA WA

by the Sixth-Grade Students of Seattle Academy of Arts and Sciences

If you kerned every pair, you would get 2,704 pairs. Now throw in punctuation marks such as ? ! " , etc. Add numerals. Include swashes and ligatures. By the time you're finished, you could end up with more than 5,000 kerned pairs.

At those levels, however, you're also using up a lot of memory. Do you really need that much kerning? Like most things in our business, the answer depends on what you need versus what you can afford. Kerning works best when it's in balance. For most text, type fonts with a couple hundred kerned pairs are fine.

If you need to kern anything beyond the most commonly used pairs, you can use applications software such as Adobe PageMaker to customize pairs. You can do this globally for a font, so that your customized kerning pairs will be used every time you use the font. Or you can customize for just one document. For display type, you can kern each letter individually if you want to take the time.

Kerning for me is a lot like washing windows. You should do it, but if you agonize over every little speck, you'll never have time to do anything else. Focus on what really matters, then move on.

(ABOVE LEFT)

Here are the twenty most common kerning pairs in our alphabet. All well-designed type fonts automatically kern these letter-pairs, as well as many more. Cheap fonts skimp here, and it shows.

(ABOVE RIGHT)

Display type, such as in this title, should be kerned by hand. Here, the designer did not specify the point size of anything in the head. Instead, she asked that each line in the head be justified and very tightly kerned at the largest point size possible. This kind of design specification would have been almost impossible to achieve with metal type; digital type made the whole job possible in just minutes.

JKLM

All typesetting is based on the original version of writing: handwriting. When ancient calligraphers wanted to draw a larger or smaller size of type, they proportioned the thickness of their strokes by eye so that the letterforms stayed in proportion optically. The best typesetting applications pay just as much attention to proportion as did the early calligraphers.

Scaling

In the old days of typesetting, when you wanted to scale type up or down to a different size, you had to carve a new set of letters. The process was slow, but you had total control of it. Nowadays, your computer can apply a mathematical formula and simply make letters bigger or smaller. To turn 9-point type into 36-point, you can just apply a factor of four, right? Wrong. Unfortunately, enlarging or reducing type is more complicated than that.

When you enlarge type evenly, the real proportions of the thin and thick strokes don't change, but they should. If they remain the same, the thin strokes look clunky, the serifs dominate too much, and the thick strokes can look a bit fat or frail. When Michelangelo carved his really big David, he made the statue's hands proportionately bigger. He knew that "correctly" proportioned hands would have looked dinky. Conversely, when you buy down-sized, street-vendor copies of Michelangelo's statue, the hands look huge as baseball mitts.

Times 12-pt.

Times 200% or 24-pt.

Times 300% or 36-pt.

Times 800%

Graphic Design
Caption (6–8pt.)

Graphic Design
Regular (9–13pt.)

Graphic Design
Subhead (14–24pt.)

Graphic Design
Display (25–72pt.)

Metal type designers had the luxury of adjusting the proportions of the different point sizes in a given typeface. They simply carved whatever looked good. Digital type suppliers should do the same thing—it's called optical sizing. But they commonly don't. Recently though, Adobe began offering optical sizing options in some OpenType fonts. The options are generally available as "Opticals" in four size categories: caption (6- to 8-point); regular (9- to 13-point); subhead (14- to 24-point); and display (25- to 72-point).

(ABOVE)

Be careful when you scale up ordinary type—the resulting display type might look clunky. Instead, you should consider ordering a special font just for super-sized type. Notice here how bad Times looks when enlarged 800 percent. A properly designed display typeface would make the crossbar of the "T" more narrow. Similarly, the narrow parts of the round strokes would also be more narrow.

(LEFT)

Note the subtle design differences in these OpenType point sizes: As the point size gets bigger, the thick strokes are made proportionately thinner so that a sense of balance between thick and thin strokes is maintained at all point sizes.

Type Families

A type family is a group of typefaces created with similar design characteristics. The most common members of a family are roman, italic, bold, and small caps. But some typefaces, such as Univers, have huge extended families consisting of variants such as semibold, extra bold, slanted, extended, and condensed.

In the old days, type foundries created families by carving new sets of alphabets. Each family was designed to resemble the parent, or roman face. But they also looked good on their own.

Digital type designers can do this, too. But it's expensive. A designer has to draw each letter, uppercase and lowercase, separately. It's a lot easier to program an algorithm that tells your computer to alter a roman letter so it mimics a new family. To make a roman X look bold, simply fatten up all the strokes.

Roman

Bold

UNIVERS

Thin Ultra Condensed	ABCDEFGabcdefg
Light Ultra Condensed	ABCDEFGabcdefg
Ultra Condensed	ABCDEFGabcdefg
Condensed Light	ABCDEFGabcdefg
Condensed Light Oblique	*ABCDEFGabcdefg*
Condensed	ABCDEFGabcdefg
Condensed Oblique	*ABCDEFGabcdefg*
Condensed Bold	**ABCDEFGabcdefg**
Condensed Bold Oblique	***ABCDEFGabcdefg***
Light	ABCDEFGabcdefg
Light Oblique	*ABCDEFGabcdefg*
Roman	ABCDEFGabcdefg
Oblique	*ABCDEFGabcdefg*
Bold	**ABCDEFGabcdefg**
Bold Oblique	***ABCDEFGabcdefg***
Black	**ABCDEFGabcdefg**
Extra Black	**ABCDEFGabcdefg**
Black Oblique	***ABCDEFGabcdefg***
Extra Black Oblique	***ABCDEFGabcdefg***
Extended	ABCDEFGabcdefg
Extended Oblique	*ABCDEFGabcdefg*
Bold Extended	**ABCDEFGabcdefg**
Bold Extended Oblique	***ABCDEFGabcdefg***
Black Extended	**ABCDEFGabcdefg**
Extra Black Extended	**ABCDEFGabcdefg**
Black Extended Oblique	***ABCDEFGabcdefg***
Extra Black Extended Oblique	***ABCDEFGabcdefg***

Here is GARAMOND (TrueType)

Here is GARAMOND italic (applied from Style menu in Word)

Here is GARAMOND italic (a separate TrueType font)

Here is GARAMOND bold (applied from Style menu)

Here is GARAMOND bold (a separate TrueType font)

Here is GARAMOND bold italic (applied from Style menu)

Here is GARAMOND bold italic (a separate TrueType font)

Here is GARAMOND semibold (a separate TrueType font)

Here is GARAMOND semibold italic (a separate TrueType font)

This system works remarkably well—until, that is, you compare such faux families to the real thing. Note how a designed italic Garamond (above) looks more natural and elegant than a faked one. The serifs are more elongated, the open counters of the round letters are more compressed, the strokes are a bit thinner. Similarly, note how different a designed bold looks compared to an obese roman (far left). The differences are especially apparent in the x-height of the letters.

Whenever you can, you should buy the designed versions of type families. Your designs will look much better. Bear in mind, however, that to use these designed versions, you have to forego using the Style option for italic or bold in the menu bar. Instead, you must use each family as though it were a different typeface. In reality, they are. Furthermore, you've got to make sure that your applications software supports this use of type families. Some applications, when told to use italic, will confuse the italic of the menu bar with the real italic of an installed font. Don't let that happen to you.

(ABOVE)

You can create bold and italic versions of a roman typeface by using these options in the menu bar, but they won't look as good as the designed versions available for purchase as separate typefaces.

fine   fine

The firefly danced in the darkness

Ligatures (right) are separate letterforms designed to eliminate the awkwardness that occurs when serifs of one letter collide with elements of an adjoining letter (left).

You should exercise care when using ligatures. If a line is loosely spaced, as this one is, ligatures look goofy because the amount of space between each half of the ligature is fixed. So here, for example, the "fi" and "fl" of "firefly" are closely spaced, but every other letter pair is more distantly spaced.

Special Features

Certain typefaces come with special design features that can add a real sense of quality to your designs. When you're out shopping for typefaces, keep some of these in mind:

LIGATURES

In some letter combinations, an element of one character can interfere with elements of neighboring characters.

In the word "fine," for example, the f's crossbar can overlap the i's dot. To avoid this problem, a special character has been designed that elides the two characters and eliminates the dot. Characters that are elided in this way are called ligatures. The most common ligatures are fi, ff, fl, ffi and ffl.

Better-designed typefaces have ligature characters. You should use them whenever typesetting a tightly spaced line. However, if a line is loosely spaced, you should not use ligatures.

1234567890

é ü rᵃ ô

The seminars will be held on July 15, 2010 and July 17, 2010.

OLD-STYLE NUMERALS

Numerals used in body text can overwhelm ordinary characters and give the numbers an emphasis that they don't need. To overcome this problem, type designers sometimes design numerals that have ascenders and descenders just like alphabetic letters. These numerals look natural in text, because they resemble the alphabet. They should not, however, be used in tables. Keep in mind that not all typefaces have this feature, however. More's the pity.

SUBSCRIPTS AND SUPERSCRIPTS

Applications software can turn any number into a subscript or superscript, simply by using ordinary numbers set small. That being said, it's better to find a typeface that has designed subscripts and superscripts, because they look in better proportion.

ACCENTS

If you do a lot of typesetting in languages that have accented letters, find a typeface that contains them as designed features. Keystroking will be easier, type will look better, you'll make fewer typos, and you will avoid the danger of encountering an imagesetter that reads a tilde as a blank rectangle.

(ABOVE LEFT AND BELOW)

Old-style numerals, with ascenders and descenders, look better in text than numerals aligned along the baseline. This is especially true if multiple numerals are set together, such as in dates. Notice how much larger the year 2010 looks compared to the other words in this sentence.

(ABOVE UPPER RIGHT)

Whenever possible, buy type fonts that are designed with separate letterforms for accents, superscripts, and subscripts. The type is better proportioned and is often easier to keystroke.

It's hard to read text with long line lengths. The eye gets lost when it tries to track one line to the next. A good rule of thumb is to never set lines longer (in picas) than twice the size of your type (in points). So 10-point text should never be set in lines longer than 20 picas. Similarly,

lines set too short look choppy. The ideal line length measures the equivalent of an alphabet and a half, when the alphabet is set with normal letter spacing.

Lines with too much leading (spacing) between them are hard to read. The best leading for typical 10- or 11-point body text is one point larger than the point size. Larger type, however, should have a point or two more leading. Display type should be leaded by hand for best visual effect.

Readability

One last issue about type is really important: readability. In the days when a designer could send a marked up wad of papers to a typesetter and let her worry about quality, readability was left largely in the hands of experts. Now the expert has to be you.

Here are some tips that will improve the readability of your text:

LINE LENGTH

It's hard to read text with long line lengths. The eye gets lost when it tries to track one line to the next. A good rule of thumb is to never set lines longer (in picas) than twice the size of your type (in points). So 10-point text should never be set in lines longer than 20 picas.

Similarly, lines set too short look choppy. The ideal line length measures the equivalent of an alphabet and a half, when the alphabet is set with normal letter spacing.

LEADING

Lines with too much leading (spacing) between them are hard to read. The best leading for typical 10- or 11-point body text is one point larger than the point size. Larger type, however, should have a point or two more leading. Display type should be leaded by hand for best visual effect.

Sometimes, due to word spacing, you can create inadvertent patterns of white space, like rivers. Rivers of white space can be very distracting, because the eye is drawn to them rather than to the meaning of the words. Correct these by revising the text, changing the line length or altering the word spacing in some of the lines.

A widow is a short line in the last line of a paragraph. Widows that are less than one-third the length of a full line should probably be fixed.

An orphan is a widow that is carried to the top of the next column or page. You should always eliminate orphans.

"Mi-nute" and "min-ute" are different words.

RIVERS OF SPACE
Sometimes, due to word spacing, you can create inadvertent patterns of white space, like rivers. Rivers of white space can be very distracting, because the eye is drawn to them rather than to the meaning of the words. Correct these by revising the text, changing the line length or altering the word spacing in some of the lines.

WIDOWS AND ORPHANS
A widow is a short line in the last line of a paragraph. Widows that are less than one-third the length of a full line should probably be fixed. An orphan is a widow that is carried to the top of the next column or page. You should always eliminate orphans.

HYPHENATION
Make sure words are hyphenated correctly. "Mi-nute" and "min-ute" are two different words. Limit the number of lines that end in hyphens. Don't stack up more than two hyphenated lines in a row.

Colored type can be very effective, but only if it doesn't fatigue the reader. Pale grays or pastels are a bad idea because the contrast between the type and the white paper is not strong enough. You need type with a density of at least 30 percent to show up well enough on white paper.

Furthermore, if you print the colored type using a screened-back halftone to create the color, you run the risk of reducing readability even more. That's because the edges of each letter will be broken up into dots, not lines, so the edges will be less distinct.

TEXT SET ALL IN CAPITAL LETTERS IS HARD TO READ. THAT'S BECAUSE PEOPLE READ BY SCANNING QUICKLY OVER ENTIRE CHUNKS OF WORDS. THE SHAPES OF THE UPPERCASE AND LOWERCASE LETTERS HELP READERS IDENTIFY WORDS QUICKLY. READERS CAN'T DO THIS WITH CAPS BECAUSE ALL THE WORDS HAVE BASICALLY THE SAME RECTANGULAR SHAPE.

COLORED TYPE

Colored type can be very effective, but only if it doesn't fatigue the reader. Pale grays or pastels are a bad idea because the contrast between the type and the white paper is not strong enough. You need type with a density of at least 30 percent to show up well enough on white paper.

Furthermore, if you print the colored type using a screened-back halftone to create the color, you run the risk of reducing readability even more. That's because the edges of each letter will be broken up into dots, not lines, so the edges will be less distinct.

CAPS

Text set all in capital letters is hard to read because people read by scanning quickly over entire chunks of words. The shapes of the uppercase and lowercase letters help readers identify words quickly. Readers can't do this with caps because all the words have basically the same rectangular shape.

Grunge type or excessively swooshed type is hard to read for the same reason: The eye cannot easily identify word shapes. Because reading is slowed down, the eye becomes tired. The reader ends up having to read each word separately, the way we did when we were first learning to read. Imagine if you had to read **Moby Dick** by laboriously sounding out each word. You'd never get out of port. You'd never meet the white whale. And you'd miss the whole point.

GRUNGE

Grunge type or excessively swooshed type is hard to read for the same reason: The eye cannot easily identify word shapes. Because reading is slowed down, the eye becomes tired. The reader ends up having to read each word separately, the way we did when we were first learning to read. Imagine if you had to read *Moby Dick* by laboriously sounding out each word. You'd never get out of port. You'd never meet the white whale. And you'd miss the whole point.

12

PAPER

A Seattle reprographics firm agreed to ink-jet an elegant invitation for a charity fund-raiser. When the designer arrived at the plant to pick up her finished work, she opened the box and saw the invitations neatly folded. "They're perfect," she said, looking at the vibrant colors. She took one out and stood it up on the counter. The edges of the invitation curled back on themselves like hair rollers. Both she and the printer stared wordlessly.

"Well, don't worry about that curl," the printer finally said. "No one will notice once they're put in the envelopes."

"They're not going in envelopes. They're standing near everyone's place setting on the tables," said the designer. "These aren't invitations to dinner. They're invitations for people to make donations. At our elegant dinner. With linen tablecloths. And crystal stemware."

"You never told me that," said the printer defensively. "I would never have laid out the job with the paper grain going that way, if I'd known. You'll have to take the invitations as is or pay for new ones."

"But they curl."

Like military spies on a clandestine mission, sometimes print buyers give out information to their printers on a need-to-know basis. We assume printers don't need to know very much about the purpose of the design; they just need to print it. So we buyers sometimes purchase paper without taking key factors into account.

When paper is formulated, it's made with certain performance standards in mind. No single paper can do everything, so mills balance one characteristic against another. If a paper has to resist tearing, for example, mills build in a lot of tear strength. But then they can't make the paper very light, because heavier weights increase tear strength. No one sends shopping bags through the mail because while they don't tear easily, they're also quite heavy.

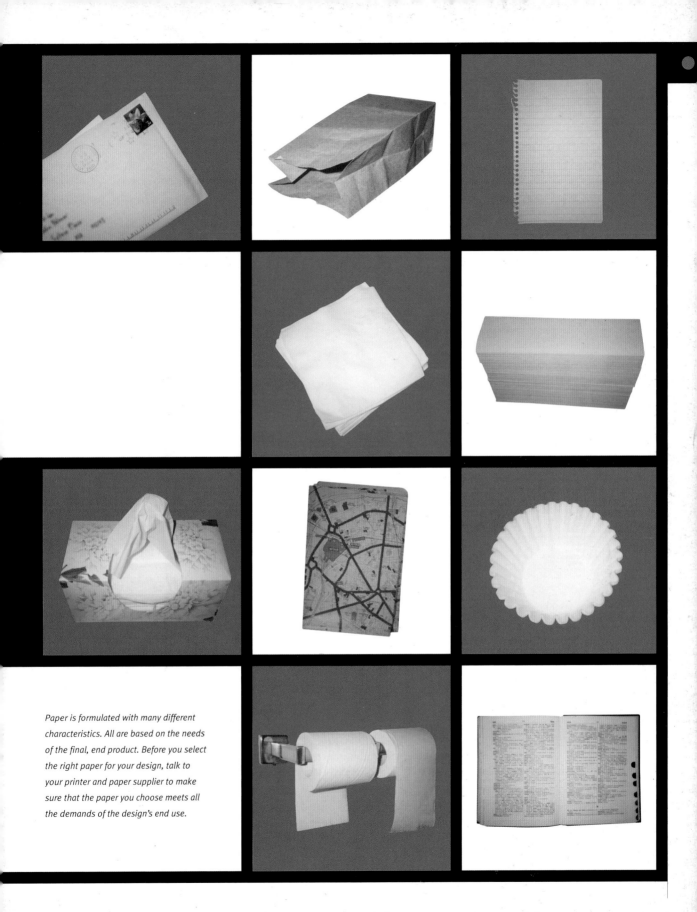

Paper is formulated with many different characteristics. All are based on the needs of the final, end product. Before you select the right paper for your design, talk to your printer and paper supplier to make sure that the paper you choose meets all the demands of the design's end use.

Cover-weight paper is usually not recommended for laser printing because it is too thick to be drawn through the printer, and the toner particles may not print properly. Here, the designer used these "disadvantages" in a creative way, creating a handmade look that resulted from a homemade desktop system.

The reason we tend not to tell the printer everything is that when many of us make paper choices, we don't base our decisions on the end use of the product. Why should the printer know what we're using the paper for when it doesn't enter our heads to select paper with that criterion in mind? We use other criteria. Designers, for example, often choose paper with their eyes. If it looks good, they buy it. Publishers, on the other hand, often buy paper with their wallets. If it's a bargain, they'll take it.

A better strategy would be to make sure that the paper you select has all the performance qualities that the job requires.

One way to do this is simply to tell your printer exactly how you're going to use the paper. The printer can decide if the paper you want will stand up to the stresses it will have to endure, whether it travels through the mail, sits on a coffee table, or ends up wrapping fish at the market.

Of course, printers are limited in the amount of paper they can stock. So if you rely solely on them to recommend paper, you will undoubtedly miss a host of other sheets that might be more interesting design-wise. If you really want design control over paper, you need to understand for yourself how to match a paper's characteristics to your needs. Here are a few things to consider:

Output Devices

The first question you must ask about your paper is: Will this work with your equipment? Different digital printing technologies have very different requirements for the papers they can accept. Toner-based technologies, for example, require very smooth finishes because the toner must be fused to the paper with heat. If a paper is too rough, the fusion doesn't work very well and the toner flakes off. Ink-jet technologies also work best on smooth surfaces because the ink droplets are small and can get distorted by heavily textured surfaces.

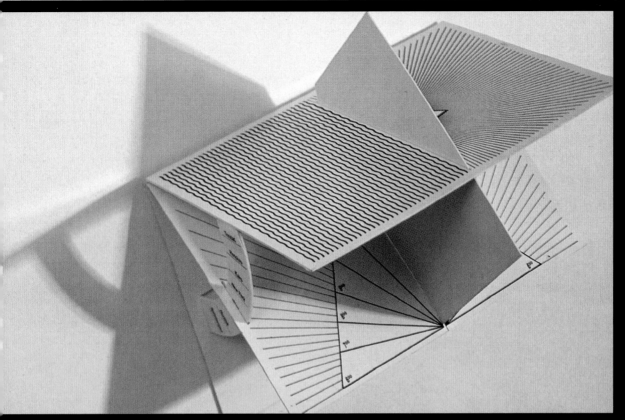

(ABOVE)

Knowing your output device's capabilities is key to choosing the right paper. Here, the designer knew that bristol stock for this hand-assembled sundial would be too thick to be printed conventionally. So instead, he printed his designs on vellum paper and hand-glued them to the sturdy bristol.

(RIGHT)

For this design, a truly thick feel was achieved by printing two separate sheets: A fairly thick, tactile sheet was used as the base, and a thin, translucent sheet was used as a flysheet.

(FAR RIGHT)

Papers like this one that have pieces of plant matter embedded in the pulp (here, bamboo) may or may not work in your digital press. Test a few sheets early in the design process.

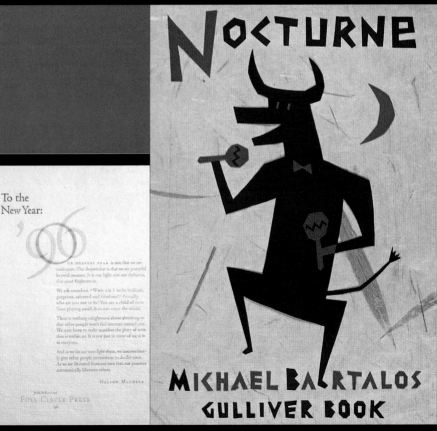

36"

24"

▨ Trimmed Waste

(ABOVE)

When designing a job, consider the size of the paper sheet you'll be printing on. It's crucial, of course, that your design is small enough to fit onto the sheet, allowing enough trim around the edges to be finished properly. But it's also wise to think about how much paper will be trimmed off and discarded. Most paper is sold by weight, so the more paper you discard, the more money you waste. Ideally, your designs should fit as tightly on the sheet as is technically feasible. In the example above, if the piece were designed slightly smaller, it could be laid out vertically, two to a column. Four columns would fit on the sheet, so we could print eight copies on one sheet instead of four.

SHEET SIZE

Paper finish is not the only limitation for these technologies, sheet size can be extremely limited. Asia, Europe, and North America all use different standard sizes, and most desktop printers can accept papers no wider than A4. They can take longer sheets if you hand-feed them. Commercial printers, on the other hand, can often accept much wider and longer sheets. If your design format doesn't fit some multiple of your continent's standard size, you will be forced to accept paper spoilage: The unused portions of paper will be tossed, although you will be charged for the entire sheet by weight.

When you're considering paper sizes, remember to think about all phases of production, not just printing. I once printed a bunch of blow-in cards at a quick-print plant that were too big for my commercial printer's bindery equipment. We had to trim each card before it would fit. Not only did this add to my expenses (and my embarrassment), but the trim looked awful. The designer had used a full bleed everywhere on the card, so when we did the trim, we cut off models' heads, part of the type describing the offer, and enough of the background design to make the final card look really stupid. We were lucky to keep our company's address on the card. When all was said and done, we should have bitten the bullet and redone the card from scratch. "Scratch" meaning, we should have found out the bindery's limitation before we even designed the piece.

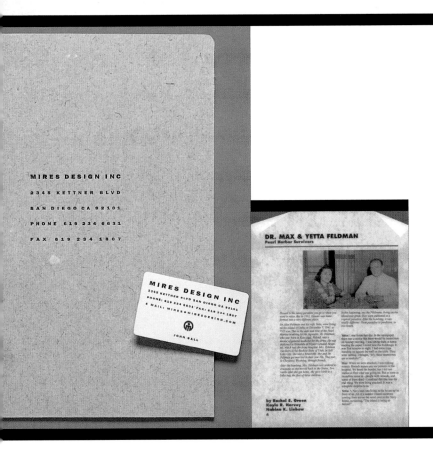

MOISTURE CONTENT

Another factor to keep in mind is whether your printing technology requires heat to set, as most toner-based and some liquid-ink presses do. If you're printing a two-sided job on a one-sided press, you need paper that retains its body and moisture when heat is applied. Most laser printers spray a charge of static electricity onto a printing drum, which then attracts toner particles that are transferred to the paper. The toner is then fused to the paper with heat.

On two-sided jobs, the paper can pick up its own charge of static, especially if the environmental humidity is low and too much of the paper's moisture gets sucked out the first time it runs through the printer. When the paper is turned to print the second side, it will curl or crease as it goes through the printer a second time.

THICKNESS

Paper thickness can be another limiting factor when it comes to matching paper with equipment, especially if the equipment is a desktop printer. Most start to jam on anything thicker than 28-pound bond. Commercial digital presses are also limited. Many cannot take paper thicker than 80-pound or at most 100-pound stock. Ink-jet-based printers tend to have a lot more flexibility than toner-based presses. If the ink is formulated properly, ink-jet printers can print on many substrates besides coated text paper: Transparencies, plastic film of all kinds, card stock, and uncoated papers are all possibilities, depending on the make and model of the press. Because the capabilities of a given digital technology are so variable, you should check ahead with your printer to make sure that your substrate will work for the printer you plan to use. If there is any doubt, ask the printer to run a few practice sheets through the press. There may be some extra expense for this service, but nothing compared to the expense of buying a load of paper that jams or that won't print at all.

Strength

Paper strength is measured in two areas: internal strength and surface strength. Internal strength is built into the paper during its manufacture. It is based on the way that the fibers in the pulp bond together. Surface strength is applied later and comes either from polishing or from adding coatings.

INTERNAL STRENGTHS

1. **Tensile strength** keeps paper from stretching too much. It's an important characteristic for web presses, where the paper is on a roll that is pulled through the press. Many commercial digital presses are web presses, as are wide-format printers. If a paper has weak tensile strength, it can tear when it's pulled. It can also distort as it goes through the press, which results in poor registration, especially on the outer edges of a sheet.

2. **Tear strength** is the ability of paper to resist tearing. Papers that will be used for packaging, bagging, or wrapping should have good tear strength. Papers that are going to be folded should have enough tear strength not to tear easily along the fold line.

3. **Mullen strength** measures the resistance that paper has to bursting. If a paper is going to be punched, stapled, wire-bound, die-cut, or otherwise punctured in some way, it should have good mullen strength.

4. **Bond strength** is the strength of the bond that keeps the pulp fibers together. It's an important characteristic for web papers, which are pulled through a press. It's also important for bags and other packaging that must hold together, even when slightly wet.

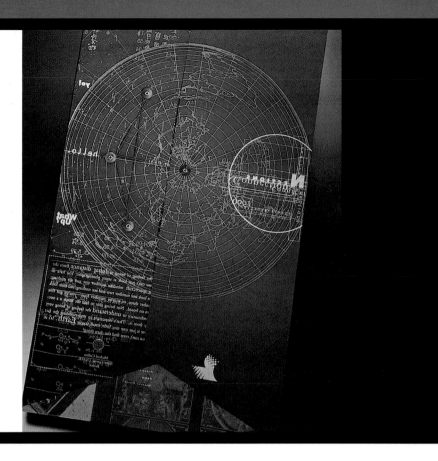

(RIGHT)

Pick strength and coating strength are necessary to make sure that ink doesn't pull off surface fibers from the paper, and that heat to dry or set the inks doesn't create bubbles and blisters under the paper. These strengths are especially important when you design jobs with heavy ink coverage, as is shown here.

SURFACE STRENGTHS

1. **Pick strength** measures the ability of paper to resist ink's tendency to pull off little pieces of coating and fiber as the ink is applied or as the paper goes through the printer. A paper with poor pick strength will lose fibers as it's printed. Not only does this make the printing on it look mottled, but you have to ask, where do the fibers go? In some presses, they go onto a rolling mechanism that prints the next sheet, which interferes even more with the ink or toner.

2. **Coating strength** is the ability of paper to hang onto its coating without bubbles, blisters, or delamination. It's an important strength for any paper that is subjected to heat, as are most papers printed with toner-based technologies.

No printer expects you to know how strong a particular paper should be. It's the printer's responsibility to make sure that the paper you want can stand up to the stresses it will undergo. However, it is your responsibility to disclose fully everything you plan to do with your finished piece. Folding, punching, binding, embossing, foil-stamping, mailing, gluing, rolling, pinning, even displaying in full sunlight all affect the kind of paper you need.

You shouldn't just tell the printer all your plans, either. You should question specifically whether the paper you'll be using can do the job. We've all received magazines in the mail with covers falling off because someone failed to select a paper that had the proper mullen strength. What a shame that a designer spent time and creative energy putting together a beautiful cover only to have it fall off for such a dumb reason as failure to communicate.

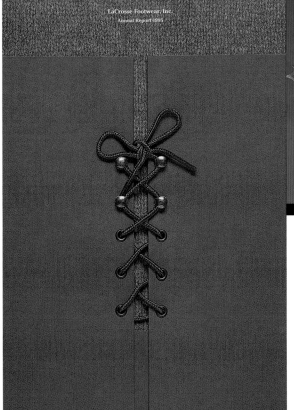

LaCrosse Footwear, Inc.
Annual Report 1995

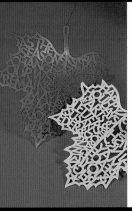

(THIS PAGE AND PAGES 158-159)
What kinds of paper strengths do you think were required for the jobs shown on this page and the following spread?

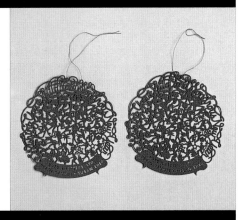

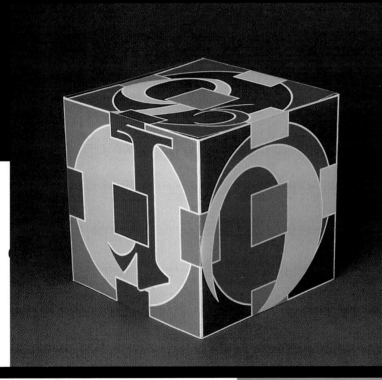

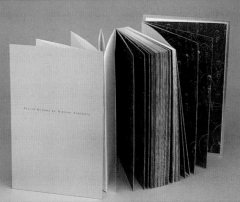

Opacity

Opacity is to paper quality as grunge is to haute couture. If a designer outfit is supposed to look like a hobo's discard, it's great. If it really *is* a hobo's castoff, then we don't want to touch it. In the same way, papers that are designed to be translucent are considered the height of elegance. Opaque papers that exhibit show-through, however, are fit only for the bottoms of bird cages.

It's these latter papers that you have to be concerned about. Show-through is the phenomenon where ink on one side of a paper can be seen on the other side because the paper is not opaque enough. It's a particular problem when you design a job that prints with heavy ink coverage on one side and light ink coverage on the other. It's generally not an issue to worry about when you're printing on only one side of a sheet, however.

Mills determine opacity by putting a black sheet behind a particular paper and measuring how much brightness the paper loses. The measurement is calibrated as a percent, which serves

(RIGHT AND BELOW)

Opacity is mainly a function of paper thickness and lignin content. The bible paper on the right is tissue-thin and has some lignin in it. It exhibits quite a bit of show-through because of its thinness. In fact, if it weren't for lignin content in the pulp, this paper would be translucent. The newsprint paper below also has quite a bit of lignin in it, but it is much thicker than the bible paper. So it exhibits much less show-through.

as the opacity rating of the paper. Nobody ever pays any attention to this number. It's far easier just to lay a sheet down on top of a strong pattern of black-and-white and see for yourself.

To check opacity, take a blank piece of paper (not a printed sheet) and put it on top of the fish below. The amount of black-and-white pattern that you can see through the paper is about the same amount of show-through you would get if you were to print both sides of the paper.

If you need opacity for your design, look for papers that have these characteristics:

1. *Thicker papers are more opaque than thin papers.*

2. *Papers made from groundwood pulp are more opaque than free sheets.*

3. *Coated papers are more opaque than uncoated.*

4. *Papers with rough finishes are more opaque than papers with smooth finishes.*

5. *Colored papers, especially dark-colored papers, are more opaque than white sheets.*

(BELOW)

To get an idea about the amount of show-through a paper might exhibit, lay an unprinted sample sheet over this fish print (or any print that shows a strong black-and-white pattern). The degree to which you can see the fish print through the sample sheet is the degree to which the paper will exhibit show-through.

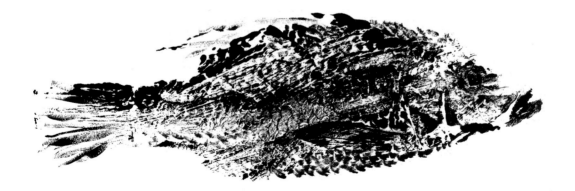

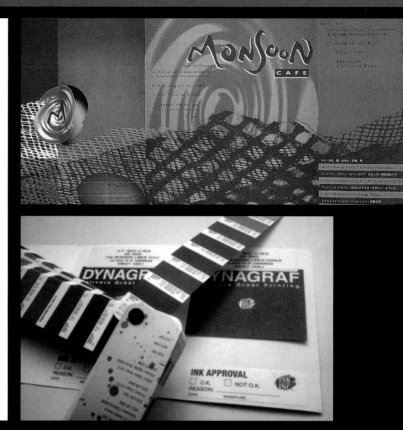

Paper manufacturers bleach white paper to make it white, but different mills use different chemicals and different amounts of bleaches. The resulting papers are white, but look at how different "white" papers appear. When you select white paper, it helps to compare your choices using unprinted sample sheets. If you look at only one sample, you won't even notice whether the white paper is blue-white, creamy white, or just plain dull.

Some paper mills add dyes to their paper pulps to make colored papers. These papers can be very effective in designs, but you must be careful when you print custom inks on them. The paper color can alter the way we see the ink color. If you are very picky about selecting a specific, custom color from an ink swatchbook, ask your printer to put samples of your ink choice on the paper you're planning to use (above right, bottom) so there are no surprises.

Color

Mills add dyes and bleaches to paper to give it color. Even white paper has a color, or at least a color cast. Some white sheets are blue-white, some a warmer yellow-white.

When you choose paper color, always look at both printed samples and plain sheets. Use the plain sheets to compare different hues. Use the printed samples to see how ink will look on the paper. Make sure the printed samples you see are printed with the same printing process and the same inks or toners that you plan to use.

Most digital printer companies are glad to throw a few sample sheets onto their press at the end of someone else's run. Since digital presses are designed to print each page as a separate entity, the printer spends little additional effort doing this for you.

You may run into difficulty if you're requesting a test run with custom inks instead of the normal CMYK. If your printer is reluctant to put a custom ink into the printer head, ask to see an ink drawdown on your paper. The printer will take a glob of ink and smear it across the paper so you can see how it will look.

The reason it's important to check this before you buy paper is that some inks (though usually not toners) can be transparent, at least to some degree. They create color by letting light through to strike the paper underneath, then they reflect the light back. But they don't reflect all the light back. Some of the wavelengths of light are absorbed by the dyes in the paper. This skews the ink colors, depending on the paper that lies underneath.

(ABOVE LEFT)

Depending on the design, sometimes it doesn't matter how paper color affects ink color. In this design, each recipient received a postcard printed on one of the four different-colored sheets of paper. The exact color of the type was not critical.

(ABOVE RIGHT)

However, in this design, ink color was vital, as each ink and each paper color were supposed to match. It was a difficult job to pull off, but the results were worth the headache.

(ABOVE)

Even black ink changes color on different colored stock. In some versions here, the black ink looks almost green, in other cases, gray. The ribbon and design, not the color, create the identity.

(LEFT)

If ink color matters, try two-colored duplex paper. Here the designer folded the paper and put the critical ink color on the paper's white side.

One quick-printer found this out the hard way when she was asked to ink-jet a purple University of Washington "W" onto some gold paper—purple and gold are the school's colors. The W came out brown instead of purple because the gold paper absorbed too much blue light. I came in on the tail end of the discussion between her and the client.

"No one's going to know the point of my design," said the irate customer. "What the hell does a brown W on yellow paper mean in this town?"

The printer tried to explain the physics of light to the man, but he was a football fan. Physics was not his forte. All he wanted was a purple W.

PERCEIVED COLOR

Even if the inks or toners you use are opaque enough to prevent the paper color from altering the color balance of your work, you should still ask to see a printed sample. Often the paper color surrounding an ink color can affect our perceptions. Take a look at the cat illustrations below to see how this works.

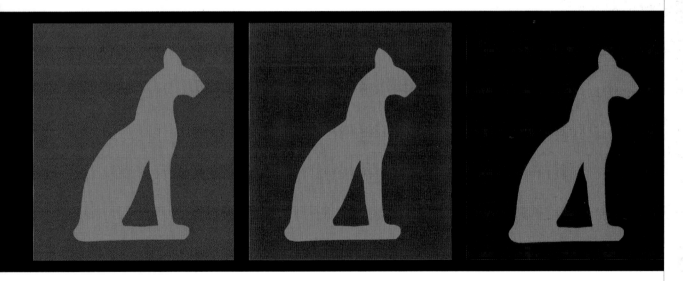

(ABOVE)

The color of paper can affect how we see the color of ink, even if there is no physical or chemical interaction between the two. Toner inks are opaque and so are not affected by the colored paper under them. However, our eyes can still perceive that ink colors vary, just from the effects of the surrounding colored paper. Do the three cats above look the same color to you? They are, you know.

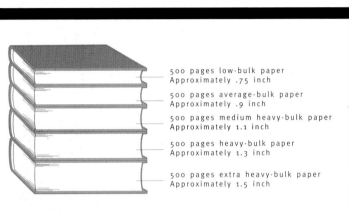

500 pages low-bulk paper
Approximately .75 inch

500 pages average-bulk paper
Approximately .9 inch

500 pages medium heavy-bulk paper
Approximately 1.1 inch

500 pages heavy-bulk paper
Approximately 1.3 inch

500 pages extra heavy-bulk paper
Approximately 1.5 inch

(ABOVE)

Papers can be made to bulk up more or less thickly. Five hundred sheets of a low-bulk paper, such as newsprint, are not nearly as bulky as five hundred sheets of cover stock. You should pay attention to this factor when you consider how people perceive value. Most people think that higher-bulk papers convey a higher sense of quality.

(ABOVE RIGHT)

The thickness of paper can also affect how it can be finished in the bindery. Thick papers, for example, do not fold well. You can see here how the ink along the edges is cracked and the corners have frayed.

Caliper

The thickness of paper is calipered in points by measuring a single sheet of paper. Note that one caliper point is .001 inches (.03 millimeters). Don't confuse it with a typeface point, which is 1/72 inches (0.6 millimeters). A caliper point measures thickness; a typeface point measures height.

Some very thick papers, such as bristol, are measured in ply rather than points. A ply is not really a measure, however; it's one layer of paper, laminated to another layer of paper. Most board papers are made in this way, with multiple layers of paper laminated to each other, just like plywood. A six-ply bristol board, for example, has six layers of paper laminated together.

Since the caliper of any one layer of paper might vary widely, knowing the ply of a board doesn't tell you anything about its real thickness. Ask for its caliper in points to find out how thick it is.

Paper caliper can have a huge impact on digital printing. For one thing, some papers might be too thick to go through a particular digital press or printer. Make sure you check this out early in the design process.

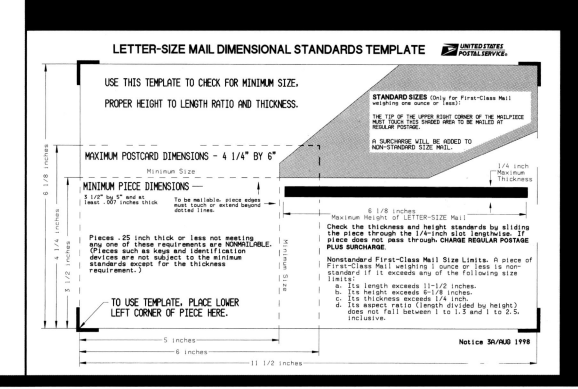

LETTER-SIZE MAIL DIMENSIONAL STANDARDS TEMPLATE *UNITED STATES POSTAL SERVICE®*

USE THIS TEMPLATE TO CHECK FOR MINIMUM SIZE,
PROPER HEIGHT TO LENGTH RATIO AND THICKNESS.

STANDARD SIZES (Only for First-Class Mail weighing one ounce or less):

THE TIP OF THE UPPER RIGHT CORNER OF THE MAILPIECE MUST TOUCH THIS SHADED AREA TO BE MAILED AT REGULAR POSTAGE.

A SURCHARGE WILL BE ADDED TO NON-STANDARD SIZE MAIL.

MAXIMUM POSTCARD DIMENSIONS – 4 1/4" BY 6"

1/4 inch Maximum Thickness

Minimum Size

MINIMUM PIECE DIMENSIONS —

3 1/2" by 5" and at least .007 inches thick

To be mailable, piece edges must touch or extend beyond dotted lines.

6 1/8 inches
Maximum Height of LETTER-SIZE Mail

Check the thickness and height standards by sliding the piece through the 1/4-inch slot lengthwise. If piece does not pass through, CHARGE REGULAR POSTAGE PLUS SURCHARGE.

Pieces .25 inch thick or less not meeting any one of these requirements are NONMAILABLE. (Pieces such as keys and identification devices are not subject to the minimum standards except for the thickness requirement.)

Nonstandard First-Class Mail Size Limits. A piece of First-Class Mail weighing 1 ounce or less is non-standard if it exceeds any of the following size limits:
  a. Its length exceeds 11-1/2 inches.
  b. Its height exceeds 6-1/8 inches.
  c. Its thickness exceeds 1/4 inch.
  d. Its aspect ratio (length divided by height) does not fall between 1 to 1.3 and 1 to 2.5, inclusive.

TO USE TEMPLATE, PLACE LOWER LEFT CORNER OF PIECE HERE.

6 1/8 inches · 4 1/4 inches · 3 1/2 inches

Minimum Size

5 inches
6 inches
11 1/2 inches

Notice 3A/AUG 1998

Caliper can also affect folding. Depending on how thick a sheet is and also on the kind of coating it may have, you might need to score a sheet before you fold. If you don't score thick paper, the paper will crack on the outside of the fold. If printing happens to fall on this line, it will flake off. Usually you don't need to think about scoring any paper thinner than 8 points, but this does vary, so ask.

If you plan to mail your piece, check caliper. Now that the United States Postal Service is so fully automated— and now that it rewards mailers who cooperate with their requirements— you need to make sure that anything you mail is thick enough to be processed by the mail center. For most jobs, paper must be at least 7 points thick. But your design can't be too thick or it will jam the USPS machinery. The Post Office has a handy little plastic ruler with a slot cut in it that you can pass your mail piece through. If it goes through easily, you're okay. But just to be sure, you might consider taking your design to the nearest USPS Business Center or post office and asking them to okay your specs. They can check that your design has the proper proportions and correct barcodes too. Believe me, nothing is worse than having the postal clerk refuse to take your mailing, or getting it all back a few days later with a note that you need to add more postage.

(ABOVE)

Paper thickness is also a big factor for direct mailing. The Post Office has stringent requirements about how thick a paper can be and still qualify for certain postage rates. To check whether your design qualifies for the best rates, slip a dummy of your design through the slot of a postal measuring device such as this one. Your piece should pass through the slot easily. If it doesn't, you might have to pay additional postage.

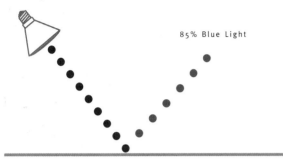

Blue Light

85% Blue Light

#1 White Paper

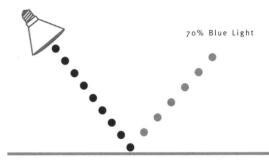

Blue Light

70% Blue Light

#5 White Paper

Coated book papers are graded based on one criterion: the amount of blue light they reflect. A #1 sheet reflects 85 percent or more blue light; a #5 sheet reflects 70 to 74 percent.

(FACING PAGE)

The highest-grade papers supply the highest-quality reproduction, but not just because they reflect the most blue light. By custom, high-grade papers also have smooth surfaces, great ink holdout, high opacity, heavy weight, and terrific overall runnability.

Grade

Paper manufacturers must be the most conservative people on earth. They never throw anything away. One of the things they have hung onto the hardest is the language they use to categorize different kinds and qualities of paper. The sheets they make are still graded based on the kind of job each paper was originally designed to handle. It may sound painfully obvious, but book papers were used to make books, newsprint for newspapers, cover stock for covers. Since the different uses of papers never overlapped in the old days, there was no need to standardize.

None of us confine ourselves to using paper the same way our forebears did, however. Nowadays, we use paper for whatever job a design calls for, never mind what the sheet itself is called. Thus, while the most common kind of printing paper is uncoated book, it is now used for books, brochures, newsletters, announcements, and other collateral material. Coated book, another common paper, is used for magazines, catalogs, brochures, calendars and posters. Cover stock is still used for covers, but it's also used for heavy posters, business cards, postcards and POP displays.

Of course, this being the paper industry, there are independent-minded mills out there who use their very own terminology to distinguish grades.

Some of these mills, for example, produce text paper, which might mean bond or uncoated book. Some make publication paper, which is really coated book. Some mills get fancy and say writing papers, not bond. Others prefer to be more down-to-earth. It's business paper, not bond.

The actual grading of each category of paper is also a happy leftover of bygone days. Bond paper, for example, is graded by its pulp content and weight. The highest quality bond is made from 100 percent cotton; five hundred sheets of it weigh 28 pounds (13 kilograms).

Coated offset paper (i.e., coated book) is graded by the amount of blue light it reflects:

#1 sheet (highest quality) reflects 85% or more blue light

#2 reflects 82-84%

#3 reflects 78-82%

#4 reflects 74-78%

#5 reflects 70-74%

The whole issue of paper grade is almost moot because of this confusion and because technically, a grade of paper is determined by a very narrow criterion. In the case of coated offset paper, it's the reflected blue light. Period. However, over the years, customers have come to expect other quality characteristics to go along with various grades. A #1 offset paper, for example, should be very, very smooth. It should not be made in the ultralight weights. It should have great ink holdout and plenty of opacity. The paper mills do respond to these customer expectations, so you can generally find higher overall quality in the higher grades of paper. But you can't necessarily count on it.

The best way to use paper grades as a selection tool is kind of like the judges who use a first cut at a Miss Universe beauty pageant. In the first cut, you can eliminate all the papers that just aren't going to make it at all. After that, you can compare a small number of sheets to each other and check out all the paper characteristics you need.

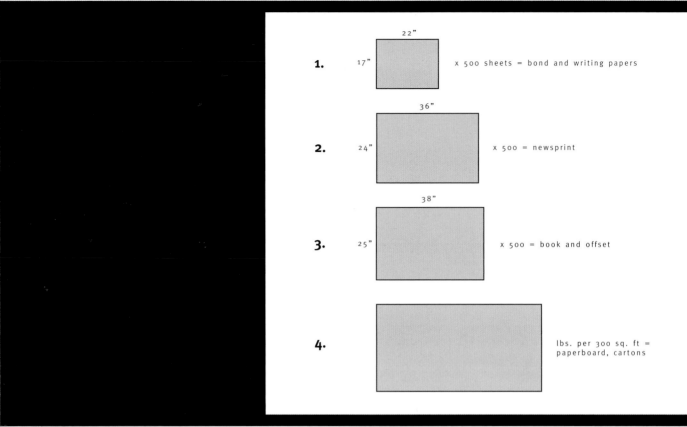

1. 22" 17" x 500 sheets = bond and writing papers

2. 36" 24" x 500 = newsprint

3. 38" 25" x 500 = book and offset

4. lbs. per 300 sq. ft = paperboard, cartons

Basis weight is measured as the weight of five hundred sheets of a given paper. Five hundred sheets of 60-pound paper weigh 60 pounds, for example. However, for historical reasons, the size of the sheets being measured can vary, depending on what kind of paper is being weighed.

Basis Weight

Basis weight is another holdover from the past. Paper mills determine the basis weight of a given paper by weighing five hundred sheets (one ream) of it. Sounds simple, until you realize that each category of paper uses different size sheets! Mills originally did this because their scales were not very accurate and could not weigh lighter-weight sheets very well. So the mills cut the lightweight papers into bigger sheets that they could weigh more precisely. Now we're stuck with these formulas:

1. 17 x 22 x 500 sheets = bond and writing papers

2. 24 x 36 x 500 sheets = newsprint

3. 25 x 38 x 500 sheets = book and offset

4. lbs. per 300 sq. ft. = paperboard, cartons

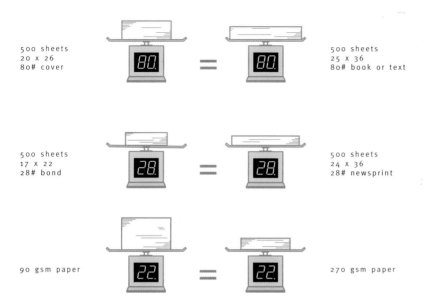

500 sheets
20 x 26
80# cover

=

500 sheets
25 x 36
80# book or text

500 sheets
17 x 22
28# bond

=

500 sheets
24 x 36
28# newsprint

90 gsm paper

=

270 gsm paper

These different sizes don't mean that you have to buy paper cut to that size. You can usually buy these papers in many different sizes. It just means that when a mill wants to figure out a paper's basis weight, it uses a different size sheet for each standardized category.

Sometimes it might pay for you to buy an equivalent sheet of paper in another category than your original design idea. If so, here are the equivalent weights:

BOND EQUIVALENTS:
- 16# bond ≈ 40# book
- 20# bond ≈ 50# book
- 24# bond ≈ 60# book
- 28# bond ≈ 70# book

COVER EQUIVALENTS:
- 50# cover ≈ 90# book
- 55# cover ≈ 100# book
- 60# cover ≈ 120# book

(ABOVE)

To determine the basis weight of paper, mills weigh 500 sheets of a given stock. But the size of sheets being weighed varies, depending on what kind of paper is measured (see the diagram on page 372). So 80-pound cover paper and 80-pound book paper both weigh the same, but the basis-sizes of the sheets is different. This makes it difficult to compare the weights of different kinds of paper. Outside of North America, basis weight is measured in grams per square meter (or grammage). So comparing the weight of one kind of paper to another is much easier.

WHEN PAPER IS BAD

ALTHOUGH BAD PAPER IS RARE IN THE DIGITAL PRINTING WORLD, OCCASIONALLY YOU MIGHT GET A BAD BATCH. HERE ARE YOUR OPTIONS FOR HANDLING THE PROBLEM:

- REJECT THE JOB. *Rejecting a roll or ream of paper might be necessary if the quality is so bad that you just can't print acceptably on it. If you do reject the job, The printer may be able to supply you with more of the same sheet from a different batch. Most printers carry enough paper in their inventory to cover emergencies, and most press runs for digital print jobs are short.*

  If you have special-ordered the paper, the printer may not have enough of your sheet to print the entire job. In that case, you might have to accept a substitute paper, a house sheet that the printer keeps constantly replenished in inventory.

  Before you agree to use the printer's house sheet, you need to ask yourself whether it matches your original paper selection. If not, would the substitute paper be different enough to bother your readers, or—more likely—your advertisers?

- REJECT THE HOUSE PAPER. *If you reject bad paper and the printer's substitute, your job will undoubtedly be delayed. You need to find out the exact length of the delay because it may involve more than mere delivery of new paper. Your printer may be so heavily scheduled that your job will be bumped far into the future.*

  Ask for a written guarantee of a new schedule from the mill and from the printer. Then ask yourself if you can stand the delay. Be sure to consider readers' expectations, distribution schedules, and promises to advertisers. Special offers may have to be altered, ads may have time-dependent information, editorial may need updating—the list of repercussions can cascade as quickly as a mudslide. This is why most print buyers accept any kind of substitute paper rather than delay.

- PAY FOR WHAT YOU GET. *If you accept the job as is, you will have to pay for it. Accepting the job means that either you sign for receipt of delivery, or you allow copies of your job to be sent directly from the printer. Most direct mail is bagged right off the bindery line, so you may not discover bad paper until you get your office copies. If this happens to you, don't expect the printer to charge you zero. After all, as faulty as the job was, you did get some use out of the product.*

- NEGOTIATE. *The size of a makegood or fee reduction that your printer may offer will depend on how harmed you were and how important your business is to the printer. Harm may be difficult to quantify. Did you lose advertisers' contracts? Did you have to give makegoods to advertisers? Did subscribers cancel? These are all straightforward consequences that you can attach a cash value to. Grayer areas might involve whether you believe you lost potential benefits (more advertisers, more sales, etc.), or even some of your reputation. Work it out.*

- PAY FOR YOUR OWN PAPER. *If you supplied the paper to your printer, then you must try to get redress from the paper mill. You'll need accurate evidence about the problem. Ask your printer to supply a detailed report. Resolving the dispute could take a very long time, and the outcome might not be to your liking. Mills have a habit of not paying too much attention to anyone other than their best customers. In the meantime, you must pay the printer for the printing and for any substitute paper supplied.*

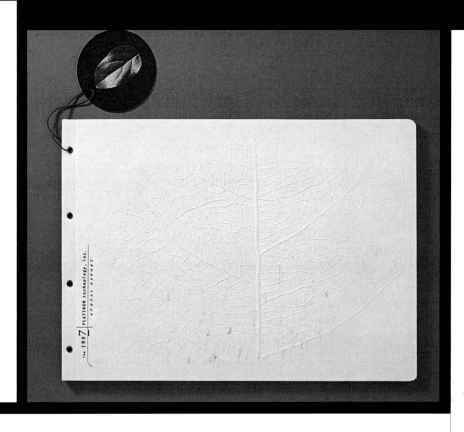

All paper is made from pulp mixed with water. When the pulp is wet, some manufacturers press shapes into it, creating an embossed design. Watermarks are one such shape, created by pressing shallow dies into the wet pulp. But other shapes can be pressed in too, such as the leaf shown here.

Pulp Content

When Chinese court official Ts'ai Lan discovered how to make paper centuries ago, he used tree bark, hemp, and rag fibers. Later papermakers in China found that mulberry and bamboo made excellent paper, too. In fact, almost any fiber that bonds together when it's wet can be used to make paper.

Most publication papers in the U.S. are made from wood fiber because it's so cheap. The fiber is pulped and used in either of two forms: groundwood papers and free sheets. In both cases, the wood is first ground up into chips, usually at a separate pulping factory. For groundwood papers, the chips are further pulped and washed, making a slurry of wood fiber and water. This is usually bleached white, and then dried. The dried pulp is shipped to the mills that actually make the paper. There it is remixed with water and beaten and refined. This is the point where the additives are put in: dyes, starches, brighteners, etc. This is also the point where recycled pulp is usually added.

This slurry, called "furnish," is then poured or sprayed out onto a vast wire mesh, the Fourdrinier paper machine. As the wet slurry flows along the mesh, water is squeezed out with rollers and flows out through the mesh. The rollers polish the paper as they press on it, but they only polish one side. The mesh side picks up the pattern of the mesh. Eventually the paper is pulled through polishing rollers at the end, which polish both sides of the paper. But the mesh (or wire side) never becomes as smooth as the top (or felt) side. Its relative roughness causes it to accept ink differently than the felt side, creating a somewhat mottled effect that makes the ink colors look grayish.

Groundwood paper contains a lot of lignin, which is a brownish, organic compound in trees that "glues" the cell fibers together. Lignin gives groundwood paper a lot of strength and opacity, but it also makes groundwood sheets less bright and white.

Paper can be made from groundwood pulp (left) that retains its lignin (a substance that gives strength to the tree's cell walls). Or paper can be made from lignin-free pulp that has had the lignin "cooked" out (above). Groundwood paper is browner and duller than free sheets, but it's also much stronger. Free sheets, on the other hand, accept ink better than groundwood and have better overall printability.

Free sheets have all the lignin chemically "cooked" out of them in the pulping stage. They are lignin-free. Such papers are whiter and brighter than groundwood sheets, but they're also somewhat weaker and less opaque. Free sheets are often coated with a mixture of clay and other chemicals to make them smoother and brighter. Depending on the thickness of the coating, its chemical composition and its method of application, these coated papers can reflect almost all the light shined upon them.

Once the paper reaches the end of the Fourdrinier machine, it is rolled up into huge logs called reels. Each log can weigh as much as 28 tons (29 metric tons) and contain 46 miles (74 kilometers) of paper. These logs are cut into smaller reels for web printing. The smaller reels can later be unrolled onto a machine, a sheeter, that cuts them into individual sheets for sheetfed presses.

All paper is essentially made this way, although boutique papers are made with less automation and on a smaller scale. Special sheets might even be made with hand-presses and might contain all kinds of added materials: rose petals, leaves, metallic fibers, seeds. These things actually tend to weaken the paper bond, so they are unsuited to most kinds of commercial printing. But for one-of-a-kind jobs, they can be very beautiful. If you do use boutique papers, be sure to test them on your equipment before you roll out your design on them. Many specialty pulps are suitable for toner-based or ink-jet digital printers, but many are not. Generally speaking, ink-jet printers are more accepting of unusual papers, laser printers less so, and commercial digital presses hardly at all.

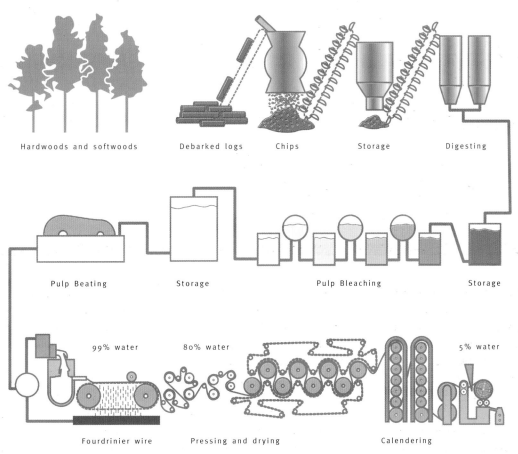

Hardwoods and softwoods   Debarked logs   Chips   Storage   Digesting

Pulp Beating   Storage   Pulp Bleaching   Storage

99% water   80% water   5% water

Fourdrinier wire   Pressing and drying   Calendering

Sizing and coating   Slit into rolls

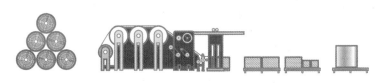

Rolls   Sheeting   Parent sheets and rolls

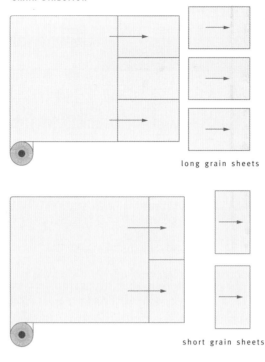

GRAIN DIRECTION

long grain sheets

short grain sheets

Grain

When wet pulp is sprayed out over a Fourdrinier wire, the pulp fibers begin to align themselves in the direction that the wire is moving. This creates a grain in the paper. When the finished paper is rolled up into logs at the end, the grain flows in the same direction as the way the paper is rolled: parallel to the outer edges of the log.

However, when the paper log is cut into smaller rolls, which in turn eventually get cut into sheets (for sheet-fed presses) or individual pages, the mill can cut the log into short rolls or long rolls. The grain is then called either short grain or long grain. Then the short grain or long grain sheets can be run through the press or your printer in such a way that the pages print with the grain running from top to bottom of the page or side to side of the page.

Why should this matter? Because paper prints with better registration when it's run grain-long. It folds more smoothly when folded with the grain but more strongly when folded against the grain. With heavier paper stock, a fold against the grain may need to be scored first so you get a crack-free fold that is also strong. Book pages that have the grain running parallel to the spine lie flat. The pages don't curl or become wavy, and they turn easily.

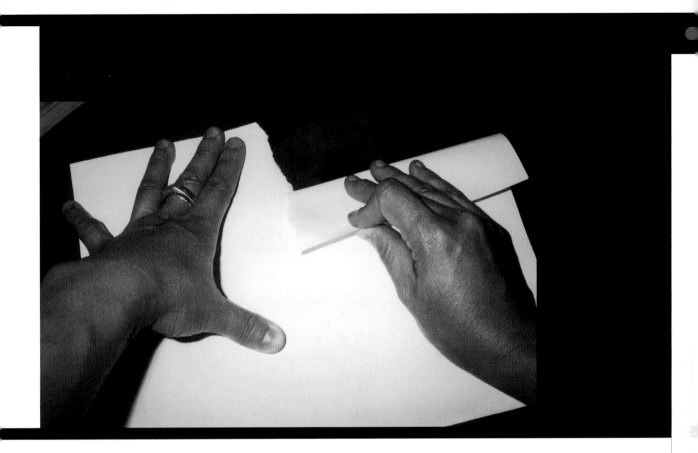

Mills tell you the grain direction of the paper by listing the grain-long measurement last. If a sheet measures 11 by 17 inches (28 by 43 centimeters), the grain runs parallel to the 17-inch (43-centimeter) side. Some mills underline the grain-long measurement, just so you know. A sheet that is called "22 x 17 inches" has a grain parallel to the 17-inch side.

If you don't know the grain of your paper, you can find out by tearing a sheet in each direction, top to bottom and then side to side. Paper tears more smoothly and easily with the grain. Tears made against the grain tear much more roughly—not in a straight line at all. Just try it with any sheet of stamps: Depending on the layout, you'll find that you can tear off a stamp easily in one direction. But in the other direction . . . ah, that's when you tear off pieces of the next stamp by accident, or rip your stamp in two, then try to glue the pieces back onto the envelope because darned if the Post Office is going to rip you off. Thank goodness for those self-adhesive stamps with die-cut edges that you simply peel off, unless they get stuck to the paper and you need a knife to tear them off, and . . . but that's another story.

(ABOVE)

If you can't determine for certain which way the grain runs on a sheet, try tearing it by hand. The paper tears easily and fairly straight with the grain; it tears unevenly against the grain.

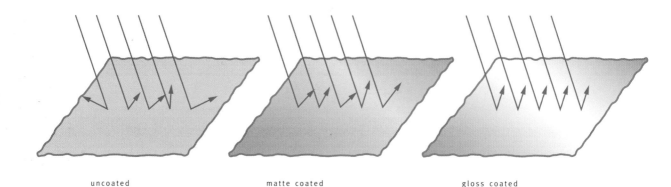

uncoated   matte coated   gloss coated

The smoothness of a paper's finish affects how much light the paper can reflect back to our eyes. Uncoated papers (left) have an uneven surface that scatters light in random directions, carrying information unseen away from our eyes. Such papers do not hold detail well and make colors look grayish. Matte-coated papers (center) are smoother and do a better job of reflecting light, but gloss-coated papers (right) are the smoothest of all and reflect light most perfectly. That's why images printed on glossy paper show fine detail and saturated colors.

Finish

Finish describes the way a paper is surfaced. Generally paper can be made with either a rough or a smooth finish.

Most digital printers work best with smooth finishes. That's because toner or ink-jet droplets are really small and they can get lost in the crevices of rough paper. In the case of toner, this might prevent good fusion of the toner to the paper. In the case of ink-jet, you might lose detail in your art-work as the ink droplets disappear into the texture.

Images tend to be brighter on smooth paper because smooth paper reflects

light back evenly, in parallel wave-lengths. Rough paper scatters light in all directions. The light that is scattered away from our eyes carries information with it. Think of printing on corrugated paper. You might not see one part of an image at all, if the curvature of the corrugation scatters light in a direction completely away from your eyes. That being said, most rough finished papers are not this rough so the information you lose is related more to intensity: Colors look less bright on rough textured paper. This is not necessarily a bad thing; it is a factor that you should incorporate into your design from the beginning.

One way to compensate for the tendency of rough finishes to scatter light is to lay on a coat of something that smoothes out the texture in the areas you are going to overprint. Foil stamping has this effect, as do various kinds of undercoats that are then overprinted later with your design.

Finishes can sometimes be too smooth for digital technology. If the paper feeding mechanism depends on friction to carry a sheet through the printer, a really slick paper surface can jam up the works. In addition, paper that has been smoothed with a coating can present ink-drying or toner-fusion problems. Not every coated paper works with this technology. Check with the mill or try experimenting before you buy.

GLOSS

Gloss is the amount of shininess a paper has, as measured by the amount of light it reflects back. Gloss can be applied merely by polishing a paper during manufacture. Papers made this way are called calendered or supercalendered.

For more gloss, mills add coatings to the paper. Some of these are shinier than others. The shiniest is cast coating, followed by: ultragloss, gloss-coated, dull-coated (also called velvet or suede), and matte.

The reason why printers like glossy paper is that it makes colors look brighter. This is partly caused by the fact that coatings seal the surface of paper and make it smoother. But colors also look brighter because shiny papers simply reflect more light. The more light you see, the more intense the colors appear.

(ABOVE)
You can print bright colors and fine detail on rough-finished paper, if you first print a layer of opaque white ink to smooth out the surface, or if you overprint foil stamping, as shown here.

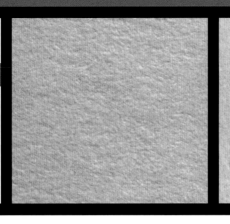

COMMON FINISHES

Mills use their own terminology to describe their finishes, so you should really check paper samples. but generally, the most common finishes are:

ANTIQUE
Slightly rough surface to simulate old-fashioned paper. It is halfway between the rougher vellum and smoother eggshell finishes.

CALENDER
Created during manufacture as the paper is smoothed between rollers. This finish is smoother than uncoated paper but not as smooth as coated paper.

CANVAS
Embossed onto dry paper to simulate a canvas weave.

CAST-COATED
Coating applied to paper and polished against a hot, smooth drum while the coating is still wet. This finish is the glossiest of all.

COCKLE
Slightly pebbly.

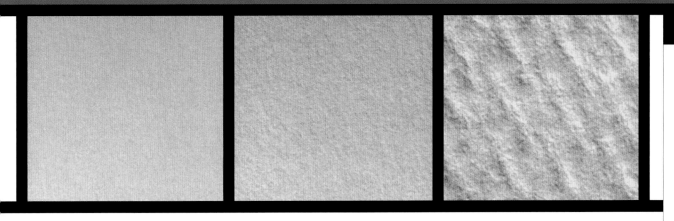

DULL
On coated paper, a coating applied to make the paper look very flat, not shiny at all. It is smoother than matte finish.

EGGSHELL
Pebbly to resemble an egg. This finish is smoother than antique.

FELT
Soft pattern that looks woven.

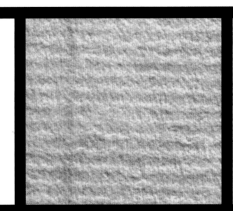

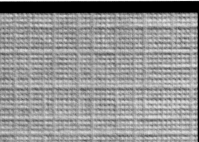

LAID
Grid pattern of parallel lines.

LINEN
Lightly embossed to resemble linen cloth.

MATTE
On coated paper, a coating applied to make the paper look flat, instead of shiny. It is a slightly rougher finish than dull-coated paper.

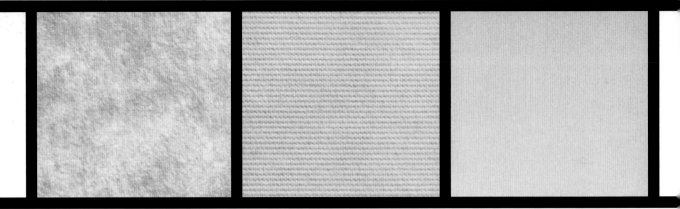

PARCHMENT
Hard-surface finish that looks almost brittle.

SATIN
Smooth finish with slightly embossed look to resemble satin. Also used as an alternate name for dull finish on coated stock.

SUEDE
Another term for dull finish.

SUPERCALENDER
Smoother than calender finish; created by pulling paper through alternating chrome and fiber rollers.

VELLUM
Fairly rough to simulate animal hides.

WOVE
Smooth finish just hinting at cloth-like appearance.

Laser printers work the same way that xerographic copiers work: First a print drum is given an electrostatic charge and a light source burns away the charge from nonprinting areas. Toner is attracted to the still-charged areas on the drum, which then transfers the toner to the paper. Then the toner is fused onto the paper by heat. Furthermore, printers and copiers feed individual sheets through the printer using surface friction.

These facts have implications when it comes to paper choices. You need to look for papers that have:

1. BALANCE BETWEEN SMOOTHNESS AND TOOTHINESS. *To feed properly, paper should have enough toothiness (rough surface) to provide the proper amount of friction for the feeding mechanism to grab each sheet separately. But to print properly, paper should have a smooth enough surface so the toner is applied evenly and, more important, so the tiny little toner particles achieve good adhesion when they're fused to the paper. Too rough a surface will prevent good fusion, and the toner will flake off.*

Papers made specifically for copiers and laser printers achieve a nice balance between smoothness and toothiness. You're usually safe when you select them, although the cast-coated, ultra-smooth papers will jam from time to time because they're so slick.

If you want to use papers not made for copiers and laser printers, you should always experiment first to see if they go through without jamming or flaking. Some will; some won't.

2. BALANCE BETWEEN HIGH AND LOW MOISTURE CONTENT. *High-speed printers and copiers that produce more than ninety pages a minute are finicky about the moisture content of paper. If the paper is too dry, static builds up on the surface and jams the equipment. But if the paper is too moist, the toner won't adhere.*

Papers made for copiers and laser printers always start out with the right moisture content, but paper moisture can vary, depending on the surrounding environment. You should always keep your printer and copier in an environment that controls humidity. Ordinary air-conditioning usually does the job adequately. It also helps if you keep the paper wrapped until you're ready to use it.

When printing on both sides of the paper, make sure you buy a sheet that is specially formulated to withstand the rigors of going through your equipment twice. Copiers and laser printers use heat to fuse toner. The first time you pass a paper through, the heat evaporates some of the moisture content in the paper fibers. You need enough moisture content left in the paper to make it through the process again.

Alternative Papers

Not all commercial papers are made from wood pulp. Some of the most intriguing papers on the market today are made from alternate fibers that would be well worth looking into.

A word of caution before you start salivating over these delicious papers: Because alternative papers are so specialized, supplies can be limited. Sometimes a mill stops making a particular paper altogether for awhile because demand is low or raw materials are short. Sometimes the paper comes back onto the market again; sometimes the mill just moves on. Some mills are completely committed to making a particular kind of paper—kenaf, for instance—so supplies are fairly reliable. But many of the alternative mills are small. When they decide to produce paper from a different fiber, they may go out of production for awhile with other fibers. Finally, some of the alternative papers are prone to market forces based more on fashion than fiber. People just get tired of them, and they disappear.

Make absolutely sure the paper you want is available in the quantity you need, when you need it. You might have to special-order the paper, in which case you must allow enough lead time for delivery. You might also consider stocking up ahead of time so you know you'll have enough. Be careful, too, about committing a major campaign to these papers. If you use an alternative sheet to establish a client's identity, what do you do when the paper disappears? Having said all that, alternative papers are worth all the hassle. They are gorgeous. Here are some of the most interesting ones available now:

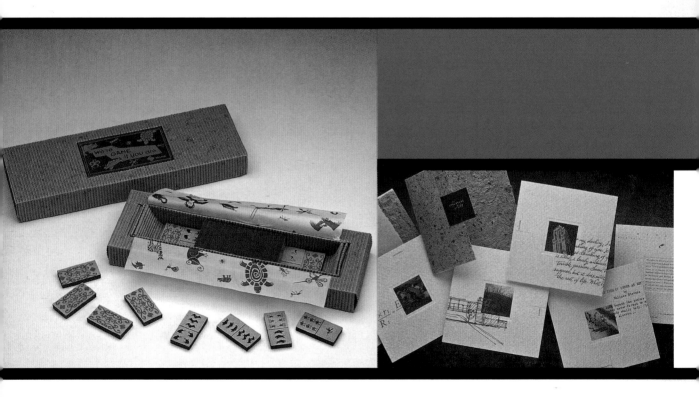

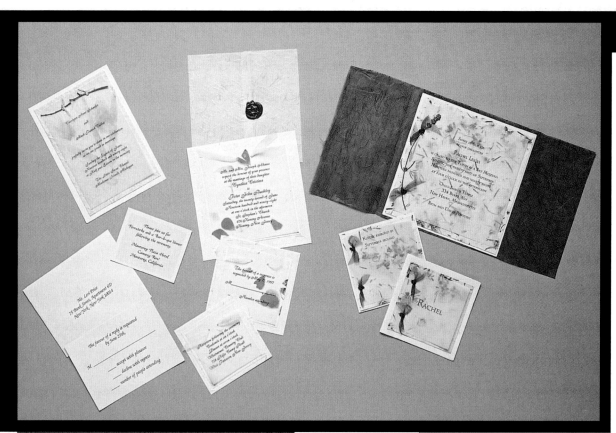

KENAF

A marrow-like plant related to the hibiscus, kenaf was originally grown in Africa but is now grown in the United States, too. It produces a warm, creamy paper that feels soft, almost floppy to the touch, like the finest bond papers. Pure kenaf paper is made without bleach. Although it contains very little lignin, it is very opaque. With a brightness reading of seventy-two, it's equivalent to the brightness of a #5 coated paper, so ink appears fairly bright on the surface. However, the creamy color makes the paper appear much less bright than a white sheet. Colors printed on kenaf appear warmer than on white paper, and ink looks softer. This can be an advantage on digital presses, which produce a very hard-edged printing dot. In addition, kenaf takes foil-stamping well, so you can get a beautiful contrast between the shininess of foil and the dull matte of the paper.

Kenaf is most often blended with other fibers, including cotton, recycled paper pulp, and hemp. Kenaf and kenaf-blends are ideal for books and collateral that strive for an old-fashioned feel, like the feeling you get when you curl up in front of a warm fire.

(ABOVE TOP)

This book about sustainable agriculture was printed on kenaf paper because the publisher thought the topic and the pulp complemented each other. Kenaf is a sustainable source of paper fiber. As an additional bonus, the soft nature of kenaf paper made the watercolor illustrations of the book look more like original watercolors.

(ABOVE BOTTOM)

Vision Paper's kenaf sheet.

HEMP

Although it is banned in the United States because it is a member of the marijuana family, hemp can legally be imported from Canada. It makes a paper that is very durable and tightly bonded. The tight bonds keep ink high on the surface for maximum brightness, however, this can create ink-drying problems. Experiment ahead of time if you're planning to use ink-jet technology. Because of its drying problems, hemp is usually mixed with other fibers, including cotton, kenaf, and wood pulp. With mixed pulps you get all the ink holdout of hemp but without the drying problems. Hemp papers are slightly crisp to the touch but with a cloth-like feel that makes for an intriguing combination.

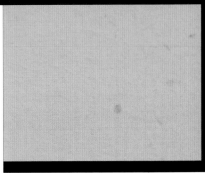

(ABOVE TOP)

Designs made from kenaf, recycled paper, and hemp. Most hemp pulp is mixed with other pulps because hemp alone forms such a tight bond that ink pools almost entirely on the surface, a bit like plastic.

(ABOVE BOTTOM)

Green Field's Hemp paper.

(ABOVE LEFT)

Crane's Crest Moonstone Grey Wove and Crane's Crest Natural White Wove are both papers made from cotton.

(ABOVE CENTER)

The designer chose 100 percent cotton paper for this restaurant postcard to link the restaurant's food image to its commitment to the environment. As a bonus, the look of the paper added to the warmth of the image.

(FACING PAGE, LEFT)

Twinrocker Double X Flax.

(FACING PAGE, UPPER RIGHT)

Paper made from agripulp (in this case, Arbokem's wheat-stalk paper) prints very like the paper made from wood pulp. Of all the alternative fibers, it is the most predictable on press.

(FACING PAGE, LOWER RIGHT)

Agripulp papers include Banana Fiber, Favini Seaweed, Domtar Weeds/Hemp/Sugarcane, and Twinrocker Heartland Cornhusks.

COTTON

Some of the finest bond papers in the world are made from cotton or cotton blends. In the past, these papers used to be made from cotton rags. Nowadays they are made from linter, an otherwise unused portion of the cotton ball. Cotton papers can also be made from recycled cotton fiber, including denim. Usually when denim is the base fiber, the papers are unbleached, allowing the familiar denim-blue color to dominate. Cotton papers can also be made from organically grown cotton, a more expensive source of supply but very correct politically for audiences who care about such issues. Cotton papers are exceptionally strong, because cotton fibers are longer than wood fibers. These papers feel soft and toothy and carry an unmistakable association with quality and excellence, especially for stationery.

One of the more intriguing cotton papers is made by Green Field from cotton that is naturally colored pale green or pale brown. The papers made from these plants keep their natural color and have no additional dyes. They look subtly different from anything else on the market. Unfortunately they can be hard to obtain at times.

fields of reams

FLAX

Linen comes from flax, and linen has long been used to make the finest writing paper in the world. In fact, many wood-pulp sheets today are given a finish to resemble flax paper. Like cotton papers, flax papers are very strong and rather toothy, in an elegant way. Also like cotton papers, they feel a little bit like cloth, though somewhat stiffer than the floppy feel you get with cotton papers.

AGRIPULP

As rural land becomes more valuable throughout the world, companies try to make every possible use of the crops that are grown. One of the more innovative ideas is to make paper out of the waste left behind when crops are harvested. Wheat stalks, rice straw, sugar cane stems, and even banana plant stems have been used as fibers for paper pulp. Usually the fibers are blended with more traditional fibers, especially recycled paper, so that the resulting papers behave more predictably on press. In fact, of all the alternate-fiber papers, agripulp fiber acts most like ordinary wood pulp paper in terms of overall runnability. In some cases, you can hardly tell the difference, especially with wheat straw fiber. However, different fibers can create surprises.

Bagasse, for example, is a very short-fiber, so the papers are thicker and stiffer but also weaker than wood pulp paper. It's best to run tests with these papers and to plan ahead, too. They're not always available in the sizes or quantities you need.

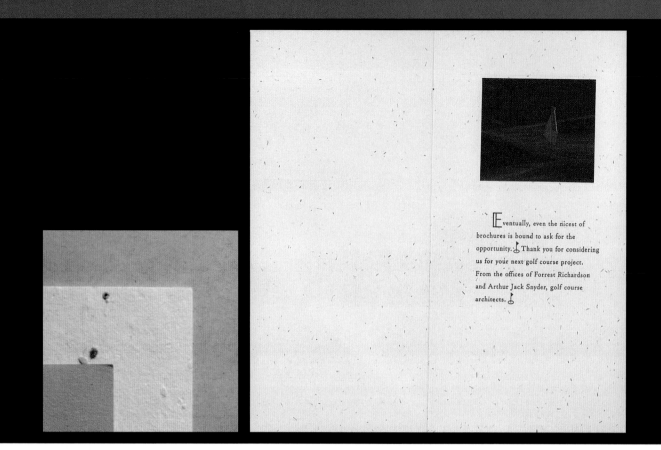

Eventually, even the nicest of brochures is bound to ask for the opportunity. ⚑ Thank you for considering us for your next golf course project. From the offices of Forrest Richardson and Arthur Jack Snyder, golf course architects. ⚑

(ABOVE LEFT)

Crane's Denim Blue, Green Field's Seeds, and Crane's Old Money papers.

(ABOVE RIGHT)

Four Corners' Golf Paper includes grass clippings from golf courses. The flecks of grass in the paper add visual interest to the design. To avoid dealing with flecks in the four-color art, the designer scanned the color images onto T-shirt transfers, hot-pressed them onto muslin fabric, and glued them into place.

(FACING PAGE)

All the papers in these designs were made from recycled paper, but the papers were made in various grades and colors. Recycled paper is now available in almost as many varieties as virgin paper.

RECYCLED

These papers are so common in the market now that they can hardly be called alternative fibers. However, there are vast differences among these papers, based largely on whether the pulp content contains post-consumer waste. Post-consumer waste is the only kind that actually keeps used paper out of landfills. It comes from paper products that have been used and discarded by consumers. This used paper is collected and trucked to a special kind of paper mill, where it is chopped up and de-inked. The de-inking can be a very tricky process because of the many different kinds of inks used today. De-inking also involves the removal of glues, coatings, varnishes, and laminates. These products, called "stickies," all need to be washed out of the recycled pulp before new paper can be made.

The other kind of recycled paper is made from "mill broke," scraps of paper left over from the manufacturing process. Mill broke has been recycled for decades. It's easy to reuse because it has never been printed or finished in any way. Technically, paper made from mill broke is recycled because the broke is thrown back into the mix. But broke never reaches the consumer in its original form; it never leaves the mill at all. So it doesn't really keep paper out of the waste stream.

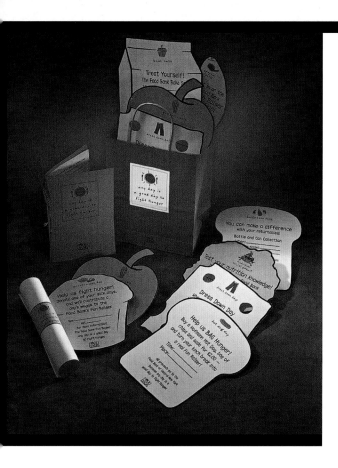

If recycling to you means keeping paper out of landfills, then be sure to check the post-consumer waste content of the paper you buy. You might be surprised at how low the percentage is in most recycled papers. The reason for the low percentage is that recycled paper pulp has shorter fibers than virgin pulp. Short fibers means weak paper. So almost all recycled sheets contain a significant amount of virgin pulp, just as a practical matter.

WHAT-THE-HECK-IS-THAT PULP?

Because paper can be made from any fiber that bonds when wet, some companies have come up with really creative pulps: grass clippings, old money, junk mail, seeds you can plant, sea grass that would otherwise clog the canals of Venice, beer labels and hops, denim jeans, coffee plants, and banana stems. Many of these papers work extremely well in laser printers and ink-jet printers. They generally aren't available in rolls however, so commercial digital web presses are out of luck.

The charm of these papers is that the pulp contains visible flecks that provide texture and color. With the right design, they can be stunning. But be aware that the flecks can occur anywhere on the sheet, including some areas where you'd rather not have them appear. For example, you wouldn't want your runway model to look more like Long John Silver just because an inconvenient fleck covered up her eye and a few too many teeth in her smile.

13

WORKFLOW

There's a scene in the movie *Top Gun* in which the intrepid hero (played by Tom Cruise) straps himself into a fighter jet, announces to the world that "I feel the need . . . for speed!" and, with no more than about three seconds of preflight preparation, he zooms off into the sky at supersonic velocity.

If only digital workflow were this easy! Your client may envision digital printing jobs whirring out the door every 20 seconds, but experienced designers know that without careful planning and preflight checks, a digital printing job can all-too-swiftly resemble a smoking pile of wreckage at the end of the runway.

The key to success is to design a workflow that makes sense. To do this you should consider two aspects of workflow:

1. In-house control of versions

2. Electronic compilation of files for printing

Versions

Years ago, when designers still sent out manuscripts to a typesetter to be typeset, my staff and I were working on an adventure-travel guidebook. The book listed more than 2,000 trips that people could take to exotic locations. Many trips went to places that we had never heard of before. We bought the best atlases we could find and hired a staff just to check place names.

Spelling all the geographic names was a major challenge for our typesetter, too. He had to take our original, correct manuscript and keystroke it into his software (no desktop publishing in those days!).

You know how some words just seem to baffle you? No matter how hard you try, you always spell them wrong. For our typesetter, Ougadougou was his Waterloo. Ougadougou is the capital city of Upper Volta. It's not really that exotic, but it's certainly not a name that you'd ever want to see spelled wrong in your book. But on the first proofs, our typesetter had consistently spelled it Ougagadougou. Just saying that name out loud had us rolling in the aisles. When our eyes stopped streaming, we sent back the proofs with the corrected name supplied.

When the second proofs came back, all was well. So we directed him to send the reprographic-paper layouts to our printer in Indiana to be plated. When the blueline proofs came back from the printer, somehow Ougagadougou had returned. My boss caught the error and came steaming into my office.

"Now, I know I had that fixed," I said, puzzled. I hadn't bothered to reread the bluelines word for word because we were in the computer age, after all. Once a correction has been made, it doesn't change. But inexplicably, Ougadougou had changed. I sat down and read the blues from cover to cover. Many of the corrections I remembered making were now missing. I called the typesetter.

"I did make those corrections," he said.

"Then what happened?" I asked. He refused to speculate. I asked the printer to send back all our original layouts. When they arrived, I saw that the typesetter had not output clean copies of the corrections. Instead, he had typeset individual words and glued them on top of our repro paper with wax. In the heat of summer in Indiana, the wax had melted and many of the corrected words had simply slid off.

I bring up this story because I'm often reminded of it when I deal with modern-day versioning issues. Unless you're a one-person design shop working in complete isolation from the real world, you will be challenged by the possibility that someone will change your work—either your text, your layout or your graphics—and you won't realize it. That is, until the worst, most embarrassing moment, of course, which usually is after the job has been printed and mailed.

The temptation not to check everything word for word or pixel for pixel in late stages of production will be overwhelming. After all, you live in the digital world, where type and pixels reside as numeric abstractions on a sacrosanct disk, invulnerable from wind, weather, or wacky typesetters. Right. If you believe that, then have I got a trip planned for you.

The reality is, whenever anyone makes a change in your digital designs, it can create a cascade effect that can reflow text and alter line breaks, create false color readings, freeze up embedded commands, and otherwise prove to be disastrous.

Original ad

Sometimes these changes can be obvious: The ad director makes the tiniest, smallest, most insignificant alteration on an ad when he proofs the "final" copy. The art director wants to tune up the skin tones in that model's face "just a tad." The copywriter realizes she has an extra hour that she didn't expect and wants to take advantage by rewriting one paragraph — it won't change the line breaks, she promises.

These in-house alterations are challenging enough. Even more challenging, however, are editorial changes that outside vendors may have to make to your designs. Perhaps you need to call in a spelling error that you just found, or your client just called to let you know that a price change has to be made in the ad copy. Sometimes when the printing vendor opens your file and makes the change, mysterious things can happen. Text can reflow completely, despite the fact that your printer is using the same font. Fonts can change. Colors can alter. Systems can crash.

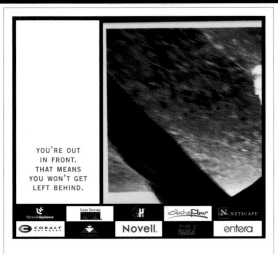

Updated with wrong version of photos

Text edit reflowing body text

Text box brought to front

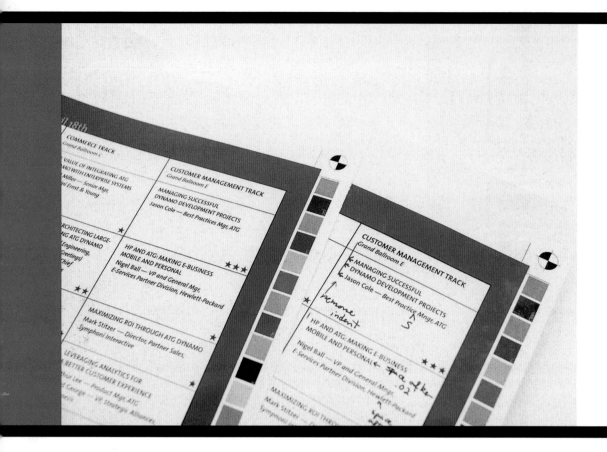

Controlling Changes

You need to control both kinds of changes, but you must do it with two different strategies.

IN HOUSE

Within your own environment, you need to set up a version control system that helps you keep track of who's changing what and when. Software programs exist that can manage your sites without a lot of nagging and herding by you. Such applications should provide:

- A secure system that lets different people check in and check out files and that records when they do so.

- A method to lock down files currently in use to prevent simultaneous modifications by others on the network.

- A way to lock out files so that only particular people can open them and change them, but anyone can look at them.

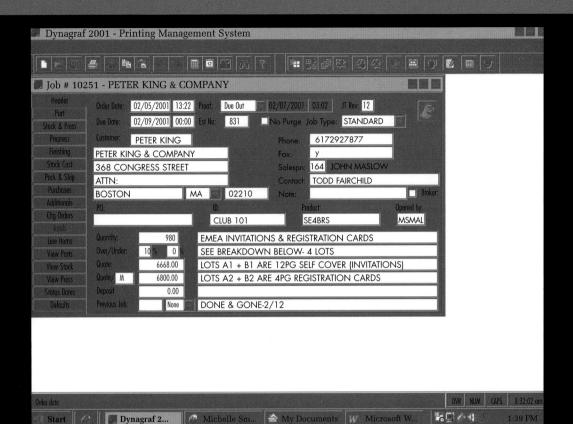

Dynagraf 2001 - Printing Management System

Job # 10251 - PETER KING & COMPANY

Header	
Part	
Stock & Press	
Prepress	
Finishing	
Stock Cost	
Pack & Ship	
Purchases	
Additionals	
Chg Orders	
Totals	
Line Items	
View Parts	
View Stock	
View Press	
Status Dates	
Defaults	

Order Date: 02/05/2001 13:22 Proof: Due Out 02/07/2001 03:02 JT Rev: 12
Due Date: 02/09/2001 00:00 Est No: 831 ☐ No Purge Job Type: STANDARD

Customer: PETER KING Phone: 6172927877
PETER KING & COMPANY Fax: y
368 CONGRESS STREET Salespn: 164 JOHN MASLOW
ATTN: Contact: TODD FAIRCHILD
BOSTON MA 02210 Note: ☐ Broker:

PO: ID: CLUB 101 Product: SE4BRS Opened by: MSMAL

Quantity: 980 EMEA INVITATIONS & REGISTRATION CARDS
Over/Under: 10 % 0 % SEE BREAKDOWN BELOW- 4 LOTS
Quote: 6668.00 LOTS A1 + B1 ARE 12PG SELF COVER (INVITATIONS)
Quote/ M 6800.00 LOTS A2 + B2 ARE 4PG REGISTRATION CARDS
Deposit 0.00
Previous Job: None DONE & GONE-2/12

Order date | OVR | NUM | CAPS | 8:32:02 am

Start | Dynagraf 2... | Michelle Sm... | My Documents | Microsoft W... | 1:39 PM

OUT OF HOUSE

To address outsourcing version changes, you need to pursue two rules.

- You and your vendors must share the same software and the same versions of that software. Don't make assumptions here; check explicitly ahead of time.

- You need to set up a way to view proofs, even when the changes are really and truly the last possible moment. Realistically, this may not be possible, but be aware that without proofs, you run the risk of creating a new problem when you attempt to solve the old one.

EMC **Club 101** 2000

Even fairly simple design jobs can employ large numbers of different software applications. How many applications do you think were used to create these designs? Hint: The answer is more than ten.

Compilation of Files

Consider how many applications must come together for an imagesetter or a digital printer to output a fairly simple design. You might employ:

- An object-oriented illustration program, such as Adobe Illustrator.

- An editing program for bitmapped color separations, such as Adobe Photoshop.

- A layout program, such as QuarkXPress or Adobe PageMaker.

- Fonts from various sources.

- Imported graphics in a variety of formats, such as EPS, TIFF, GIF, JPEG, etc.

- A trapping program, such as Adobe InProduction.

- A validation or preflight program such as Enfocus PitStop.

- A workflow automation program, such as Callas PDF Toolbox.

- A compression tool, such as TIFF or JPEG.

To print on any digital printing device, all these different applications must come together to produce one document that can be read by your output device.

In the past, the language that brought all these elements together and communicated them to the output device was PostScript. PostScript language converts many different digital schemes into one

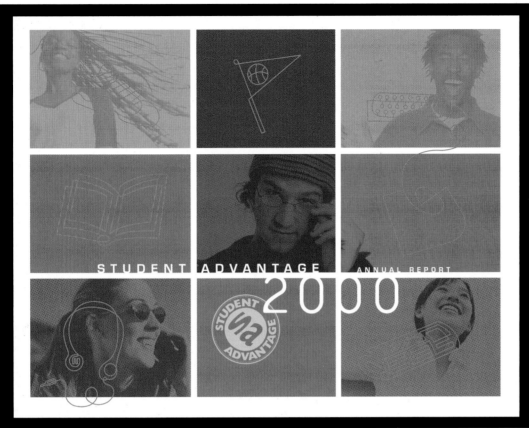

STUDENT ADVANTAGE   ANNUAL REPORT

2000

scheme that arranges data into lines of dots, called rasters. Before anything can be printed, it must be rasterized (RIPed).

PostScript is still universally used to RIP graphics applications. But PostScript is limited. It cannot accept all software programs. When a RIPing device receives PostScript instructions that it doesn't recognize, it halts or crashes.

Service bureaus and printers try to accommodate the almost infinite number of software programs in the marketplace by buying and installing the most common applications. Many attempt to satisfy customers by buying the same software that the cus-

tomers like, so that they can support the designs that customers submit. But service bureaus and printers can't buy everything. Now and then, a customer embeds a file or graphic that simply won't RIP. This usually happens at the end stage of production, when there is no time left in the schedule. Customers become very unhappy if their designs fail at this point.

To solve this problem, vendors urged programmers to come up with some kind of standardizing, over-arching software. Adobe PDF (Portable Document Format) is the answer that is coming to dominate digital printing more and more. PDF is a language that is platform- and media-independent.

You don't need to separate text files, fonts, image files, or vector illustrations. PDF can incorporate everything into one file. Furthermore, PDF can compress data, making it easy to send extremely large files across the Internet without tying up your equipment for eons. Best of all, you can design your own workflow system. Here's how:

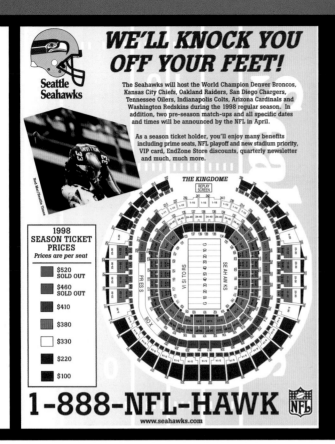

To Build Your Own Confidence, Build Your Own Workflow

When you're learning to fly an airplane, they don't start you out on a jumbo jet (too expensive) or a jet fighter (too fast). No, they start you out on something like a Piper Cub—an airplane so simple that all the parts are visible, so slow that a new pilot has plenty of time to look around and figure out how it all works, and so inexpensive that that you can afford to own one yourself.

Recent developments have made it possible to get started in digital printing workflow the same way, using PDF as the core technology. At this point, so many different vendors support PDF that it is now practical

to build a complete digital workflow environment on your own personal computer, inexpensively, in a completely do-it-yourself manner.

In fact, not only is it possible to construct a do-it-yourself digital workflow environment, doing so is by far the best way to acquire an in-depth understanding of how digital workflow works.

Your first step toward digital production is to convert the PostScript file output from your layout program (typically a program like PageMaker or QuarkXPress) into a PDF file. Among the higher-end products are Adobe

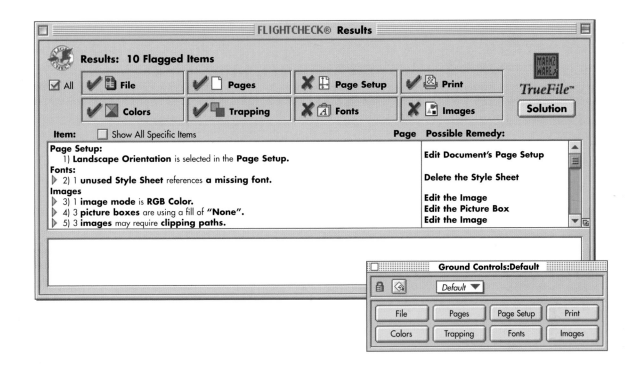

Acrobat and Agfa Apogee Create, while at the low end there is the shareware product Ghostscript. Even at this very first step, however, it is entirely possible to "crash and burn." You have to keep in mind all the things we talked about in previous chapters. For example, did you remember to embed all the fonts you need into the PDF document? Do you know whether the fonts are Type 1, TrueType, or some even more modern format, and does your RIP engine care? Are all the bitmap graphics in the document of sufficiently high resolution? Was the trapping handled in the layout program, or are you going to handle it yourself later on in the digital print cycle?

Many of these problems can be detected by verification software, which essentially performs a preflight check on the PDF file. Many such verification packages are available on the market.

It used to be the case that PDF files could not be readily altered, but the modern software programs have changed this: It is now perfectly possible to change fonts, add words, tweak the position of graphics elements, and alter the color balance of individual graphic elements within Acrobat. Major changes, however, require a return to the starting layout program most of the time.

(ABOVE)

Preflight applications such as this one are essential for good workflow. They can flag potential RIPing problems that would cause your job to crash. They can also remind you to send all the necessary files to your printer. You might think this last point is a no-brainer, but a recent survey among service bureaus showed that the most common problem is that clients don't include all the font files needed to RIP their designs.

Variable-data printing is likely
to play a very important role in any twenty-first century
career in print production.

You can be reasonably assured that a PDF file that passes the verification stage will RIP without crashing, but this does not mean that the results are guaranteed to be good. Innumerable layout problems like poor kerning, insufficient bleeds, bad color balance, insufficient pixel resolution, and banding can occur, and may require you to return to the beginning to fix.

Most of the verification software programs do not attempt to deal with the next stages of digital production: trapping, imposition, and separation. Typically these are handled by separate applications. This is a rapidly evolving area in which new software products appear on a monthly basis — your best bets for keeping up-to-date

in these areas are to check with your printer ahead of time to see what you might need to do in-house and what may be performed by the printer on the printer's workstation.

But if you become reasonably conversant with a PDF program such as Adobe Acrobat, a validation program like Enfocus PitStop, a separation and trapping tool like Adobe InProduction, and an imposition and workflow automation tool like Latana CrackerJack, you should be capable of RIPing onto ink-jet, dye-sublimation, liquid toner, and dry toner presses, in four or more colors.

Congratulations! You have achieved the digital equivalent of flying a Piper Cub . . . now it's time to begin upgrading your skills.

Reach Out to Clients Through Variable-Data Printing

If you are lucky, it will not be until after you have finished your own do-it-yourself digital workflow system that one of your managers, in a highly excited state, will approach you waving a trade journal article about a hot new marketing tool called "variable-data printing which allows you to individualize every single message that you print."

"I've got a great idea!" he or she will say. "Let's start customizing all our print jobs for our individual customers! Here's a Zip disk with our customer database. Can you have something printed by next week? Oh yeah, and we want to put it on the Web too!"

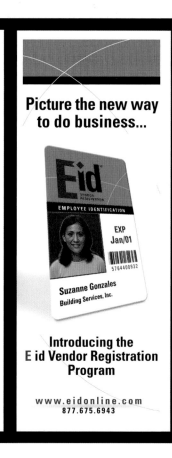
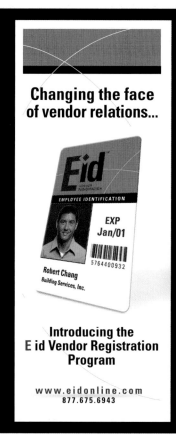

This may sound like a nightmare— and it can be. Unless, that is, you have anticipated that this day will come, and have prepared for it. Because the plain fact is, variable-data printing is likely to play a very important role in any twenty-first century career in print production.

The main challenge you are going to face is this: Companies that know a lot about business and database management (such as IBM and Xerox) are generally not too strong at high-end printing. And conversely, companies that know a lot about high-end digital printing (such as Agfa, Indigo, Heidelberg, and Xeikon) are generally not too strong at business database management. But all these companies, and dozens more, are scrambling furiously to enter the market for high-quality, variable-data digital printing.

The paradoxical result is that the overall business of high-quality variable-data printing is going to be a big success, but most of the individual products will not survive. A shakeout is inevitable.

As a designer, you can save yourself a lot of grief by being proactive in this area. Identify a product in your client's portfolio that would clearly benefit from variable-data printing: Such products can be as varied as billing statements, business proposals, catalogs, direct mail, and posters. Then contact the vendors of your favorite layout programs: You can be completely confident that most of them now offer a variable-data interface.

(ABOVE)

Using variable-data printing, the designer of this job was able to provide a service to his client that was impossible prior to the invention of on-demand digital printing. With variable-data printing, an entire press run of brochures can be printed, and each brochure can be completely different from the one before.

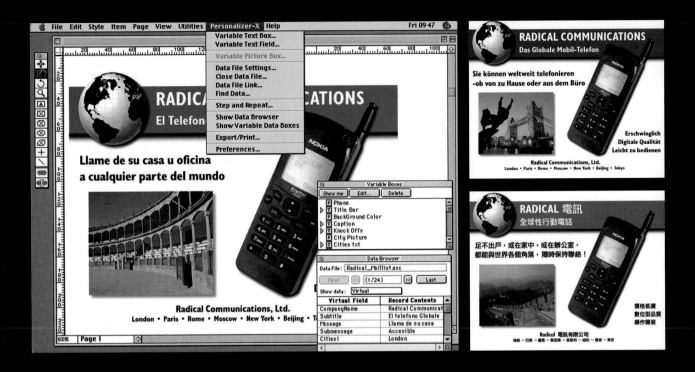

Now work out the kind of variable-data assignment you would like to receive from your client, as a do-able increment on your existing digital workflow system. Concentrate mainly on a smooth and reliable production flow; don't worry too much about the marketing or artistic aspects (which will be taken care of later). How will you interface to the database? Once you have a good idea of the kind of variable-data job you would be prepared to tackle as a reasonable first job, approach your client and say, "Look, this is the kind of variable-data printing job we are presently set up to do. Let's give it a try and see how it

works." In this way, you can reliably arrange to fly a Piper Cub for your first variable-data mission. Your chances of surviving the mission and enjoying the trip will be correspondingly greater, and you will look like a hero to your clients.

There are some not-so-obvious considerations that enter into variable-data printing. A key issue is that a digital press that prints a page every 3 seconds cannot be efficiently driven by software that takes 20 seconds to RIP each page.

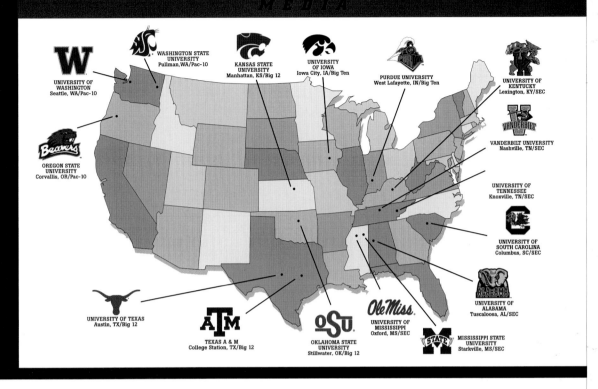

W — UNIVERSITY OF WASHINGTON, Seattle, WA/Pac-10

WASHINGTON STATE UNIVERSITY, Pullman, WA/Pac-10

KANSAS STATE UNIVERSITY, Manhattan, KS/Big 12

UNIVERSITY OF IOWA, Iowa City, IA/Big Ten

PURDUE UNIVERSITY, West Lafayette, IN/Big Ten

UNIVERSITY OF KENTUCKY, Lexington, KY/SEC

VANDERBILT UNIVERSITY, Nashville, TN/SEC

OREGON STATE UNIVERSITY, Corvallis, OR/Pac-10

UNIVERSITY OF TENNESSEE, Knoxville, TN/SEC

UNIVERSITY OF SOUTH CAROLINA, Columbus, SC/SEC

UNIVERSITY OF TEXAS, Austin, TX/Big 12

TEXAS A & M, College Station, TX/Big 12

OKLAHOMA STATE UNIVERSITY, Stillwater, OK/Big 12

Ole Miss — UNIVERSITY OF MISSISSIPPI, Oxford, MS/SEC

UNIVERSITY OF ALABAMA, Tuscaloosa, AL/SEC

MISSISSIPPI STATE UNIVERSITY, Starkville, MS/SEC

When PostScript was originally written, this problem was not anticipated. It was thought that a RIPing engine, such as an imagesetter, would be given one job to do, and it could chunk away at it for an appreciable amount of time. Eventually it would spew out film that would go on to be made into printing plates that would then be used to print many, many copies. The paradigm was RIP once, print many.

Variable-data digital printing requires a different paradigm: RIP and print, RIP and print, RIP and print really, really fast. That's because, with variable-data digital printing, the RIPed file is essentially the final printed piece.

Different digital printers have come up with different ways to speed up the RIP so that their printers don't sit around waiting while the RIPing device thinks about what to output. Commonly, these vendors try to segregate elements of your design that do stay the same from one copy to the next. These elements are RIPed once. Then little sidecar RIPs can process the design elements that are different and plug them into the final output. Because the amount of data used to create the differences is smaller, the process goes faster.

Unfortunately, it will be awhile before new standards emerge in this area, and in the meantime, the vendors all tout their own (proprietary) solution. There is no perfect solution to this, except to encourage your vendors to embrace open standards as they emerge.

Another not-so-obvious consideration is that your client may be very unwilling to let the company's proprietary customer database travel off-site to a commercial printer. They worry about this because, in principle, it would be easy to extract the company's database, especially now that text in PDF can be saved to rich text format (RTF).

This fear can lead to ludicrous situations in which large-capacity Xeikon presses suddenly appear in-house, with a corresponding decrease in your business (if you are an independent design firm) or an increase in your responsibilities (if you work for one of these corporations and they snag you into this before you can run away). This is where a proactive relationship with your client and/or management and marketing can pay big dividends.

One of the most important reasons to maintain rigorous protocols in your workflow process is that when a last-minute digital printing job comes in the door (above left), you will have the systems in place to handle it as well as the other jobs already in the pipeline (above right) —without causing you or your staff to burn out.

Maintain Situational Awareness

Lastly, to create a sensible digital workflow, you should know what every pilot knows: how vital it is to maintain situational awareness. Situational awareness is knowledge of where the airplane is, what direction it is headed, and what is likely to happen next. Without good situational awareness, nasty crashes are almost inevitable.

Digital print production is like that too. You can maintain your own situational awareness if you:

1. Control and master all the details of your own digital workflow.

2. Get serious about keeping up-to-date on developments.

3. Be proactive in dealing with your clients and/or your management: Let them know what you can and cannot do with exciting new resources before they get too creative.

4. Be progressive yet incremental in the jobs you tackle. Don't tackle new technologies unless and until your present digital workflow environment is calm, stable, and productive — at least, within reason.

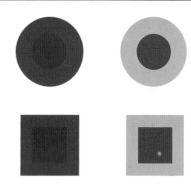

Trapping is a way to butt two or more colors against each other so that white space doesn't show between them when they're printed. As the paper goes through the printer, minor variations in registration can occur. The printing device can put one color down in one area, but then the paper can shift slightly and mis-register when the printer puts the second color down on the paper.

To avoid this problem, designers must overlap the two colors. The question is: Which colors overlap and which underlie? You have two choices:

- You can spread (enlarge) the lighter color into the darker color.

- You can choke (reduce) the lighter color into the darker color.

You use a spread trap when the background color is darker than the image it surrounds; use the choke trap when the background color is lighter than the image it surrounds.

You can set traps in many different software applications and at different stages in the design process: when you create a graphic; edit the graphic; or layout the pages. Most of these software applications have tried to automate trapping for you; several have default traps built in.

The problem is that different output devices have different trapping requirements. Before you set any traps, you must find out what the overlap requirements are (especially the amount of overlap) for the particular output device you will be using. Then set traps accordingly.

Some printing devices are extremely finicky and idiosyncratic. Your printing house should be able to tell you ahead of time all the information you need to set proper traps. Or your printer might just tell you not to set any traps at all. If the printing device is extremely idiosyncratic (as all flexographic presses are, for example), the printer may prefer to set all the traps once your job is in the production pipeline.

If you do set your own traps, you should make them during late stages of design. It's usually not a good idea to set traps in your individual illustrations or graphics because, under certain circumstances, if you have to resize your art, the traps don't convert to the new size.

14

BINDING AND FINISHING

One of the most gratifying things about a new technology is the thought that you can help people you were never able to help before. Take midlist book authors, for example. In their dreams, they are the next frontlist Stephen King, signing thousands of books for hordes of eager readers at each whistlestop on the promotion circuit. In reality, however, midlist books often wind up on the remainder tables at Barnes & Noble. Then they go out of print.

It's not the lack of royalty checks that hurts so much, although that is painful. It's the sense that one's unique artistic interpretation of the world is no longer around to speak to readers.

Luckily the Author's Guild has recently sponsored a partnership with an on-demand book publisher who promises to print one book at a time for a reasonable price. As one midlist author thrilled, "Each time an order is placed, a single copy of the book is printed. The result: one book per happy reader, and the end of dusty remainders."

More than 600 midlist authors have signed up to join the digital print revolution. What makes this revolution possible is not just the digital printing devices that can cheaply image one copy at a time. It's also bindery and finishing machines that can efficiently trim, fold, staple, or glue one copy at a time.

Many of these machines are linked directly to the printing device, so all the finishing happens in one fell swoop.

In other cases, trimming, folding, and binding machines are offline operations, sometimes so far offline that they happen in a different location and with a different company altogether. Either way, the goal of finishing and binding a digitally printed piece is speed: You need enough speed in the bindery to keep up with the speed of the printer. Without it, your job will stall in bottlenecks. If that happens, then on-demand printing might take on a whole new meaning, as your clients demand to know where their printing is.

The best way for you to stay on the sunny side of your clients is to remember this simple rule: Always start at the finish and work backwards. Before you design anything, you need to discuss finishing with

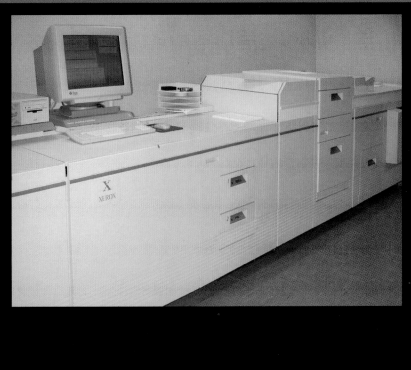

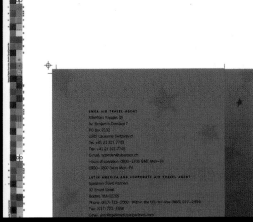

your printer. Most particularly, you need to know two pieces of critical information:

• What finishing options are available?

• What are the design specifications?

This is important even if you're printing only a single-page design, such as a poster. The poster may require no folding or binding, but it will require trimming if you want your image to bleed off the sides.

That's because in all printing, mechanical limitations prevent a printer from covering a sheet completely with a printed image. The printers need a certain amount of blank paper to grab onto to feed through the printing units. This is not a problem if you plan to keep white margins in your finished design, of course. But you still need to know the dimensions that your printing device can image.

Similarly, folding and binding equipment may require some extra paper to grab onto. The extra paper is trimmed off during processing but is absolutely necessary to plan for in the design stages. You don't want to fill a sheet with your design, only to find out later that you haven't allowed enough blank space for the equipment to function.

Another reason to check finishing specs before you design anything is that, as you fold and gather paper, parts of the image may become lost in the folds and trims. Images that used to line up may no longer do so. Binding methods, even simple staples in the upper left corner of a school book report, can obscure images.

(ABOVE LEFT)

Simple trimming and folding jobs might be able to run in-line on an all-in-one printing/finishing system such as this one. More complicated jobs might require off-line finishing, adding to the lead-time.

(ABOVE RIGHT)

Even simple finishing jobs, such as a one-page poster that needs no folding or stapling may require off-line trimming. Check with your printer to make sure your design allows enough trim space.

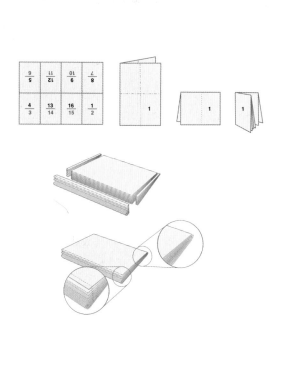

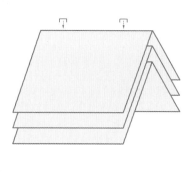

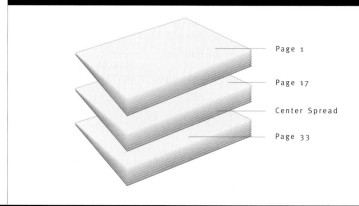

Page 1

Page 17

Center Spread

Page 33

(ABOVE LEFT)

If your job needs folding and trimming, you should ask your printer for a folding dummy before you start designing anything. The folding dummy shows trim lines, bleed lines, imposition, and center lines. If your job is to be saddle-stitched, you should also ask your printer to indicate how much creep (the forward movement of two-page spreads during folding) will occur.

(TOP RIGHT)

Saddle-stitched binding nests one folded signature on top of another on the bindery line. The signatures are then stapled along the folded center line.

(BOTTOM RIGHT)

Perfect binding stacks one folded signature on top of another. The bound edges are then glued or stitched to a cover.

Another technical issue can arise too: The imposition or arrangement of your pages on a press sheet can affect the image size. Any time you print multiple pages on a single printing sheet, this issue can arise. Different styles of imposition result in different image area dimensions.

Because the specifications for each job can vary widely, your best strategy is to ask your printer for a folding dummy (also called a folding layout). The dummy should be lined out with trim marks, bleed marks, fold lines, and center lines.

It should also show the layout of all the pages in imposition order, if your design is a multiple-page job. If your design needs die-cuts or drilling, then the folding dummy should show those, too.

Here are some parameters to consider, as you think about the kind of folding dummy you may need.

Binding Methods

There are two basic ways to bind pages together. Saddle-stitching folds a page or signature in two and drapes the folded piece over a V-shaped saddle, nesting one piece on top of another and fastening them all together along the center fold line.

Perfect binding stacks one page or one signature on top of another and fastens them together along the side in various ways.

All saddle-stitching works essentially the same way, no matter how many signatures are involved. At the start of the bindery line, a folded signature drops onto a V-shaped saddle, with half the pages draped on one side and half draped on the other side. The line conveys the signature to the next station, where the next signature is dropped on top of it. The signatures are carried down the line until all the signatures have been assembled. Then a stitcher staples them together on the center fold, using two, three, or more wire staples. Then the assembled booklet is trimmed on three sides.

By contrast, perfect binding can be done in many different ways, although all involve a similar approach. A folded signature is fed folded and unopened into the first station of the bindery line. The line carries it to the next station, where another folded signature is dropped on top, making a stack. After all the signatures have been stacked, one on top of another, they are bound together and trimmed.

Different methods do this differently, but essentially what happens is that the signatures are bound together by glue, sewn together with thread, or stitched with staples. At some point, the spine side is roughened or milled off and the cover is attached, sometimes with glue, sometimes with stitching. Eventually the three sides of the book are trimmed to final size.

The method of binding can have a large impact on how much image area you have to work with, and how much image gets lost in the gutter or trimmed off. It can also affect how flat the pages lie when the book is open, and how durably the spine can resist weakening with use. Here is a rundown of the most common forms of perfect binding:

Perfect Binding (closed)

Perfect Binding (open)

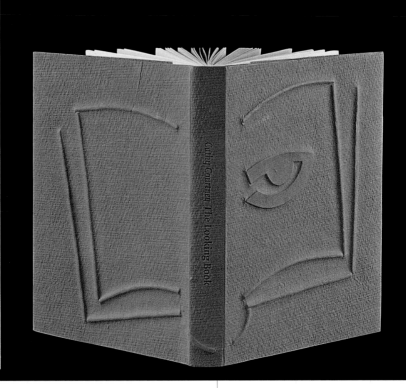

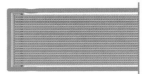

Side-Stitching (closed)

Side-Stitching (open)

PERFECT-BINDING

The signatures are assembled by stacking one on top of another on a bindery line. The signatures are not draped or opened, as with saddle-stitched jobs. The spine edges of the signatures are milled off and glue is applied. The cover is wrapped on and pressed against the glue, then the three remaining sides are trimmed.

The book does not lie flat when opened. In fact, if the book is opened too widely, the glue on the spine can crack, causing the binding to fail.

SIDE-STITCHING

The signatures are assembled by stacking one on top of another on a bindery line, which then runs them through a side-stitcher. The stitcher staples the signatures together by shooting two or three staples through all the signatures along the spine side, inset a fraction of an inch.

The edges of the signatures on the spine side are then milled off and roughened, and glue is applied. A cover is wrapped on and pressed against the glue. Then the other three sides of the book are trimmed to size. The pages do not lie flat when the book is opened, but the binding is very durable.

Channel Binding (open)

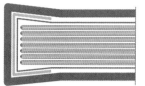

Channel Binding (closed)

Channel Binding (open)

CHANNEL BINDING

The signatures are assembled in a stack and trimmed. Then they're put into a cover, like a case. A metal channel on the cover is compressed, gripping the pages inside.

The metal channels are available in different colors. The pages do not lie flat when opened.

Case-Binding Assembly

1

2

4

3

5

CASE-BINDING

Case-binding is done in two stages. In one stage the case (outer cover) is manufactured. In a separate stage, the body of the book is assembled. Then the two parts are glued together.

1. The case is made by cutting thick paperboard or other rigid material into three pieces: one for the front cover; one for the back cover; and one for the spine. A book covering is cut out of cloth or leather big enough so that it can overlap the three pieces of the case. The case pieces are glued onto the covering, leaving enough room between the three pieces so that the book can be folded. The lapping pieces of the cover are folded over and glued on the inside.

2. The body of the book is assembled much like any other kind of perfect binding. Endpapers may be glued to the first and last pages of the book at this point. Endpapers can be decorative and are often made of heavier stock than the body stock.

3. Then the assembled signatures may be glued together along the spine, or they may be sewn together in different ways.

4. A strip of gauze is glued to the spine, so that the gauze extends outward on each side of the spine.

5. Paste is applied and the book is glued inside the case. Books made in this way "float" inside the hard case. This helps them open flatter than they otherwise would. The spine is also more durable than if the spine was glued directly to the case itself.

Lay-flat Binding (open)

Lay-flat Binding (open)

LAY-FLAT BINDING

This binding method attempts to blend the strength and durability of case binding with the cost-effectiveness of machine perfect-binding. The inside of the book is assembled as with any perfect binding method. The pages are trimmed, and a flexible adhesive is applied to a strip of reinforced crepe lining, which is wrapped over the spine and extends around a portion of the first and last book pages. This is what binds the book pages together; it is also what holds the cover onto the book. The softback cover is glued to the sides of the front and back pages of the book, so the book "floats" between the covers.

The key to this process is the glue, a special kind of cold glue called polyurethane reactive (PUR) that stays flexible throughout its life. The book lies flat when opened.

ADVANTAGES AND DISADVANTAGES OF BINDING METHODS

PERFECT-BINDING

1. Can bind single sheets or cards

2. Can print text or graphics on the spine

3. Many different binding styles and materials available

4. Signatures don't creep

5. Direction of paper grain is crucial—the grain must run parallel to the binding edge

6. A certain portion of the image area may be lost in the gutter

7. Must have an overall thickness of at least 1/8 inch

8. Expensive

SADDLE-STITCHING

1. Must bind folded signatures, so the minimum page count of a signature is four pages

2. Has no spine, so cannot print text or graphics here

3. One style of binding available; can vary the number of staples used

4. Signatures creep, meaning that as one signature is nested on top of another, it must be slightly larger than the one below it for the trimmed edges to line up evenly

5. Direction of paper grain doesn't matter for most papers, so you can use grain-long or grain-short papers

6. No portion of the image area is lost in the gutter

7. Cannot be thicker than approximately 1/2 inch (13 millimeters), and at that size, the binding is weak

8. Relatively cheap

Comb-binding (open)

Tape Binding (open)

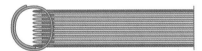

Comb-binding (closed)

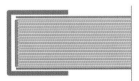

Tape Binding (closed)

Comb-binding (front)

PLASTIC COMB-BINDING

This kind of binding is very similar to wire spiral-binding, except that the binding material is plastic and is usually much wider than wire.

The signatures and cover are assembled like wire spiral-bound books, and holes are drilled. The holes can have many different shapes: square, rectangle, circle, or oval. The plastic binding can be of many different colors. It is fairly durable but not as strong as wire binding. The book lies flat when opened.

TAPE BINDING

All the signatures and cover are assembled and trimmed. Then a strip of flexible cloth tape that contains glue is applied on the edges of the spine side and heated. The glue melts and spreads, gluing the stack of signatures together.

The tape is available in several different colors. The book lies flat when opened.

Screw and Post Binding (open)

Screw and Post Binding (front)

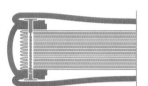

Screw and Post Binding (closed)

SCREW AND POST BINDING

This is a form of side-stitch binding in which the signatures are fastened together with posts held on by screws instead of staples. The signatures are assembled in a stack and trimmed on all sides. Holes are drilled along the spine side. Posts already attached to the cover are threaded through the holes, and a screw head is screwed on to hold everything in place. The process is slow because it must be done by hand.

The book does not lie flat when opened, but the screws can be unscrewed to accommodate more pages at will.

Single Wire Spiral-Binding (front)

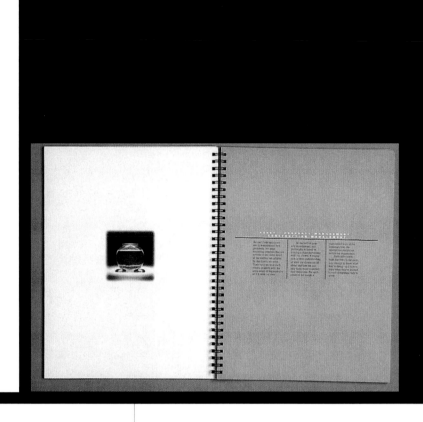

WIRE SPIRAL-BINDING

The signatures are assembled by stacking one on top of another. A cover is wrapped on and the pages may be trimmed at this point along all four sides. Holes are then drilled through all the pages. The holes may be square or round. Then wire is threaded through the holes. The wire can be threaded singly or doubly, in different spiral patterns.

Most wire is silver, but you can get colored wire too. The book lies flat when opened. Unlike other forms of perfect binding, which use glue to stick the pages together, spiral-bound books can be printed with bleeds out to the edges of all four sides. However, while you can bleed an image out to the spine edge, it will be punched with holes and partly obscured by the wire.

Wire Spiral-Binding (open)

Wire Spiral-Binding (closed)

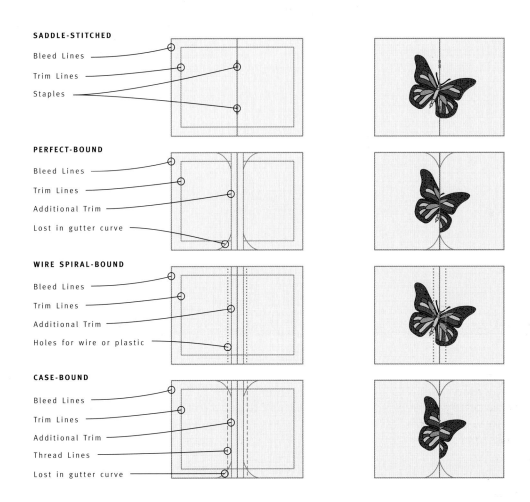

SADDLE-STITCHED

Bleed Lines

Trim Lines

Staples

PERFECT-BOUND

Bleed Lines

Trim Lines

Additional Trim

Lost in gutter curve

WIRE SPIRAL-BOUND

Bleed Lines

Trim Lines

Additional Trim

Holes for wire or plastic

CASE-BOUND

Bleed Lines

Trim Lines

Additional Trim

Thread Lines

Lost in gutter curve

Lost in the Gutter

Depending on the binding method you choose, a certain amount of your design is going to be compromised in the middle. With some methods, actual holes are drilled in the gutter area, or staples are punched through the center fold of gutter. With other methods, the image is not actually mutilated, but because the pages don't open fully, portions of the design can curve into the gutter and be lost from view.

As you design your job, you should keep bindery limitations in mind and adjust your designs accordingly. You may want to back the image away from the gutter altogether. Or you may decide to choose a binding method that minimizes the loss of image. At the very least, you need to know specifically how much image will be affected by the bindery. Ask your printer for a ruled-up folding dummy in page-reading order. Open the dummy in a natural way, not pulling the pages apart more than a reader would, and see for yourself.

You may want to laminate your printed piece after it has been produced, especially if the inks you use are water-based (as most ink-jet printers' inks are). Laminates protect ink and paper from scuffing, flaking, running, and fading. They are usually available offline and can be made from many different kinds of plastics. You should choose one that is somewhat porous, if possible. It will allow the paper to adjust to changes in atmospheric humidity, preventing paper curl. Also pay attention to how thick the laminate is. Thicker plastic protects better but may overwhelm the design, giving it the feel of a driver's license. You can also decide between a glossy or a dull laminate. Choose the one that enhances your design best, as you would with a glossy or matte varnish.

If you need to laminate a large piece of printing, such as a poster or a banner, then consult with the printer. Some laminating machines can crease large-format paper, creating unsightly lines and folds in the finished piece. You may need to print a backup copy or two, in case things go wrong. Ask about the spoilage rate and get a recommendation as to how many extra copies would be reasonable.

This happened to me on a job I was doing for a political candidate. Her campaign staff had ink-jet-printed the voting records of hundreds of precincts onto a giant map of the city. They wanted to laminate the map so that they could assign door-belling volunteers to the best areas.

The printer fed in the first map, and the machine creased it badly. "Not to worry," I said. "I've come prepared." I hauled out another copy and halfway through, the machine stopped. It had run out of plastic. The printer had to back the map out with only half of it coated.

"You'll have to be satisfied with that," he said. "I can't put the map through the machine again."

I looked at my two crashed and burned designs and heaved a sigh. What to do? Two copies were all I had made. Should I give my client the creased map or the half-laminated one? Neither choice was calculated to make me look like I had a clue about what I was doing. I looked more closely at the creased map. By some chance, the creases all seemed to run through precincts that wouldn't vote for my client if she was running for dog-catcher. So that's the map I gave her. I'm not sure she ever noticed, but I sure did, every time I walked into her headquarters. Three weeks later, she lost the election.

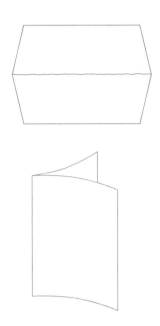

Folding Preflight

If you've ever tried making a Japanese crane out of origami paper, you know how frustrating folding can be. The paper curves in some directions and won't lie flat. Creases may not be straight. The folds weaken the paper fibers, so if you're not careful, your crane's beak will flop down like a piece of overcooked spaghetti. I know mine always did.

In the same way, folding your digitally printed jobs can be frustrating too. Your printer may not have the proper folding equipment. Paper may tear or crumple as it goes through the machine. The paper can wave and curve, without lying flat.

To avoid these mood-breaking moments at the end of the production line, you need to check with your printer early in your design process to make sure of three things:

1. **Will your paper work in the machines?** Paper needs to be the right thickness and weight to be folded. Papers that are too lightweight may not go through a machine without tearing. Papers that are too heavy and thick may not go through the machine at all, or if they do, they may need to be scored first to give a clean fold. Scoring is an off-line process that you'll need to pay for separately.

Papers also need to have the right finish to withstand folding. The finish of some highly glossy papers will crack along fold lines, creating unsightly blemishes. You also need to consider the grain of the paper as you fold it. Folds that parallel the paper grain are preferred by most designers because the folded paper lies flat afterward. This is particularly important if you're printing multiple-page designs that will be perfect bound. The first fold should always be parallel to the grain.

(ABOVE)

Signatures can be folded either with the grain (top left) or against the grain (bottom left). Most signatures are folded with the grain because paper that is folded this way lies flat; paper folded against the grain can curl, although the folds are stronger and less apt to tear.

(ABOVE)

Whenever you have a complex folding job
like this one, you should get a folding dummy
(facing page) from your printer and make sure
that your art works properly with the folds.

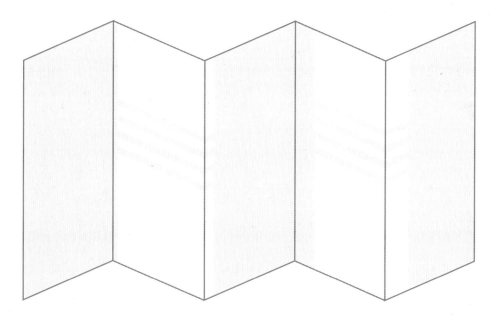

Sometimes, however, you may want to fold perpendicular to the grain. Folds may not lie as flat, but they are stronger. Talk to your printer to get the best recommendation.

2. **Will your designs work in the machines?** When a job is folded, the accuracy of the fold does not match the accuracy of print registration. Registration that may be accurate to within a thousandth of an inch in print may decline to an accuracy of 1/8 inch in folding. If your design calls for a perfect match across fold lines, you may be disappointed. I've seen this many times with four-color envelopes, where the design of the flap is supposed to match the design on the body of the envelope. One memorable mailing for the local zoo

showed an elephant whose trunk was sticking out of his ear.

Misalignment is even more problematic with page designs that are folded more than one time. Each time the page folds, it may lose 1/8 inch accuracy, compounding the problem with each fold.

As you design your folds, you should also be careful about tracking the sequence of copy from one panel to the next. What may be an obvious sequence to you may not be to your reader, who has not been living with the design night and day, as you have. If the text sequence is not obvious, your message may be lost. One way to mitigate this problem is to make each panel of your piece become a stand-alone panel.

3. **Can your printer fold your design in the way you want?** There are many ways to fold a printed sheet, especially when you use more than one fold. Combination folds can be parallel to each other, or they can be perpendicular to each other. Folds can nest into each other or stack on top of each other. Paper can be folded symmetrically or asymmetrically. The possibilities are almost endless, and folding machines are not standardized. You should check with your bindery.

Having said that, there are a few folds that are fairly common:

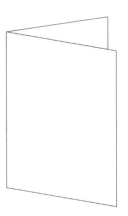

SIMPLE FOLD

One fold, made either with the grain or against the grain, along the short dimension of the paper or along the long dimension.

SHORT FOLD

A simple fold that is not folded symmetrically—one side is longer than the other.

BARREL FOLD

Two simple folds in which the outer edges of the page are folded in toward each other. Depending on where you make the folds, the edges can meet in the middle or overlap each other.

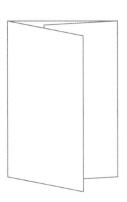

OVERLAPPING BARREL FOLD

A barrel fold in which the paper is folded asymmetrically, so one panel overlaps another.

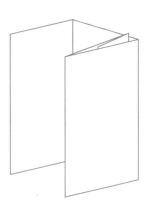

COMPLEX BARREL ROLL (ROLLING FOLD)

A barrel fold with more than two simple folds. You can start on one side of the page, fold short, fold over short again, and fold over short again, as many times as you want.

GATEFOLD

A class of barrel fold that has an additional fold in the center of the paper. Depending on where the folds are, the gates can be the same size or different sizes.

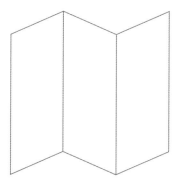

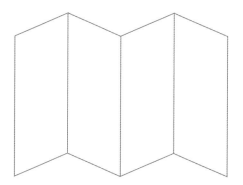

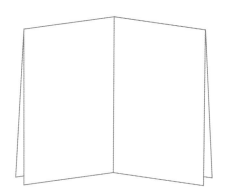

ACCORDION FOLD
A multiple fold where the first fold bends in and the next fold bends out.

MULTIPLE ACCORDION FOLD
An accordion fold with more than two folds, each fold bending in and out successively.

FRENCH FOLD
A multiple fold in which the paper is first folded in one direction, then folded perpendicular to the first fold. Sixteen-page signatures on offset presses are usually folded in this way.

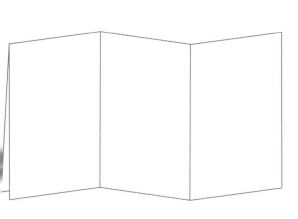

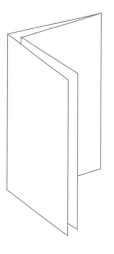

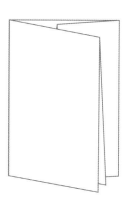

COMBINATION FOLDS
Multiple folds that combine features of simple folds. For example, you can combine a French fold with an accordion fold. Maps are often folded in this way.

PARALLEL FOLD
A combination fold that combines a barrel fold with an accordion fold.

COMBINATION FRENCH AND OVERLAPPING BARREL FOLD
Complex folds like this one are sometimes used for large-format brochures. Be careful when designing such folds; it is not always clear how a reader should track each page. You should consider designing each page so it can be read independently.

THE MAILING ISSUES YOU SHOULD ADDRESS ARE:

- WIDTH AND HEIGHT OF YOUR FINISHED DESIGN—*not only the absolute dimensions but their proportions*

- THICKNESS OF YOUR FINISHED DESIGN

- BINDING METHOD—*not much of an issue for first-class mail but important for all other mail classes*

- CONTENT—*there are certain savings for book rate and certain costs for mail that contains advertising*

- QUANTITY—*different classes have different minimum quantity requirements*

- INKS—*some inks will goof up the USPS automatic scanners, especially fluorescent inks and some metallics*

- PAPER GLOSSINESS AND FINISH

- PAPER TEXTURE OR PRINTED PATTERNS THAT MAY CONFUSE THE SCANNER

- CONTRAST NEEDED BETWEEN THE PRINTED DESIGN AND THE PRINTED ADDRESS—*especially if you're overprinting the address onto a colored background*

- WINDOW SIZE AND PLACEMENT

- WINDOW COVERINGS—*if any*

- BARCODES—*including size, location, and inking*

- ADDRESS LOCATION

- ADDRESS SORTING REQUIREMENTS

- PERMITS

Pleasing Mr./Ms. Postal Delivery Person

If you plan to mail your piece, you should check with the United States Postal Service before you begin designing anything. This is especially true if you print in larger quantities and hope to benefit from the USPS discount program.

The USPS discount program operates on one simple principle: The more automated your job, the cheaper your postage. The savings can be substantial if you use barcodes and if you presort and prestamp your mail. But the specifications can be daunting.

Few things will send your stomach crashing through the floor faster than a postal service worker who opens your sack of mail and finds that your design is too wide or too fat, or that you used the wrong inks or the wrong contrast on the labels. The USPS may dump you easy or they may dump you hard, but dump you they will.

Fortunately the USPS is perfectly happy to help you ahead of time by providing the right specs. They will even go over a folding dummy with you and help you make corrections before you print. You can access this service at any USPS Business Center around the country. To find a USPS Business Center near you, call 1-800-238-3150.

(ABOVE)

The Post Office rewards mailers who design jobs that fit the system's automated equipment. Here stacks of mailers in three different sizes all qualify for automated sorting — and lower postage fees.

(FACING PAGE LEFT)

Designs that don't fit the postal service's equipment are thrown into the reject bin, to be returned to sender for expensive remakes or expensive additional postage. Don't let this happen to you.

GLOSSARY

A

Accordion fold: In binding, a series of parallel folds where the first fold bends in and the next one bends out.

Acid-free paper: Paper that contains no acid or acid-producing chemicals.

Additive color: Color produced by combining red, green, and blue light in varying intensities. Computer monitors use additive color, whereas the printing process uses subtractive color.

Against the grain: Folding or printing performed at right angles to the grain direction of the paper.

Agripulp: In paper-making, a pulp made from agricultural waste such as wheat straw, rice straw, hops stems, banana stems, and the like.

Ambient light: Light surrounding an area or object. Outdoor ambient light is all the light from the sun. Indoor ambient light is all the light supplied by light bulbs and/or incoming sunlight from windows, as well as reflected light bouncing off walls and objects.

Analog proofing system: A system that makes proofs through analog (or physical) processes, as opposed to a digital proofing system that makes proofs through digital (or electronic) processes.

Antialiasing: A technique that smoothes jagged edges in text and line art on a computer screen by slightly blurring pixels in edge areas.

Anti-offset spray: A dry vegetable starch powder used to help prevent wet ink from transferring from one sheet of paper to another.

Aqueous coating: A water-based paper coating designed to overprint, protect, and enhance printed images.

Artifact: A visible defect in a digital image, often caused by hardware or software limitations.

Automatic image replacement: A process in which low-resolution FPO (For Position Only) images are automatically replaced by high-resolution images before the final pages are produced.

B

Banding: An undesired phenomenon in which visible bands mark the borders where one tone graduates into another tone.

Barrel fold: In binding, two or more simple folds in which the outer edges of the pages are folded in toward each other.

Baseline: In typesetting, an imaginary, horizontal reference line along which all letters in an alphabet, all typefaces, and point sizes align.

Basic size: The standardized dimensions of a given sheet of paper for the purpose of measuring the sheet's basis weight. Basic sizes for different kinds of paper differ.

Basis weight: The weight of one ream (500 sheets) of paper, cut in the basic size for that particular grade.

Bézier curve: A smooth, mathematical curve whose shape is determined by control points; much used in object-oriented graphics programs (such as Adobe Illustrator) to draw smooth curves.

Bible paper: A kind of paper stock, made originally for bibles and dictionaries. It is very lightweight (usually well under 20-pound stock) and rather opaque for its weight.

Bindery: The department within a printing plant that handles trimming and binding. Some companies operate as specialized binderies for printers.

Binding: The fastening of assembled sheets or signatures along one edge of a publication. The binding process also includes folding, gathering, trimming, stitching, gluing, and other finishing steps.

Bit: In computers, the smallest unit of information defining one of two conditions: on or off.

Bit depth: The number of bits that can be captured by a scanner or shown on a display. An 8-bit image is limited to 256 colors: a 24-bit image can show up to 16.7 million colors.

Bitmapped: A gray-scale or color image stored as a collection of pixels, with minimal or no data compression.

Black plate: Also referred to as the black printer, this printing plate is used along with cyan, magenta, and yellow plates in four-color (CMYK) process printing. Also called the key plate, its purpose is to enrich the contrast of the final reproduction.

Black-and-whites: Originals or reproductions in which black is the only color.

Blanket: A rubber material that is clamped around the cylinder on a printing press, to which the image is transferred from the printing plate, and from which the image is transferred to the paper.

Bleed: The portion of an image that extends beyond the trim area of a page.

Bleed allowance: The degree to which a bleed must extend beyond a document's trim to allow for variations in cutting and folding.

Blend: An area in an image that transitions from one color (or gray level) to another. Also known as a graduated tint, graduation, or vignette.

Blind image: An image on a printing plate that has lost its ability to hold ink and fails to print.

Blueline: An imposition proof made from stripped film negatives or positives used to check the position of page elements before printing.

BMP: A format for storing bitmapped images in compressed form, conceptually similar to JPEG, PICT, GIF, and TIFF, and mostly used with Windows.

Body: The viscosity or consistency of an ink.

Bond paper: A grade of paper that often has cotton content and is used for letterheads.

Bond strength: The ability of paper fibers to hold together.

Book paper: A grade of coated or uncoated paper generally used in books and other publications.

Bootlegged font: A digital type font copied (often illegally) from a previously programmed type font. Bootlegged fonts typically do not contain the mathematical programming that ensures smooth curves and sharp edges, so when the type is scaled up or down, it may show jaggedness or blurriness.

Bounce: An undesirable mechanical press registration resulting from the lead edge of the sheet bouncing away from the press head stops.

Break for color: To separate the elements of a design to be printed in different colors.

Brightness: In paper, the amount of blue light a given sheet reflects. This term is used to grade different paper stocks.

Brochure: A pamphlet of two or more pages that is folded or bound.

Broke: In paper manufacturing, the paper that is spoiled during the manufacturing process, usually returned to the pulping process to be made back into virgin paper.

Bump: Ink applied from a fifth plate in four-color process printing to strengthen a specific color. Also referred to as a touch plate.

Burn: To expose light-sensitive emulsions on proofs or plates in a vacuum frame with high-intensity light.

Byte: In computers, the standard unit of measure for files equal to eight bits (see bit); a megabyte equals 1,048,576 bits.

C

Chalking: A printing defect, caused by improper drying of ink, in which the pigment becomes chalklike and falls off the page, often because the ink vehicle has been absorbed too rapidly into the paper.

Channel binding: A form of perfect binding in which pages are assembled and trimmed, then placed inside a cover or case, which has a metal channel that is compressed to hold the pages.

Choke: A trapping technique in which one color area is made slightly smaller to allow for misregistration on press. It is used in conjunction with a spread, in which another color area is made slightly larger.

CMYK: Cyan, magenta, yellow, and black, the four inks used to reproduce full-color (or four-color) printing.

Coated paper: Paper with a smooth clay-coated surface.

Coating: An emulsion, varnish, or lacquer applied to a printed surface to give it added protection or to produce a dramatic special effect.

Coating strength: In paper, the ability of coating to resist delaminating or blistering.

Color calibrate: To fix, check, or correct the gradations of color on a color monitor.

Color cast: In photography or printing, an overall tinge or shade. A picture with a pink cast has an overall tinge of pink.

Color control strip: A series of color bars printed on press sheets designed to help press operators monitor and detect problems with color balance, registration, dot gain, and other printing-related factors.

Color correction: The process by which color values in images are adjusted to correct or compensate for errors in photography, scanning, or separation.

Color key: An analog proofing system that used pigmented acetate overlays to represent four-color images.

Color proof: A full-color reproduction of a design made photomechanically or digitally.

Color reduction: The process by which the number of colors in a digital image is reduced so it can be saved at a smaller file size or displayed on an 8-bit monitor.

Color separation: The process of separating artwork into component electronic files or films of cyan, magenta, yellow, and black in preparation for printing.

Commercial printer: A printing company that focuses primarily on print runs of 5,000 or more using half-size and full-size printing equipment.

Continuous tone: Artwork that contains a continuous gradient of tones from dark to light. Continuous tones cannot be printed by a press; the tones must be broken up into small dots (halftones).

Contract proof: A proof that has been signed by the print buyer and designated as the official proof to be matched by the printer on press.

Contrast: In photography and printing, the amount of gradation between tones, especially between highlights and shadows.

Conventional printing press: A printing press that applies ink to a substrate by using a physical printing plate. Such presses may be offset, gravure, flexographic, or letterpress.

Cotton paper: Paper made from cotton fibers rather than, or in addition to, wood fibers.

Cover stock: A variety of heavier papers used for the covers of catalogs, brochures, booklets, and similar publications.

Cromalin proof: An off-press proofing system (trademarked by DuPont) that involves laminating successive layers of CMYK toner onto a light-sensitive, sticky substrate with the use of color toners.

Cropping: Cutting out portions of unwanted artwork in a layout.

Curl: The distortion of a sheet of paper due to absorption of moisture or differences in coating from one side to another.

Cyan: One of the subtractive primary colors used as a part of the four-color process inks (cyan, magenta, yellow, and black); blue.

D

Densitometer: An instrument that measures optical density of colors, dot gain, and other printing elements, used to monitor and control consistency throughout a press run.

Depth-of-field: In photography, the zone of acceptably sharp detail in the background and foreground of a subject.

Die cut: A letterpress technique that uses sharp steel rules to make cuts in printed sheets.

Digital sheet-fed press: A printing press that applies ink or toner onto a substrate via digitized commands rather than with printing plates. The substrate is fed into the press one sheet at a time.

Digital web press: A printing press that applies ink or toner onto a substrate via digitized commands rather than with printing plates. The substrate is fed into the press continuously from a roll; individual pages are created at the end of the line when a blade cuts the pages off the roll.

Direct-to-plate: In printing, the process whereby digital layouts are transmitted electronically to a plate-making apparatus, without the intervening process of making film negatives first.

Distributing rollers: Rubber-covered rollers that transfer ink from the ink fountain and into the ink train of a printing press.

Dot: A single element of a screen-lined image.

Dot gain: The physical gain in size of halftone dots, caused by ink sinking into the substrate and spreading out.

Dot-matrix: A digital printer that "types" small dots to make patterns that form characters.

DPI: (Dots Per Inch). The measure of an input or output device's resolution.

Drier: A substance added to ink to make it dry more quickly.

Dryback: The tendency of an ink to dull and lighten as it dries and is absorbed into the paper

Dull finish: A flat clay coating applied to paper that is duller than gloss coating, and slightly smoother than a matte coating.

Dummy: A preliminary layout showing the size, shape, form, and general style of a printed piece, including folds.

Duotone: A two-color halftone reproduction from a black-and-white or color photograph.

Dye-sublimation: A form of digital printing in which a computer-controlled scan-head heats special dyes to such high temperatures that they transform directly from a solid to a gaseous state. The vaporized dye is then transferred to the substrate.

E

Emulsion: A light-sensitive coating on one side of a photographic film, proofing materials, or printing plates that faces a light source during exposure.

EPS: (Encapsulated PostScript). A popular graphics file format based on Adobe Systems' PostScript technology.

Exposure: The process of producing an image on a light-sensitive emulsion-coated material, such as film, proofs, or plates.

F

F-stop: In photography, a measure of the size of the lens opening, or aperture on a camera. The larger the number, the smaller the opening. Each f-stop doubles the amount of light reaching the film.

Feeder: The section of a sheet-fed printing press that separates the sheets and feeds them in position for printing.

Felt side: The top side of paper made on a Fourdrinier wire. When finished or coated, it is smoother than the reverse side (see *wire side*) and accepts ink better.

File compression: Any of a large number of software protocols for storing a file at a reduced storage size; most commonly used in desktop publishing to reduce the size of image files (see *lossless compression* and *lossy compression*).

Fillers: White pigments such as clay, titanium dioxide, and calcium carbonate that are added to paper to improve its opacity, brightness, and printing surface.

Filling in: A condition on a printing press in which the ink fills the area between halftone dots.

Finish: In paper, the surface characteristics of a sheet. In the bindery, a general term covering trimming, folding, binding, off-line varnishing, and the like.

Flax: A slender plant whose stems can be spun into fiber to make linen or paper.

Flexography: In printing, a process that prints by using raised images on a flexible printing plate made from rubber or soft plastic.

Flier: A one-page, unfolded printed promotional piece.

Fold mark: Horizontal or vertical lines printed outside the final image area on a sheet of paper to indicate where it should be folded.

Font: In typesetting, a complete set of all the characters (upper- and lowercase letters, numerals, punctuation marks, superscripts, subscripts, small caps, and other characters) that make up one typeface.

Form rollers: The inking or dampening rollers that directly contact the plate on a printing press.

Fountain roller: The roller in offset lithography that feeds ink or water to the inking or dampening roller systems.

Fountain solution: A mixture of water, gum Arabic, and other chemicals used to dampen the plate and keep non-printing areas from accepting ink.

Four-up: The imposition of four items to be printed on the same sheet of paper.

FPO: (For Position Only). A low-resolution or simulated version of a graphic that is used as a placeholder in initial proofing and layout stages.

Free sheet: Paper made by cooking wood chips to break down chemicals and remove lignin.

French fold: In binding, a multiple fold in which the paper is folded first in one direction and then folded perpendicular to the first fold.

Furnish: In paper manufacture, the mixture of pulp, water, dyes, clays, and chemicals poured out onto a Fourdrinier wire. As the water is removed the furnish bonds into paper. Also called *slurry.*

G

Gamma: A measure of brightness and contrast in photographic images.

Gang: The random combination of several images on a proof. Also, the combination of unrelated jobs on one press sheet.

Gang run: A print run in which two or more print jobs are combined.

Gatefold: In binding, a multiple fold that combines a barrel fold with a simple fold down the center line of the paper.

Gathering: The process of assembling folded signatures in proper sequence in preparation for binding.

GIF: Graphic Interchange Format. A lossless (or more recently, lossy) format for storing bitmapped images in compressed form, conceptually similar to JPEG, PICT, BMP, TIFF, and the like. GIF supports animation but does not support a full range of colors.

Gloss: A paper's ability to reflect light.

Gradation: A smooth transition of shades between black and white, between one color and another, or between one color and white. Also called a gradient.

Grade: A general term categorizing different qualities of paper. Grade can mean a category of paper, a class, a rating, a finish, or even a brand.

Grain: The direction in which the paper fibers line up.

Grain long: A sheet of paper whose fibers are aligned parallel to the long side of the sheet

Grain short: A sheet of paper whose fibers are aligned parallel to the short side of the sheet.

Grammage: In paper, the basis weight as expressed in grams per square meter.

Gravure: In printing, a process that prints by using cylinders that contain cells to hold the ink, which is transferred to the substrate.

Gripper: A set of pincers that holds and transfers paper through the printing press.

Gripper edge: The leading edge of paper as it passes through a printing press.

Gripper margin: The unprintable edge on which the paper is gripped as it passes through a printing press.

Groundwood: Paper stock that is made by mechanically grinding up wood into chips.

Gutter: The inner margins of two facing pages in a publication.

H

Hairline register: To register color separations within one half (0.5) point.

Halation: An undesirable blurred effect in photographs, proofs, printing plates, and printed pieces that resembles a halo, usually occurring in highlighted areas or around bright objects, caused by dust particles or improper contact.

Halftone: The reproduction of an image through the process of shooting an original, continuous-tone image through a grid (screen) that breaks up the continuous tones into discrete dots of differing sizes. Also a term for artwork that has been screened in this way.

Hard dot: A dot in photographic images, proofs, and printed pieces that has no noticeable halation around its edges.

Hard proof: A tangible proof, such as laser paper, film, or any of various proofing mediums.

Hatching: The reproduction of continuous tones through the drawing or etching of fine dots and/or crossed or parallel lines.

Hemp: A plant whose fibers are commonly used to make rope, cloth, and paper.

Hexachrome: A trademarked term for a six-color printing process developed by Pantone Inc.

Hickey: A spot or imperfection in a printed piece due to foreign particles becoming adhered to the printing plates.

Highlight: The brightest or lightest part of a photograph.

Hints: In digital typography, mathematical algorithms used to turn pixels on and off in such a way as to make typeset characters look smoother and crisper.

Histogram: In digital prepress, a graph that displays the tonal range of a given image.

House sheet: Paper stock always kept in inventory on a printer's floor.

HTML: (Hypertext Markup Language). One of many markup languages used to create digital graphics and text. HTML is especially useful in Web design, but it is gradually being supplanted by WYSIWYG languages.

Hue: The attribute of a color that distinguishes it from other colors.

I

Image area: The viable area of a press sheet that can be printed, surrounded by nonimage areas, or margins.

Image assembly: The process of stripping film negatives in position prior to proofing and plate making.

Image editing: The process of changing and manipulating photographs and other graphics and images, usually performed electronically using software applications.

Imagesetter: A device designed to reproduce graphics and type at high resolution onto film, proofs, or printing plates. Also referred to as an image recorder.

Impose: To arrange and position pages for a predetermined press sheet size to meet press, folding, and bindery requirements.

Imposition: The layout of individual pages of a multipage design on a press sheet so that, when the sheet is folded after printing, the pages are in correct, sequential order.

Impression: The printed image caused by the applied pressure from the printing plates, blanket, and impression cylinders, as the paper is printed.

Impression cylinder: The cylinder on a printing press that comes in contact with the press sheet and presses the sheet against the image carrying image-carrying blanket.

Ink holdout: A characteristic of the surface of a paper sheet that keeps ink from sinking into the paper fibers. Papers with good ink holdout keep ink on the surface, so colors look more saturated and details are finer.

Ink-jet printing: A digital printing process that applies ink to a substrate by spraying tiny droplets of ink through computer-controlled nozzles.

Inkometer: A device that measures the tack, or cohesion, of printing inks.

Ink trap: The capacity for one ink color to print over another ink color smoothly.

Insert: A printed piece that is not part of the original publication but is bound into a magazine, newspaper, or other printed piece.

J

JPEG: (Joint Photographic Experts Group). A lossy format for storing bitmapped images in compressed form, conceptually similar to BMP, PICT, GIF, TIFF, and the like. JPEG best supports continuous tone images.

K

Kenaf: A plant related to hibiscus whose fibers can be used to make paper.

Kerning: In typography, the space between letters. To kern is to adjust the letter spacing so the letters appear closer together or farther apart than they normally would.

Kerning pairs: Two letters that have been moved closer together than they would normally be, to make those letters appear optically spaced as evenly as nonkerned pairs. Most digital type fonts are programmed with a certain number of kerned pairs of letters.

Key: A color-coded legend that explains symbols or identifies colors to be printed in a piece of artwork, such as a color key.

Keyline: Artwork for offset reproduction that shows outlines indicating the exact shape, position, and size of halftone elements, line illustrations, and text.

Knock-out: To remove the background color on which type or graphics are being printed.

L

Laid paper: Paper in which the surface finish shows a visible pattern of parallel lines.

Laminate: (v) The process of applying a plastic film to a printed piece for protection or appearance; (n) the plastic film itself.

Laminate proofs: Proofing systems that consist of several layers of pigmented proofing materials adhered to a substrate in sequence to form a single layer; a substrate.

Lamination: A plastic film applied to a printed piece for protection or appearance.

Laser printing: A printing process that employs a laser beam to charge a drum, which in turn attracts toner particles that are transferred to paper and set by heat.

Lay-flat binding: A form of perfect binding in which the pages are assembled and trimmed. Then a strip of reinforced crepe is glued onto the spine and a portion of the first and last pages with flexible glue. A case (or cover) is then glued onto the first and last pages, so the pages "float" within the case.

Leading: In typography, the space between lines of type; also called line spacing.

Letterpress: In printing, a process that prints by using raised images on flat plates. The raised images are inked, and then paper is pressed against them.

Ligature: In typography, two or more letters designed to print together as one unit so that one letter does not interfere with the other.

Lightfastness: The ability of paper to resist fading or yellowing when exposed to light.

Light table: A table made for assembling film negatives that has a translucent top with a light source underneath.

Linen finish: Paper in which the fibers form a linen, or woven finish.

Lignin: The substance in trees that gives strength to wood cells. If left in paper, lignin adds strength and opacity but lessens brightness.

Lithography: In printing, a process that prints by using flat plates that employ water to repel ink from non-image areas.

Lossless: A data compression scheme that reduces the amount of data needed to store an image but without any loss of data. When a lossless image is uncompressed, it contains exactly the same data as the original.

Lossy: A data compression scheme that reduces the amount of data needed to store an image by throwing away some pixels of information. When a lossy image is uncompressed, it may be slightly different from the original.

Loupe: A magnifying lens held close to the eye to examine printing. The most common loupes are eight-power, which enlarge images by a factor of eight.

LPI: (Lines Per Inch). The number of rows of halftone cells per inch, also referred to as screen frequency.

M

Machine coated: Paper that is coated on one or both sides on a paper machine.

Magenta: One of the subtractive primary colors (cyan, magenta, yellow, and black) used for four-color process inks.

Makeready: The process by which printing plates are hung on a conventional press and inked to the proper density and color balance.

Markup language: In computer programming, a language that requires the user to keystroke lines of commands to produce text and graphics. The user cannot see the design until the commands are output, in contrast to WYSIWYG languages, which display text and graphics directly on a monitor.

Matchprint: A proofing system made from film for the purpose of proofing four-color materials to be printed; a popular contract proofing system.

Matte: A dull, clear coating applied

to printed materials for protection or appearance.

Matte finish: A clay coating on paper that is dull, without gloss or luster.

Mechanical: Camera-ready artwork that includes text, photos, illustrations, and so forth. A mechanical can be in the form of an artboard, a digital printout, or a digital file ready for high-resolution output.

Metamerism: A phenomenon in which colors perceived by the human eye appear different when viewed by an artificial lens, such as a camera lens.

Midtone: In printing and photography, the range of tones in the middle between highlights and shadows.

Mockup: A visual presentation of a design or page layout that approximates what the final printed piece will look like.

Moiré: An unwanted pattern of printing dots caused by halftone screen angles that conflict with each other, creating a discernible pattern of squares; often occurring when previously screened halftones are screened again, or when screened halftones are used to reproduce patterns that already have a screen or grid pattern in them (such as houndstooth checks).

Monochrome: A one-color image or page.

Mottle: An undesirable printing effect in which solid areas appear spotty and uneven.

Mullen strength: The ability of paper to resist bursting.

O

Offset printing: In printing, a process that prints by using flat plates (deployed either flat or wrapped around a cylinder) to pick up ink from an ink fountain (or trough) and transfer it to a rubber blanket. The blanket then presses against the substrate to print the image.

One-sided press: A press that can print only one side of a substrate at once (as opposed to a perfecting

press, which can print both sides of the substrate at the same time)

One-up: To impose only one finished piece on a press sheet.

Opacity: The ability of paper to keep printing on one side from showing through on the other side.

Orphan: A widow carried to the top of the next column or page of type.

Out-of-register: A print-production error in which the color separations for an image are not properly aligned.

Overexposed: A photograph that has been exposed to too much light. Overexposed photos look washed out and lack a full range of tones, especially deep shadow tones.

Overprint: To print over an area that has already been printed.

Overrun: The number of printed copies exceeding the amount of the specified print run.

P

Packing: Sheets of calibrated material that are placed between printing plates, blankets, and the cylinders they are attached to, and that provide proper printing pressures between the cylinders.

Page layout: The assembly of the elements on a page, including text and graphics. Also called page composition.

Page proof: A layout of pages as they will appear in the publication or printed piece.

Pagination: The process of arranging the pages of a publication in proper sequence.

Pantone Matching System: A system of inks, color specifications, and color guides for reproducing spot colors.

Paper spoilage: The amount of paper discarded during the printing process because it has been spoiled by a number of factors: poor registration, printing flaws, folding flaws, poor color balance, bad paper, and the like.

PDF: (Portable Document Format). A file format created by Adobe that allows users to view and print documents independent of the applications used to create the files.

PE: (Printer's Error). A mistake made by the printer after the originals have been submitted by the client.

Perfect-bound: A method of binding in which signatures are folded and collated on top of one another and held together by adhesive.

Perfecting press: A press that can print both sides of the substrate at the same time.

Perforate: To cut or provide cut marks for the purpose of tearing out the perforated element on a printed sheet.

Pica: A unit of measurement used by printers and designers, equivalent to approximately $1/6$" (4 mm).

Pick strength: The ability of a paper surface to resist fraying into little fragments when sticky ink is applied.

Picking: Paper, or ink particles on previously printed press sheets that adheres to blanket or impression cylinders

PICT: A standard file format that allows for the exchange of graphic images (usually bitmapped) graphics file format developed by Apple for use on the Macintosh.

Pigment: The solid particles in ink or proofing materials that act as colorants.

Pixel: Short for "picture element," a single dot in an on-screen image.

Plate: Aluminum composite sheets with emulsion coatings that represent the image to be printed and are used to transfer inked images to the blankets and onto the paper.

Plate cylinder: The cylinder of a printing press on which the plate is mounted.

Platemaking: The process of exposing and developing printing plates for press runs.

Ply: In paper, one of several sheets laminated together to form extremely thick, heavy board-papers. Six-ply board means that six sheets of paper were laminated together to make one board.

Point: In typesetting, a measure of type size. One point equals $1/72$" (0.35 mm). In paper, a measure of the thickness of paper. One point equals 0.001" (0.25 mm).

Positive: Film in which the black and clear areas are the same as the original, as opposed to a film negative.

PostScript: A printing technology developed by Adobe Systems that permits high-quality output of digital images. Adobe licenses the technology to manufacturers of printers, image-setters, and other output devices.

Prepress: The process of preparing all output elements in preparation for printing.

Press check: The visual examination of press sheets during the makeready process to determine that all elements and colors are correct and in register.

Press proof: A final color proof made on a printing press to verify color and printing quality.

Press run: The physical act of operating a printing press for a particular project; also refers to the total number of copies to be printed.

Press sheet: A single printed sample pulled at random during or after a press run that represents the quality and content of the range of sheets from which it was taken.

Print run: The total number of copies of a publication to be printed; also called a press run.

Printer's spread: The imposition of pages as they will be assembled and reproduced on press.

Process color: Four-color reproduction of the full range of colors by the use of four printing plates, one for each of the primary colors: cyan (process blue), magenta (process red), yellow (process yellow), and black (process black).

Progressive proof: Press proofs made from each separate printing plate, showing the sequence of printing as well as the result after each color plate is added to the image.

Proof: A predictable representation of what the printed job should look like.

Pulp: Fibers that are separated mechanically or chemically, then dried into thick sheets. Mixed with water and other chemicals, it becomes furnish to make paper.

Pulp content: The nature of fiber used to make pulp. Pulp content can include any fibers that bond together when wet, including wood, bamboo, cotton, rice, mulberry, kenaf, hemp, flax, and used paper.

PUR: (Polyurethane Reactive). A special kind of cold glue that always stays flexible, making it a good choice for lay-flat binding.

R

Rasterization: The process of converting mathematical and digital information into a series of dots using an image setter.

Rasterized image: An image that has been converted into a bitmap for every pixel in that image.

Reader's spread: The sequential layout of a printing project for design layout purposes that shows pages in the sequence in which they will be read.

Ream: 500 sheets of paper of any given standard parent size.

Reduction: A photographic or digital process in which an image is made proportionally smaller.

Reflective art: Artwork that must be photographed by light reflected from its surface for reproduction, such as photographs and drawings.

Registration: The process of placing two or more overprinted images in such a way that the images align exactly over each other.

Registration mark: Crosshairs or other graphic elements applied to originals, proofs, and printing plates used to establish proper image alignment.

Reprint: To print a project again using the original materials.

Resolution: The degree that a device can record or reproduce sharpness of detail.

Retouch: To alter a photograph or illustration, either manually or digitally.

Reverse: To print an image or text in the opposite of the background color, such as white type on a black background.

RGB: (Red, Green, and Blue). The three primary components of white light.

Right-angle fold: Two or more folds that are at right angles to each other.

RIP: (Raster Image Processor). Hardware and/or software that converts all files to bitmapped images that can be output on an imagesetter at very high resolution, thereby producing film or data files that can be printed on a commercial press.

Roll-fed press: A web-fed press that uses rolls of paper.

Rosette: The flowerlike pattern created when the four CMYK color halftone screens are printed in register at the traditional angles.

S

Saddle-stitching: A kind of binding method in which signatures are nested on top of each other along a "saddle" bindery line and stitched together with staples.

Saturation: A measure of the purity of a color, determined by the amount of gray it contains. The higher the gray level, the lower the saturation.

Scale: To reduce or enlarge an image or a page proportionally.

Scan-head printing: A form of digital printing in which a printing head controlled by a computer is driven (or "scanned") across a substrate in order to apply ink. The two main forms of modern scan-head printing are ink jet and dye sublimation.

Scanner: A device used to turn hard copy output such as paper or slides that captures images on paper or transparencies and converts them into digital information for the purpose of manipulating and reproducing on the computer.

Scoring: The process in which paper is compressed along a straight line to break the fibers and allow the sheet to be folded without cracking.

Screen: Short for halftone screen. The reproduction of continuous-tone artwork, such as a photograph, by screening the image into dots of various sizes. When printed, the dots merge to give the illusion of continuous tone.

Screen angles: The angles at which halftone screens are placed in order to avoid undesirable screen patterns, called *moirés*.

Screen frequency: The number of lines per inch (LPI) or dots per inch (DPI) in a halftone screen.

Screen ruling: The number of lines or dots per inch in a halftone screen.

Scum: An undesirable film of ink that prints in the nonimage areas of a plate in offset lithography.

Selective binding: A process that allows distinct copies of a publication to be assembled with different signatures. The process is controlled by a computer, which directs the bindery line to drop the correct signatures into place. It is often combined with ink-jet printing, also controlled by a computer, which may print a unique message onto each copy of the publication.

Separation: The process of breaking a full-color image into four colors (cyan, magenta, yellow, and black) that can be printed together to simulate full color.

Serif type: Letters whose ends terminate in circles and cross strokes.

Service bureau: An organization that provides output services to graphic designers and printers in the form of scanning, film output, paper output, and color proofs.

Set back: The predetermined distance from the gripper edge of a press sheet to the beginning of the printed image.

Set-off: The accidental transfer of inked images from one side of a press sheet to the backside of the sheet above or below it.

Shadow: In photography or printing, the darkest part of an image.

Sheet-fed press: A printing press that uses a stack of precut sheets of paper.

Sheetwise: To print one side of the paper with one set of plates, then to turn the sheet over and print the other side with another set of plates.

Short fold: In binding, a simple fold that is folded asymmetrically so that one side is longer than the other.

Short-run color: A printing job printed in color in a small quantity. The term is relative and depends on the capability of the printing press and the economics of the process. Short-run for a gravure press might be any quantity less than 100,000. Short-run for an offset press might be any quantity less than 5,000. For digital presses, short-run can refer to a quantity as small as one copy.

Show-through: In printing, the amount of printing on the reverse side of a sheet that is visible on the front of the sheet under normal viewing conditions.

Side guide: A guide on sheet-fed presses that positions the sheet sideways as it feeds into the printing press.

Signature: In printing, a sheet folded at least once and usually more than once, to form individual pages or panels in a publication.

Simple fold: In binding, a single fold.

Skid: A platform that holds a pile of cut sheets.

Slurry: See *furnish*.

Soft dot: A dot in photographic images, proofs, and press sheets that has excessive halation around its edges.

Soft proof: A proof of an image or page layout on a computer monitor.

Specification: The characteristics of typeset copy, a color expressed in percentages, or any set of specific instructions for reproducing an image or a page layout.

Specular highlight: In photography or printing, a highlight that reflects a light source directly. When printed, specular highlights have no dots at all.

Spine: The back of a bound book (hard- or softcover) that connects the two covers.

Spot color: A single solid (or screened) color printed using one separation plate, as opposed to a process color printed using two or more separation plates.

Spot varnish: a clear coating applied to a particular area of a printed piece that provides protection as well as a dull or glossy appearance, depending on the type of varnish.

Spread: Two facing pages of a publication.

Step-and-repeat: The process of repeating an image or a group of images by "stepping" it into position using a predetermined measurement.

Stochastic screening: An alternative to conventional screening methods in which an image is color separated using fine, randomly placed dots rather than geometrically aligned halftone dots.

Stock: The type of paper or other material that will be used for printing.

Stream feeder: The most common type of sheet-fed press paper feeders that sends overlapping sheets of paper toward the grippers on a printing press.

Strip: To assemble film on a flat before proofing and plate making.

Strip in: To manually affix a film negative to another piece of film.

Subscript: In typesetting, a character set smaller and slightly below the baseline of type; used most commonly in chemical and mathematical equations and in footnotes.

Substrate: In printing, any printing surface that accepts ink. The most common substrate is paper, but substrates can also be plastic, metal, wood, fabric, or glass.

Subtractive color: Color produced by using cyan, magenta, and yellow inks printed on white paper to absorb, or subtract, the red, green, and blue portions of the spectrum in the printing process.

Subtractive primaries: Cyan, magenta, yellow, and black (CMYK). The colors used for process color printing inks.

Supercalendared: A paper finish that has been applied mechanically by smoothing the paper over chrome and fiber rollers during manufacture. The finish is smoother than ordinary calendaring but less smooth than coatings.

Superscript: In typesetting, a character set smaller and slightly above the x-height of type; used most commonly in chemical and mathematical equations and in footnotes.

T

Tack: The property of cohesion of particles in printing inks.

Tear strength: The ability of paper to resist tearing.

Template: A preformatted document that is protected from overwriting and can be used repeatedly to create new documents.

Tensile strength: The ability of paper to resist stretching without bursting.

Text paper: Any fine-quality printing paper.

Thermal-wax printing: A form of digital printing in which dots of waxy dye are heated to melting point and transferred to the substrate.

TIFF: Tagged Image File Format. A lossless format for storing bitmapped images in compressed form, conceptually similar to JPEG, PICT, GIF, BMP, and the like. TIFF best supports continuous tone images.

Tile: To break a page or image into smaller units so that it can be printed.

Tint: A solid color that has been screened to less than 100 percent to create a lighter shade of that particular color.

Tonal range: The difference between the brightest and the darkest tone in a photograph, proof, or printed piece.

Tooth: A descriptive term referring to the rough surface of a paper finish.

Transparent ink: A printing ink that does not conceal the color underneath.

Trapping: In printing, the process whereby one ink is printed over another. In prepress, the process whereby one color is lapped over another so that when printed, no white space shows between the two overlapped colors.

Trim: To cut the excess paper from the edges of a printed piece after it has been printed, folded, or bound.

Trim mark: Vertical or horizontal lines placed outside the image areas of a press sheet to indicate where the paper should be cut.

Trim size: The size of a printed piece after it has been trimmed.

Two-up: The imposition of two items to be printed on the same press sheet.

Typeface: The design of one particular style of type. Originally, typeface meant the printing surface of a letter of type.

U

Uncoated: Paper with no finish coating applied to it.

Underexposed: A photograph that has been exposed to too little light. Underexposed photos look dark and lack a full range of tones, especially in highlight areas. The deep shadow tones may lack detail as well.

Underrun: The production of fewer printed pieces than originally specified.

Unders/overs: The amount of printed material that is under or over the originally specified print run.

Unit cost: The price to print per piece.

Unsharp masking: In digital prepress, an algorithm that increases the contrast at the edges of objects. You can control the amount of unsharp masking you use, as well as the level at which the computer will apply the mask or not (the threshold), and the number of pixels surrounding each edge that will be affected (the radius).

UV coating: A protective, ultraviolet, transparent finish applied to a printed piece.

V

Vacuum frame: A vacuum device used in proofing and platemaking that holds materials in close contact during exposure.

Variable-data printing: A form of digital printing in which each printed piece is different from the one before. The difference might be as simple as an address label or as complex as an entire design.

Varnish: A thin, clear coating applied to a printed piece for protection or special effects.

Vector curve: A mathematical description of smooth curves, also called *Bézier curve.*

Vehicle: The fluid component of a printing ink that carries the pigment.

Vellum finish: A toothy paper finish that absorbs ink quickly.

Vendor: A supplier of goods or services, such as a printer, bindery, or a service bureau.

Viewing booth: A booth constructed in such a way that color art (both originals and reproductions) can be seen under totally neutral light. Viewing booths are painted with neutral gray walls and are illuminated with color-corrected lights at 5,000 K.

Viscosity: The properties of tack and flow in liquids, such as printing inks.

Visible spectrum: White light diffracted by a prism into bands of visible color arranged by their respective wavelengths, ranging from violet to indigo, blue, green, yellow, orange, and red.

W

Washup: The process of cleaning the rollers, plates, blankets, and other elements of a printing press after a press run.

Waterless printing: A method of printing without water in which the plates consist of metal for image areas and rubber for nonimage areas for printing without water.

Watermark: A design that is impressed on a sheet of paper during the paper making process.

Web: A roll of paper used in web printing (as opposed to sheet-fed printing).

Web press: A printing press that uses paper from a continuous roll (a web). The paper is threaded through the press units and is cut and folded into signatures at the end of the line.

Web tension: The amount of pull applied to a web of paper on a web-fed press.

Weight: The density of paper measured in pounds.

Wet trapping: The process of applying layers of ink in rapid succession while the ink is still fluid.

Widow: In typesetting, the last line of type in a paragraph that is less than one-third the width of the line above.

Wire side: The side of paper lying against the Fourdrinier wire during manufacture. The wire side of paper is less smooth than the felt side and accepts ink differently.

With the grain: To fold or feed paper into a printing press or folding machine parallel to the paper's grain direction.

Work and tumble: The process of printing one side of a sheet of paper, then turning the sheet over from gripper edge to the tail edge, using the same set of plates to print the second side.

Work and turn: The process of printing one side of a sheet of paper, then turning the sheet over from left to right using the same gripper and set of plates to print the second side.

Wove paper: Paper that has a uniform surface and a soft, smooth finish.

WYSIWYG: (What You See Is What You Get). Initialism describing a computer monitor's ability to display layouts more or less as they would appear when output by a printer. WYSIWYG is pronounced WHIZZ-ee-wig.

X

X-height: In typesetting, the height of the lowercase letter x.

Y

Yellow: One of the subtractive primaries (cyan, magenta, yellow, and black) used in four-color process inks.

ART AND PHOTOGRAPHY CREDITS

page 291
artist John Sidles
contact sidles@u.washington.edu
copyright © 2000

page 323
photographer Dennis Swanson
contact www.studio101west.com
copyright © 1999

page 339
designer Maury Sharp
courtesy Seattle Academy
contact csidles@mail.isomedia.com
copyright © 2000

page 78
photographer Kevin Morrill
contact www.workbook.com/portfolios/morrill
copyright © 2001

page 80
photographer Marie Mueller
contact csidles@mail.isomedia.com
copyright © 2001

page 82
photographer Kathy Baxter
contact csidles@mail.isomedia.com
copyright © 2001

page 84
courtesy Nathan Hale High School
contact csidles@mail.isomedia.com
copyright © 1998

page 86
artist Jo Sherwood
contact 505-983-6916
copyright © 2001

page 298
design firm Peter King + Co.
designer Garet McIntyre
contact www.peterkingandcompany.com
photographer Aaron Washington
contact 617-710-9094

page 332
design firm Miriello Grafico
designer Michelle Aranda
paper Chipboard (cover);
Gilbert Esse (interior)

page 340
artist John Hegnauer

page 79
photographer Zoe Campagna
contact 212-768-6027
copyright © 2001

page 81
photographer Marie Mueller
contact csidles@mail.isomedia.com
copyright © 2001

page 83
photographer Marie Mueller
contact csidles@mail.isomedia.com
copyright © 2001

page 85
photographer Constance Sidles
contact csidles@mail.isomedia.com
copyright © 2001

page 87
courtesy Rob Phillips
contact csidles@mail.isomedia.com
copyright © 2001

page 87
photographer Keitaro Yoshioka
contact 617-542-0096
copyright © 2001

page 87
courtesy Rob Phillips
contact csidles@mail.isomedia.com
copyright © 2001

page 89
photographer Kevin Morrill
contact www.workbook.com/portfolios/morrill
copyright © 2001

page 89
photographer Kathy Baxter
contact csidles@mail.isomedia.com
copyright © 2001

page 90
courtesy William Booker
contact 425-827-4862
copyright © 2001

page 90
photographer Keitaro Yoshioka
contact 617-542-0096
copyright © 2001

page 93
photographer Constance Sidles
contact csidles@mail.isomedia.com
copyright © 2001

page 94
studio Invisible Imports
photographer Joan Richardson
contact www.invisibleimports.com
copyright © 2001

page 94
photographer Kevin Morrill
contact www.workbook.com/portfolios/morrill
copyright © 2001

page 96
photographer Kathy Baxter
contact csidles@mail.isomedia.com
copyright © 2001

page 98
photographer David Katz
contact dmkatz@earthlink.net
copyright © 2001

page 99
photographer Marie Mueller
contact csidles@mail.isomedia.com
copyright © 2001

page 101
studio Invisible Imports
photographer Joan Richardson
contact www.invisibleimports.com
copyright © 2001

page 101
photographer Marie Mueller
contact csidles@mail.isomedia.com
copyright © 2001

page 101
photographer Marie Mueller
contact csidles@mail.isomedia.com
copyright © 2001

page 103
photographer Zoe Campagna
contact 212-768-6027
copyright © 2001

page 104
photographer Constance Sidles
contact csidles@mail.isomedia.com
copyright © 2001

page 105
photographer Constance Sidles
contact csidles@mail.isomedia.com
copyright © 2001

page 106
photographer Todd Fairchild
contact www.peterkingandcompany.com
copyright © 2001

page 107
photographer Alex Sidles
contact csidles@mail.isomedia.com
copyright © 2001

page 108
artist Jane A. Gildow

page 110
photographer Todd Fairchild
contact www.peterkingandcompany.com
copyright © 2001

page 111
artist Nathan Bulmer
contact 206-236-6120
copyright © 2001

page 112
artist Nathan Sidles
contact csidles@mail.isomedia.com
copyright © 2001

page 113
artist Kathy Baxter
contact csidles@mail.isomedia.com

page 122
photographer Keitaro Yoshioka
contact 617-542-0096
copyright © 2001

page 123
studio Invisible Imports
photographer Joan Richardson
contact www.invisibleimports.com
copyright © 2001

page 127
design firm Peter King + Co.
designer Ann Conneman
contact www.peterkingandcompany.com
photographer Aaron Washington
contact 617-710-9094

page 133
artist John Cameron
contact 617-338-9487

page 136
photographer Kevin Morrill
contact www.workbook.com/portfolios/morrill
copyright © 2001

page 148
artist Nathan Bulmer
contact 206-236-6120
copyright © 2001

page 152
photographer Zoe Campagna
contact 212-768-6027
copyright © 2001

page 153
studio Disario Photography
photographer George Disario
contact 978-463-3372
copyright © 2001

page 158
studio Disario Photography
photographer George Disario
contact 978-463-3372
copyright © 2001

page 159
studio Disario Photography
photographer George Disario
contact 978-463-3372
copyright © 2001

page 160
photographer Keitaro Yoshioka
contact 617-542-0096
copyright © 2001

page 161
photographer Todd Fairchild
contact www.peterkingandcompany.com
copyright © 2001

page 162
photographer Keitaro Yoshioka
contact 617-542-0096
copyright © 2001

page 352
design firm Lionel Ferreira
designer Lionel Ferreira
paper French Construction;
French Durotone

page 353
design firm Sagmeister, Inc.
designers Stefan Sagmeister & Veronica Oh
contact 212-647-1789
paper Chipboard

page 353
design firm Bob's Haus
designer Bob Dahlquist
paper Simpson Teton (base); Millers Falls
EZ Erase typing paper (flysheet)

page 353
design firm Michael Bartalos
paper Handmade

page 355
design firm Mires Design, Inc.
designers John Ball & Miguel Perez
paper Handmade (folder); Rising
Drawing Bristol, 4-ply vellum (card)

page 355
courtesy Seattle Academy
contact csidles@mail.isomedia.com
copyright © 2001

page 356
design firm Miriello Grafico
designer Ron Miriello
paper Gilbert Esse

page 356
designer Babsi Daum
paper Various

page 357
design firm Visual Dialogue
paper Monadnock Revue; Astrolite

page 357
design firm Matsumoto, Inc.
designer Takaaki Matsumoto
paper Carolina board lined with
white corrugated

page 358
design firm Louey/Rubino Design Group
designer Robert Louey
paper Hopper Cardigan

page 359
artist Anna Wolf
paper Sundance Felt

page 359
design firm Costello Communications
designer James Costello
paper Hopper Protera

page 359
design firm Arts & Letters, ltd.
designer Craig Dennis
paper Neenah Environment;
Appleton Currency

page 359
design firm Arts & Letters, Ltd.
designer Craig Dennis
paper Neenah Environment;
Appleton Currency

page 360
design firm Cahan & Associates
designer Bill Cahan
paper Riegel Jersery Leatherette

page 360
design firm Mires Design
designer Deborah Horn
paper Champion Carnival

page 360
design firm Parachute Design
designer Heather Cooley
paper Strathmore American; ProTac
Pressure Sensitive; Curtis Corduroy

page 361
design firm Ashley Booth Design
designers Helene Skjelten & Ashley Booth
paper Multiart Silk

page 361
design firm Mires Design
designer Deborah Horn
paper Champion Carnival

page 361
design firm Matsumoto, Inc.
designer Takaaki Matsumoto
paper Van Nouveau

page 362
design firm Jeanette Hodge Design
paper Newsprint

page 362
design firm Sagmeister, Inc.
designers Stefan Sagmeister & Mike Chan
contact 212-647-1789
paper Lightweight bible paper

page 363
artist Nathan Sidles
contact csidles@mail.isomedia.com
copyright © 2001

page 364
design firm Vrontikis Design Office
designer Kim Sage
contact 310-446-5446
paper Fox River Confetti

page 365
design firm Wages Design
designer Ted Fabella
paper Champion Benefit

page 365
designer Sigi Ramoser
paper Anders Reflex Hochtransparent

page 366
design firm Spielman Design
designer Amanda Bedard
paper Fox River Confetti; Frida Flack
(card with no ribbon)

page 366
design firm Spielman Design
designer Amanda Bedard
paper Strathmore Writing Natural

page 368
design firm Visual Asylum
paper Potlach McCoy Gloss

page 371
design firm Peter Felder Grafikdesign
paper Zöchling Black (box);
Chromocard (cards)

page 375
design firm Pressley Jacobs Design
designer Amy Warner McCarter
paper Alpha Cellulose (cover);

page 376
design firm Pangborn Design, Ltd.
designer Dominic Panghorn
paper Corrugated cardboard

page 381
design firm Vaughn Wedeen Creative
designer Steve Wedeen & Pamela Farrington
paper Kraft chipboard (cover);
Vintage Velvet (interior)

page 386
design firm Cross Colours Ink
designer Joanina Pastoll
paper Various Mondi products

page 386
design firm Hornall Anderson Design Works
paper Strathmore Beau Brilliant (cards);
Tai Chiri (outer wrap); Gmund Boch
(sticker); Gliclear (envelope)

page 387
design firm Woodson Creative
designer Laurel Shippert
paper Various

page 387
illustrator Michael Bartalos
paper Various

page 387
design firm blackcoffee design
designers Mark Gallagher, Laura Savard
paper Chipboard

page 388
design firm Sixth Street Press
paper KP Products Vision Paper

page 389
design firm Vrontikis Design Office
contact 310-446-5446
paper Crane's Old Money; Kenaf; Eco Paper Hemp

page 390
design firm Jeanette Hodge Design
paper Cotton handmade

page 392
design firm Richardson or Richardson
designers Forrest Richardson & Debi Mees
paper Four Corners Golf Paper

page 393
design firm Mark Russell Associates
paper Various recycled stocks

page 402
design firm Jeff Fisher LogoMotives
designer Jeff Fisher
contact www.jfisherlogomotives.com
copyright © 2000

page 405
design firm Jeff Fisher LogoMotives
designer Jeff Fisher
contact www.jfisherlogomotives.com
copyright © 2000

page 407
design firm Jeff Fisher LogoMotives
designer Jeff Fisher
contact www.jfisherlogomotives.com
copyright © 2000

page 408
design firm Cahan & Associates
designer Bob Dinetz
paper Warren Patina

page 408
design firm Troller Associates Graphic Design
designer Fred Troller
paper Beckett RSVP

page 413
design firm @KA
designer Albert Kueh

page 414
design firm Thomas Manss & Company
designer David Law
paper Various

page 415
design firm Cahan & Associates
designer Kevin Roberson
paper Cougar Vellum (cover)

page 419
design firm Gee + Chung Design
designers Earl Gee & Fani Chung
paper Simpson Starwhite Vicksburg

page 420
design firm Bailey Lauerman & Associates
paper French Construction

page 423
design firm @KA
designer Albert Kueh
paper Ivorex

page 424
design firm Vrontikis Design Office
contact 310-446-5446
paper Fox River Confetti

RESOURCES

The following companies also supplied artwork used in this book.

ArtToday.com
5232 E. Pima Rd.
Suite 200C
Tucson, AZ 85712 USA
520.881.8101
www.arttoday.com

CMB Design
608 Sutter St.
Suite 200
Folsom, CA 95630 USA
916.605.6500
www.cmbdesign.com

Gardner Design
3204 East Douglas
Wichita, KS 67208 USA
316.691.8808
www.gardnerdesign.net

Graphic Arts Technical Foundation (GATF)
200 Deer Run Rd.
Sewickley, PA 15142-2600 USA
412.741.6860 or 800.910.GATF
www.gain.net

Heidelberg USA, Inc.
1000 Gutenberg Dr.
Kennesaw, GA 30144 USA
888.472.9655
www.heidelbergusa.com

Image Wise Packaging
920 24th St.
Sacramento, CA 95816 USA
916.492.9900

Paul Baker Printing, Inc.
220 Riverside Ave.
Roseville, CA 95678 USA
916.969.8317
www.pbaker.com

ACKNOWLEDGMENTS

It's a colorful life no matter where you are, and there are plenty of colorful folks we are indebted to for their humor and support, both on a personal and professional level.

For starters, we'd like to send our thanks to Rockport's Kristin Ellison for her patience, professionalism, and hard work. Thank you as well to Stephan Beale, for fine copyediting and technical know-how. A very heartfelt thanks as always to the Blonde Bombshell, whose color is and always shall be, pure gold.

Graphic designers have numerous resources on the Web, but one of the best resources around is ArtToday.com. Many of the images in this book came from ArtToday and over the years, they've been a godsend for many of the projects we've worked on. We'd like to thanks them and all of the wonderful artists and photographers whose contributions make this an invaluable site for all designers.

Special thanks to Heidelberg USA for graciously sharing images and cutting-edge information, and to the Graphic Arts Technical Foundation (GATF) for granting permission to reproduce elements of their excellent process control forms for commercial printers.

We'd also like to thank Audrey Baker of Paul Baker Printing for sharing practical expertise and images.

As with all things in life we'd like to thank our families, Dale, Dottie, Ma, Pop, Pookie, Anne, Terry-Bob, and Kathy.

—B.K. and R. S.

A NOTE ON TRADEMARKS

Trademarked names are used throughout this book. We are using the names only to describe, inform, and advise readers about various aspects of computer and printing products and to the benefit of the trademark owner, with to intention of infringement on the trademark.

Products included in this book are identified for information only and the authors and publisher assume no responsibility for their efficacy for performance. While every attempt has been made to ensure that the details described in this book are accurate, the authors and publisher assume no responsibility for any errors which may exist, or for any loss of data which occur as a result of such errors.

ABOUT THE AUTHORS

CONSTANCE SIDLES is a production consultant and business writer with twenty-five years of experience in print production. She has been a production editor for several publications and for eighteen years has operated her own production consultancy that specializes in production planning, color printing, and troubleshooting for commercial clients and publications. Additionally, Sidles has written more than 450 feature articles and has won two Maggie awards for best nonfiction feature article. She presently writes regular columns for *HOW* Magazine and is the author of *Great Production by Design* (North Light Books), *Printing: Building Great Graphic Design Through Printing Techniques*, and *Pre-Press: Building Innovative Design Through Creative Pre-Press Techniques* (both by Rockport Publishers).

RICK SUTHERLAND is vice president of project development for Lone Wolf Enterprises. In addition to being an author, he has edited dozens of professional texts, including architectural, interior design, landscape design, and engineering books.

Prior to joining Lone Wolf Enterprises, Sutherland was, for fifteen years, part-owner of Paul Baker Printing, a multi-million dollar commercial printing company in California, where he served as production foreman, production manager, and for several years, as the lead sales account representative.

Sutherland has an extensive printing production background, gleaning years of craftsmanship from master printer, Jake Jacobbsen, and turning that into ten years of experience as the lead multicolor sheet-fed press operator with printing companies focused on advertising agency expectations and quality.

BARB KARG has a twenty-plus-year career as a journalist, graphic designer, and screenwriter. Part of desktop publishing since its inception, she has developed many publications from the ground up, and set up complete production and editorial systems for publishers in print and on the Web. As executive vice president and director of operations of Lone Wolf Enterprises, a professional book production company, she is responsible for overseeing the production and editorial departments. A self-professed publishing "lifer," she holds a B.A. in English and Creative Writing from the University of California, Davis.

Karg is the author and designer of *Dancing Hamsters, Gothic Garden, and Cyber Conspiracies: The 501 Funniest, Craziest, and Most Bizarre Web Sites You'll Ever See*, and coauthor and designer of *The Dark Eye: The Official Strategy Guide*.